PARLIAMENT AND POLITICS IN LATE MEDIEVAL ENGLAND

PARLIAMENT AND POLITICS IN LATE MEDIEVAL ENGLAND

J. S. ROSKELL

THE HAMBLEDON PRESS

The Hambledon Press 1981
35 Gloucester Avenue
London N.W.1

History Series 7

ISBN 0 9506882 8 2(Cased)
ISBN 0 9076280 7 9 (Paperback)
ISBN 0 9506882 7 4 (Volumes I and II cased)

British Library Cataloguing in Publication Data

Roskell, J. S.
    Parliament and politics in late medieval England
    – (History series; 7)
    Vol. 1
    1. Legislative bodies – England   History – Addresses,
    essays, lectures
    I. Title   II. Series
    328. 42'09   JN515

Printed in Great Britain by
Biddles Ltd, Guildford, Surrey

CONTENTS

Acknowledgements

The articles reproduced here first appeared in the following places and are reprinted here with permission.

I   *Manchester Guardian*, 30 May 1953.

II   *Bulletin of the Institute of Historical Research*, vol. xxix (1956).

III   *Bulletin of the John Rylands Library*, vol. 50 (1968).

IV   *B. I. H. R.*, vol. xxiii (1950).

V   *Nottingham Medieval Studies*, vol. 3 (1959).

VI   *B. I. H. R.*, vol. xxiv (1951).

VII   *English Historical Review*, vol. lxviii (1953).

VIII *B. J. R. L.*, vol. 46 (1964).

PREFACE

It will readily be perceived by readers of this two-volume collection of papers that, ever since the publication (by the Chetham Society in 1937) of my book entitled *The Knights of the Shire for the County Palatine of Lancaster (1377-1460)*, I have been concerned to write about the medieval English parliament mainly in relation to the Commons, the elected representatives of the shires and towns, whose attendance, demanded by the Crown, converted parliament into a representative parliament. More than a hundred years ago now William Stubbs believed that the Commons had, in the course of the fourteenth century, come to occupy the *foremost* place among the three 'estates' comprising parliament. Here Stubbs exaggerated; and historians like A. F. Pollard and, more powerfully, H. G. Richardson and G. O. Sayles argued differently, the tendency of their writings being greatly to diminish the significance of the rôle of the Commons in the medieval parliament, not least in the field of politics. But, then, that reaction resulted in a counter-reaction. And how firmly established now is that counter-reaction may be gathered from a reading of a recently published collection of essays, by a number of scholars of this present generation, entitled *The English Parliament in the Middle Ages* (Manchester University Press, 1981). Undoubtedly, the greatest single contribution to the counter-reaction was made, in a long series of papers ranging in time of production from 1925 to 1965, by the late Sir Goronwy Edwards, writing mainly from the constitutional angle. The late K. B. McFarlane, too, made a notable contribution, writing mainly from the social and political angle. Their work, as and when published, encouraged me in mine. But my own independent reading of the evidence of the records of the medieval parliament and of contemporary chronicles had led me, even at an early stage, to become one of those who, in the great debate over parliamentary origins, were concerned to demonstrate that the rôle and functions of the Commons in the medieval parliament were not merely noteworthy but of fundamental importance, which was, after all, Stubbs's *basic* conviction. The general drift of a number of the papers re-published in volume I of this collection is in support of that contention. The medieval Commons were important because of what they did, but this was always partly because the members of their house were who they were.

THE ENGLISH MONARCHY,
POWERS AND LIMITATIONS, IN THE MIDDLE AGES

Since feudal times we have moved as a nation from subjection to a proprietary monarchy into conditions in which in many ways it is the community that is proprietary. In the Middle Ages our crowned rulers thought of themselves as possessing their realm as hereditary overlords of it and as being personally responsible for its government, and of their administrative officials as being immediately answerable for their conduct to them.

When first we can discern some of the main features of English monarchy in Anglo-Saxon times we find that a claim to the throne was normally based on membership of the royal family, outside the limits of which the Witenagemot or national assembly was not likely to stray when it exercised its regular function of electing the king. Primogeniture did then perhaps assist a claim but did not constitute a special right. Not even after the Norman Conquest for some long time : after 1066 five kings were to go their way before an eldest surviving son followed his father on the English throne in the person of Richard I.

It was, nevertheless, only to be expected that the succession to the throne would be assimilated to feudal rules of inheritance. Had not Henry I's writs spoken of his realm as though it were a feudal honour? Did not the king succeed to the possession of land himself and to the suzerainty of his vassals' lands as well as to his royal rights and prerogatives? Was not the sovereign "dominus" as well as "rex"? At the accessions of Henry I (1100), Stephen (1135), and John (1199), none of whose titles to reign* was clear-cut, their claim was bolstered up by an appeal to the election or consent of clergy and people. But from the beginning of the thirteenth century for nearly three hundred years the rules of succession to real property were dogmatically applied to the succession to the throne, except at the revolution which brought in Henry IV in 1399.

The principle of hereditary succession may perhaps be said to have been most clearly established when Edward II was able to reckon his reign from the day after his father's death; and with the accession of Richard II (1377), Edward III's grandson and heir, and with the application of what lawyers call the principle of representative primogeniture, we may say that the crown had become a birthright. And so doubtless it would have remained had there not been occasions of usurpation and of disputed or disputable succession when formalities of popular election and consent (sometimes even parliamentary consent) proved useful in supporting a title that was shaky on hereditary grounds alone. Especially at times when violent remedies were found for constitutional and political ills in the form of the depositions of kings the old notion of election and consent was refurbished.

How importantly the coronation was regarded is clear from the fact that down to Henry III (himself included) our kings reckoned their accession and the legally effective beginning of their reign from its date. In this ceremony of inauguration there took place the king's anointing with holy oil, the delivery of the regalia, and the enthroning. In a society based fundamentally on rank and dignity those of the king were supreme. The king was an estate in himself: his royal "dignitas" was his own. At his coronation, when his claim to rule was transmuted into a right to rule, this was solemnly recognised; he became by the rite of the anointing, which was regarded as more important in the medieval period than the act of crowning, a "persona mixta", something more than a mere layman, in some sense one of the Lord's anointed. But the coronation service also emphasised that his distinctive position as anointed king rested on his being accepted by the people over whom he was set to rule, an acceptance which might take the form of election, recognition, or mere acclamation.

The king's elevation was also conditioned by his sworn oath, in which was outlined, in an elementary but impressive way, his primary duties to give peace to God's Church and the people, to put down wrongdoing, and to be just in his judgments and merciful. From the second half of the tenth century the traditional form of this threefold oath remained substantially unchanged until 1308, when (for the coronation of Edward II) it was recast in order to make the king promise to grant and preserve good laws and customs, and when a fourth clause was added to make him promise to observe laws to be chosen by the people or community; this fourfold oath then endured with but little alteration until after the Glorious Revolution of 1688. From time to time additional royal promises may have been made, but the oath itself, threefold and then fourfold, was all but sacrosanct; it enshrined a living principle that kings only forgot to their cost; here was the ark of the constitutional covenant.

Both Edward II and Richard II, like Edward I before them, seem to have regarded their coronation oath as including an undertaking to maintain their own prerogative rights as a duty to themselves. But that was not the view of their subjects, who stressed only the obligation to observe the law and custom. It was this view that was dominant. The grounds mainly alleged for the deposition of Edward II (1327) were his insufficiency and negligence, but not the least of the charges preferred against him was his contravention of his coronation oath. The point was even more strongly urged during the reign and at the deposition of Richard II. After the political crisis of 1387-8 Richard was compelled to take the oath again; and in 1399, in the record and process of his deposition, the clauses of the oath were given in full as a preface to the list of charges against him, and chief in the catalogue of his demerits were his misdeeds and illegalities that constituted breaches of the coronation oath: formally he was deposed for perjury.

The authority of our medieval kings was limited by the prevailing general theoretical recognition of the sovereignty of law, and of the existence of private rights which their own must not unjustifiably conflict with or deny. Their view of public utility and their resulting domestic policies must be brought to the touchstone of law and custom. It was in this sense that Bishop Stubbs thought of our two greatest exponents of the arts of medieval kingship, Henry II and Edward I, as being "in their better actions defenders of the law, in their worse actions captious defenders of their right." Their political and constitutional situation compelled our medieval sovereigns to entertain some respect at least for the sanctions of legality. If they failed to do so it was at their peril.

Practically the medieval English king's power was limited because he was compelled to get a lot of the work of administration done, especially local administration, by decentralising public functions into the private hands of vassals, lay and ecclesiastical, who frequently derived their franchises from the possession of large landed estates; and also because in his own central administration, especially as its work became more complex and complicated, he was forced to delegate administrative functions to his officials and their ministries, such as the Exchequer and the Chancery. But the king himself was never simply the "dignified" head of the State but its primary "efficient" part as well. All its commands ran as writs in his name and became ineffectual with his death; his household was the hub of the machine of government, and he himself was the mainspring of its activities.

How true this is was so often shown by the way in which the accession of a new king could change decisively the whole existing complexion of politics, especially the relationship between the king and his barons. The king must rule as well as reign. Edward II was the first king after the Conquest who was not "a man of business", and he was deposed as "inutilis". His reign had seen an attempt to distinguish between the crown and the person of the king, and some development of the notion that the king could be constrained to act in the proper interests of the crown by those who had sworn allegiance to it as well as to him; but this doctrine of capacities was rejected as false and alien.

What really mattered in medieval English political life was that the king should govern responsibly, not who should be responsible for government. This was never but exceptionally in question. All would really be well if only the king and his magnates concurred on policy, although, in baronial eyes, this was only likely if they advised him what to do. At times they felt his hand over-heavy on themselves, particularly in matters of feudal finance, and there were ways in which the king might be more generally tyrannical. The promises of the coronation oath were too vaguely worded to restrain the king except in his conscience, so that after the Conquest it became for a time usual for the king to amplify and expand his oath by granting a special coronation charter (sometimes laid on the altar of the church of his consecration and later dispatched in copies throughout the land for public appreciation). This was the case with most of the Norman kings and with Henry II.

They sometimes promised, quite explicitly, reforms of a legal character and in their judicial and feudal practices. But these coronation charters often turned out to be little more than bids for popular support, coronation largesse, incidental expenses best written off and forgotten. Richard I and John felt that they could dispense with them, and the latter's first general charter, Magna Carta of 1215, "the great capitulation", was different from all its predecessors (including its prototype, the coronation charter of Henry I), in that it came at the end of a period of oppressive rule on the part of its *grantor*, and in circumstances not of national trust and expectation (however misplaced) but of national disgust and despair.

Hence its so-called "sanctions" clause, providing for a committee of the barons authorised by the king to compel him to observe the charter. Rightful resistance must be saved from the taint of rebellion. It did not work, for the selfsame general reason that the baronial scheme of government did not work in 1258-63, when the barons took charge of the royal administration of Henry III, in order to reform it: the barons at such times could neither get on with the king nor get on without him. The problem was one of rights as well as of right, and a just balance between the king's and his people's rights would best be secured when both king and people agreed what was for the common profit of the realm. Promises of reform of royal government in the shape of royal charters, or their confirmation, that is, royal acts of self-limitation, were proved unsatisfactory by the recurrent crises of the thirteenth century (e.g. in 1215, 1233, 1258, 1297).

Gradually it came to be realised that it would be better if the scheme of government itself provided checks both on the royal power and on that feudal anarchy into which baronial reform movements tended to degenerate. It was in royally summoned parliaments that methods to do this were contrived, so that neither the realm should suffer periodic turmoil and uncertainty nor the monarchy acts of disrespect and disregard. Eventually these parliaments came to meet frequently and ceased to be exclusively ministerial and aristocratic. By the beginning of Edward III's reign (1327) the elected Commons were an essential part of them. The "community of the realm" was no longer the feudatories alone; and it was the introduction of the representative principle into the structure of parliaments which suggests, perhaps more forcibly than does anything else, the transition from a more feudal than national to a more national than feudal conception of the realm.

Consent thus became more broadly based, whether we have in mind taxation or legislation, so much so that by the end of the fourteenth century it had become an axiom that what parliaments did only parliaments could undo. Parliament was bringing to a focus the unity of the realm as something other than that of a feudal state, and also was steadily promoting the idea that the king must regard his office as a trust. It was these developments which permitted Sir John Fortescue, a mid-fifteenth century Chief Justice, to speak of the government of England as a "dominium politicum et regale", under which there was a measure of participation by subjects in government; the participation he envisaged was the sharing of the many in parliament rather than the few in council. Before absolutist notions bedevilled English constitutional development under the Tudors, Fortescue had recognised that if the monarchy was to be controlled it must be by parliamentary limitations. The kingdom might be a piece of real property; in his view it was, nevertheless, property of a public character, the kingship was a public office, and the "prince" was a public person. His theory, however, fell short of the doctrine of parliamentary sovereignty, and the problem of whether the King or the King in Parliament was supreme was left for later theorists to postulate and for later political happenings to solve.

II

THE PROBLEM OF THE ATTENDANCE OF THE LORDS IN MEDIEVAL PARLIAMENTS

When, in his brilliant essay, *The Evolution of Parliament*, Pollard discussed the problem of attendance in medieval parliaments, he was mainly preoccupied with the elected commons.[1] This was not because he was unaware of the fact that there were many medieval occasions when the parliamentary attendance of the lords was defective. Indeed, he went so far as to say that there was 'hardly a parliament of the first half of the fourteenth century the opening of which had not to be postponed owing to defective attendance', and that the defect was 'always due to the absence of prelates and magnates'. Here, the moral which Pollard intended to point was not simply the lack of seriousness attaching (in

[1] A. F. Pollard, *The Evolution of Parliament* (2nd edition, London, 1926), especially pp. 316–20, and Appendix II (pp. 386–429). On one occasion Pollard referred to the 'scanty presence of members in medieval parliaments' (*op. cit.*, p. 332). Speaking of the boroughs, he remarked that 'the effort of Edward I to compel attendance at parliament had a waning success under his son and grandson'. ('History, English, and Statistics', *History*, xi. 23). Again, speaking more generally: 'members elected were regarded merely as a panel, from which a far smaller attendance was actually secured'; and again, 'it seems clear from the writs *de expensis* that election did not mean attendance, and that the large number of elections recorded . . . may convey an exaggerated impression of the importance of the commons in parliament' (*The Evolution*, p. 116). Regarding the commons, Pollard's notion was that there was no readily obedient response to the royal call to co-operate in parliament, either on the part of local communities (especially the boroughs) by enforcing the parliamentary attendance of their representatives, or on the part of individual knights of the shire or burgesses by being willing to submit to re-election. These ideas were disposed of (*a*) by Miss McKisack (*The Parliamentary Representation of the English Boroughs during the Middle Age* (Oxford, 1932), chapter iv), who disproved Pollard's assumption that absence of enrolment of the writs *de expensis* of parliamentary burgesses was evidence of their failure to attend parliament (see Appendix A of this article), and (*b*) by Professor J. G. Edwards (*Essays in Medieval History presented to T. F. Tout* (Manchester, 1925), 'The Personnel of the Commons in Parliament under Edward I and Edward II'; 'Re-election and the Medieval Parliament', *History*, xi), who undermined Pollard's notion of the rarity of proper parliamentary experience among the knights and burgesses. (See also J. S. Roskell, *The Commons in the Parliament of 1422* (Manchester, 1954), chapter iii.)

his opinion) to the habitual absence from parliament of so many of the elected commons, but also the supreme importance for parliament's proper functioning of the presence of the lords. In his view, the absence of prelates and magnates was 'a fatal defect in a parliament', whereas the absence of the knights and burgesses was not so prejudicial.[1] The question of how far in practice the lords reacted to the perennial challenge of their indispensability in parliament was, however, one to which he did not devote particular attention. This was something of a strange omission, if only because he made clear, by the way in which he so pertinaciously tackled the problem of the commons' attendance, his appreciation of the relation between the political importance of any one element in parliament's constitution and the number of those who composed it. He was certainly at least in no doubt of the significance of the absenteeism of the vast majority of the lords in modern times: it was for him 'a political portent' that at the Restoration the lords 'denied their obligation to obey the royal summons to parliament, while claiming the right to come if they chose', so that 'disobedience to the writ of summons became common form with the peers as time went

---

[1] *The Evolution*, p. 115. Pollard went on to note that 'when, later on, measures are taken to compel attendance at parliament, they are applied to magnates long before they are enforced upon knights of the shire or burgesses'. He perhaps ought, at this point, to have made clear that (as we shall see) the first record evidence of the lords being actually fined does not appear until the mid-fifteenth century, long after the commons had come to be considered essential to the working of parliament. Regarding their earlier position he might have been expected to remark that the fourteenth-century tract, the English *Modus tenendi parliamentum*, included the commons as well as the lords among those who were to be fined for non-attendance (*Modus tenendi parliamentum*, ed. T. D. Hardy (London, 1846), p. 29), the implication of its author surely being that a full attendance in parliament on the part of the representatives of local communities was as necessary as a full attendance on the part of the lords who represented only themselves. Fortunately, there is no shortage of other (and safer) evidence that Pollard was not always or exactly right in regarding the lords as alone essential to the proper conduct of parliament, especially in the period after the summoning of the commons became absolutely regular, that is, from the beginning of Edward III's reign. As we shall have cause to notice later on, some of Edward III's earlier parliaments were impeded by the absence of prelates and magnates, but their absence alone may well have been remarked in the parliament-roll because it alone was remarkable. Certainly, from then on the commons had their recognized functions in parliament, and the most important, presenting petitions and consenting to taxation, were vital. In any case, it was not the king's motive in summoning them to parliament to seek the silent consent of absentees. When on 5 April 1340, after a session of only eight days, Edward III adjourned parliament for a fortnight, no knight of the shire, citizen or burgess, just as no prelate, earl, baron or councillor, was to leave if he could not get back to expedite 'les busoignes le Roi et des Communes'. The parliament summoned to meet on Friday, 6 October 1363, was adjourned over the week-end by Chief Justice Green, because 'pluseurs des Prelatz, Grantz *et Communes* . . . ne sont pas uncore venuz' (*Rot. Parl.*, ii. 114, 275). There were many similar occasions when parliament got off to a late start, and for the same reason, in 1368, 1372, 1376, and January 1377 (*ibid.*, ii. 294, 309, 321, 361), and so on well into Richard II's reign, until with the parliament of 1386 the session for once began on the appointed day. One of the reasons sometimes given for the postponement of parliament's opening in the early years of Richard II's reign is perhaps rather significant: that some sheriffs had not returned their writs, a procedure upon which obviously depended the roll-call and the establishment of the bona fides of knights and burgesses (*ibid.*, iii. 3, 32, 55, 71, 88, 122, 132, 144, 149, 166, 203).

on'.[1] That medieval conditions might contain a not entirely dissimilar index did not apparently occur to him, at least not as regards the prelates and magnates.

Enough has perhaps been said to warrant an enquiry into the question of the attendance of the lords spiritual and temporal in the parliaments of the medieval period. It will have, I believe, at any rate the value of showing to those who may still regard as valid Pollard's theory that the commons were reluctant to attend parliament and were frequently absent in large numbers, that such a failure to face their obligations would only have been a characteristic shared by many of those who were actually summoned directly to parliament by individual writs. There are reasons to believe that, as regards the commons' unwillingness and failure to attend, Pollard very much overstated (to say the least of it) a charge which, even if it had been proved, certainly ought never to have been pressed home against them alone. The enquiry may well have some relevance to the problem of the political standing of the Lower House, for the absence of the lords from parliament on a large scale might be regarded as a factor influencing in certain circumstances the political authority and value of the commons' proceedings.

Let us first of all recapitulate briefly certain well-known facts about the prelates and magnates individually summoned to medieval parliaments. Normally, the attendance of the two archbishops of Canterbury and York and their nineteen suffragans, including the four diocesans of Wales, was demanded by the king. If a diocese was vacant, the writ of summons was addressed to the keeper of spiritualties; if a bishop was *in remotis agens*, to his vicar-general. The number of the regular clergy summoned varied considerably in the earlier phases of parliament's growth, but the tendency was for it to decrease and with comparative rapidity: Edward I summoned seventy abbots and priors to the great parliament of 1295, whereas by the beginning of his grandson's reign in 1327 the number of the religious had declined to nineteen. By the end of the century their number had been lifted to twenty-seven, round which figure it remained fairly constant. In 1341 the lay peers summoned numbered fifty-three; in 1377, they were sixty; in 1399, fifty; in 1413, thirty-eight; in 1449, forty-eight; in 1453, fifty-six; and at the end of Edward IV's reign, forty-five. At times of foreign campaigning, when the nobility frequently participated in considerable force, the total number of lords spiritual and temporal might fall to little more than sixty (as under Henry V, after 1415), but in the meantimes of peace or unsustained military activity, as in Richard II's reign and later on in Henry VI's, it might rise to nearly a hundred and sometimes even over-top that figure.

In the fourteenth century, parliament was summoned to meet, on an average, every eleven months; in the fifteenth, parliaments were newly summoned with

The Evolution, p. 314; p. 307.

roughly only half that frequency. In the later time, however, there was very much greater recourse to the practice of prorogation. And this meant, in fact, that there was no very serious overall difference between the two centuries in the number of separate sessions and occasions for attendance. There were, of course, single years when no parliament met at all, and occasionally, especially in the fifteenth century, there were times when for two or three years on end parliament did not come together; and practice might vary even within the compass of a single reign, a rapid frequency being followed by a very intermittent recourse to parliaments. But a rough average attendance in parliament of once a year, however long or short a session turned out to be, was something of a burden for prelates and magnates summoned time after time. And for this, and because of personal reasons operating in the case of individual men—old age, illness, preoccupation with royal business, and so on—one would expect to find some degree of incompleteness in attendance quite inevitable. Attendance on a scale resulting on most occasions in a tolerably comprehensive representation of the two estates comprising the Upper House of parliament was, doubtless, frequently accepted by the Crown as sufficient for normal purposes. Those present were in any case regarded as capable of binding those who failed to attend in answer to their summonses: absence, like silence, could be taken to imply consent. Even so, an individual summons to a prelate or magnate commanded his personal attendance, and was meant to be obeyed. The lords were firmly enjoined to come, and in no wise to fail. In 1305 was introduced into the writ the additional admonition, 'omnibus aliis pretermissis', which was used until 1334; this formula was then changed for 'omni excusacione voluntaria cessante', a phrase immediately modified to 'omni excusacione cessante', which thenceforward became a normal inclusion.[1] Already, the writs that had gone out ordering parliament to meet at Northampton on 24 April 1328 and at Salisbury on 16 October following, had stated that it was not the royal intention to admit any proctor of prelate or magnate to excuse his personal attendance.[2] The writs summoning to Westminster for 16 March 1332 had said that no proctors or 'excusatores' would be admitted except for evident necessity. Those arranging for the parliament of 30 September 1331 had referred to the frequent postponement of parliament's business because of the absence of prelates and magnates who did not come on the day appointed but much later. The writs for the parliament of 3 February 1339 stated that absence would not be excused because, on account of the frequent failure of prelates and magnates to attend, the king's business had been obstructed in some parliaments, 'nonnullis parliamentis'. When parliament was summoned to meet in mid-January 1349 certain exonerations by patent were suspended, and the writs not only said that absence would not be

[1] *Reports from the Lords' Committees touching the dignity of a peer* (London, 1820–9), iii. 168.
[2] *Ibid.*, iv. 381, 386.

excused, but those to the prelates and abbots stated in addition that proxies would not be admitted. In the writs for the parliament of November 1355 immunities from attendance were again waived, and the abbots forbidden once more to appoint proxies.[1] Between 1362 and 1371 the writs re-extended the prohibition to bishops as well.[2] How far it was successful we may perhaps judge from the fact that from the last occasion of its formal use in the writs summoning the parliament of February 1371, there have actually survived the letters of proxy of no fewer than seven bishops and eleven abbots.[3] From 1372 to 1379 the writs continued merely to say that absence would not be excused, and from 1379 to 1399 that absence would not be excused except for infirmity. Then, with the accession of Henry IV there is an end put to these periodic variations on this theme, and the writs thenceforward simply require personal attendance without any corroborative phraseology.[4] However soon, and for however long or short a time, new phrases in the writs of summons became common form, some significance may surely be attached to the circumstances which prompted their first inclusion or their later replacement by a formula of greater urgency.

But quite apart from the note of compulsion in the writs of summons themselves, there are not wanting other indications that, however highly our medieval sovereigns valued silence, they preferred presence to absence on the part of those lords whom they desired or felt themselves obliged to summon. They did not mean their parliaments to be travesties. Sometimes, of course, royal offices or commissions, or national policy, involved the absence of an individual prelate or lay magnate from parliament. Such a contingency, however, frequently if not invariably was met by a *vacatur* of his writ or the sending of a second writ of explicit discharge. (This, of course, assumes that he had been summoned: if a lay lord were out of the country, no writ issued.) During the fourteenth and fifteenth centuries, times of war or agitated relations with Scotland, there were periodic remissions of attendance on account of military preoccupations or engagement in negotiation in that quarter, sometimes in favour of one or more of the northern prelates and lay magnates of those parts as well: in February 1313 the bishops of Durham and Carlisle were ordered to send proctors and to keep themselves at home, and ten northern barons were commanded not to leave Northumberland, in spite of their parliamentary summonses, without special royal order;[5] two years later, when the situation in northern England was more serious still, all the prelates of the province of York, including the

[1] *Reports from the Lords' Committees touching the dignity of a peer* (London, 1820–9), iv. 408, 403, 501, 578, 607.
[2] *Ibid.*, pp. 631–47.
[3] Parliament and Council, Letters of Proxy, Public Record Office, S.C. 10/29, 30.
[4] *Reports on the dignity*, iv. 680–759.
[5] *Parliamentary Writs* (Record Commission, London, 1827–34), ed. F. W. Palgrave, vol. ii, division ii, p. 91, nos. 51–2.

abbots, were told to resort to proctorial representation, and nearly a score of lay barons from north of Trent were instructed to ignore their summonses and look to defence; in September 1320 the primate of York and his suffragan of Carlisle, because of their embroilment in Anglo-Scottish negotiations, were excused coming to the Westminster, Michaelmas parliament;[1] in January 1337 the writs of prorogation from York to Westminster addressed to the earl of Angus and four other magnates were not sealed, because they were on active service in Scotland;[2] in July 1346 there was a wholesale discharge of the prelates and magnates of the north country from personal attendance in parliament (the prelates were to send proxies) to enable them to meet the Scottish invasion that was to come to grief at Neville's Cross;[3] in 1372 the two northern bishops and certain northern nobles were excused parliamentary attendance at their discretion, but if, after weighing the business for which parliament was to assemble, they decided not to come, they were each to send a proctor or attorney with full instructions and authority to act;[4] in July 1388 the bishops of Durham and Carlisle, the earl of Northumberland and seven other northern temporal lords were ordered to stand to the defence of their region against the Scots;[5] halfway through the first session of the parliament of July 1433 the council agreed that Lords Dacre and Fauconberg might be excused from parliament for the better keeping of the truce with Scotland; and it was on the grounds of threat from the northern kingdom that, only nine days before the parliament of February 1449 was due to meet, the bishop of Durham, the earl of Westmorland, and six other magnates were excused attendance by writs of privy seal.[6] These instances of discharge by writ for obviously valid reasons of national expediency (with the possible exception of the case of 1433, when Dacre and Fauconberg certainly came to the second session of that parliament) are practically all of that type that I have been able to discover for a period of a century and half. Discharge was not glibly conceded, and when it did happen to be granted, it was in the shape of an explicit and formal exoneration, and normally under the great seal.[7]

There were, of course, other formal acquittances from personal attendance made by the Crown as of royal grace and favour to individual prelates and nobles, mainly on the grounds of illness or old age. These exemptions, issuing in the form of letters patent under the great seal, were usually granted for life, but could be (if rarely) for very short periods or even a single parliament; and in

---

[1] *Parliamentary Writs* (Record Commission, London, 1827–34), ed. F. W. Palgrave, vol. ii, division ii, p. 435, nos. 22–5; p. 436, nos. 30–1; p. 138, no. 41; p. 139, no. 42; p. 230, no. 35.

[2] *Cal. Close Rolls, 1333–7*, p. 736.   [3] *Ibid., 1346–9*, p. 146.

[4] *Ibid., 1369–74*, p. 463.   [5] *Ibid., 1385–9*, p. 604.

[6] *Proceedings and Ordinances of the Privy Council, 1386–1542* (Record Commission, London, 1834–7), ed. N. H. Nicolas, iv. 174; vi. 65.

[7] If our records of the council, however, were fuller, more discharges conceivably might have been found for the fifteenth century, issuing as writs of privy seal.

most cases involving prelates they required the beneficiary's representation in parliament by proxy. A list of them from the beginning of Edward III's reign until the end of the fifteenth century comprises some twenty-three bishops, eight abbots, and sixteen temporal lords.[1] This is not an impressively large number at all when the length of the period is taken into consideration. It is obvious, moreover, that they fall, with one or two exceptions, into certain well-defined phases: between 1340 and 1361, in Richard II's reign and at the very beginning of Henry IV's, and in the second half of Henry VI's and the opening years of Edward IV's reign. And the biggest effect on attendance which these royal concessions ever occasioned at any one time was in January 1398, when three bishops, two abbots, and three temporal lords stood free to be absent either by exemptions for life or by privileges of more limited scope: at the parliament then held at Shrewsbury the bishops of Lincoln, Bath and Wells, and Durham, the abbots of Gloucester and Glastonbury, the earl of Oxford, John de la Warre, and Robert de Lisle of Rougemont, were exonerated, and of these the first two bishops and all three temporal lords were near the end of their life and could hardly have been expected to travel, discharge or no discharge. The sum of absences, for example, in the November 1355 parliament, attributable to Edward III's licences, was no more than three bishops, one abbot, and two lay peers; absences excused by Henry VI and Edward IV together would have affected, for instance, in the closing stages of the parliament of 1463–5, no more than four bishops and three lay peers. And these were high-water marks in the tide of exonerations from parliamentary attendance by royal grant. There were no discharges at all originating under Henry V, and at the end of his reign none, dating even from an earlier period, was in being.

For the most part, royal exonerations by patent were not readily granted, and their collective effect at any one time was of no very great moment. Even so, there were a few occasions when it was felt needful to insist that the privilege which they conferred should be waived. When, for example, parliament was summoned to meet at Westminster on 19 January 1349 in order to consider the three-cornered negotiations recently held at Calais with the French and Flemings, and when all the writs included an unusual additional clause that absence would not be excused, Bishop Bransford of Worcester was ordered to attend, notwithstanding his immunity for life (granted him in 1342); the abbots of Oseney, Thornton, and Thorney, were similarly specially summoned to appear, despite any previous charters or patents of discharge. No prelates or abbots might send proctors, except Archbishop Zouche of York, Bishop Northburgh of Lichfield, and Bishop Hethe of Rochester. The same suspensions of immunity were repeated when parliament was prorogued (because of the Black Death)

---

[1] See Appendix B.

until after Easter, by which time it had had to be abandoned.[1] Bransford's successor at Worcester, Raynold Briene, and also Bishop Pascal of Llandaff similarly found their patents of exemption of no avail when the parliament of 23 November 1355 was summoned; this time abbatial representation by proxy was once more prohibited expressly. Again, the abbot of Evesham, exonerated for life in January 1375 and not summoned with the other abbots on 1 December 1376, was separately summoned by writ of 16 January following to attend parliament in person eleven days later, without prejudice to the future exercise of his privilege.[2]

Although formal exonerations were on the whole remarkably few, and when granted might even be temporarily suspended, there is no dearth of evidence suggesting that personal attendance at parliaments by prelates and magnates, however insistent and corroborated was the language of the writs of summons, very frequently fell short of the royal ideal. This was so in those late thirteenth and early fourteenth century assemblies when prelates and magnates met to afforce the special sessions of king and council described as parliaments. During the Westminster parliament of Michaelmas 1278 there took place in the king's chamber the ceremony in which Alexander III of Scotland did homage to Edward I and, by the mouth of Robert de Bruce, earl of Carrick, swore fealty: out of the thirteen earls summoned to the parliament, only six (Bruce included) were present, along with four bishops.[3] We need not be surprised at the fewness of the bishops: a month or so before a parliament was to meet at Northampton on 20 January 1283, the archbishop of Canterbury, when ordering the bishop of London to make his citation of the clergy of the province in pursuance of the royal writs, intimated that the bishops might be all the more willing to come because he intended to consecrate the bishop-elect of Hereford at the same time and place. Again, when in the parliament of May 1290 Edward I secured an aid for the marriage of his daughter, those who made the grant included no more than six bishops and the same number of earls.[4] The long-drawn-out disturbance of the former cordial relations between the king and baronage which followed the grave constitutional crisis of 1297 possibly had the effect of 'gingering up' baronial interest in their parliamentary duties.[5] But at what proved

---

[1] *Reports on the dignity*, iv. 578–9, 581–2.

[2] *Ibid.*, p. 672; the abbot of Evesham had recently been embroiled with the earl of Warwick, and may have requested to be summoned on this occasion (*Chronicon Anglie, 1328–1388*, ed. E. M. Thompson (R. S.), pp. 393–4).

[3] Palgrave, *op. cit.*, i. 7.   [4] *Ibid.*, p. 10; p. 20.

[5] The famous letter sent to Pope Boniface VIII after discussions during the Lincoln parliament of Hilary 1301 (in which the barons asserted the direct dominion of the English Crown over Scotland and denied the papal claim to interfere) was sealed by (among others) as many as seventy-five out of the ninety earls and lay barons summoned to the parliament (Palgrave, *op. cit.*, i. 102, no. 42). Not all who sealed, however, were present in the parliament (cf. J. H. Round, 'The Barons' Letter to the Pope', *The Ancestor*, vi. 189).

to be Edward I's last parliament, which met at Carlisle in January 1307, the attendance, both prelatical and baronial, seems to have been woefully thin, even allowing for the season and the remote place of meeting. A list survives of those summoned, with highly interesting if sometimes puzzling annotations against their names in the shape of dots and crosses as well as verbal remarks.[1] Those listed as summoned were the prince of Wales, eleven earls, eighty-six barons, two archbishops, nineteen bishops, and forty-eight abbots; 167 prelates and magnates in all. It would appear that perhaps no more than forty-one, almost certainly no more than fifty-seven, including in each case only six secular

---

[1] The Chancery Vetus Codex, P.R.O., C. 153/1, faithfully copied by Palgrave (*op. cit.*, i. 183 *et seq.*).

In this list the word 'hic' is put against the names of the prince of Wales, the earl of Lincoln, and eight barons. Against each of the names of twenty-three magnates (including three of the ten marked 'hic') is a dot. There is a dot, too, against the names of the archbishop of York and five other bishops (Carlisle, London, Chichester, Worcester, and Coventry and Lichfield, the treasurer, who were certainly present), and against the names of five abbots (Holm Cultram (near Carlisle), Peterborough, Waltham, Tichfield, and Torre). Now, in the large collection of letters of proxy for this parliament, there is not one of these secular prelates and abbots who excuses his absence. Moreover, from a comparison between a similarly annotated companion list of knights of the shire and burgesses and a list of the writs *de expensis* for attendance, it appears that every knight, and every burgess (except four), who is marked with a dot was given a writ *de expensis*. It would seem that a dot signified attendance. If this is so, it may be conjectured that the annotation 'hic' meant 'present when (or perhaps before) parliament began', and that a dot signified attendance then or (more probably) later in the session (dots being placed against ten of the twenty-seven magnates specially re-summoned on 22 February). Assuming this to be a correct deduction, we may then calculate an attendance of no more than thirty lay magnates, six secular prelates, and five abbots. What difference of signification was meant to be conveyed by a cross being placed against a name—this symbol is laid only against the names of lay magnates—it is difficult to say. But even if we were to assume that it too denoted attendance, we should need to add only sixteen more lay magnates, and we should then calculate our attendance as forty-six lay magnates, six secular prelates, and five abbots: fifty-seven in all. No symbol or annotation appears against the names of five earls and thirty-five lay barons, and eight of the rest were marked as excused and did not attend, the earl of Surrey, for example 'excusatur quia in Wallia de licencia Regis'. It could, of course, be urged that so far as the lay magnates are concerned the only safe index of absenteeism, and even then only in the first six weeks of the session, is the list of three earls and twenty-four others who were specially re-summoned on 22 February to attend on pain of forfeiture, to whom should be added as absentees the eight magnates excused from coming. This would be to postulate an attendance, even at that stage of the parliament, of sixty-three lay magnates out of the ninety-eight summoned. If a dot in the annotated list means attendance, to these sixty-three must be added ten out of the twenty-seven specially re-summoned magnates against whose names in the list dots are placed, making seventy-three in all. But to add these ten to the list of those present is not only to accept the annotated list but to admit that it was being kept up to date long enough for the attendance of these previously recalcitrant magnates to be recorded in it. Regarding the bishops and abbots dotted present in the list, we can have a fairly quiet mind, because we know that none of them sent proxies, and that at least ten of the remaining fifteen bishops and at least thirty-five of the remaining forty-three abbots certainly did. Even if we ignored the annotated list altogether and assumed that all bishops and abbots who did not send proxies did in fact attend, the bishops and abbots attending would only number eleven and thirteen respectively. If the sixty-three lay magnates be added to these, we have a total attendance of eighty-seven. If we use the annotated list only to swell the total of lay magnates in attendance to the maximum limit of seventy-three, but ignore it for the prelates, even then our total would be only ninety-seven out of 167 summoned.

prelates and five abbots, attended. Certainly, letters of proxy from no fewer than ten bishops have actually survived, and the thirty-five extant abbatial letters of proxy show that the abstention of the regulars was quite as serious as that of the bishops. Again, when nearly six weeks had passed from the date when parliament had been due to begin, writs were sent out (on 22 February) enjoining personal attendance, on pain of forfeiture, on Thomas earl of Lancaster, the earls of Warwick and Angus, and twenty-four more lay magnates. It appears that none of these three earls and only ten of the other twenty-four so threatened subsequently attended.

It has already been remarked that there were times, especially in the fourteenth century, when parliaments got off to a bad start for want of prompt appearance on the part of both lords and commons, but mainly, it frequently appears, on the part of the lords. It would not do to prejudge the issue by assuming that, because parliaments did not as a rule last long, failure to make an early arrival meant no arrival at all. It is, nevertheless, very tempting to believe that this was sometimes the case: that when parliament did get under way, it was often with an attendance that was not completely satisfactory, either then or later in the session. There is, of course, no question that the business of parliament was frequently impeded by dilatory appearance on the part of those individually summoned, and on occasion dislocated or even vitiated altogether for want of the lords' attendance. Such phenomena were by no means entirely novel when Edward of Carnarvon followed his great father in 1307. But from this time forward there would appear to have been more official notice taken of default, and one inference might be that the problem was becoming more acute. This is not very surprising, in view of the contemporary aggravation of more frequent sessions by the summoning of parliament on numerous occasions to York and elsewhere far away from the capital. (Between 1314 and 1335 parliament met oftener away from Westminster than it did there, and no fewer than eleven times at York.) This may very well have encouraged a 'stay away' habit, especially on the part of the prelates of the southern province, whose aversion to the northern metropolitan city in particular became almost a part of their professional duty as suffragans of Canterbury: an ecclesiastical factor of importance. Mainly because of the absence of several prelates and magnates, the business of the parliament summoned even to Westminster for 8 July 1313 could not be fully dealt with, and on 26 July fresh writs were issued for the early holding of a new session on 23 September. We are given some indication of the number of bishops and abbots and other regulars absent from the July session in the list of recipients of special writs sent out on 26 July and 13 August, not only calling their attention to the retarding of parliament's business, but also requesting loans of the kind already contributed by those prelates who had recently managed to attend. From the list of addressees it is clear that in July

1313, out of seventeen secular prelates summoned, the archbishop of York and the bishops of Durham, Lincoln, Rochester, Hereford, Bangor, and St. Asaph had been absent from the parliament; that although the bishops of Salisbury, Norwich, Ely, and Llandaff had attended to begin with, they had left before the king had put to the prelates the matter of the loan; and that at least twenty-eight out of the fifty abbots and other regulars summoned had either not attended at all or had similarly taken themselves off.[1] How many of the temporal lords had been absent is not known. But only a week before parliament was due to come together again on 23 September, writs prohibiting an intended tournament at Brackley (ominous occupation, perhaps ominous rendez-vous) were sent to Thomas earl of Lancaster and five out of the nine other earls summoned to the parliament, and parliament had, in fact, met before (on 24 September) safe-conducts were issued to Lancaster, Hereford, and Warwick.[2] There is no reason to believe that in this time of great political disaffection and threatening civil war, the attendance of the lay magnates was any better than that of the ecclesiastics. Less than a year and a half later, at the Hilarytide parliament of 1315, a petition was put forward by Roger Mortimer of Chirk which could not be determined without the common assent of the magnates: 'nec sunt hic ad presens tot quot requirentur; ideo expectet proximum parliamentum'. Similarly a petition of Griffin de la Pole, regarding his right to the land of Powis, was postponed, 'pur ceo qe plousours de grant Seigneurs, Prelatz et autres ne sont pas a ore a cest Parlement, et eux qe cy sont ne voillent emprendre de juger chose qe touche le tretiz sanz assent de toutz'.[3] And so it went on in this unquiet time. On 28 January a year later (1316), the day after parliament was due to come together at Lincoln, the earl of Lancaster and other magnates had not come, and parliament marked time: on 5 February the earl and other 'proceres' were still absent; three more days passed, and by then the earls of Hereford, Richmond, and Pembroke had arrived, but Lancaster and others not; only on 12 February could the causes of summons be declared 'in pleno parliamento', by which time Lancaster had appeared. The prelates had not shown up satisfactorily either: the chancellor had been ordered to scrutinize their letters of proxy and excusation, and a committee, consisting of the chancellor, treasurer, and one of the justices, was set up to do this and to report to the king those who had failed to come or send sufficient proxies, with a view to further (unspecified) action. There are actually extant the letters of excusation from as many as eight bishops

---

[1] Palgrave, *op. cit.*, vol. ii, division ii, Appendix, p. 64 (no. 2), p. 65 (nos. 7, 9).

[2] Rymer, *Foedera*, iii. 438–9. To facilitate Warwick's appearance, steps had already been taken to postpone certain assizes against him in the bishopric of Durham, and the holding of other assizes in the northern shires had also been deliberately deferred because of the parliament (Palgrave, *op. cit.*, ii. 102–3, nos. 25–6).

[3] *Rot. Parl.*, i. 289, nos. 70, 71.

on this occasion. Four of these had also sent their apologies for absence to the parliament of the year before, when there had been at least an equal number of bishops away from Westminster; and certainly in 1316 no fewer than twenty-eight out of the religious declined to come in person and sent proxies instead.[1] The number of absentees among the prelates and abbots was, however, undoubtedly greater than this. For Archbishop Reynolds of Canterbury, whose letter of proxy is not extant, did not come to Lincoln: on 16 February he was sent a royal writ calling attention to the unanimous grant of a subsidy in his absence by such of the clergy of his province as had attended the parliament, but requiring him to summon convocation to give that general approval which had been so obviously lacking at Lincoln. Clearly, the 'turn-up' at the parliament had been miserable, and his mandate saw fit to ignore all reference to the grant. A meeting of the northern convocation of York was also deemed necessary.[2]

There were perhaps special reasons why the higher clergy were not pulling their weight at this time. The clergy generally, with some of the foremost bishops at their head, were taking exception to the forms of citation used by the Crown, and there was the added complication of the Canterbury-York dispute. Besides, there was ever an almost inevitable 'wastage'. It was so in convocation, and it was also regularly to be so, for example, in the later provincial chapters of the black monks. Travel meant travail, and, as a matter of course, all sorts of conventions composed of persons individually summoned, including those of the superior *gradus* of parliament (as Stubbs[3] once judiciously remarked), took on something of the appearance of representative assemblies, because so many of those summoned preferred to send proxies.

The Lincoln experience of 1316 was by no means unique so far as the prelates are concerned. Their absence continued to be a feature of parliamentary sessions in this period of clerical dissatisfaction, as well as later. It was so even in the critical York parliament of 1322, when the Ordinances of 1311 were repealed and much else of importance was done. At the southern convocation in the previous December, when the reversal of the Despensers' exile was demanded of the clergy, as many as ten of the seventeen bishops of the province had not come. To the York parliament as many as ten came, but without their archbishop; and only three suffragans of Canterbury went to both assemblies.[4] The attendance of the regulars at York was doubtless as deplorable as usual: the letters of proxy of over half of those summoned have actually survived,

[1] Palgrave, *op. cit.*, ii. 156, nos. 17–20, P.R.O., S.C.10/3, nos. 177–227; the bishops of Lincoln (even he), Lichfield, Ely, London, Rochester, Worcester, Hereford, and Llandaff excused themselves.
[2] Palgrave, *op. cit.*, ii. 158, no. 29; p. 162, no. 45.
[3] W. Stubbs, *The Constitutional History of England* (Oxford, 1880, Library Edition), iii. 527.
[4] Palgrave, *op. cit.*, vol. ii, division ii, Appendix, p. 173, no. 44; vol. ii, division ii, p. 259, no. 78.

including those of the heads of even such houses as Bridlington, Kirkstall, and Welbeck, in the diocese of York itself.[1] The absenteeism of the prelates, secular and religious, from another York parliament of some ten years later—the parliament summoned for 4 December 1332—was so much more serious than usual that it could not be overlooked, and the abstentions of the lay peers were also very substantial. Admittedly this parliament was the third of the year, but Edward III needed backing for his personal desire to support Edward Balliol, the English candidate for the Scottish throne, who had recently had some military success in the northern kingdom and had got himself crowned. The session began on a Friday and was promptly 'continued' over the weekend, and then for yet another day, because of the 'non venue des Grantz'. No panels of triers of petitions could be appointed, and so petitions were not received. Deliberations did, however, begin, and lasted until, when parliament was theoretically a week old (Friday, 11 December), the *gradus* separately and then together advised the king that for want of attendance on the part of the prelates and magnates they did not dare nor were able to counsel him to do more than prorogue parliament for nearly six weeks (until 20 January 1333). In the meantime, although there was no need to re-summon those who had attended the session, the absentees were to be specially charged to come, the writs drawing their attention to the serious results of their recent absence. The roll of this parliament itself discloses that of the higher clergy only the archbishop of York, the bishops of Carlisle and Lincoln, and the abbots of York and Selby had been present. And this evidence is exactly confirmed by the writs of re-summons sent to the absentees. The list of those to whom they were sent further makes clear that at least five of the eleven earls summoned had failed to get to York, together with no fewer than thirty-seven out of the sixty-six other magnates.[2] Archbishops, bishops, abbots, priors, earls, and barons present had numbered no more than forty out of 129 summoned.

Whether the young Edward III was subjected to further humiliations of this sort when war with Scotland again required parliaments to meet at York in 1334 and 1335 is not known. But even after 1336, when for the rest of his long reign parliament always assembled at Westminster, there were certainly some occasions when the attendance of the lords was distressingly sparse. When on 5 April 1340, after a suspiciously short session of a bare week, parliament was adjourned for a fortnight (until Wednesday in Easter week), those who had come were told not to go away unless they could be sure of getting back.[3] Certainly, the abbots and priors had followed their habitual line: as many as twenty-one of their letters of excusation and proxy have survived for this

[1] P.R.O., S.C.10/7, nos. 344, 345; S.C.10/8, no. 364.
[2] *Rot. Parl.*, ii. 67; *Reports on the dignity*, iv. 418–19.
[3] *Rot. Parl.*, ii. 114.

parliament.[1] Fortunately, we are not left entirely in the dark about attendance in the first brief session of this spring parliament of 1340. The roll of the parliament gives us, in addition to the names of one or two other magnates, a list of the secular prelates and the earls who were there in time to hear the causes of summons declared 'en especialte' on the second day: Archbishop Stratford and seven of his sixteen suffragans who were able to come, did so, and so did the bishops of Durham and Carlisle, but without their primate; and seven of the thirteen earls summoned were there, too. In other words, roughly only half the bench of bishops was filled, and half of the comital seats. The list in the roll appears to be complete, because an examination of the personnel of the panel of triers of petitions, and of the committees set up to deal with 'les notes de Flaundres', the 'chevance de Brussell', the merchants of England, the alien priors, the keeping of the Scottish March, the 'busoignes de Gascoigne', and the keeping of the Isles and the sea-coasts, affords no further names regarding these two superior parliamentary *gradus*.[2] Limited though this evidence is— we are left unaware of the attendance of those of merely baronial rank—it is less unsatisfactory than the little evidence that remains regarding the next parliament of July 1340, when the king himself was in the Netherlands. There he was in urgent need of immediate supplies and sent special word home by the earls of Arundel and Gloucester and Sir William Trussell in order to secure prompt relief: the 'grantz' searched all possible ways and means to this end, but when they made a proposal to help with their wool, only Archbishop Stratford, the bishops of London and Chichester, the earl of Arundel himself and sixteen other lords subscribed.[3] Such a piece of evidence is perhaps merely faintly suggestive of a thin 'turn-up' of the prelates and lay peerage.

Of attendance at the next parliament but two, which met nearly four years later on Monday, 7 June 1344—and by then no parliament had been convened for a year—the evidence is, by way of contrast, quite positive. In spite of the fact that the southern convocation had supposedly been in session at St. Paul's for the past week, when parliament met to hear the chancellor's opening speech, of the prelates and greater magnates only the archbishop of Canterbury, the bishops of Chichester, Bath and Wells, and Ely, and the earl of Huntingdon were present 'ensemblement od ascuns des abbes et barons, et chivalers des counteez', etc. It was now revealed that in the convocation 'nul des grantz Prelatz' had appeared except the primate and his suffragans of London, Chichester, Ely, and the elect of Hereford, 'dont il (i.e. the king) se merveill trop'. Another cause of royal concern was the failure of the 'Grantz' to appear on the day of summons. Regarding the bishops, the king was enough dis-

---

[1] P.R.O., S.C.10/22, 23 (nos. 1084–1112).
[2] *Rot. Parl.*, ii. 112 (the bishop of Hereford was *in remotis agens*), 113–14.
[3] *Rot. Parl.*, ii. 118.

gruntled ('mal appaiez') to order the primate to deal with the contumacy of his clergy, but declared that for his part he would do to those who disobeyed his writs what was behoveful. Those who had appeared for the openings of convocation and parliament, he heartily thanked ('mercia molt'), and then ordered an adjournment pending further arrivals. On the second day, the bishops of London and Carlisle joined the handful of prelates in parliament, and perhaps the bishop of Lichfield (*Cestrensis*) came too or was expected, because he appears among the triers of petitions. By Thursday, the fourth day, Lichfield was certainly present at the declaration of the causes of summons, and the bishops of Salisbury and Lincoln are now recorded as present for the first time. This brought the tally of bishops to ten (including the primate) out of the twenty-one summoned. Of the twenty-six regular clergy summoned, only the abbots of Westminster and Reading and the priors of Coventry and Rochester were there to hear the formal opening speech. As many as eight out of the thirteen earls appeared then also. We are left in the dark about the extent of absenteeism among the other magnates, because the short list of five named barons present ends with the words 'et autres barons et baneretts'.[1] In spite of the fact that on the second day it had already been decided to ascertain which lords were absent, so that a written list could be supplied for the king's benefit 'pur ordeigner tieu punissement come lui plerra', it is doubtful whether many more bishops, abbots, earls, or barons came along. For the lists of triers of petitions add no names to those already collected, except the abbots of St. Albans and St. Augustine's, Canterbury. Neither do any fresh bishops, earls, or barons appear among the names of those thirty-one prelates, abbots, and magnates who on 23 June, three days before the end of the parliament, met to advise Edward III about France, with the sole exception of Sir Nicholas de Cantilupe. The ranks of the regulars, however, had by now increased to seven: the abbots of St. Albans, Westminster, Abingdon, Waltham, Reading, and Hyde by Winchester, and the prior of Coventry were now listed as present.[2] The king's threats had seemingly borne fruit, at any rate in this direction, because, before the session opened, of these heads of houses the abbots of St. Albans, Abingdon, Waltham, and Reading had certainly sent letters of excusation.[3] The extant letters of the regulars appointing proxies to this parliament number twenty. Those of the bishops extant number eight (including none from those whose attendance is referred to in the notices on the parliament-roll). Attendance in this parliament of 1344 would seem to have been almost as irritating to the government as in that of York, nearly twelve years before.

[1] *Rot. Parl.*, ii. 146–7. Technically the sees of Hereford and Norwich were vacant, but writs had issued to the new bishop of Norwich as 'electus' and to Hereford as 'electus confirmatus'.
[2] *Ibid.*, p. 148.
[3] P.R.O., S.C.10/23, nos. 1137, 1143; S.C.10/24, nos. 1156, 1158.

It is impossible to judge whether there was any improvement in the next parliament. Over two years passed before it met on 11 September 1346. But the situation was on this occasion abnormal in more than one sense: Edward III himself was over in France, where he had just won the battle of Crécy and begun the long siege of Calais; many of the nobility were with him; and the situation on the northern borders towards Scotland involved the expressly allowed absence from parliament of the northern prelates and abbots and eleven lay magnates. Sir Bartholomew de Burghersh's description of the recent campaign on the third day of the session was heard, the parliament-roll tells us, by Archbishop Stratford and only half his suffragans (London, Winchester, Salisbury, Norwich, Chichester, Ely, Hereford, and St. Asaph); of the twenty-five abbots and priors individually summoned, only the abbot of Westminster and the prior of the Hospital of St. John were there; none of the five earls not overseas had then appeared; of the eleven barons summoned, only two were present (Segrave and Berkeley) with Baron Wake, who had been excused with the other northerners: fourteen all told, nine of them secular prelates.[1]

Not until we come to the roll of the parliament of November 1355 do we meet with a like piece of evidence about the lords' attendance. The king had adjourned parliament for two days, 'par cause qe ceux qi furent somons . . . ne furent pas plenerement venuz', and then Chief Justice Shareshull announced to the lords and commons that Sir Walter Manny would explain the reasons for the meeting, arising as they did out of the diplomatic and military situation: of the twenty-one secular prelates summoned, the two archbishops and five bishops of the southern province alone were present, along with five out of eight earls.[2]

We have long to wait before such detailed evidence of the lords' attendance in parliament is again forthcoming in the rolls of the parliaments themselves. But, apart from the terms of the writs of summons with their steady insistence that excusation from personal attendance would not be accepted and their periodic order to the bishops and abbots not to appoint proxies, there is at our disposal a certain amount of interim data which, however imprecise it may be, suggests that a poor attendance on the part of the spiritual and lay peers was a recurrent, if not fairly constant, feature of the parliamentary situation. When the first parliament of 1348 came together on Monday, 14 January, there had to be adjournments from day to day, until Thursday, before Chief Justice Thorpe declared the causes of summons, because the 'grantz et autres' were not 'pleinement venuz'.[3] The first parliament to meet after the Black Death was summoned for Wednesday, 9 February 1351. For want of full attendance, the king's commission to begin the session was not read until the Friday, when seemingly Arundel was the only earl as yet present. The weekend passed. Even

---

[1] *Rot. Parl.*, ii. 158.   [2] *Ibid.*, p. 264.   [3] *Ibid.*, p. 164.

then, because the king 'avoit certeines Novels qe pluseurs des Grauntz somons . . . qi n'estoient pas lors venuz vendreient hastiement a Londres par cause du Parlement', there was a further adjournment for a day (until Tuesday) before the session was formally opened.[1] It is relevant to note that this parliament lasted for only another fortnight. In the next parliament of January 1352 and in the great council of September 1353, there were similar postponements of the opening formalities. At the parliament of November 1355 there was again a delayed start.[2]

That this dilatoriness was misliked by the king is clearly indicated by the inclusion in the writs of summons to the very next parliament (which met on 17 April 1357) of an order to appear on the first day.[3] In 1360 began a departure from the general rule of summoning parliaments to begin on a Monday, and in that year, and in 1361, 1362, and 1363, parliament was called to meet on a Friday, a Sunday, a Thursday, and a Friday respectively. There may have been here a deliberate intention to anticipate an originally decided date and discount the first weekend of the session as a period of grace for the late arrivals. But this experiment, if experiment it was, was short-lived, and in 1365 Monday resumed its position as the generally accepted day for the beginning of parliaments. The difficulty of getting off the mark remained. Those individually summoned to the parliament of Monday, 4 May 1366, were instructed in the writs to be there on the Sunday, so that parliament could be begun on Monday morning.[4] Failure to attend promptly on the part of those who did attend, was a commonplace.

The rolls of the later parliaments of Edward III frequently, and those of the early years of Richard II invariably, tell the old story of adjournments for want of attendance at the advertised start of a session.[5] Sometimes the clerk of the parliament went out of his way to be a little more explicit than usual about the reason: in January 1380 an adjournment of one day was made because 'une grande partie des Prelatz et Seigneurs . . . n'estoient encores venuz, a cause de grant pluvie et autre male temps q'avoit este les trois ou quatre jours devant'. At Northampton in the following November there was an immediate adjournment, the reason given being the delays caused by perilous roads and 'le outrageous cretyn de eawe q'estoit sourdez des grantz et continueles pluuyes et tempestes'. Begun on a Monday, parliament was not formally opened until the

---

[1] Rot. Parl., ii. 225.   [2] Ibid., pp. 236, 246, 264.
[3] Reports on the dignity, iv. 611-12.   [4] Ibid., p. 639.
[5] This was so in 1368 (Rot. Parl., ii. 294), 1372 (ibid., p. 309), 1376 (ibid., p. 321), January 1377 (ibid., p. 361), October 1377 (ibid., iii. 3), 1378, at Gloucester (ibid., p. 32), 1379 (ibid., p. 55), January 1380 (ibid., p. 71), November 1380, at Northampton (ibid., p. 88), 1381 (ibid., p. 98), May 1382 (ibid., p. 122), October 1382 (ibid., p. 132), February 1383 (ibid., p. 144), October 1383 (ibid., p. 149), April 1384, at Salisbury (ibid., p. 166), November 1384 (ibid., p. 184), 1385 (ibid., p. 203).

Thursday, and even then 'des ditz Seigneurs Temporeles y avoit moelt petite nombre'. An additional reason for this was alleged to be that John of Gaunt ('Monsr d'Espaigne') was still in the Scottish March 'avec grant partie des Contes et Barons del Roialme'. Certainly a week before this Lancaster was still at Berwick-on-Tweed, and so were the earls of Warwick and Suffolk, but the only other lords involved in the recent commissions of September and October to deal with breaches of the truce, were Archbishop Neville of York, the prior of the Hospital of St. John, and Richard Lord Scrope.[1] At the outset of the first parliament to be summoned after the dislocations of the Peasants' Revolt (that of 3 November 1381), 'grant partie des Prelatz et Seigneurs' had still not come, but the long postponement of the proper opening of this session was clearly due, in the main, to the difficult business of getting Lancaster and Northumberland to meet without an explosion of feeling. In the next parliament (May 1382) there was reported the same thin attendance of prelates and lords at the beginning of the session, and this time at least there is more than a hint that failure to attend promptly turned out to be failure to come at all: before the parliament ended, certain 'ordinances et establissementz' were agreed upon, one of which was to the effect that 'toutes singulers Persones et Communaltees q'averont desore la sommonce de Parlement, viegnent desenavant as Parlementz par manere come ils sont tenuz de faire', and that if anyone such 'soi absente ou ne viegne mye a la dite somonce, s'il ne se purra resonablement et honestement ent excuser devers le Roi nostre Seigneur, soit [il] amerciez et autrement puniz selonc ce qe auncienement a este usez deinz le Roialme . . . en ce cas'.[2] We are perhaps not entitled to doubt the literal correctness of the rolls of the autumn parliament of this year (October 1382) and of the mid-Lent parliament of the next (February 1383), when they state that, although on the first day 'le greindre partie des Seigneurs et autres' were not come to town, after a two-day delay 'la greindre partie' of the lords were then present. But certainly there was little change for the better when parliament met in the spring of 1384 (29 April) at Salisbury: the absence of Lancaster and other commissioners for redressing violation of truces with Scotland[3]—the earl of Northumberland and Lords Neville, Clifford, Scrope, and FitzWalter—was the formal reason for the postponement of the chancellor's opening speech for as much as a week. But, in addition to Lancaster and his colleagues, there were also absent 'ceux Prelatz et Seigneurs as queux pur diverses causes s'avoient ent fait excuser devers nostre dit Seigneur le Roi'. Evidently, not until after 9 May, when parliament had already been met eleven days, did Lancaster and other 'grantz Seigneurs' arrive, his brothers of Cambridge and Buckingham among them. It is not surprising that the lists of triers for this parliament are short

---

[1] *Rotuli Scotiae*, ii. 27, 29.   [2] *Rot. Parl.*, iii. 124.   [3] *Rot. Scot.*, ii. 58–9.

ones, nor that the chancellor had announced that 'le Roi defende a touz qe nul se depart de ce Parlement sanz especial congie de lui devant le fin de mesme le Parlement, sur peril q'appent'.[1] Whether the November session of this same year (1384) was better attended or not, there is little to show, but certainly no fewer than nine bishops sent letters of excusation.[2]

The parliament of October 1386 was the first for ten years to see the session begin on the day appointed in the writs of summons. Thenceforward, until 1413, prompt starts alternated with adjournments for want of prompt attendance, and then, from the beginning of Henry V's reign, parliament regularly came to be opened on the day stipulated in the writs. We must believe the parliament-rolls on this point. There is no reason, however, as we shall see, to think that prompt starts meant an adequate initial attendance in the fifteenth century. In the meantime, even during the Merciless Parliament of 1388, the lords' attendance was not all that was desirable from at any rate the point of view of the Lords Appellant, who were then in political control. When the first session of this parliament, which perhaps marks the highest point of pressure of the aristocratic theory of government between 1311 and 1422, was adjourned for over three weeks because of Easter, it was felt necessary to issue fresh writs of summons to the lords and to warn them to appear (the lords spiritual, not by proxies) on the day before the resumption, under the threat of a heavy penalty to be limited by the king and the lords who did come. Moreover, seven temporal peers (William de Dacre, John de Welle, John Grey of Codnor, William Botreaux, John de la Warre, John de Montague, and Philip Despenser) were specially ordered to appear, having taken no heed to come at all during the first session, 'in nostri contemptum manifestum'. What attendance was like in the session after Easter, there is no means of knowing, but it is very likely that some saw fit to be circumspect, or were otherwise sickened by a return to the political savagery of Edward II's time, and so stayed away: whether the lords came in force or not, when more of Richard II's friends, Sir Simon de Burley and Sir James Berners (among others) came to be condemned for treason, there were absent—so the charge against John Lord Cobham ran at Shrewsbury nearly ten years later—'plusours autres Piers du Parlement qi soy leverent et ne voloient mye seer en tiel Jugement'.[3] Absence as well as presence might be regarded as a paying investment in bitter circumstances like these. It depended on one's point of view, degree of involvement and temperament, no doubt.

Probably the excitement of such a situation worked in favour of a good attendance. Certainly, if no more than seven lay peers had been absent from the first session of the Merciless Parliament, it would appear so (although these seven magnates may well have been king's friends singled out for particular

---

[1] Rot. Parl., iii. 167; ibid., p. 166.   [2] P.R.O., S.C.10/35.
[3] Reports on the dignity, iv. 727, 729; Rot. Parl., iii. 245, 381.

treatment). But at a time of no special impending agitation, in January 1397, for example, before Richard II had decided to prepare the *coup* he made in the following summer, a poor attendance on the part of the lords had once more evidently become far from abnormal. On the second day of the session, the chancellor had warned the lords to come each day at nine o'clock at the latest, no lord being absent without the king's special leave. And then, on the third day, 'les Communes vindrent devant le Roy et les Seigneurs en Parlement et prierent qe toutz les Seigneurs Espirituelx et Temporelx qi feurent absentz soient envoier de venir au Parlement'. That the commons were not referring to lords who were up in town but careless of their duty, is made quite clear in the king's answer: the chancellor stated that if what the commons asked was done, 'ce serroit tre long delaie du Parlement', but that, nevertheless, 'y pleust au Roy q'en esploit du Parlement q'il serroit envoiez de novel pur les Seigneurs qi feurent bien pres'.[1] As it turned out, parliament was dissolved before three weeks had passed, and if perhaps a short session could already be anticipated— and no direct taxation was being demanded—to re-summon any but those who lived close-by would have been pointless. But the significant thing to note in the royal answer is that not only did it confirm the commons' complaint, but showed what this did not, namely, that there was a number of lords who lived within easy reach ('bien pres') and who had yet neglected to attend the parliament. Most significant of all—rather hardly for Pollard's theory of the negligent attitude of the commons to their own parliamentary attendance—it was actually the commons who had complained of the unsatisfactory attendance in the Upper House.

It will, of course, be generally recognized that nobody can know the precise extent to which, for the duration of any medieval parliament, the lords spiritual and temporal—or for that matter anybody else—attended its daily sessions. The nearest thing to an attendance-list of the lords—if not essentially a register of attendance itself—is supplied by the Fane fragment of the Lords' Journal of 1461,[2] a much later copy of a summary of day-to-day attendance for a part of a session only. It is a happy survival, but nevertheless unfortunate in the sense that it relates to the first parliament of a new reign after a dynastic revolution, when parliamentary attendance was hardly likely to be typical. And for only one session of another parliament is there a list of lords, for whose absence a tariff of fines was actually imposed in the exchequer by parliamentary authority: the third proper session of the parliament of 1453–4.[3] And so the collection of letters of excusation from attendance in parliament, and of appointment of par-

---

[1] *Rot. Parl.*, iii. 338.

[2] *The Fane Fragment of the 1461 Lords' Journal* (New Haven, Yale Univ. Press, 1935), ed. W. H. Dunham, junior.

[3] See below, pp. 189–92.

liamentary proxies, written to the king (or as letters patent) by absent bishops, abbots, and lords temporal, deserves special consideration. Such letters form the bulk of the series of Parliamentary Proxies kept in the Public Record Office as Parliament and Council, S.C.10.

First surviving from Henry III's reign, the letters of this series reach down to the time of Henry VIII. So far as the letters of proxy or attorney of lords temporal go, there is nothing until 1307, and then there are complete gaps between 1339 and 1401 and between 1426 and 1529. These form but a small collection. In the period 1307 to 1339 only twenty such letters survive, involving no more than seven lords. They begin with the appointment of the dean of Wells by John de Beauchamp de Somerset, seignur de Hacche, 'a treter, ordener, et assenter en mon noun ensemblementes ove les autres seigneurs de la terre' at Carlisle in January 1307, and then there are the letters of Robert de Vere, earl of Oxford (1319, 1322, 1328, and 1330), Robert FitzWalter the father (1322), John de Warenne, earl of Surrey (1322, December 1332), Robert de Clifford (1329), William la Zouche of Haryngworth (1331, January 1332 [his proctors to be 'en mon leu et pur moy a ces tretitz et parlantes . . . a un d'eux plein poair totes choses affaire que a moy apendeit en ces parlantes et tretitz . . .'], March and November 1332, 1333, 1334, 1335, and 1336), and of Henry, earl of Lancaster and Leicester (March 1332, 1334, and 1339).[1] The little group of nineteen letters in this category dating from 1401 to 1426 are entirely made up of the appointments of proxies by Edward Courtenay, earl of Devon (in 1401, 1404, 1406, 1407, 1410, 1413, 1416, 1417, and 1419), and Thomas Lord de la Warre, clerk (in 1414, 1416, 1417, 1419, 1420, 1421, 1422, 1425, and 1426).[2] Forming so small, and so obviously fragmentary, a collection, these letters are but of little help with the general problem of the attendance of the lay peers.

The case is rather different with the bishops and abbots. Their surviving letters of proxy are very sparse indeed until the end of Edward I's reign, but the series from then on (to 1447, after which there is a wide gap until 1523), although demonstrably time and time again very incomplete, does occasionally contain enough letters relating to a single parliament to be very revealing of their lack of attendance. The extant letters excusing attendance at the Westminster parliament of Hilary 1315, for instance, number nine in the case of the bishops, and in the case of the abbots and priors, twenty-two; at the Lincoln parliament a year later, ten and twenty-eight, respectively. There have survived ten bishops' letters excusing their attendance at the York parliament of 1332–3; as many as twelve letters appointing bishops' proxies to parliament in May 1335, again at York; nine bishops' letters for each of the parliaments of November

---

[1] P.R.O., S.C.10/52, nos. 1–16, 28; S.C.10/14, no. 672.

[2] S.C.10/52, nos. 16A–27; S.C.10/47, no. 2315; S.C.10/48, nos. 2373, 2385.

1384 and January 1393. The collection, incomplete though it is, shows absence
on the part of individual bishops sometimes for parliament after parliament:
for example, Bishop Wouldham of Rochester appointed proxies to excuse his
absence at Westminster in 1313, at York in 1314, at Westminster again in
1315, and at Lincoln in 1316; Bishop Swinfield of Hereford was absent from
every parliament (for which these letters of excusation are extant) from 1307
until his death ten years later; Bishop Shrewsbury of Bath and Wells excused
himself from certainly no fewer than seven out of nine parliaments or councils
between 1348 and 1357 before he secured (in 1361) a royal patent of exemption
for life; Bishop Stretton of Coventry and Lichfield sent proxies to every one of
the eight parliaments between 1373 and 1380, and probably carried on in this
way until his death in 1385 (he certainly did not attend in 1382 and 1384);
a later occupant of his see, John Burghill, Richard II's former confessor, was
absent from certainly two out of every three of Henry IV's parliaments, including even the Coventry session of 1404; Bishop Lancaster of St. Asaph sent
letters excusatory to no fewer than twelve out of the fifteen parliaments that sat
between 1416 and 1432. There were some parliaments—for instance, in 1335
(York), 1337, and 1344—when not one of the four Welsh bishops came in
person. We need not be surprised if we happen to light on evidence that suggests that an attendance of no more than half of the bishops was nothing out of
the ordinary.

There have actually survived the letters of excusation of more than half of
the abbots in the case of each of no fewer than forty parliaments in the course
of the fourteenth century. In 1337 certainly no less than twenty abbots and
priors, out of thirty-two summoned, sent letters of excusation, and two years
later the number of extant letters is the same, and again in 1340 and 1344. The
surviving letters of excusation for the successive parliaments of 1391, 1393,
1394, 1395, and January 1397 (by which time twenty-seven abbots and priors
were being regularly summoned) number respectively 16, 19, 19, 17, and 16.
An examination of the record of the heads of individual monasteries, as revealed
by their letters of proxy, suggests that in the vast majority of cases it was really
exceptional for an abbot to attend parliament in person. To avoid tedium, may
I draw attention to a few particular instances only. The surviving letters of
excusation and appointment of proxies of the abbots of Peterborough relate to
roughly two out of every three of the parliaments of the fourteenth century; for
only four out of the twenty-three parliaments which met in Richard II's reign
are such letters missing in the case of the head of this great Benedictine abbey.
Between 1385 and 1425 the abbots of Thorney sent letters of excusation, which
are extant, to all parliaments save six. There is no letter of proxy from the abbot
of Evesham excusing his attendance at the parliament of 1411, but otherwise
he excused himself from every one of Henry IV's parliaments. The number of

surviving letters of excusation written by the abbot of Westminster is a small one. Doubtless he was a normal attender of parliaments meeting in the precincts of the palace on the other side of his own abbey wall. But he certainly at times absented himself from even Westminster sessions, in January and March 1340, January and March 1348, October 1382, November 1391, and January 1394; and when there was travelling to be done, as to York in 1318, 1319, 1322, 1328, 1332, 1333, and 1335, or to Salisbury in 1328, Winchester in 1330, and Northampton in 1380, the abbot of Westminster shared the aversion of the majority of his brother abbots and abstained from personal appearance. The collection of letters is at any rate complete enough to show that to none of the eight parliaments which sat between 1372 and 1381 did the abbots of St. Mary of York, St. Benet's Hulme, Evesham, and Ramsay come; or again, the abbots of Peterborough, Bury St. Edmund's, St. Mary of York, Selby, St. Benet's Hulme, Thorney, and Gloucester contented themselves with sending proxies to each one of the five parliaments which met between November 1391 and January 1397. In view of these deductions, derived though they are from an obviously incomplete collection of letters, it should be a cause of no amazement to find that, whenever it happens that there is a record of the lords' attendance in parliament on a particular occasion, the regular clergy individually summoned appear as seldom present in more than bare handfuls at best, and generally in only ones and twos. The paucity of attendance on the part of the abbots, if the large number of letters of excusation were not itself evidence enough, could perhaps be conjectured from the fact that, in the medieval period, the absentees—and those summoned were almost all Benedictines—did not appoint other parliamentary abbots to act as their proxies. This, some of them were doing in the very last parliaments to which they were ever summoned, that is, before the Dissolution; in 1523 and 1529 this was certainly the case. This suggests a last flickering of interest—and understandable it was in the circumstances—before their light was put out. Theoretically, the secular prelates and regulars in the Upper House had long outnumbered the lords temporal, and, theoretically, the Dissolution had the effect of reducing the spiritual peers 'from more than a half to less than a third of the whole house'.[1] In practice, however, the Dissolution can have had but little effect on the day-to-day composition of the lords in session, in view of the habitual, large-scale absenteeism on the regulars' part.

It remains to consider the evidence of a series of fragments of information from both the parliament-rolls and the records of great councils of the later medieval period and mainly of fifteenth century date, in which from time to time appear lists of prelates and magnates assisting at particular ceremonies in

---

[1] A. F. Pollard, *Evolution*, p. 303.

these assemblies or consenting to particular acts. I am proposing to deal in this context with the evidence from great councils as well as from parliaments, because of the obvious relationship between attendance in the one and in the other type of assembly (which is not, of course, to suggest that great councils were equal in status and authority with parliaments).

The first of such notices concerns a letter written about the middle of February 1395 to Richard II, then engaged on the earlier of his two military expeditions in Ireland, requesting him to return, because of the Scottish situation. The duke of York was then holding parliament as 'custos', and the letter was subscribed by him and the five earls of Derby, Arundel, Warwick, Salisbury, and Northumberland 'et autres seigneurs du parlement', and then come some more names (in another but contemporary hand), comprising the earl of Devonshire and eight other lords temporal. This was only fifteen out of the thirty-seven lay magnates summoned, some of the nobility being, of course, with the king (and accordingly not summoned). Six of the eight earls summoned were clearly present. The evidence regarding the other peers must be regarded as inconclusive; but it is doubtful whether many more were in fact present, because no principle of selection can be discerned in the list.[1]

What proved to be Richard II's last parliament (although not the last to be summoned in his name) met on 17 September 1397. During a first session of no more than a fortnight it repealed the parliamentary commission of 1386 as a treasonable usurpation of the royal authority, and brought about the condemnation of the late duke of Gloucester, the earls of Arundel and Warwick, and Archbishop Arundel of Canterbury, for their share in the disaffection of the years, 1386–8. On Sunday, 30 September, the day after the adjournment of parliament to Shrewsbury, following mass in the abbey church of Westminster, the lords spiritual and temporal came before the altar of the Confessor's shrine to take an oath to maintain the acts of the session. That what parliament was going to be required to do was of great consequence had been already made clear, and in ample time, before it met: the writs of summons had been issued two months in advance (on 18 July), and eight of Richard's supporters among the nobility, six weeks before Parliament met, had (at Nottingham) appealed of treason those three of the former Appellants of 1388 against whom it was now intended to proceed. Such was the king's temper at this time of his *coup*, that to fail to attend the parliament would be to run grave risk of a charge of treason; it would be an even greater risk for those who, having attended, did not come to swear to uphold what had been done. And, in fact, a remarkably high number of the upper aristocracy attended the ceremony in the abbey[2]: all the dukes, the one marquis (Dorset), and all the earls (except Devonshire) were there, sixteen

---

[1] *Proc. and Ord. P.C.*, i. 59.   [2] *Rot. Parl.*, iii. 355–6.

altogether. And of the thirty-six other temporal peers summoned, no more than eleven were absent. Regarding these last, the attendance of Lord De la Warre and Lord Cobham probably ought, moreover, to be discounted, of the former because he had been exonerated by patent as long ago as 1382 (although he was now, on 14 October 1397, to secure a renewal of his discharge), and of the latter because he was very likely already under arrest pending his trial for treason at Shrewsbury in January following. Besides, six of the remaining nine absent barons were from the north of England. No stronger testimony than this, if it were required, could be adduced to prove Richard II's complete and fearful dominance of the nobility at this crisis in his affairs. The attendance of the bishops was even more satisfactory: Archbishop Waldby of York, his two suffragans of Durham and Carlisle, and eleven out of the sixteen suffragans of Canterbury were present at the abbey ceremony. It was naturally impossible for Archbishop Arundel to be present on this occasion, because he stood condemned of treason and under sentence of banishment—he had of course attended the parliament—and Bishop Buckingham of Lincoln and Bishop Erghum of Bath and Wells were excused by their patents of exemption. If, among those who attended the parliament, we include the bishop of Norwich, who was among the triers of petitions but not present at the oath-taking on 30 September, no fewer than sixteen out of the twenty secular prelates summoned[1] attended the parliament, and of the four who did not, two were not bound to come. It should, of course, be remembered that the southern convocation had been convened for 8 October. This may have helped with the bishops. It had seemingly no effect on the habitually slack attendance of the regulars: of the twenty-five abbots summoned, only two, the abbot of Westminster and his neighbour of St. Albans, were present at the ceremony at St. Edward's shrine, along with one of the two priors summoned, the prior of the Hospital of St. John of Clerkenwell. What was the measure of the lords' attendance when parliament reassembled at Shrewsbury on 27 January 1398 to continue its work, there is, unhappily, no means of knowing.

Two years to the very day from Richard II's triumph on 30 September 1397 he was deposed, and Henry of Bolingbroke's claim to the Crown accepted, in a convention of the estates. Now, in 1399, in these circumstances of dynastic revolution, and especially in view of the impending coronation of the new king and all that this involved in the performance of hereditary services and in the doing of homage and swearing of fealty, the lords were under heavy duty to attend. It was certainly to their general interest to do so. And, as in Richard II's last parliament, so in Henry IV's first, the evidence shows that their attendance was very numerous. A collation of the evidence of the lists of triers of petitions,

---

[1] Seventeen suffragans of the province of Canterbury had been originally summoned, but Bishop Gilbert of St. David's had died in the meantime.

of the deputation which had been to see Richard II in the Tower on Michaelmas Day, of the record of the arraignment of the Appellants of 1397, and (most importantly) of the list of all those lords who on 23 October 1399 advised on the manner of the deposed king's future safe-keeping,[1] shows that of the twenty secular prelates summoned (the see of Bangor was technically still vacant) the two primates and fifteen bishops certainly attended, the remaining three summoned being Bishop Erghum of Bath and Wells, who enjoyed a patent of discharge for life, Tideman of Winchcombe, bishop of Worcester, Richard II's former physician, and Bishop Merks of Carlisle, the ex-king's close supporter, who on 28 October was to be given over into the protective custody of the abbot of St. Albans; that of the sixteen members of the higher ranks of the lay peerage only the earls of Devonshire and Oxford were not present, and of the remaining thirty-four barons summoned only eleven more were absent; that the attendance of the abbots was comparatively good, too, nine being present out of twenty-five summoned (there being no mention of the prior of the Hospital or of Coventry). Out of all those ninety-seven summoned, there were no fewer than sixty-three certainly in attendance at Henry IV's first parliament, the overwhelming preponderance of absentees being among the regular clergy. Never again perhaps was Henry IV to see so many of his prelates and magnates gathered together in either parliament or great council.

In the first five years of his reign Henry IV did not find it convenient to meet parliament again oftener than three times, the intervals being bridged by the holding of great councils. At the first of these councils, the one summoned to meet at Westminster less than three months after the dissolution of the 1399 parliament (namely, on 9 February 1400), not unnaturally the attendance was somewhat sparse. It came together to consider means of levying war against France and Scotland, and all the bishops present granted an aid in money, and the lay magnates one in the form of a quarter's free military service.[2] The bishops made up a respectable contingent: the two primates and eleven out of the eighteen bishops of the two provinces. (Carlisle was vacant.) The lay magnates, on the other hand, numbered no more than five earls and fifteen others, little more than half the number of those present in the recent parliament, and only two out of every five of the whole lay peerage. On the crucial day of the vote of supplies no more than thirty-three lords in all had been present. The increasingly harassed king can hardly have been comforted by the lords' attendance at subsequent assemblies, whether these were fully parliamentary or not. When, in the second parliament of the reign (which met in January 1401), Chief

---

[1] *Rot. Parl.*, iii. 416, 449, 426–7.

[2] *Proc. and Ord. P.C.*, i. 105–6. Privy seals requiring contributions were to be sent to the abbots. Whether they had been summoned is not known. If they had not been summoned, this might suggest that the futility of calling them in was fully realized, for seemingly none of them attended.

Justice Thirning declared the causes of summons, he saw fit to warn both lords and commons that none 's'absente hors de mesme le parlement, ne departe ascunement d'icell hors du ville tan qe il soit finiz', which conceivably might point to an unsatisfactory initial attendance. However this may be, when, early in March, towards the end of the session, all the lords temporal present were party to a judgement of treason against the Ricardian nobles who had been killed or executed in the futile revolt of January 1400, they comprised the prince of Wales, the duke of York, and as many as eight out of the ten earls, but no more than fourteen out of the remaining thirty-five lay peers.[1] Some three months later (at the end of June 1401), apparently only four of the earls, along with no more than fifteen other temporal lords, attended a meeting of a great council held to advise about the expediency of engaging in war with France and the restitution of Richard II's widowed queen, Isabel of Valois.[2]

Not until Henry IV's seventh regnal year are we next vouchsafed any reliable evidence bearing upon this problem of the lords' attendance in parliament. Henry IV's sixth parliament met on 1 March 1406, and was first adjourned on 3 April to meet (after Easter and the Garter Feast) on 25 April; there was a second recess from 19 June to 13 October, from which date the third and last session lasted until 22 December. That the beginnings of the second and third sessions had each to be postponed, the former for four days and the latter for five, partly because of an inadequate presence of both lords and commons, is perhaps not very surprising in these circumstances of heavy demands for parliamentary service. But even in the second session, and at a favourable season for travelling, the attendance of the lords was far from what it might have been. That this was so is indicated by the list of those who on 7 June 1406 sealed the exemplification of the statute entailing the Crowns of England and France on Henry IV and the heirs male of his body.[3] A convocation of the southern province was then in session at St. Paul's, and Archbishop Arundel and eleven out of the other sixteen secular prelates summoned (the sees of York, Durham, London, and Rochester being vacant) sealed the instrument. But of the twenty-five abbots summoned to the parliament only those of Westminster, St. Albans, Waltham, and Shrewsbury sealed, along with the prior of the Hospital of St. John. Incidentally, no fewer than nineteen abbatial letters of proxy actually survive for this parliament. Of the temporal lords, the duke of York and five (out of the seven) earls affixed their seals, together with eighteen out of the thirty-two barons summoned. This adds up to a total presence of forty-one peers out of eighty-four summoned, slightly under a half. It should be remembered that of those present on this occasion, Arundel and two of his suffragans

[1] *Rot. Parl.*, iii. 454, 459 (the earl of Warwick and Lords Roos and Cobham appear among the triers (455).
[2] *Proc. and Ord. P.C.*, i. 144.   [3] *Rot. Parl.*, iii. 576.

(Winchester and Exeter), and the duke of York, the earl of Somerset, and six of the other temporal peers (Roos, Grey of Codnor, Furnival, Willoughby, Burnell, and Lovell) were all members of the council recently appointed on 22 May, when the king's physical weakness necessitated the transference of the work of government to its control.[1] Excluding councillors, we get a balance of thirty peers present out of seventy-three. It is hardly surprising that, on the last day of this second session (19 June), the lords temporal, wishing to postpone to the next session their final decision on the character of the risings of the late Archbishop Scrope of York, the late earl marshal, the earl of Northumberland, and Lord Bardolf, asked the king 'de comander toutz les Seigneurs temporelx, peres de Roialme, d'estre presentz pur la cause suisdite, et qe null d'eux soit absent a icell fait'.[2] At the end of the third and last session of this long parliament (on 22 December), the recent statutory restrictions imposed on the royal succession were found unsatisfactory and a return to the parliamentary arrangement of February 1404 was recommended. The request was added that the new act should be promulgated under the seals of all the lords spiritual and temporal, 'si bien presentz come absentz'.[3] Whether or not a greater measure of absenteeism in this winter season of the year than in the previous June prompted this new requirement, there is no knowing, although it looks as though it might have done so.

There is no similar evidence about the number of lords attending Henry IV's later parliaments of October 1407, January 1410, and November 1411, but some evidence has survived of the attendance at a great council held at Lambeth on 19 March 1411, to which Henry IV himself came.[4] The southern convocation was at this time in session at St. Paul's. The lords present, who considered and advised certain financial measures, were made up of the two archbishops and ten bishops, two abbots (one being Westminster), the prince of Wales, the duke of York, five earls (including Dorset, the chancellor), and eleven other peers (including Scrope of Masham, the treasurer): thirty-two prelates and magnates in all.

After there had died down all the attractive excitement of Richard II's deposition and the accession of a successful royal rebel leading a great coalition of the baronage in arms, what a few and chronologically dispersed fragments of evidence seem to tell us about the attendance of prelates and lay magnates in two of Henry IV's parliaments and three of his great councils, is that roughly two out of every three of the secular prelates, a mere handful at best of the heads

---

[1] *Rot. Parl.*, iii. 572.   [2] *Ibid.*, p. 606.
[3] *Ibid.*, p. 582. (The escort of Henry IV's daughter, Philippa, for her marriage with Eric of Denmark had taken out of the country, between early August and roughly Christmas, only Bishop Bowet of Bath and Wells and Lords FitzHugh and Scrope of Masham.)
[4] *Proc. and Ord. P.C.*, ii. 7.

of the monastic houses, and perhaps seldom more than half of the lords temporal, but generally including most of those of the dignity of earl and above, might be expected to come: in all a body of peers regularly no stronger in numbers than from thirty to forty odd, of whom an appreciable proportion were under a special obligation to attend as members of the council.

The evidence for Henry V's reign is very meagre, and what little there is comes, for the most part, from a time when the attendance of the temporal lords was very much affected by the conquest of France, and when some of the higher clergy were away from England, either with the king or as members of the national delegation to the general council of the church at Constance. The first piece of information relates, however, to a great council which assembled in the parliament chamber at Westminster in the middle of April 1415:[1] it met before the French war had begun, in fact, in order to provide for the government and defence of the country in the king's absence and to discuss military wages during the impending expedition to Normandy. The lords, whom the king thanked for their coming 'et de lour prompte obeissance a son mandement et envoie', were the two archbishops and eight bishops (half of those available, the see of Lichfield being vacant, and the bishops of Salisbury and of Bath and Wells at Constance), five abbots and one prior, all the four dukes, nine out of the eleven earls, but no more than fourteen other peers: a gathering of forty-three lords all told. How many had been summoned we do not know, but the moment was prospectively very important, especially for so many of the forty-three lay magnates who had been summoned to the last parliament (of November 1414) and of whom only nineteen (the rest being abroad) were to be summoned to the next (of November 1415). The other two pieces of evidence for Henry V's reign relate to attendance in parliament proper; and they are similar in character. In October 1416 parliament met for the third time within a twelve-month and proceeded, before its dissolution some four weeks later, to add to its recent acts of financial generosity by granting to the victor of Agincourt, now ally of the Emperor Sigismund, two whole tenths and fifteenths. Three parts of these subsidies, it was provided, were to fall due at Candlemas 1417, the remaining moiety at Martinmas following. In the meantime, the lords agreed, loans might be raised on the security of the last half-subsidy voted; the chancellor was empowered to issue letters patent or other warrants promising repayment without charge for the seal; and, for further security of creditors, 'toutz les Seigneurs Espirituelx et Temporelx esteantz presentes, des quelx les nons sont desoubz escriptz' offered surety that they would never agree to the annulment of the undertaking to repay.[2] The spiritual lords, who underwrote this guarantee, comprised Archbishop Chichele, eight bishops (including Beaufort of Winchester,

---

[1] *Proc. and Ord. P.C.*, ii. 155-7.   [2] *Rot. Parl.*, iv. 95-6.

the chancellor) out of the thirteen available,[1] three abbots (those of Waltham, Battle, and St. Albans) and the prior of the Hospital of St. John. Of the lords temporal, all four dukes, six of the nine earls, but of the twenty-four other lay lords only seven, were present. Altogether the lords numbered no more than thirty out of seventy-seven summoned, and of those thirty certainly no fewer than eleven were members of the council.[2] The raising of loans to the Crown on the security of parliamentary and clerical taxation resulted in an identical proceeding three years later, in the Westminster parliament called by the duke of Bedford for October 1419.[3] The convocation of the southern province had also been convened at St. Paul's for a fortnight after the opening of parliament, and this may account for the slightly better attendance of bishops and the considerably less unsatisfactory attendance of abbots. For now the lords spiritual offering assurance for repayment of loans comprised the archbishop of Canterbury, ten of his fourteen available suffragans,[4] to whom must be added as present Bishop Langley of Durham, the chancellor, that is, twelve secular prelates out of eighteen summoned, and as many as eleven abbots and one prior out of the twenty-six regulars summoned. Of the three earls not engaged in France, Northumberland and Devon were not present, only Westmorland being named; and of the thirteen barons summoned, only six appear in the list of those—all the lords present—undertaking to guarantee loan repayments. As near as makes no matter, of the sixty prelates and magnates summoned no more than half attended.

Not until twenty years of Henry VI's reign had passed was the nominal numerical strength of the lay peers summoned to parliament equal to what it had been just before Henry V embarked on his first expedition to France. The interest of the nobility in the French conquest was not sustained to the same degree after as before Henry V's death in 1422. And during the early years of Henry of Windsor the number of writs of summons to lay peers never reached the low level of Henry V's last parliament (of December 1421) when only fifteen such were issued. Mainly owing to the overseas military preoccupations of some of the magnates, however, not until Henry VI's coronation parliament of 1429 did the number of writs to lay peers rise above thirty, and not until 1442 above forty. Any consideration of evidence bearing on the subject of the parliamentary attendance of the lay lords in the first half of Henry VI's reign must take into account the absence from England of at any rate some militarily active and politically interested members of their estate who, had they been in a position

[1] Robert Hallum of Salisbury, Nicholas Bubwith of Bath and Wells, and John Catterick of Coventry and Lichfield were at Constance, and Richard Clifford of London and John Wakering of Norwich were either there or on their way to the General Council. The see of Chichester was vacant.

[2] *Proc. and Ord. P.C.*, ii. 157.   [3] *Rot. Parl.*, iv. 117–18.

[4] Bishop Catterick was still out of England, and the sees of Worcester and Rochester were now vacant.

to be summoned, would more likely than not have obeyed their writs and fulfilled their parliamentary duty. Counterbalancing perhaps the effect of this
factor, however, was the sense of aristocratic solidarity in the face of the difficulty of a royal minority, aggravated as it was by the ambition of the duke of
Gloucester, who for the greater part of the first seven years of the reign was
Protector: the difficulty prompted, and aristocratic solidarity made possible, the
adoption of the notion that during Henry VI's minority the exercise of the royal
authority should be vested in the lords spiritual and temporal when met together
in parliament, great council, or ordinary council. With the tide of aristocratic
participation in government flowing so strongly at this time, a discernible
upward trend in the parliamentary attendance of the lords might have been
expected to occur. If this did happen to be so, what evidence there is from this
period of Henry VI's minority, or even from later in his reign, does not reflect it.

How many of the lords came into the first parliament of Henry VI which
met in November 1422 to decide and sanction a form of government for the
duration of the king's immaturity, is not known. But Archbishop Chichele and
six of the bishops, five of the parliamentary abbots and the prior of Coventry had
been members of the funeral cortège bringing the body of Henry V on the last
stretch of its journey from Paris to Westminster; and on 5 November, two days
before the entombment and four before parliament was to meet, all the secular
prelates mentioned, now joined by Bishop Fleming of Lincoln, met the duke of
Gloucester and thirteen other lay peers in order to consider Gloucester's commission to hold parliament on the king's behalf[1]: twenty-two lords in all, without
any of the regular clergy present. The royal funeral and the weighty business
of this session probably ensured a satisfactory attendance. Of attendance in the
second parliament of the reign of 1423–4, nothing is to be gathered. But from
the rolls of most of the other parliaments of Henry VI's minority there are wisps
of information to be gleaned giving a momentary picture of attendance in the
Upper House. On 30 April 1425 the third parliament of the reign met at Westminster, and in the course of the first fortnight of the session there came to a
head the dispute between the earl marshal and the earl of Warwick over
the former's claim to a seat of greater dignity among his peers. Eventually
the controversy was resolved by restoring to the earl marshal the ducal title
of his father, annulled in 1399. In the meanwhile, on 14 May, before the suit
began, the Protector and the other lords of parliament present had taken oaths
to be impartial[2]: those so sworn were Archbishop Chichele, only four of his
thirteen available suffragans[3] (despite the fact that the southern convocation was
in session at St. Paul's), together with the two suffragans of the metropolitan

---

[1] *Proc. and Ord. P.C.*, iii. 5–6.   [2] *Rot. Parl.*, iv. 262.
[3] The sees of Bath and Wells, Lincoln, and Bangor were vacant, and Bishop Polton of Chichester
was out of England.

see of York, which was itself vacant; two abbots (Ramsey and Reading) out of the twenty-six regulars summoned; and of the twenty-seven temporal lords summoned, the dukes of Gloucester and Exeter, the earls of Stafford and Northumberland, and eleven other peers. This is not an exhaustive list of the peers attending the parliament: from the lists of triers of petitions must be adduced three more abbots (Westminster, Glastonbury, and York); there is a reference in the roll to the appearance of John Lord Talbot;[1] and, of course, the parties to the dispute themselves were present. All these lords totalled, however, no more than thirty out of the sixty-nine altogether summoned. Relatively small though this number is, it is worth mentioning that another list of sixteen lords present on 1 June, when they guaranteed repayment of Bishop Beaufort's loans to the king,[2] adds no fresh name at all to the earlier list except that now the treasurer, John Stafford, appears as bishop of the previously vacant see of Bath and Wells. Of the thirty-one lords comprised in these lists, it is important to note that as many as fourteen were members of the royal council.

Before the end of this year, 1425, another but far more serious quarrel than that between Mowbray and Beauchamp had sprung into flame between Protector Gloucester and his uncle, the chancellor, Bishop Beaufort of Winchester, and there was active threat of civil war. Beaufort appealed to Bedford, who returned from France, and parliament was summoned to meet well away from the excited capital, at Leicester, on 18 February 1426. As in the previous year, so now, on 4 March, all the lords spiritual and temporal present in the parliament swore an oath to behave impartially.[3] To their number must be added the two disputants. From which it is clear that the lords attending the parliament comprised Archbishop Chichele and nine of his thirteen suffragans (the sees of Lincoln, Norwich, Ely, and Bangor being vacant) and the two northern suffragan bishops of Durham and Carlisle (the see of York being still vacant), that is, twelve of the sixteen secular prelates summoned; six abbots out of the twenty-six regulars summoned; and all four dukes, both earls (only Northumberland and Stafford being summoned), and eighteen out of the remaining twenty-three lay peers summoned. This was a remarkably full assembly of lords, there being a serious defection only on the part of the abbots, and it is doubtful whether before 1450 the lords were ever again to attend parliament in such numbers, except in 1433. Forty-two prelates and magnates were in attendance out of a total of seventy-one summoned, but one out of every three present, it should be remembered, was a councillor—the primate, four bishops, and nine lay peers.

Two years later, at the beginning of March 1428, when five weeks of the second session of the parliament of October 1427 had passed, there was trouble

---

[1] *Rot. Parl.*, iv. 275.   [2] *Ibid.*   [3] *Proc. and Ord. P.C.*, iii. 189.

again with Duke Humphrey of Gloucester, who was now demanding from the lords a definition of his authority as Protector and refusing to attend parliament until he had an answer. A statement was accordingly made by 'universi et singuli Domini Spirituales et Temporales tunc ibidem presentes', embodying their view of what had transpired in the parliament of 1422 when Gloucester had been given his title and office, their interpretation of what powers the office had been intended to confer, and their request that the duke should be content and attend parliament as was his duty.[1] The lords subscribing this answer were Archbishop Chichele, Archbishop Kemp of York (the chancellor), and nine of the eighteen available bishops (Beaufort of Winchester being out of England), four abbots (Westminster, Glastonbury, York, and Hyde by Winchester) out of the twenty-seven regulars, the duke of Norfolk (the only other duke summoned, now that Exeter was dead, being Gloucester), three out of the five earls, and eight out of the twenty-one other lay magnates summoned: fifteen lords spiritual and twelve temporal peers. Including the Protector himself, the sum comes to twenty-eight out of seventy-five summoned, and of these twenty-eight as many as sixteen were members of the continual council.[2] The lists of triers of petitions for this parliament add not a single fresh name to this number.

Before we come upon any further evidence of the lords' attendance in parliaments proper, we have, in the extant minutes of the royal council, a number of pieces of evidence of attendance at great councils. The first of these relates to the great council held in the spring of 1429. The attendance is recorded for a session on 17 April, and for another on 3 May.[3] In the earlier one, the matter at issue was of considerable, immediate importance: whether Henry Beaufort, now elevated to the Roman cardinalate, should be allowed, as bishop of Winchester, to officiate as prelate of the Garter at the impending festival of the Order, doubt having arisen on the formal grounds that his right to the see itself was open to question as incompatible with his new dignity. That on this occasion he should refrain from officiating was decided by the two archbishops and twelve bishops, four abbots, and thirteen temporal peers: a presence, if we include the cardinal himself, of thirty-two lords. In the later session, which met to determine in pleno parliamento [sic] Sir Richard Neville's right to the title and place in parliaments and councils of Thomas, late earl of Salisbury, his father-in-law, the attendance was fewer by ten, but five lay magnates who had not appeared on 17 April now did so. A conflation of the two lists gives us, therefore, a total of thirty-seven peers attending one or both of the two meetings. How many lords had been summoned we do not know, but of those who came, no fewer than eighteen—roughly a half—were members of the continual council. Two and a half years later, on 6 November 1431, another great council met and the

---

[1] Rot. Parl., iv. 327.   [2] Ibid., v. 407; Proc. and Ord. P.C., iii. 213.
[3] Proc. and Ord. P.C., iii. 323, 325.

question of Cardinal Beaufort's right to the see of Winchester was again tabled:[1] on this occasion, the lords (who eventually declined to act in Beaufort's absence) were the two primates (Kemp of York being chancellor) and ten of the seventeen bishops available,[2] two abbots, the two dukes of Gloucester and Norfolk, three of the six earls, and three other lay peers—twenty-two in all. Some three weeks later, on 28 November, when (to discuss payment of the king's retinue in France and an increase in the salary of the duke of Gloucester) there was another meeting of the great council of which the attendance was recorded, twenty-seven lords were present: the two archbishops, twelve bishops, three abbots, the duke of Norfolk, two earls, and seven other lay lords.[3] Taken together, the two lists give us thirty-one peers in all, of whom eleven were members of the royal council.

In July 1433 parliament came together at Westminster in a situation perhaps more critical than any that had supervened since Henry V's death; the duke of Bedford himself, after an absence from England of over six years, had arrived from France with the main object of composing differences among the nobility at home, in order to make possible a serious renewal of the French war. The gravity of the situation seems hardly to have been properly sensed by the peerage as a whole. What their attendance in the first session of this parliament was can only be guessed. But when the second session had run its course for nearly three weeks the lords' attendance was deemed unsatisfactory for the purposes in hand so that, on 1 November, fresh writs urging them to appear were issued to four bishops, eighteen abbots and the prior of Coventry, the three earls of Northumberland, Salisbury, and Westmorland, and to thirteen other lay peers: a deficiency of thirty-nine out of eighty-eight summoned.[4] These special warnings certainly had some effect. On 3 November the commons drew attention to the growth of crime and lawlessness and the danger of riotous assemblies, and they proposed that an oath to keep the peace should be taken by all the members of the parliament. All the lords present agreed, and they and also 'alii absentes, et ad idem parliamentum postmodum venientes' were accordingly sworn.[5] Altogether these comprised the Cardinal of England, the two metropolitans, and eleven bishops; thirteen abbots and the prior of the Hospital of St. John; all the four dukes, all save one of the ten earls (Westmorland being the exception), and eighteen of the twenty-eight other lay peers. Those who sooner or later took the oath numbered fifty-nine: thus, before the session ended, after special pressure on the absentees, a two-thirds attendance had been secured. A comparison of the list of absentees on 1 November and the list of those who

---

[1] *Proc. and Ord. P.C.*, iv. 101.

[2] Beaufort himself and Bishop Robert FitzHugh of London were out of the country.

[3] *Proc. and Ord. P.C.*, iv. 104–5.   [4] *Reports on the dignity*, iv. 887.

[5] *Rot. Parl.*, iv. 422.

eventually took the oath discloses that all four bishops, eleven out of the nineteen regulars, and ten out of the sixteen lay peers, so urgently re-summoned, failed to come in, although they had ample time in which to do so, for parliament was still sitting on 18 December, seven weeks after the special re-summonses had issued.

Before parliament next met, in October 1435, a great council, to which both lords and commoners were summoned, had assembled at the end of April and the beginning of May 1434, to discuss war policy.[1] On this occasion there were present Cardinal Beaufort, the two archbishops, and eight of the bishops (including the chancellor), the three dukes of Bedford, Gloucester, and York, six of the earls, and ten other lay peers: thirty prelates and magnates in all. Difficult though were the problems facing parliament when it met in 1435, shortly after the three-fold disaster of Bedford's death, the breakdown of negotiations for peace at Arras, and the defection of Burgundy from his long-standing English alliance, the attendance of the lords was apparently even less satisfactory than it had been at times in the parliament of 1433, and no more satisfactory than in the great council of 1434. That this was so seems certainly likely if we examine the constitution of the Upper House on 29 October 1435 (nearly three weeks after the opening of the session), when it approved a modified version of the duke of Gloucester's offer to undertake the safe-keeping of Calais and other towns and fortresses in the March.[2] Those lords present were Archbishop Chichele and eight out of the seventeen bishops summoned, two abbots, the duke of Gloucester, four out of eight earls, and eight other lay lords: no more than twenty-four peers in all out of eighty summoned, and half of them members of the ordinary council. This undoubtedly, however, did not represent the total attendance of lords in this parliament, for the lists of triers alone add another seven lords spiritual and three lay peers, assuming that we may trust the lists of triers for evidence of appearance.

In summing up the evidence for the minority of Henry VI, we may say that the magnates attending particular sessions of parliaments and great councils, where certain matters to be decided were often sufficiently important to require the listing of the lords present, appear to have been only a fraction of those summoned, generally below a half and only very infrequently more than that proportion. The archbishops and bishops attended respectably well, and so did the members of the upper aristocracy. Those who did come were quite consistent in their attendance, but then so many of these were members of the royal council with a special duty to come and a special interest in coming. The proportion of those summoned who were not under so particular an obligation, but who came nevertheless, was necessarily sometimes a very small fraction. And

---

[1] *Proc. and Ord. P.C.*, iv. 212.   [2] *Rot. Parl.*, iv. 484.

regarding this period, for which we have (comparatively speaking) so rich a record of the actual occasional presence at parliaments and great councils, it is difficult to avoid the conclusion that at meetings of both these types of assembly the lords were frequently no more than an ample session of the continual council, afforced by only a small number of other peers.

Although between 1435 and 1449 parliament met five times, a large gap opens up in the sort of evidence we have been discussing. A great council met on 24 February 1439 and was attended by Cardinal Beaufort, the two metropolitans, seven bishops, four abbots and the prior of St. John's, the two dukes of Gloucester and York, seven of the earls, and fourteen other lay magnates: thirty-eight lords in all.[1] But not until we come to the roll of the parliament of 1449–50 do we find any more material bearing on the lords' attendance in parliament offered by that particular central source. We have, however, an early seventeenth-century copy of a list of lords attending parliament in June and July 1449, discovered by Mr. A. R. Myers.[2] This list relates to the third session, held at Winchester, of the parliament which had originally met at Westminster in the preceding February. Those lords listed as present at Winchester were Cardinal Kemp, archbishop of York, Archbishop Stafford of Canterbury, eleven out of the eighteen available bishops (the see of London being vacant), the two abbots of Westminster and Gloucester, the duke of Suffolk alone out of the four dukes summoned, four out of the six earls, the two viscounts, and eleven out of the thirty-six other lay peers: thirty-three lords in all out of ninety-five summoned, roughly a third. And no less than ten, even perhaps as many as fourteen of the thirty-three, were members of the regular council.

As Mr. McFarlane[3] sums up the situation in England in the autumn of 1449, 'for a decade the country had been slowly getting out of hand, [now, especially in view of the *débacle* in France] it was ripe for revolution and civil war'. Both before and after a new parliament met at Westminster on 6 November 1449 there had been ministerial changes. Early in its second session, which began on 22 January 1450, the duke of Suffolk was committed to the Tower

---

[1] *Proc. and Ord. P.C.*, v. 108.

[2] A. R. Myers, 'A Parliamentary Debate of the mid-fifteenth century', *Bulletin of the John Rylands Library*, xxii. 15. W. H. Dunham junior, in 'Notes from the Parliament at Winchester, 1449', *Speculum*, xvii. 410, decided that the list is one of the lords attending parliament. The debate of the copy he regarded as either having taken place in the council or as being the proceedings of a 'committee' of the lords. Personally I should prefer to regard it as held in a meeting of the council, for ten of the fourteen lords taking part in the debate had certainly been present in a single meeting of the council only five days before parliament was re-opened at Winchester. But it could quite well have been held in a single meeting of the lords in parliament, of whom councillors were even usually an important proportion of those present and of whom the actual numbers in attendance bore (as usual) no close relation to the number of those summoned to parliament. This latter fact Mr. Dunham seemingly did not suspect when he spoke of a 'committee'.

[3] 'England: The Lancastrian Kings, 1399–1461', *Cambridge Medieval History*, viii. 405.

on suspicion of treason, and on 7 February the commons formally impeached him. A month went by before a majority of the lords agreed that Suffolk should answer, which, in the second week of March, he did by denying all charges. A few days later, on 17 March, he repeated his denial before the king and lords assembled in the palace in 'the innest chambre with a gavill wyndowe over a cloyster', when the king banished him of his own authority. The lords present, and the roll of the parliament[1] says that Henry VI had sent for 'all his Lordes both Spirituell and Temporell then beyng in Towne', comprised Cardinal Kemp, Archbishop Stafford, and thirteen of the eighteen bishops (the see of Chichester being vacant since the recent murder of Adam Moleyns); of the twenty-six regulars summoned, the abbots of Westminster and Gloucester and the prior of the Hospital; the duke of Buckingham and Suffolk himself (Norfolk being absent, and his uncle, York, away in Ireland); six of the nine earls; both the two viscounts; but no more than eighteen out of the thirty-three other lay magnates summoned and not excused. The lords' total attendance was forty-six out of the ninety-two summoned and liable, precisely a half.

The last decade or so of Henry VI's reign was a period of increasingly violent contest between what, as time went on, emerged more clearly defined as Lancastrian and Yorkist parties. In 1450 the pendulum swung in favour of Richard of York, but his policy, incoherent as it sometimes was at this time, gained little ground during the next three years, and the parliament which met at Reading in March 1453 was Lancastrian in its sympathies. This parliament, whose course was marked by military disaster abroad and political unrest at home, ran for four sessions, the last beginning at Westminster on 14 February 1454. By then, for nearly three months York had been in control, Henry of Windsor having suffered in the late summer of 1453 a lapse of his never very considerable mental powers; and on the day before parliament reassembled the premier duke was given a commission to hold the parliament. The two archbishops, eight bishops, six earls, and ten other lay peers, twenty-six lords in all, were already present to agree to this act.[2] Facts suggest that the lords were loth to overlook the queen's claim to a regency, and not until 27 March 1454 was York made Protector during the king's incapacity, by which time Queen Margaret's five-month-old son had been recognized as prince of Wales. Many of the lords, it seems, had showed their reluctance to commit themselves personally by staying away from parliament altogether in this difficult time. York had evidently chafed at the resulting delay, for when the session was a fortnight

---

[1] *Rot. Parl.*, v. 182. Edmund Lacy, bishop of Exeter, and William Aiscough of Salisbury had patents of exemption for life; the latter came to the parliament, the former did not. Thirty-five lay magnates of the rank of baron were summoned, but Lords Lovell and Audley were excused for life.

[2] J. F. Baldwin, *The King's Council in the Middle Ages*, p. 197.

old a petition (of uncertain origin) was made, formally addressed to the king, drawing attention to the non-appearance of 'dyvers and mony Lordes of this Lande as well Spirituell as Temporell' and proposing *ad hoc* fines.[1] The petition was adopted. This was to be the only occasion in the history of the medieval parliament on which there is record evidence of fines being actually imposed on the lords for non-attendance, although there had certainly been earlier occasions when mulcts had been threatened. The fines, which were to be leviable in the exchequer, were graduated according to dignity or rank: £100 for an arch-bishop or duke, 100 marks for a bishop or earl, and £40 for an abbot or baron.[2] The petition itself included provisos limiting or waiving fines in certain cases, sometimes for obvious reasons. The absent bishops of three of the four Welsh dioceses (Bangor, St. Asaph, and Llandaff) were to pay only £20 each. The duke of Somerset and Lord Cobham, 'beyng in prison', were exempted; so were Lords Rivers, Wells, and Moleyns, who were overseas on royal business, together with Lords Beauchamp and St. Amand, who were 'abought the Kynges persone in the tyme of his infirmitee'. More generally, those lords who could satisfy the council of bodily frailty or illness were to be fined at its discre-tion. The list of fines, for the levy of which process was entered in the exchequer in Easter term following,[3] taken along with the above recognized exemptions, discloses that the lords attending parliament at the end of February 1454 were the two archbishops, ten bishops, five abbots, the prior of the Hospital, the three dukes of York, Norfolk, and Buckingham, eight out of twelve earls, both

---

[1] *Rot. Parl.*, v. 248.

[2] The fines bear some resemblance, at least regarding the upper ranges of parliamentary society, to those tariffs proposed in the English *Modus tenendi parliamentum*, where the fines were £100 for an archbishop or earl, and 100 marks for bishop or baron. Fines for absence from parliament were frequently inflicted in Ireland in this period, even on representatives, a practice with which the duke of York, as ex-lieutenant of Ireland, was inevitably familiar (cf. H. G. Richardson and G. O. Sayles, *The Irish Parliament in the Middle Ages*, chapter 10).

[3] Memoranda Roll of the Exchequer, Queen's Remembrancer, Easter term, 32 Henry VI, P.R.O., E. 159, Communia, Recorda, mem. XXXVI. The lords absent without excusation and subjected to fine according to the tariff imposed by parliamentary authority were as follows: the bishops of Chichester, Worcester, St. David's; the abbots of Peterborough, Colchester, Bury St. Edmund's (elected after the issue of the writs of summons and so later exonerated), St. Albans, Selby, Glastonbury, Malmesbury, Battle, Shrewsbury, Cirencester, Gloucester, Thorney, Evesham, Ramsey, St. Austen's Canterbury, Winchcombe, and Reading, and the prior of Coventry (exonerated because not elected at the time of summons); the duke of Exeter; the earls of Richmond, Arundel, and Northumberland; Lords Berkeley, Poynings, Botreaux, Dacre of Gilsland, Audley, Abergavenny, Clifford, Grey of Wilton, Vessy, Grey of Rougemont, Percy of Egremont.

Moderations of fines on the alleged grounds of 'syknesse or feblenesse' after 'juste and indifferent examinacion' by the lords of the council were made regarding the following: the bishops of Exeter (80 marks), Bath and Wells (80 marks), Bangor (£20), St. Asaph (£20), Llandaff (£20), and Rochester (20 marks); the abbots of Bardney (£20), St. Benet's Hulme (£20), and Croyland (£30); the earl of Westmorland (50 marks); Lords Grey of Groby (£20), Hungerford senior (£20), Scrope of Masham (40 marks), Zouche of Haryngworth (40 marks), Lovell (40 marks), and Hoo (£20).

of the two viscounts, and no more than fourteen out of the thirty-seven other lay peers summoned: a total presence of forty-five out of one hundred and five lords. A large proportion of those attending parliament were, moreover, members of the royal council. In fact, the formal constitution of the council was becoming once again so enlarged as to make one of its well-attended sessions hardly, if at all, different from a poorly-attended session of the Upper House of parliament: for example, when on 15 March 1454 the lords in parliament consented to the creation of Edward of Lancaster as prince of Wales, they numbered only twenty-two, whereas the lords of the council who, on the same day, empowered a group of physicians and surgeons to prescribe medicines and drugs for the king's malady, numbered twenty-eight.[1] These two lists of peers, together with (i) a list of twelve lords named on 23 March as a deputation to Henry VI at Windsor (to try to explain to him that Cardinal Kemp, the chancellor, was dead), (ii) lists of twenty-six lords who met on 30 March and 1 April (to consider the promotion of Bishop Bourchier of Ely to the primacy and of William Grey to Ely), and (iii) a list of twenty-eight lords who on 2 April witnessed the livery of the great seals to a new chancellor (the earl of Salisbury): all these lists[2] add to the names of those who had been attending parliament at the end of February no more than the bishop of Worcester, the abbots of Gloucester, Battle, and Selby, and Lords Abergavenny, Fauconberg, and Willoughby (the last two of whom had not originally been summoned). In fact, the lists of lords party to business in the parliament chamber at various times between 15 March and 16 April, the eve of parliament's dissolution, include, all told, no more than fifteen spiritual and twenty-three temporal lords: thirty-eight in all, of whom exactly half were members of the royal council at this time.[3] More lords than these were probably in London and in some sense attending parliament. But, although writs of *non omittas* to the sheriffs ordering execution of the fines for non-attendance were being issued from the exchequer early in April, and parliament continued to sit until 17 April, few of the absentee lords seem to have seen the point of being fined and attending parliament as well, *ex post facto*. And when, apparently at the end of the parliament, by which time the lords 'present nowe late in oure parlement' had each agreed to supply free a force of men for the rescue of Calais from siege, and some of them to go in person, the council sent out letters to absentee lords to lend money or raise men at their costs for the same purpose, the recipients included six bishops, nineteen abbots and the prior of Coventry, the two dukes of Norfolk and Exeter, the five earls of Richmond, Pembroke, Northumberland, Arundel, and Westmorland, and twenty-six other lay magnates: a final absence on the part of fifty-nine lords

---

[1] *Rot. Parl.*, v. 249; *Proc. and Ord. P.C.*, vi. 167.
[2] *Rot. Parl.*, v. 240, 450; *Proc. and Ord. P.C.*, vi. 169, 355.
[3] *Rot. Parl.*, v. 249; 240, 450; *Proc. and Ord. P.C.*, vi. 169, 171, 172, 173, 174, 355.

in all.[1] The decision at the end of February 1454 to make large fines for non-attendance had clearly had but a slight effect on the number of lords in parliament: at the end of the session, of those summoned far more were still absent than present.

Regarding the general problem of the lords' attendance in parliaments, not too much should perhaps be read into the comment offered on the lords' attendance in this last session of the 1453–4 parliament by this imposition of fines. However ill-equipped he was to fulfil it, York may well at this stage of national deterioration have felt himself to be a man with a mission to preserve what he doubtless still regarded, even after the birth of a Lancastrian heir-apparent, as his own royal inheritance. A generation later, his son Richard was to convert a Protectorship into a royal title. York may have already entertained similar ideas. Hence, perhaps, a feeling of frustration on his part, at a time when he needed all the support from the Upper House of parliament that he could get in his struggle for the regency, at its failure to be more than representative, especially at the defections in the lay baronage. Hence, perhaps, the fines. However this may be, the fact that fines were imposed in 1454 does not necessarily mean that this moment marked an abnormal and unprecedented low ebb of the lords' attendance in parliament. Certainly, the absence of fines in the past (so far as we know) does not mean that the attendance of the lords had been always satisfactory, or even tolerably so. But now if ever was the time when the Upper House ought to have been complete, if the lords were to act as the repository of that residual authority in the state, which they had certainly claimed for themselves when Henry VI had been incapable of government for other reasons than did now apply. Perhaps now, in the period of 'cold war' between the factions, rather than in 1460, was the pass sold by the peerage to the Yorkists. For now, when York only with difficulty secured his first Protectorship, so many of them stood aside. The abstention of so many lords from parliament early in 1454 came at a critical enough juncture in the conflict between the houses of Lancaster and York. In the context of a discussion of the lords' observance of their duties of parliamentary attendance, however, what happened in 1454 is no more than an important incident. So many had often failed to come before, especially just when they were needed, and would do so again in moments of great stress.

Before Henry of Windsor recovered his sanity about Christmas 1454, York was able to restore 'a measure of conciliar government'. But his troubles with the generality of the lords seem to have continued to embarrass him. On 18 July 1454, in a great council which had first met on 25 June, following a motion that the duke of Somerset be given his liberty on bail York refused to

---

[1] *Proc. and Ord. P.C.*, vi. 175–7. Of these fifty-nine lords, seven had been in attendance at some time or another during the previous month, but presumably had failed to stay for the whole session.

assent without the advice of the judges and also without the agreement of 'mo lords than be here at this tyme'.[1] Perhaps the actual threat of a repetition of fines, however, did some good, because, although the only lords present on this occasion—sixty-seven of the lords of parliament had been summoned[2]—were the archbishop of York, ten bishops, one abbot, the two dukes of York and Buckingham, three earls (including Salisbury, the chancellor, and Worcester, the treasurer), and six other named lay peers—twenty-three in all, of whom thirteen were members of the reconstituted council—when another great council was summoned for 21 October, special writs of summons were sent to no more than the bishop of St. David's, the earl of Shrewsbury, and eleven other lay peers, recalling their summonses to the earlier meeting, which they had failed to attend. The earlier summonses, the new writs stated, they had chosen to ignore, 'yevyng ful straunge example to other of disobeissaunce', and this time they were warned to obey, otherwise 'it shal give us cause to entrete you in suche wise as shalbe thought unto us by th'avis of oure saide Counsaill according to youre disobeissaunce'. But when this autumnal great council had a session on 13 November, to establish certain regulations for the royal household, only the two archbishops, eight of their suffragans, the two dukes of York and Buckingham, six earls, and eight other temporal peers were then present: no more than twenty-six in all, and twenty of them members of the ordinary council. Not one of the lords specially warned to appear was among them.[3]

When parliament next assembled on 9 July 1455 less than seven weeks had passed since the Yorkist victory at St. Albans, where Somerset, Northumberland, and Stafford had met their death. Either the tense situation, or the prospect of a repetition of the fines for absence of the last parliament, brought up the parliamentary abbots to Westminster in great strength of numbers, for it was they who made the attendance of the lords very respectable on this occasion, at any rate in the first short session of three weeks. On 24 July, when the lords each took the oath to remain loyal to Henry VI and to resist any who did not, twenty of the twenty-seven religious were among their number. So were the two archbishops and eleven bishops, the two dukes of York and Buckingham (Exeter, as in 1454, and Norfolk being absent), six out of the eleven earls, the two viscounts, and only seventeen of the remaining thirty-six temporal lords. There was need to agree that 'all other Lordes beyng not present, shuld at theire commyng make the seid othe and promisse'.[4] It is doubtful whether more than a handful at most came in after this during the first session, which continued for

---

[1] Proc. and Ord. P.C., vi. 206–7.   [2] Ibid., pp. 184–6.   [3] Ibid., pp. 216–7, 233.
[4] Rot. Parl., v. 282; Proc. and Ord. P.C., vi. 247–8. The bishop of Durham was doubtless excused because of the recent attack by the Scots on Berwick-on-Tweed, and the bishops of Bath and Wells and Exeter were discharged for life. The earls of Northumberland and (presumably) Westmorland were exonerated because of the northern situation. And so probably also were Lords Scrope of Masham and FitzHugh. Lord Audley had a patent of exemption for life.

no longer than another week, and the list of sixty lords who took the oath to Henry VI almost certainly represents the sum of those then in attendance. For a comparison with the lists of triers of petitions and of the members of the five lords' committees set up at the beginning of the session[1]—and together they supply thirty-seven names—yields the additional evidence of the presence of only the bishops of Salisbury and Rochester, bringing the total of the secular prelates up to fifteen and the whole total of the lords up to sixty-two out of the 101 summoned (eight of whom were free not to come): a two-thirds attendance, with the biggest proportional deficiency among the ranks of the lesser baronage, only half of whom were present.

On 31 July 1455 parliament was prorogued to 12 November, by which time the king's mental health had suffered a relapse. Shortly before parliament reassembled after the recess, most of the lords who were in fact to attend this second session were already present at Westminster. From the list of the twenty-four lords present at a meeting on 6 November (which recommended to Pope Calixtus III the promotion of the Yorkist earl of Salisbury's son, George Neville, to the vacant see of Exeter), and from the list of those thirty-eight lords who met on 10 November and subscribed the duke of York's commission to conduct the parliament in place of the king—he was appointed Protector again a week later—it appears that certainly no fewer than forty-one peers were now ready to begin the second session.[2] But records of further meetings on 4 and on 11 December, when parliament was prorogued, do not suggest that this number was materially increased during its course.[3] The number of lords present at one or another of these four meetings in November and December was fifty, being comprised of the two archbishops, fourteen bishops, fifteen of the regular clergy, the two dukes of York and Buckingham (Norfolk and Exeter being never mentioned), five out of the eleven earls, both the two viscounts, and no more than ten of the thirty-six other lay peers, out of a total number summoned of 100: an attendance of exactly a half. This estimate of the lords present is entirely confirmed by the list of sixty-five lords who were to be the recipients of letters of privy seal issued on 15 December, four days after the prorogation.[4] These writs recalled their earlier writs of summons proper, notwithstanding which they had 'forborne youre attendaunce, . . . beyng absent at youre plesire'; all excuses were to be laid aside, and they were to attend on the date to which parliament had been adjourned (14 January 1456); failure to do so would involve them in the king's displeasure, and 'ye and all othre that come not shall renne into like paynes, or gretter, as have been in oure [reign?] afore this tyme and leide upon such as have absented theim and forborn to come to oure Parlement for the tyme beyng'. Five of the ten bishops so addressed

---

[1] *Rot. Parl.*, v. 279.   [2] *Foedera*, xi. 367; *Rot. Parl.*, v. 453.
[3] *Proc. and Ord. P.C.*, vi. 265–7; *Rot. Parl.*, v. 454.   [4] *Proc. and Ord. P.C.*, vi. 279–82.

had actually attended, certainly on one or two occasions, during the recent session, and so had eight of the twenty abbots, one of the eight earls, and another lay peer, and perhaps *their* attendance had been merely unsatisfactory, or perhaps they had not attended in the first session of the parliament. But there is no mention at all in the lists of the lords present at meetings in the second session of November–December 1455 of any of the remaining fifty of the absent addressees of these privy seal writs of special summons. What the attendance was like in the Upper House in the third session of this parliament, which began, after the king had come to his senses, on 14 January 1456 and which sat until parliament was dissolved on 12 March following, there is no knowing.

The next three and a half years were a period of an uneasy, formal peace between the royalist and Yorkist groups. No parliament met in this time, but there was a succession of great councils. One at Coventry in January 1457 seems to have been attended by upwards of fifty prelates and magnates, the prelates and abbots being in good evidence, the attendance of the lower ranks of the lay peerage, however, once again being very defective.[1] Another great council at Westminster a year later was very poorly attended by every *gradus*.[2] A year later again and, early in 1459, preparations for civil war were being actively put in train by both parties. And when parliament next met, at Coventry on 20 November 1459, it was to celebrate the recent Lancastrian victory in the field and the dispersal of the Yorkist lords, and to secure their proscription for treason. The appearance of the situation was to prove deceptive, but the attendance of the lords in this openly partisan assembly was such as virtually to demonstrate a feeling of confidence in the royalist cause as well as respect for the Lancastrian line. For the list of those lords who, on 11 December, when the parliament had been in session for three weeks, took an oath of allegiance to Henry VI and acknowledged Prince Edward as his heir,[3] comprises the names of no fewer than sixty-six out of the ninety-seven summoned. Of the twenty-one secular prelates, only the aged Bishop Beckington of Bath and Wells, who had been discharged for life from parliamentary duties in 1452, and his brethren of Rochester and Bangor did not take the oath. Fourteen abbots were there to take it, and the two priors summoned, the three dukes of Exeter, Norfolk, and Buckingham, five of the eight earls (Devon, Westmorland, and Oxford being absent), the two viscounts, and twenty-two out of thirty-six other lay peers summoned. Ironically enough, this last proper parliament of the Lancastrians—that of October 1460 was virtually a Yorkist parliament called in Henry VI's name, and the Readeption parliament of 1470–1 may be ignored—was possibly the best attended of any parliament summoned by a member of that dynasty.

---

[1] *Proc. and Ord. P.C.*, vi. 333.   [2] *Ibid.*, pp. 291–3.   [3] *Rot. Parl.*, v. 351–2.

There is little record evidence to illustrate the lords' attendance in the parliaments of the rest of the fifteenth century. One important exception, however,
is that relating to a part of the first session of the first parliament of Edward IV,
which met at Westminster on 4 November 1461, for which there are lists of
day-to-day attendances in the *Fane Fragment of the Lord's Journal*.[1] The activities of this first Yorkist parliament may well have been promoted by a political
faction, as Mr. W. H. Dunham junior says, but an analysis of these attendance-
lists discloses an extraordinarily full presence of the peers in the period covered
by the journal. The number of peers summoned but not listed and of peers
summoned and/or listed but not in attendance, was no more than nine spirituals
and eleven temporals against a recorded total attendance of thirty-nine spirituals
and thirty-eight temporals. Roughly four out of every five peers were present.
Only three of the bishops did not come, and one of these (Beckington of Bath
and Wells) was discharged for life; the other two were the Welsh diocesans of
St. David's and St. Asaph. How important was evidently regarded the need to
attend this first parliament of the new reign can be especially gathered from the
fact that as many as twenty-one abbots were present. Attendance at daily
meetings was remarkably large too: the smallest number of peers present on any
one of the recorded occasions was forty-seven, and the largest presence was as
high as sixty-seven. It is, in a sense, unfortunate that this extraordinary piece
and form of evidence relates to a parliament which, being the first of the newly
restored legitimate branch of the royal family, was summoned in extraordinary
circumstances, circumstances which warranted, as they explain, the fullness of
the lords' attendance on this occasion.

There is no knowing how soon or to what extent in Edward IV's reign
there was any reversion to earlier conditions of slack-gaited or haphazard
attendance. A most important great council,[2] which met on 3 July 1471 after the
brief Readeption of 1470–1, and where oaths were taken to accept Edward IV's
son and heir as king on his death, was attended by only half the secular prelates
and by no more than three out of every five of the lay peers: a gathering of only
thirty-four of the lords of parliament. There were none of the regular clergy
present at all. And, although we do not know how many peers had been summoned, it may well be that Edward IV was not able to command a fuller and
more constant obedience on the part of his lords to his writs of summons than
had earlier been the case. Certainly, when, on 1 February 1474, after its short
fourth session, parliament was prorogued until May following, the chancellor
felt the need to declare to both lords and commons that if any neglected to come
in person on the appointed day and attend parliament, the king would ordain
'pro sui punitione' by act of parliament, 'quod punitio hujusmodi aliis timorem

---

[1] *The Fane Fragment*, pp. 93–5.   [2] *Cal. Close Rolls, 1468–76*, pp. 229–30.

incuteret de cetero taliter delinquendi'.[1] Whether there was any notable change in the lords' attendance at the later Yorkist and the earliest of Tudor parliaments, there seems to be no way of learning. Henry VII's parliament of 1485 appears to have been well attended. The session was nearly a fortnight old when, on 19 November, oaths were taken by the lords not to receive criminals, give livery, or commit the offence of maintenance: those so sworn numbered thirteen of the eighteen secular prelates summoned, seventeen out of the twenty-seven abbots and priors, the two dukes of Bedford and Suffolk, eight out of the eleven earls summoned, but no more than eight of the twenty-two other lay peers. If we add those five others who figure among the twenty-five lords appointed as triers of petitions, we have a total known attendance of fifty-three out of eighty-two summoned in all.[2] But this, of course, was the first parliament of a new reign—indeed, of a new dynasty.

From 1509 onwards we are able to draw on the invaluable information of the consecutive series of the *Lords' Journals*. These demonstrate that the lords' attendance in the earlier parliaments of Henry VIII was not materially different from what seems to have been generally the case in the previous century. The day-to-day records of attendance in the Upper House during, for example, the parliament which met (after a gap of some two years) on 5 February 1515, show that in its first session the two archbishops, ten bishops, thirteen abbots, ten out of the fifteen peers of the rank of earl and above, and sixteen of the twenty-nine other lay peers came into parliament at one time or another: a total attendance of fifty-one out of the ninety-five lords spiritual and temporal summoned. During the second session of this parliament, which began on 12 November following, four more bishops came and two more abbots than before, but the temporal lords were two fewer: the total attendance was fifty-five. Only forty peers came to both sessions. Four bishops, eleven abbots, three earls, and nine other temporal lords came to neither. In Henry VIII's later parliaments, beginning with the Reformation parliament of 1529–36, the lords' attendance underwent an important change for the better, the overall attendance going up into the seventies, and when Henry VIII met parliament in January 1542 the attendance on the very first day of the first session was over fifty, notwithstanding the removal of the regular clergy from the scene. Something of a falling-off in attendance came with Edward VI: for instance, in the third session of his first parliament (in November 1549) only three out of every five lords were present. Under Elizabeth I, however, the lords' attendance seems to have recovered the high level eventually reached under her father, and, for example, in the first session of her third parliament, which met in April 1571, as many as three out of every four lords summoned attended at one time or another during its course.[3]

[1] *Rot. Parl.*, vi. 99.   [2] *Ibid.*, p. 288; Wedgwood, *History of Parliament, Register*.
[3] *Journals of the House of Lords*, i. 19 *et seq.*; p. 166; pp. 355 *et seq.*; pp. 668 *et seq.*

Whether in the Old English witan, or in the *curia regis* or *commune concilium* of the Norman and Angevin kings, or in the later medieval parliament, archbishops, bishops, abbots, and lay magnates had a long tradition of obligatory service. In the post-Conquest, feudal period, counsel was an immaterial form of aid due to the king from the great men of the land, prelates and *proceres* alike, in virtue of their fealty or homage. The lords spiritual and temporal, when summoned to parliament, were expected to attend. Formally granted exonerations from personal appearance, whether for a special occasion or for life, were never more than a few at any one time. Appearance by proxies or attorneys was in constant use, at least among the churchmen: this was in a sense inevitable, being a common phenomenon in all kinds of medieval assemblies and courts. But such a practice was the object of royal disapproval on occasion, certainly in the fourteenth century, and the whole emphasis of the language of the writs of summons was on the needfulness of personal attendance. That frequent attendance in parliaments was likely to be found burdensome by the many might be deduced even as early as 1258, for when in the Provisions of Oxford it was laid down that parliament should meet at fixed intervals three times a year it was agreed that no more than twelve magnates, additional to those appointed as members of the baronial council of fifteen, need come together, 'pur esparnier le cust del commun'. Certainly in the fourteenth century there is no shortage of evidence that the lords' attendance was frequently spasmodic, and at times so embarrassingly scanty as to have a very deleterious effect on parliament's capacity to proceed with its business: in fact, now and then, parliament had to be abandoned altogether on this account. The heavy fines for failure to attend, proposed in the *Modus tenendi parliamentum*, a treatise which is to be attributed to this century, confirm the seriousness of the problem. And perhaps the recurrent petitions (fourteen in the century between 1344 and 1444) against the exoneration of the free tenants of peers of parliament from contributions to the wages of the knights of the shire have some bearing on the subject: if many of those peers were not attending parliament, any such exemption of their tenants was likely to be regarded as even more unjustifiable.[1] However this may be, at the end of the fourteenth century there was one occasion when even the commons felt called upon to complain of a poor 'turn-up' on the part of the lords. The fifteenth century was to witness instances of claims on the part of individual magnates for precedence over one or more of their compeers, but in this there is probably more of a recognition that the lay lords were hardening into a parliamentary peerage based on the hereditary principle, than a suggestion that they were generally finding their parliamentary occupation more congenial and less of a burden than before. Although, for the most part, the clerks

---

[1] L. C. Latham, 'Collection of the Wages of the Knights of the Shire in the Fourteenth and Fifteenth Centuries', *Eng. Hist. Rev.*, xlviii. 455–64.

who made up the rolls of the parliaments of the fifteenth century were not so ready to reveal the king's dissatisfaction with abstentions from parliamentary attendance as had been their predecessors of the previous century, there is evidence in the rolls and elsewhere of a different kind to suggest that the attitude of the ecclesiastical and lay baronage to parliamentary service had undergone no important change for the better. The attendance of the parliamentary abbots was evidently throughout the medieval period even normally deplorable; so much so, that the theory that 'during the middle ages the spiritual peers . . . always outnumbered their temporal colleagues', and that the Tudor period (with its monastic dissolutions) saw 'the reduction of the spiritual peers from more than half to less than a third of the whole house',[1] is a myth if we think in terms of actual attendance and not merely of the chancery lists of those individually summoned. At some times of great political stress, when clearly it was to their interest to do so, certainly the secular prelates and the lords temporal turned up in great force (as in 1388, 1397, 1399, 1426, and 1433). On the other hand in the very difficult circumstances of the later years of Henry VI's reign, abstention from attendance in some parliaments was even at the time regarded as serious, and this led to the first recorded fines for absence levied by parliamentary authority. The attendance of the secular prelates, by and large, was relatively satisfactory. But, though so many of the bishops were ex-civil servants, to whom Westminster was in a sense always a 'home from home', even their attendance was dependent for its fullness on the circumstances of the moment. The dutifulness of the lay nobility was very much conditioned by political interest and also by status: members of its upper ranks attended very well on the whole, but the barons and bannerets, so it would appear, only very indifferently even as a regular thing.

What all this meant, from the time when, in the later fourteenth century, the royal council began to contain a substantial and generally increasing number of prelates and magnates, was that the Upper House of parliament was frequently no more than an ample session of the continual council afforced by a comparatively not very significant number of other peers. And the fact that there was seemingly no very material difference between the attendance of the lords at great councils and their attendance in parliaments, suggests that parliaments rather than great councils were summoned for purposes to the pursuance of which the presence of the elected commons was deemed to be, and indeed really was, most needful. In fact, it would perhaps not be going too far to say that, in practice, parliaments were called in order to get together a full meeting of the ordinary council, afforced by as large a number of other lords as possible, and so that they should meet the elected commons. The political influence of

[1] A. F. Pollard, *The Evolution*, pp. 303–4.

the commons—their recognized place in the parliamentary procedures of taxation and legislation apart—was undoubtedly growing in the late medieval period, partly at least as a result of (and as indicated by) the quickening rate of the gentry's permeation of borough representation and the consequential levelling-up of the general social character of the Lower House.[1] That this was so is also suggested by the way in which, in the first half of the fifteenth century, shire and even borough elections became (for the first time) the recurrent subject of legislative enactment. And that the successful management of the commons in the royal interest was an important factor in the successful management of any parliament is more than hinted by the growing royal habit of handsomely recompensing the commons' speaker, expressly for his managerial services in the office. To these considerations must now be added the fact that there were many later medieval occasions when attendance in the Upper House was so weak as to make of parliament no more than a full meeting of the council, reinforced by not many other peers, face to face with a Lower House, in which the gentry were coming to preponderate and which grossly outnumbered the lords. Some of the basic factors which by the end of the sixteenth century were securing to the commons an important measure of political initiative in parliamentary affairs were already more than portended in the later medieval period. And not the least of these were the evident eagerness of the gentry to attend parliament, even as burgesses if county seats were not available to them, and the contrastive, chronic reluctance of so many of the prelates and magnates to observe their elementary duty of obedience to their individual writs of summons. That this reluctance seems to have been eventually very much weakened under our Tudor sovereigns, in whose time originated the patents of creation of the majority of the sixteenth century nobility, was due partly to their own inherent royal strength and to the respect which it commanded, but partly also perhaps to the fact that this new, non-feudal nobility, to a far greater extent than had been the case with the medieval aristocracy, was drawn from that class in English society that had long supplied the men who established and nourished the traditions of the commons in parliament.

APPENDIX A

On the subject of the parliamentary attendance of the medieval commons, Professor McKisack, in Chapter iv of her book, *The Parliamentary Representation of the English Boroughs during the Middle Ages*, not only showed that absence of enrolment of the writs *de expensis* of parliamentary burgesses was not evidence of their failure to attend parliament, but

---

[1] J. S. Roskell, *op. cit.*, chapter vii.

also that it was not even evidence of their failure to be paid. She also used the interesting morsel of evidence from the *Anonimalle Chronicle of St. Mary's, York* (ed. V. H. Galbraith (Manchester, 1927), p. 80) that the Good Parliament of 1376 saw the meeting of as many as 280 knights and esquires, citizens and burgesses, which points to a full attendance of the commons on this occasion. She noticed, besides, the roll-call of elected representatives in the late fourteenth-century parliaments, which she properly regarded as suggesting some interest on the part of the government in the attendance of the commons, including the burgesses. Her pertinent query, why a handful of boroughs occasionally sought formal exemption from the obligation to return burgesses if the same result could be secured with impunity simply by their burgesses failing to attend, was also somewhat damaging to the view propounded on this topic on *The Evolution of Parliament*: that they sought exoneration suggests that they needed it, and knew that they needed it.

One or two fresh pieces of evidence may be vouched in support of Professor McKisack's view. It is true that when the Salisbury parliament of April 1384 had been in session for more than a week, no elected barons from the Cinque Ports had arrived. But, then, the council sanctioned the sending of another writ to the warden of the Ports, formally calling his attention to their absence and ordering the deficiency to be repaired within a week (*Reports from the Lords' Committees touching the dignity of a peer* (London, 1820–29), iv. 710). This, like the roll-call of knights and burgesses, surely suggests the vigilance of the administration regarding the attendance of the commons. During the second session of the Merciless Parliament, in May 1388, the controller of the wool customs and subsidies at Bishop's Lynn petitioned the Crown for leave to appoint a deputy for the duration of the parliament, because he was attending it as one of the town's parliamentary burgesses (*Cal. Pat. Rolls, 1385–9*, p. 439): this was certainly taking his parliamentary attendance (and his port office) seriously. Again, during the second session of the long parliament of 1406, the speaker regarded it as necessary to request the king—and the clerk of the parliament saw fit to engross this petition on the roll —to license the absence from parliament of Richard Clitheroe (one of the two Kentish shire-knights), who had recently been made a fleet-admiral and was required at sea, and to ask further that the king and lords would allow Clitheroe's fellow-knight to appear in parliament in their two names, to act as if both were present (*Rot. Parl.*, iii. 572). Whatever else the petition may imply, it surely suggests scrupulosity, not on the score of the appearance of the knights (which, judging from the writs *de expensis*, was by this time never much in doubt), but even on the score of the knights' continuing attendance. And as regards the attendance of parliamentary burgesses, the tendency in the fifteenth century for resident burgesses to give place to non-residents and outsiders (members of the local gentry, careerists of the professional administrative class, and royal and other retainers) implies an incentive and a competitive eagerness to serve in parliament that are not at all compatible with non-attendance. Moreover, the boroughs that were most affected by these developments, were just those smaller towns whose elected representatives had been, in Pollard's view, most prone to non-attendance at an earlier time (J. S. Roskell, *The Commons in the Parliament of 1422*, chapter vii). So that, even if we were compelled still to accept Pollard's notion that in the fourteenth century abstention from parliamentary attendance on the part of the burgesses was serious, and were obliged accordingly to correct a misleading impression of the size of the commons given us by the electoral returns, we should not need to take his warning so much to heart when dealing with the fifteenth century.

APPENDIX B

List of lords spiritual and temporal exonerated from service in parliament, 1327–1500.

[I have not included in this list those abbots or priors who, they and their successors, were discharged in the period from parliamentary service as not holding of the Crown by barony: Bristol (1341), Thornton (1341), Sempringham (1341), Beaulieu (1341), Spalding (1341), Oseney (1341), Leicester (1352), Lewes (1365).]

Wulfstan Bransford, bishop of Worcester, was granted on 21 June 1340 exoneration from coming to parliaments or councils on account of infirmity and because he had undertaken to celebrate the anniversary of Edward II in the abbey of Gloucester; he was to appoint a proctor (*Cal. Pat. Rolls, 1338–40*, p. 546); 3 May 1342, renewal for life (*ibid., 1340–43*, p. 431); he died 6 August 1349.

Nicholas de Cantilupe (lay peer, summoned 1336–54) excused on 13 February 1346 from coming to parliaments (*ibid., 1345–8*, p. 48); died July 1355.

John de Warenne, earl of Surrey (born *c.* 1286), on 13 October 1346 excused for life, but to send attorney (*ibid.*, p. 196); died June 1347.

Hugh de Courtenay, earl of Devon, excused (because of ill health) for life, on 10 February 1347, but to send attorney (*ibid.*, p. 528); died May 1377.

Simon de Burcheston, abbot of Westminster, excused on 26 June 1347 for two years in order to attend to conventual business (*ibid.*, p. 350).

Roger Northburgh, bishop of Coventry and Lichfield, because of long royal service and loss of sight, discharged for life on 20 November 1348, but to send a proctor (*ibid., 1348–50*, p. 211); died 13 December 1358.

William Hereward, abbot of Cirencester, on grounds of age and infirmity, excused on 17 February 1350, for life (*ibid.*, p. 476); died 25 April 1352.

Simon de Aumeney, abbot of Malmesbury, on 12 January 1351 was excused attendance at the next parliament (*Cal. Close Rolls, 1349–54*, 279).

John Pascal, bishop of Llandaff, on 4 May 1351 exonerated for life (to celebrate anniversary of Edward II), but to send proctor, *Cal. Pat. Rolls, 1350–4*, p. 70); died, 11 October 1361.

Thomas de Horton, abbot of Gloucester, excused for life on 6 March 1352, but to send proctor (*ibid.*, p. 236); resigned 1377.

James de Audley (lay peer, summoned 1330–85), on 20 April 1353 exempted for life (*ibid.*, p. 425); on 14 October 1382 secured inspeximus and confirmation (*ibid., 1382–5*, p. 172); died 1 April 1386.

Reginald Briene, bishop of Worcester, on 30 March 1354 excused for life (to celebrate anniversary of Edward II), but to send proctor (*ibid., 1354–8*, p. 31); died 10 December 1361.

Ralph of Shrewsbury, bishop of Bath and Wells, broken by age, on 26 January 1361 excused for life, but to send proctor (*ibid., 1358–61*, p. 530); died 14 August 1363.

Robert de Lisle of Rougemont (lay peer, summoned 1357–60), exempted for life on 24 November 1368; inspeximus and confirmation, 20 October 1379 (*ibid., 1377–81*, p. 392); died *c.* 1399.

John of Ombersley, abbot of Evesham (to celebrate the anniversary of Edward II at Gloucester with four monks), excused for life on 3 January 1375, but to send proctor (*ibid., 1374–7*, p. 41); died 30 October 1379.

John de la Warre (lay peer, summoned 1371–97), on account of bad sight, discharged for life on 5 November 1382 (*ibid., 1381–5*, p. 185); further exemption for life on 14 October 1397 (*ibid., 1396–9*, p. 226); died 27 July 1398.

Walter Frowcester, abbot of Gloucester (to celebrate anniversary of Edward II), on 25 May 1383 excused for life, but to send proctor (*ibid.*, *1381–5*, p. 273); died 1412.

John Tymworth, abbot of Bury St. Edmunds, excused on 7 October 1383 for three years after restitution of temporalities, in consideration of a long vacancy, but to send proctor (*ibid.*, p. 321).

John de Buckingham, bishop of Lincoln, because of age and infirmity, discharged for life on 3 December 1384, but to send proctors (*ibid.*, p. 484); died 10 March 1398.

John Chinnock, abbot of Glastonbury, on 23 July 1386, excused for life unless summoned by special order under the signet (*ibid.*, *1385–9*, p. 202); died 1420.

Thomas Brantingham, bishop of Exeter, on 26 August 1389 (six days after dismissal from treasurership of the exchequer) exempted for life in consideration of great age and debility and long royal service (*ibid.*, *1388–92*, p. 102); died 23 December 1394.

Richard Fitz Alan, earl of Arundel, in political disgrace, exempted for life on 30 April 1394 (*ibid.*, *1391–6*, p. 405); executed, 25 September 1397.

Ralph Erghum, bishop of Bath and Wells, on 9 November 1395 excused for life because of weakness and age, but to send proctors (*ibid.*, p. 635); died 10 April 1400.

Walter Skirlaw, bishop of Durham, on 8 October 1397 exempted for life, after the next parliament of Shrewsbury, because of long royal service and great age, with licence to appoint a proctor (*ibid.*, *1396–9*, pp. 211, 221); died 24 March 1406.

Aubrey de Vere, earl of Oxford, aged about sixty, on 29 November 1397 exempted from coming to the next parliament at Shrewsbury on account of incurable infirmity, but to appoint proxies (*ibid.*, p. 279); died 23 April 1400.

John Fordham, bishop of Ely, on 4 December 1399 exonerated for two years (*ibid.*, *1399–1401*, p. 141).

John Bourghill, bishop of Coventry and Lichfield, on 5 January 1401 licensed to be absent from next parliament (*ibid.*, p. 403).

Thomas de la Warre, clerk, summoned as a baron, licensed on 10 January 1402 to be absent from parliament for three years without incurring penalty or molestation, notwithstanding any mandate to the contrary (*ibid.*, *1401–5*, p. 32).

Edmund Lacy, bishop of Exeter, on 13 February 1435 exempted for life, being prevented from riding on horse-back by a long-standing disease of the shin-bones, but to appoint proctors (*ibid.*, *1429–36*, p. 453); died September 1455.

William Heyworth, bishop of Coventry and Lichfield, on 12 December 1439 exonerated for life because of ill health and old age, provided he appoint proctors (*ibid.*, *1436–41*, p. 362; *Foedera*, x. 740); died 13 March 1447.

William Ayscough, bishop of Salisbury, on 11 July 1443 exempted for life, in consideration of attendance on the king's person, but to appoint proctors (*Foedera*, xi. 41); murdered, 29 June 1450.

William Lovell (lay peer, born *c.* 1397, summoned 1425–55), on 4 February 1446 exempted for life because of long royal service, provided that he and his heirs hold their places in parliaments and councils at will; exemption for life repeated, because of infirmity, on 17 May 1453 (*C.P.R.*, *1441–6*, p. 401; *ibid.*, *1452–61*, p. 74); died 13 June 1455.

John Tuchet, lord of Audley (lay peer, born *c.* 1398, summoned 1421–55), on 26 October 1447 discharged for life (*ibid.*, *1446–52*, p. 113); killed at Bloreheath, 1459.

Adam Moleyns, bishop of Chichester, then keeper of the privy seal, on 9 December 1449 granted indulgence to abstain from secular employment, including attendance at parliaments and great or secret councils, in view of bodily (including eye) weakness, long labours

ATTENDANCE OF THE LORDS IN MEDIEVAL PARLIAMENTS

in the royal service, and his desire to give attention to his diocese and fulfil vows of pilgrimage (*ibid.*, p. 297; *Foedera*, xi. 255); he was murdered on 9 January 1450.

Thomas Beckington, bishop of Bath and Wells, on 18 June 1452 discharged from parliamentary and conciliar attendance because of age and infirmity (*C.P.R.*, *1446–52*, p. 558; *Foedera*, xi. 311); died 14 January 1465.

Henry Bromflete, lord Vescy (lay peer, summoned 1449–67), on 13 May 1456 exempted for life, retaining all privileges if he attend parliament of his own will; on 15 February 1462 secured a renewal of the patent (*C.P.R.*, *1452–61*, p. 285; *ibid.*, *1461–7*, p. 115); died 16 January 1469.

John de la Bere, bishop of St. David's, on 15 February 1457 exempted for life because of ill health (*ibid.*, *1452–61*, p. 337; *Foedera*, xi. 386); he had been 'graviter amerciatus' by authority of parliament for non-attendance in spite of a former similar exemption, but this is not to occur again; he resigned and died *c.* 1460.

Walter le Hert, bishop of Norwich, in February 1460 exempted for life, because of age and long royal service and a desire to occupy himself in his spiritual office, but was to appoint proctors; any future attendance is not to prejudice his privilege of absence (*C.P.R.*, *1452–61* p. 642; *Foedera*, xi. 470); died 17 May 1472.

John de Vere, earl of Oxford, on 12 November 1460 (when 52 years old) exempted for good service to the Crown in England and France and because of infirmity, but to have all privileges if he come voluntarily (*C.P.R.* *1452–61*, p. 645); executed, February 1462.

Ralph Butler, lord Sudeley, on 26 February 1462 exonerated for life because of age and weakness (*ibid.*, *1461–7*, p. 72); died February 1474.

John lord Beauchamp of Powick, on 24 October 1462 exempted for life on account of old age and debility (*ibid.*, p. 213); died April 1475.

Laurence Bothe, bishop of Durham, on 15 April 1464 (two days before restitution of temporalities, in the king's hands since December 1462) excused for next three years (*ibid.*, p. 325).

William Bothe, archbishop of York, on 10 August 1464 exempted for life, but to appoint proctors (*ibid.*, p. 341; *Foedera*, xi. 531); died 12 September 1464.

John Arundel, bishop of Chichester, on 3 September 1474 excused for life because of old age, but to appoint proctors (*C.P.R. 1461–7*, p. 358; *Foedera*, xi. 532); died 18 October 1477.

Fulk Bourchier, lord Fitz Wareyn (first summoned, 1472), on 26 May 1474 exonerated from attendance against his will (*C.P.R.*, *1467–77*, p. 443); died, September 1479, aged thirty-three years.

A CONSIDERATION OF CERTAIN ASPECTS AND PROBLEMS OF THE ENGLISH *MODUS TENENDI PARLIAMENTUM*

THE English *Modus Tenendi Parliamentum* is an anonymous treatise of uncertain date, but produced not later than the fourteenth century.[1] Written in Latin, it purports to be a description of how an English parliament had been held in the time of Edward the Confessor and since, how it had been habitually summoned, who composed it, what officials of the Crown should attend and record its transactions, how it should be begun, what it should do, how it should end, where its records should be deposited, and the rest.

The earliest extant manuscripts of the *Modus* belong to the reign of Richard II. But they themselves point to an earlier origin. Most historians would be prepared (on the basis of the work of M. V. Clarke[2] and W. A. Morris[3]) to ascribe the original production of the treatise to the second half of Edward II's reign; and I am myself ready to accept Professor Morris's closely defined date of 1321, with which Miss Clarke's conjectures (independently arrived at) do all but precisely agree. Professor Galbraith's more recent dictum on this point of dating is that " Neither [of these two writers] is far out ".[4]

The main reasons for accepting the particular date of 1321 are that the *Modus* (article XVII) would assign to the earl steward (then Thomas, earl of Lancaster), the earl constable (then

---

[1] The best text so far available is that based on a collation of sixteen early manuscript versions and printed in the appendix of M. V. Clarke, *Medieval Representation and Consent. A study of early parliaments in England and Ireland with special reference to the Modus Tenendi Parliamentum* (1936), pp. 374-84. My references to particular articles of the *Modus* are in accordance with the enumeration of her text. [2] Clarke, op. cit.

[3] W. A. Morris, " The Date of the ' Modus Tenendi Parliamentum ' ", *English Historical Review*, xlix. 407 ff.

[4] V. H. Galbraith, " The Modus Tenendi Parliamentum ", *Journal of the Warburg and Courtauld Institutes*, xvi (1953), 84.

Humphrey, earl of Hereford), and the earl marshal (then Thomas, earl of Norfolk), an important part in arranging for a committee of twenty-five representatives of parliament (if parliament could not achieve a majority decision) to settle cases of great difficulty, including dangerous discord between the king and magnates or between magnates ; that in the spring and summer of 1321 it was possible that some such procedure might be needed to effect the banishment of Hugh Despenser the younger, Edward II's over-mighty chamberlain ; that in that year Lancaster was sympathetic to, and Hereford was actually involved in, a rising in the marches of Wales directed against this " favourite " ; and that these two major earls were then, after a period of political separation, once again actively allied against the court party until their untimely deaths in March of the following year. Might not the *Modus* be identified with the " quidem tractatus ex antiqua consuetudine ordinatus et approbatus ", which, according to the Pauline Annals,[1] the earl of Hereford and his confederates, in their advance on London in 1321 to depose and destroy the Despensers, " fecerunt in scriptis . . . ante adventum . . . parliamenti "? Whatever might be thought of this suggestion, it may perhaps be said that the main political purpose of the *Modus* was to emphasize the significance of the part which ought to be played in parliament by the higher baronage in the circumstances of a Lancastrian " come-back " and, to put the matter crudely, to secure the support of the representative elements in parliament for Lancaster's programme—the old Ordainers' policy with some important changes—of using parliament as an instrument for controlling the king and the government of the country. The *Modus* is, of course, much more than this. But here, it may be thought, is one of its chief political aims.

Stubbs once referred to " the proved worthlessness " of the *Modus*.[2] He later relented, at least to the extent of calling it " a somewhat ideal description of the constitution of parliament "

---

[1] *Chronicles of the Reigns of Edward I and Edward II* (R.S.), ed. W. Stubbs, p. 293. I see no reason to accept Miss Clarke's identification of this *tractatus* with the treatise on the office of the steward of England (op. cit. p. 242).

[2] W. Stubbs, *The Constitutional History of England*, Library edition (Oxford, 1880), iii. 465.

or " a theoretical view for which the writer was anxious to find a warrant in immemorial antiquity ".[1] Professor Galbraith has recently termed it " a paper constitution ", but considers it worthy of serious consideration as such.

The venerable antiquity of the parliament which the *Modus* describes we may, of course, reject as quite inane or even fatuous. What the treatise says of the functions of the serjeants-at-arms in attendance upon parliament, the usher and crier of parliament, and the principal and secondary clerks and official members of the king's council, of the sealed duplicate warrants of the elected clerical and lay representatives, of the roll-call of those sum- moned, of the seating arrangements (doubtfully stated to be under the control of the hereditary steward of England), of the opening sermon before parliament and the *pronunciatio* of its causes of summons by the chancellor or chief justice or their deputy, of the proclamation of a time-limit for the submission of petitions and complaints, of the order of deliberation upon the business of the king and his family and of the realm, and of the auditing of petitions in the order of their filing, may well be true, even though such particulars cannot all be verified from the rolls of the parliaments themselves. (These records are, of course, very uninformative regarding such details in the period when the *Modus* was written or, for that matter, at any time in the Middle Ages.) But what the tract says on the very important questions of the position of the king in parliament, of parliament's composi- tion, and of its political and tax-voting functions, in other words, about the nature and purposes of parliament, cannot be seriously regarded as authentic or as worth-while evidence of what par- liament was, how parliament worked, or what parliament did at any time in its early history. Regarded, however, simply as a political pamphlet,[2] whose text is made more life-like and realistic by what we may call its antiquarian details, the *Modus* still deserves proper consideration. This is so, if only because it was evidently composed by someone who cared enough about English government to wish to reform parliament drastically in

---

[1] Stubbs, *Select Charters* (9th edn.), p. 500.
[2] I accept Professor Galbraith's ideas on this point.

certain of its aspects, and was able to do so according to a reasoned plan.

If we regard the parliamentary " antiquities " of the *Modus* as merely incidental and only its political content or " message " as crucial, we can—as Professor Galbraith has suggested—cease to decry the " misstatements " alleged against the *Modus* as aberrations or anomalies or departures from current practice. These are in all conscience difficult to account for in a treatise obviously composed by a " professional ", but this need not be the case if we regard them as proposals (however extravagant in themselves) in a large and well-ramified scheme of parliamentary reform. The *Modus* is a political pamphlet. All of what is odd or eccentric in it ought to be considered not as statements of fact— that they are so represented in the tract is beside the point—but as projects for reform. If we were to translate the title of the tract into modern English, that title might well be, as Professor Galbraith has said, " How to hold a—perhaps *the*—parliament ". On this hypothesis, each and every " misstatement " of the *Modus* has its own intrinsic value, especially when it is clearly related to the whole, common purpose of the tract.

Thus far with Professor Galbraith. It is, however, on a matter arising out of this last point that to some degree I part company with him. Because to one particular article (article II) of the *Modus* (to which I shall eventually return), the especially important article which provides for the summoning of two proctors for each archdeaconry (not each diocese, as was current practice), he takes exception on the grounds that it " looks like a plain mistake ". If it is taken as an account of existing parliamentary practice, the *Modus* is full of mistakes. That is to say, it contains some statements about parliamentary practice that cannot be verified, some statements that can be contradicted. It seems to me unwise—if we are to take the tract at all seriously as a piece of political propaganda or as proposals for reform—to discriminate in this way between its " mistakes ", regarding some as deliberate and others as accidental, especially if we accept Professor Galbraith's view (and I think that we may) that " the author knew his subject minutely and at first hand ".

Of unusual theory and practice there is certainly no lack in the

Modus. At first sight the most surprising features of the tract are to be found in articles XVII and XXIII, those respectively entitled " De Casibus et Iudiciis Difficilibus " and " De Auxiliis Regis ". The former I have already referred to as suggesting a Lancastrian inspiration for certain parts of the *Modus* and as likely to appeal to the higher baronage.[1] But in the committee of twenty-five persons appointed (in article XVII) to resolve disagreements in parliament on difficult questions where there is discord (between king and magnates or among the magnates) serious enough to hazard the peace of the realm, a place is found for the representation of the clerical proctors and knights of the shire, citizens, and burgesses. These together make up three of the five *gradus* of parliament.[2] Indeed such a place is afforded these representative elements as would give them a large majority in this committee over those of its members who were bishops, earls, and barons, a majority of eighteen[3] over seven.[4] Almost as surprising as this preponderance of elected representatives over prelates and magnates in the committee is the preponderance, among the lay commoners, of the citizens and burgesses. For, although citizens and burgesses comprise together only one of the five parliamentary *gradus*, they figure on this committee of twenty-five as though they were two separate *gradus*, being represented by five citizens and five burgesses (the knights of the shire, too, being five in number).

Startling, too, is the reference in the *Modus* to all the members of every *gradus* as " pares parliamenti ". This " parity ", so " clearly at variance with contemporary practice " (as Professor Galbraith puts it), is sustained in the article " De Auxiliis Regis " : although a demand for an extraordinary financial grant to the king is to be considered by each *gradus*, all the " pares parliamenti " are to consent and, lest there should be any doubt

---

[1] The standing of the great lords in that single one of the six *gradus* which (in the *Modus*) embodies the lay magnates was likely to be enhanced if individual summonses were restricted to earls and barons and those with landed estate comprising not less than 13⅓ knights' fees (article III, " De Laicis ").

[2] In counting five I omit the *gradus* of which the king was the sole member.

[3] The 18 comprise 3 clerical proctors, 5 knights of the shire, 5 citizens and 5 burgesses.

[4] The 7 comprise 2 bishops, 2 earls and 3 barons.

of what this means, two knights of the shire are to have a greater voice than a " maior comes Anglie ", and all the proctors of a diocese (provided they agree) than their bishop. The theoretical justification for such a remarkable suggestion is that the presence of the " communitas regni ", glossed a few lines later as " communitates cleri et laici ", is alone essential to a parliament's proper constitution and valid operation, provided that members of the other *gradus* entitled to individual summonses have, in fact, been summoned. The " communitas parliamenti ", made up of proctors of clergy, knights, and citizens and burgesses, personifies the " tota communitas Anglie " : the prelates and lay magnates represent no one but themselves. This was a proposal clean contrary to the earlier policy of the Lords Ordainer of 1310, who had then regarded themselves as entirely competent to speak for the community of the realm and had all but ignored the elected commons when devising their programme of reform of the royal administration and household.

If the *Modus* was the work of somebody bidding for Lancastrian support—and there is more than a suggestion that its author was aware of the doings of Lancaster's private parliament held at Sherburn in Elmet (Yorkshire) in June 1321—it only serves to show how far Lancaster may have been prepared to go to secure the assistance of the middling elements, lay and clerical alike, in English society, and, therefore, how precarious the earl's situation had become at that time. But, as Tout once put it, " behind the narrow circles of barons and bishops, courtiers and officials, who were the permanent governing classes, lay the great masses of the smaller landed proprietors and of the traders of the towns, who, if still unable to lead, were now competent to take a side." " For their support ", he went on, " both parties to the main conflict eagerly competed at every great crisis. We are now [under Edward II] getting to the period when these lesser folk were almost in a position to turn the scale."[1] And certainly we need only look at the ranks of the " contrariants " (of 1322 and later) to perceive how crucial to Lancaster and his kind was the support of (at any rate) that class which supplied the knights of

[1] T. F. Tout, *Chapters in the Administrative History of Mediaeval England*, ii. 190-1.

the shire. 1321 would not be the first time that the support of the knights, or even of the clergy, knights, and burgesses together, had been seriously canvassed when king and barons were mutually hostile. We may think back to 1213, to 1261, or, with greater relevance still, to 1265, when for the first time knights and burgesses sat together in parliament, or we may look forward only a little way to their part in the events of 1327. Was Lancaster perhaps taking up again, where his great predecessor in the earldom of Leicester and the stewardship of England (Simon de Montfort) had laid down, the design of leading the middling classes over " the frontiers of political responsibility " (Miss Clarke)? Certainly, Lancaster in 1321 was well aware of the claim of the office of steward of England (appurtenant to his earldom of Leicester) to carry with it a guardianship of the common weal. This claim is writ large in the Lancastrian treatise on the Stewardship, with no fewer than seven of the earliest manuscripts of which copies of the *Modus* were, very significantly, actually written up or associated.[1] Following Miss Clarke,[2] we need only remark the close correspondence between what is advocated in article XVII of the *Modus* (" De Casibus et Iudiciis Difficilibus ") and the provision in the treatise on the Stewardship for the election in parliament, by the steward and constable, of the committee of twenty-five persons. In the latter treatise the twenty-five were to be composed of earls, barons, knights of the shire, citizens, and burgesses. In the *Modus* the twenty-five were to be chosen by the earl steward, the earl constable, and the earl marshal (" vel duo eorum ") from all the " pares regni ". This means that they were to include two bishops and three clerical proctors as well as lay magnates and lay representatives. The inclusion of representatives " pro toto clero " in the version of this proposal in the *Modus* is a notable amendment.

Quite the best part of Miss Clarke's treatment of the *Modus*

[1] Clarke, op cit. p. 358.

[2] Ibid. p. 244 : Miss Clarke was surely right in assuming that the tract on the Seneschalcy came before the *Modus*, and that the author of the *Modus* knew and used it. Both tracts most probably belonged to c. 1321. The reference in the treatise on the Seneschalcy to the time of Edward the Confessor when Earl Godwin was exiled, is worth comparing with the attribution of the parliament of the *Modus* to the reign of the same king.

in her book, *Medieval Representation and Consent*, is in regard to those ecclesiastical issues and problems of the early fourteenth century to which it refers. She saw in the tract " a definite prejudice in favour of the rights and dignity of the Church " or " a decided bias towards the ecclesiastical side ".[1] In fact, she went so far as to describe the *Modus* as " an ecclesiastical manifesto ".[2] Accordingly she gave more serious consideration than Professor Galbraith has been prepared to do to certain " misstatements " (*alias* reforms) in article II of the *Modus*, entitled " De Clero ". This chapter relates to the summoning of the higher and lower clergy to parliament. It states that archbishops, bishops, abbots, priors, " et alii maiores cleri " who hold lands of the Crown by barony are bound to be summoned and to come to parliament by reason of this tenure. Ecclesiastics of lesser dignity are normally not to be individually summoned to attend, unless they happen to be " de consilio regis " or their presence is deemed necessary and advantageous to parliament, and even then they ought to be asked (not ordered) to come and are entitled, when doing so, to receive expenses from the king. And then, by summonses directed in the first place to archbishops, bishops, and exempt ecclesiastics, arrangement is to be made for the election, by deaneries and archdeaconries, of two proctors for each archdeaconry to represent their clergy in parliament. Here was an important change. For current practice was that cathedral chapters and *dioceses* should be represented, respectively by one and two proctors. Miss Clarke at this point[3] suggested that if one purpose of the *Modus* was to counteract the ever-increasingly powerful tendency in Edward II's reign for the lower clergy to secede from parliament and to grant or withstand the king's financial demands upon their spiritualities only in their own provincial councils or convocations, the obvious answer was to give the lower clergy a greater numerical representation in parliament. Surely she was right. This would associate them there on a comparable basis with the lay commons. Moreover, with the three *gradus* of the " communitates cleri et laici " (the proctors of the clergy, the knights, and the burgesses) in joint

[1] Clarke, op. cit. pp. 16, 18.   [2] Ibid. p. 20.
[3] Ibid.

sessions with the two *gradus* of prelates and lay magnates, would then rest control over taxation.

The inception, in 1295, of Edward I's scheme for including representatives of the lower clergy in parliament had unfortunately all but coincided with the papal bull *Clericis laicos* of 1296. And since then the English clergy had followed a policy of obstruction to the royal plan. This they had done by objecting to the form of their summons (reinforcement of the " praemunientes " clause in the parliamentary writs convening the archbishops and bishops by a provincial letter issued by the archbishop, acting upon a royal mandate and citing his clergy to parliament as if to a provincial council), by declining to obey the extra-provincial citation, and by exploiting the difficulties likely to arise from the chronic dispute over primacy between the archbishops of Canterbury and York, when either was summoned to a parliament meeting in the other's province. Could the lower clergy, despite their wish to be separate from parliament, be induced to return to it willingly by reforming the system of their direct representation there in such a way as to give them greater numbers and presumably, therefore, a stronger voice ? Such an intention seems to be the drift of the argument of the *Modus*.[1]

That a considerable increase in the number of the clerical proctors in parliament would theoretically[2] accrue from the reform proposed by the *Modus* in article II is undoubted. On paper, under this new dispensation, the clerical proctors returned from the archdeaconries of England and Wales would number 120 instead of the usual 65 elected proctors from cathedral chapters and dioceses. The number of elected proctors would be almost doubled. We should not have regarded the total number

---

[1] One objection of the clergy—sometimes at any rate—was that parliament was a lay court which they therefore ought not to attend. This difficulty is not met by the *Modus*.

[2] I say " theoretically ", because it occasionally happened that one person acted as proctor for more than one ecclesiastical dignitary or body of clergy : for example, to the York parliament of 1322 was sent Master David Fraunceys as proctor for the bishop of St. David's, the archdeacons of St. David's, Carmarthen, Cardigan and Brecknock, and the cathedral-chapter and the clergy of the diocese of St. David's, each appointment being by separate letter (P.R.O., S.C.10/8, nos. 358, 367, 373, 376, 377, 387, 397).

of the clergy in parliament below the rank of bishop, abbot and prior as so remarkably changed by article II of the *Modus*, had we not made a distinction between those of the middle clergy normally summoned as individuals (the priors or deans of cathedral chapters and archdeacons) and those clergy who were as a rule proctorially represented (the cathedral and diocesan clergy). The elimination in article II of the *Modus* of the cathedral deans (11 in number), of the archdeacons (60), of the single proctor for each cathedral chapter (23), and of the two proctors for each diocese (42), accounted in all for as many as 136 clergy.[1] The total number of clergy in parliament below the rank of bishop, abbot, and prior, would have been, therefore, in fact, diminished by 16 if the plan of the *Modus* had ever been made effectual. It was only the elected proctors whose number would have been drastically increased. In other words, what the author of the *Modus* intended here was to effect an important shift of the balance of the representation of the clerical order in parliament away from the dignitaries to the rank and file of the Church, as well as to raise the numbers of his separate *gradus* of the proctors of the clergy in the reformed parliament envisaged in his tract. The enhanced localism of the electoral units, rural deaneries and archdeaconries, is also worth remark.

Professor Galbraith dismissed these proposed changes of the *Modus* with their restriction of proctorial representation to archdeaconries, observing that " it looks like a plain mistake ", and that " perhaps the author was misled by the practice of the Convocation of the northern province ". My own feeling, and I use Professor Galbraith's own words against him here, is that the *Modus* is " most valuable when it is most at fault, for

---

[1] Admittedly, in article IX there is a reference to deans among those prelates and clerks required to appear on the fifth day of parliament and in article XII to archdeacons among the *gradus*. Such inclusions are, however, quite inconsistent with article II, which provides for the *regular* summoning of only prelates and other clerics who hold by barony, and also with article XXVI, where the second *gradus* is composed " de archiepiscopis, episcopis, abbatibus, prioribus, per baroniam tenentibus " and the third *gradus* " de procuratoribus cleri ". In taking the clause to imply the exclusion of deans and archdeacons and proctors from cathedrals and dioceses, I have followed Miss Clarke's conclusion on this point (op. cit. pp. 18-19, 326).

when it is wrong it is wrong to a purpose ".[1]   Even if the plan of
the *Modus* for representation by proctors from archdeaconries was
grounded on the practice of the convocation of York, where the fewness of the episcopal sees (York, Durham, and Carlisle) made recourse to such a system obviously preferable to one based on dioceses,
that need not detract from the sincerity of the proposal.   But in the
province of Canterbury itself, in fact, representation of the lower
clergy by archdeaconries would have appeared not at all unreal
or even novel.   In the first quarter of the fourteenth century
the existing arrangements for the election of diocesan proctors
(apparently to both convocation and parliament) in at least the
great diocese of Lincoln were based upon a system whereby the
rural deaneries elected proctors who chose one for their archdeaconry to join with the proctors of other archdeaconries for the
purpose of finally electing two proctors for the diocese.   And a
similar system of pre-elections in at any rate archdeanconries,
preliminary to a final diocesan election, was being employed at
this time in the diocese of Salisbury also.[2]   Moreover, it was not
unknown for the election of the two proctors for those dioceses
which were divided into only two archdeaconries, to be made
directly by these archdeaconries, one proctor being elected from
each.   In 1307, 1316 and 1318[3] the two archdeaconries of the
bishopric of Winchester (the archdeaconries of Winchester and
Surrey) each elected one proctor to parliament, so supplying the
two required from the diocese without any further election being
needed.   In 1309 the archdeaconry of Lewes elected one proctor
to parliament,[4] and it may be conjectured that the other archdeaconry of the diocese of Chichester (that of Chichester itself)
elected the second diocesan proctor required.   Similarly in 1318
the archdeaconry of Durham elected one proctor to parliament,[5]
and presumably the other archdeaconry of the diocese (Northumberland) did the same to make up the diocesan complement.   For
the same parliament the archdeaconry of Gloucester made its
own election of a proctor,[6] and perhaps the archdeaconry of

---

[1] Galbraith, op. cit. p. 94 and n. 2.   [2] Clarke, op. cit. pp. 327-9.
[3] Clarke, op. cit. pp. 328-9, 329, n. 1 ; Parliament and Council, Parliamentary
Proxies, P.R.O., S.C.10/5, nos. 247, 248.   [4] S.C. 10/2, no. 55.
[5] S.C. 10/6, no. 256 A.   [6] S.C. 10/6, no. 263.

Worcester (the other archdeaconry of the diocese of Worcester) supplied his fellow. There are actually a few cases where a single archdeaconry sent up two proctors independently to parliament : Salop in 1307,[1] Hereford in 1309,[2] and Stafford (one of five archdeaconries in the diocese of Lichfield) in 1309.[3] It is important to recognize that in all these instances the body making the return of proctors was expressly stated in the letter of proxy to be the clergy of the archdeaconry, and where there were two archdeaconries in a diocese the election of a proctor in one archdeaconry was clearly made independently of the election in the other, although such separate elections in all probability resulted from a common acceptance of so convenient a usage by the bishop and diocesan clergy together. Moreover, we should not forget that there were as many as five dioceses in the southern province (Canterbury, Rochester, Ely, Llandaff, and St. Asaph) and one in the northern province (Carlisle), where there was a single archdeaconry only, so that in these dioceses the proposal of the *Modus* to have proctorial representation by archdeaconries would have made no actual change. But clearly, that on one side, archdeaconries (and sometimes even rural deaneries) were already in occasional use as ecclesiastical electoral units outside the limits of the northern province. And, as Miss Clarke says, " the direct representation of archdeaconries laid down in the text [of the *Modus*] was probably intended to standardize a practice sometimes actually followed ".[4] The requirement, in the *Modus*, of proctors from archdeaconries instead of from dioceses (as was normal) was, to my mind, no slip.

Article II of the *Modus* would have had some other effects on clerical representation in parliament than simply to double the numbers of the proctorial element there (although whether its author was aware of them may be doubtful). To confine proctorial representation, as he evidently intended, solely to archdeaconries would to some extent have had the remarkable effect of co-ordinating the parliamentary representation of the lower clergy with that of the lay folk of the communities of the shires.

[1] Clarke, op. cit. p. 329.
[2] S.C. 10/2, no. 62.
[3] S.C. 10/2, no. 61.
[4] Op. cit. p. 329.

In by no means all, but certainly in many, cases a shire would have been similarly and equally represented in its ecclesiastical and lay aspects, respectively by two clerical proctors and two knights of the shire.   For, as A. Hamilton Thompson once made clear,[1] the archidiaconal system was founded in the main upon the county divisions, the more important exceptions being almost invariably supplied by the larger counties.   Almost half of the shires were exactly, or so nearly as makes no matter, coterminous with archdeaconries, which carried the name of their shire itself.   In the large medieval diocese of Lincoln, for instance, there was " a nearly symmetrical example of division by counties " into archdeaconries.   It would be unwise, perhaps, to press the implications of this fact with regard to the *Modus*, but it seems that in the larger context of the operation of the ecclesiastical and secular jurisdictions generally in England the territorial identity or correspondence of shires and archdeaconries has not been given the attention it may deserve.

Of one other corollary of article II of the *Modus*, I feel sure, its author was not at all unaware.   In his " model " parliament not only would he substitute the general proctorial representation of the clergy on the basis of archdeaconries for representation by dioceses, but he would omit altogether the proctorial representation of cathedral chapters and abolish the personal attendance (normally required under the " praemunientes " clause of the royal summonses to the bishops) of the deans[2] of cathedral churches and of archdeacons.   And here, it seems to me, a prosopographical approach to the problem has something to recommend it.

It is well known that the political tendencies of Edward II's reign stressed the baronial as against the professional, official element in parliament.   Mr. Richardson and Professor Sayles[3] have shown that under Edward I " the conduct of the business of parliament was throughout very largely in the hands of

[1] A. Hamilton Thompson, " Diocesan Organisation in the Middle Ages : Archdeacons and Rural Deans ", *Proceedings of the British Academy*, xxix (Raleigh Lecture), 165-7.   [2] And priors.
[3] H. G. Richardson and G. O. Sayles, " The King's Ministers in Parliament ", *English Historical Review*, xlvi, 532 ; xlvii, 202.

trained lawyers and administrators ", primarily though not exclusively in the hands of the more important Chancery clerks, royal officials of whom some received their own individual summons to parliament ; that under Edward II the inclusion of magnates among the triers of petitions was " deliberately designed to restrict the authority of the official class " ; and that, after the political " feudal reaction " of the middle years of Edward II's reign, " the official class did not recover the predominance that had been theirs under Edward I ". But Chancery clerks, at any rate on occasion, continued to be well represented on committees of the council performing parliamentary business, as Mr. Richardson and Professor Sayles's work itself makes clear. Article XV of the *Modus*, where the duties of the principal clerks of parliament are described, suggests that its author wished to diminish the part played by the judicial and other official elements in examining parliamentary petitions, and to give a bigger share in this work to all the proper members of parliament, the " pares parliamenti ". Miss Clarke[1] also saw in these changes a step towards the emergence of common petitions as the basis for legislation. Be that as it may, it is here sufficient to notice in the *Modus* a certain antipathy to any restoration of royal officials to that central place in parliament which undoubtedly they had once held but were in process of losing or had lost. For there is implicit, I believe, in the proposed reform in the *Modus* of the character of the representation of the lower clergy, with its concomitant exclusion of the proctors of cathedral chapters and the abandonment of the personal attendance of deans of cathedrals and of archdeacons, summoned as such, something of the same " anti-official " bias.

There can certainly be no doubt that many of the king's clerks would have been affected in their ecclesiastical capacity by the reform of clerical representation in parliament proposed in article II of the *Modus*. One only needs to investigate the composition of the secular cathedral chapters at the time about when the *Modus* was composed, to appreciate the relevance and significance, in this respect, of the abandonment of their direct representation in parliament as proposed by the tract.

[1] Op. cit. pp. 234-5.

One effect of the collusion between the Crown and the Papacy over provision to ecclesiastical benefices, of the exercise of royal rights of patronage during episcopal vacancies, and of the sympathy towards the king's needs felt by the bishops (more than half of whom at this time had formerly been king's clerks themselves),[1] is clear to see in the frequent possession of cathedral prebends by the clerks of the Chancery and of other branches of the royal administration. The most lucrative prebends were those of York, Lincoln and Salisbury. Cathedral prebends generally were sinecures and could therefore be enjoyed in plurality and without obligation to residence (certainly when held by king's clerks), and usually only a small minority of canons undertook residence in their cathedrals. Even so, the connection of non-resident English-born canons with their chapters was never merely nominal.[2] And if a list is compiled of cathedral prebends held by king's clerks in 1321 (the putative date of composition of the *Modus*) it is difficult to imagine that the election of parliamentary proctors from the cathedral chapters went uninfluenced by that element in their constitution.[3] Many king's clerks held prebends in not a few cathedral churches. For example, among the canons of York (whose complement was now stabilized at thirty-six) were, in 1321, the following thirteen king's clerks : William Airmyn, " custos rotulorum cancellarie " (with two prebends), Robert Bardelby, and Henry Cliff, all three of them masters in Chancery and joint-custodians of the Great Seal in this year ; two other Chancery clerks, Richard Airmyn (a younger brother of William), and Peter de Dene ; Thomas de Charlton, a former controller of the Wardrobe and recently keeper of the Privy Seal ; Robert Wodehouse, a baron of the Exchequer who received his own individual writ of summons to parliament in 1321 ; Hervey

[1] Kathleen Edwards, " The Political Importance of the English Bishops during the reign of Edward II ", *English Historical Review*, lix, 312.

[2] For a general review of the situation of the royal clerks in the secular cathedral chapters, see K. Edwards, *The English Secular Cathedrals in the Middle Ages*, chapter I (" The Canons and their Residence "), especially pp. 84-88, and W. A. Pantin, " *The English Church in the Fourteenth Century* ", pp. 59-61.

[3] In compiling these lists I have mainly used H.M. Stationery Office, *Calendars of Patent Rolls, Close Rolls* and *Papal Registers*, and J. Le Neve, *Fasti Ecclesiae Anglicanae*, ed. T. Duffus Hardy.

Staunton, chancellor of the Exchequer, who was similarly summoned; Roger Northburgh, keeper of the Wardrobe; and Master John de Nassington (official of the court of York), John de Merkingfeld, Robert de Appleby, and Master Nicholas de Ros.[1] William Airmyn, Robert Wodehouse, and Roger Northburgh were also at this time in possession of canonries at Lincoln. Here their fellow-prebendaries then included Master Robert Baldock, in 1321 controller of the Wardrobe and keeper of the Privy Seal; two other king's clerks, Robert de Pickering and Thomas de Clifford; and three more masters in Chancery, Richard Carmel, Master John de Stratford and (with two prebends) Master Gilbert de Middleton, the last two being important ecclesiastical lawyers as well as king's clerks, respectively as dean of the Court of Arches and official of the Court of Canterbury, and both of them independently summoned to parliament in 1321. Fourteen prebends at York and ten at Lincoln were thus held at this one time by king's clerks, some of them important office-holders in the royal service. And if we look further afield into the constitution of the chapters of the remaining seven secular cathedral churches in 1321, we find at least seven king's clerks at both Salisbury and London, five at Lichfield, and four at Hereford.[2] In naming these men we need not go outside the group of those eighteen king's clerks already listed above, except to mention another seven : Adam de Herwyngton, canon of Hereford and in 1321 keeper of the writs and rolls of the Common Bench, who was individually summoned to parliament in that year; Gilbert de Stapleton, canon of Salisbury and the king's escheator north of Trent, who similarly received his own summons to parliament; Nicholas Huggate, another canon of Salisbury, a

[1] There was nothing unusual about the constitution of the York chapter in 1321 : discussing it in the primacy of Archbishop William Greenfield about a decade earlier, A. Hamilton Thompson was able to notice " the remarkable prominence of Yorkshire-born clerks, alike in offices of state and in the chapter of York, which continued throughout the greater part of the fourteenth century " (*Publications of the Surtees Society*, cxlv, " The Register of William Greenfield, Archbishop of York, 1306-15 ", ed. W. Brown and A. Hamilton Thompson, p. xv; *Victoria County History, Yorkshire*, iii. 378).

[2] Were we able to identify more king's clerks and more cathedral canons, our list would surely be somewhat larger.

Chancery clerk who was keeper of the Wardrobe of Prince Edward of Windsor and was later (in November 1326) to become controller of the King's Wardrobe ; John de Everdon, also canon of Salisbury ; Master James de Ispania, illegitimate nephew of Eleanor of Castile, canon of St. Paul's and of Salisbury, and in 1321 a chamberlain of the Exchequer ; Roger Waltham, another prebendary of London, who in 1322 became keeper of the King's Wardrobe ; and John de Husthwayt, canon of Lichfield, a former keeper of the Great Wardrobe (1295-1300). Looking at the matter from a somewhat different angle, we see William Airmyn, the most eminent of the masters in Chancery in 1321, then installed at York, London, Lincoln, Lichfield, Hereford and Salisbury ; Roger Northburgh, keeper of the King's Wardrobe, with canonries at York, Lincoln, London, Wells, Hereford and St. David's ; Thomas de Charlton, prebendary at York, Salisbury, London and Lichfield ; Robert Wodehouse, baron of the Exchequer, canon at York, Lincoln and Hereford.

Unfortunately, it is not possible to say what precise effect the membership of cathedral chapters enjoyed by king's clerks had on capitular representation by proctors in parliament : how often, for instance, king's clerks who were cathedral canons themselves acted as proctors for their chapters. The number of letters of parliamentary proxy emanating from cathedral chapters in Edward II's reign and preserved in the Public Record Office (Parliament and Council, Letters of Proxy) is only a small fraction of the whole of that generally incomplete collection for the reign.[1] Not many more than a score of such capitular letters have, in fact, survived for the reign in the Public Record Office, so that the normal current practice of a particular chapter or of chapters in general regarding their proctorial representation cannot be determined. The nearest approach in the collection for this period to a series of such letters is that relating to the cathedral chapter of York. But here in 1315, 1316 and 1317,[2] the parliamentary proctors chosen were generally canons who were king's clerks : in 1315, Adam de Osgodby and Robert de Bardelby, then senior masters in Chancery, along with John de Merkingfeld,

[1] P.R.O., S.C. 10/1-11.
[2] S.C. 10/3, nos. 126, 147 ; S.C. 10/4, nos. 168, 193.

a recent chancellor of the Exchequer (1310-12) ; in January 1316, John de Hustwace (*alias* Husthwayt ?) and Master Nicholas de Ros, both king's clerks, and Robert de Cotingham ; in June 1316, Osgodby and Bardelby again ; and in 1317, the two latter and Merkingfeld once more. It is unhelpful to find that one half of the remaining extant capitular letters of Edward II's reign came from Welsh cathedrals where it was not so usual to give prebends to king's clerks. But from among the few other letters it may be noted that the monastic chapter of Worcester in 1319 appointed one of its monks and Thomas de Evesham, a king's clerk, as its proctors,[1] and that the chapter of Salisbury in 1322 appointed two of its canons, one of whom was Master John de Everdon, a king's clerk and former baron of the Exchequer, who in the next year (1323) was to be admitted as dean of St. Paul's.[2] If the author of the *Modus* was aiming in article II of his treatise to exclude royal officials from the representation of the lower clergy in parliament, some measure of success was likely to accrue if the proctorial representation of the cathedral chapters were abandoned. To secure this end he was evidently also prepared to abandon the direct representation of those cathedral chapters which were monastic in constitution.

Article II of the *Modus* also conflicts with established practice in its implied advocacy of an omission of the deans of cathedral chapters and of archdeacons from among those personally summoned to parliament. They had regularly been summoned since 1295 whenever the " praemunientes "clause was included in the parliamentary summonses of the archbishops and their suffragans. An examination of the state of the nine English secular cathedral deaneries in 1321 reveals that, of the seven that were occupied by Englishmen, three were certainly then filled by king's clerks : the dean of York was Robert de Pickering, professor of civil law and formerly archdeacon of Northumberland (already met with as a canon of Lincoln) ; at Lichfield was Stephen de Segrave, formerly archdeacon of Essex, who early in 1321 had been a commissioner for negotiating with Robert I of Scotland and who was soon (in 1324) to become archbishop of

[1] S.C. 10/6, no. 290.   [2] S.C. 10/8, no. 384.

the Irish province of Armagh; and at Wells was the recent
keeper of the Wardrobe of Edward I's widow, Queen Margaret
(who died in 1318), John Godelegh, who in 1327 was to become
bishop of Exeter. If we investigate the state of the fifty-two
English archdeaconries in 1321, the results are more surprising. As many as twelve of them were occupied by car-
dinals or other members of the Avignonese Curia. The occupants
of no fewer than sixteen of the remaining forty English archdeaconries were king's clerks, some of whom we have already
encountered among those provided with cathedral prebends.
In the diocese of York, with its five archdeaconries, William
Airmyn, keeper of the rolls of the Chancery, was archdeacon of
the East Riding; Roger Northburgh, keeper of the Wardrobe,
archdeacon of Richmond; Adrian de Flisco, a royal kinsman and
king's clerk, archdeacon of Cleveland. In the diocese of Durham,
one of the two archdeacons, he of Northumberland, was a former
keeper of the Privy Seal who was personally summoned as a
king's clerk to parliament in 1321 : Thomas de Charleton (also
archdeacon of Wells). In the extensive bishopric of Lincoln,
with its eight archdeaconries, were Master John de Stratford, a
master in Chancery, archdeacon of Lincoln ; Richard de North-
wode, king's clerk, archdeacon of Stowe ; Edmund de London,
master in Chancery, archdeacon of Bedford ; and Master Gilbert
de Middleton, master in Chancery, archdeacon of Northampton.
In the diocese of Norwich, which had four archdeaconries, were
William Harleston, master in Chancery and sometime joint-
keeper of the Great Seal, archdeacon of Norfolk ; and Alan de
Ely (perhaps no longer a king's clerk but in royal service in 1310),
archdeacon of Sudbury, who in 1324 became archdeacon of
Suffolk. Among the five archdeacons of the diocese of Coventry
and Lichfield was a former royal escheator north of Trent and
(under Edward I) constable of Bordeaux who had gone abroad
with Edward II in 1313: Richard Havering, archdeacon of
Chester. The archdeacon of Middlesex in the London diocese
(where were five archdeaconries) was Robert Baldock, controller
of the Wardrobe and keeper of the Privy Seal, who in 1323 was
appointed to the archdeaconry of Lincoln. Gilbert de Stapleton,
king's escheator north of Trent, as archdeacon of Berkshire

administered that one of the four archdeaconries comprising the bishopric of Salisbury. One of the two archdeaconries of the diocese of Chichester, that of Chichester itself, was under Robert Leyset (or Lesset), who had been a king's clerk and the constable of Bordeaux as long ago as 1293-4 but was perhaps no longer occupied with royal business at the centre of affairs. In the diocese of Bath and Wells, Robert Hereward, king's clerk, was archdeacon of Taunton. And perhaps Master Hugh de Statherne, to whom Edward II had granted the archdeaconry of Gloucester in the diocese of Worcester in 1318, during an episcopal vacancy, was a royal clerk, for certainly most of the appointments to archdeaconries made *sede vacante* were of king's clerks. The proportion of king's clerks among Englishmen occupying deaneries and archdeaconries as revealed by these identifications was two out of every five. Their number is all the more significant, of course, because, being civil servants, they are not likely to have abstained to any appreciable extent from personal attendance in parliament when summoned under the " praemunientes " clause. And we must not forget that the absence of the rank and file of the clergy from parliaments was so recurrent as to be a source of serious irritation and dissatisfaction to the royal administration on such occasions (as, for example, in 1316, 1319, 1321, and 1322).[1] In other words, deans of cathedrals and archdeacons who were king's clerks could be better relied upon to attend parliament than deans and archdeacons who were not king's clerks.

In the light of these enumerations, may we not fairly ask whether article II of the *Modus* was not an attempt to exclude the more important of the king's clerks from parliament in their capacity as proper members of the *gradus* of the lower clergy and, *ipso facto*, restrict their parliamentary rôle to that of mere assistants or technical experts ? The suggestion gains point from the fact that among those royal justices, officials, and others " de consilio regis " actually in receipt of a personal summons to parliament in 1321 were Dean Pickering of York, Archdeacon Charleton of Northumberland and Wells, Archdeacon Middleton of Northampton, Archdeacon Stratford of Lincoln, and

[1] Clarke, op. cit. pp. 135-44.

Archdeacon Stapleton of Berkshire, and four other king's clerks from our list of the prebendaries of secular cathedrals (Hervey de Staunton, Robert de Wodehouse, Adam de Herwyngton, and Master John de Nassington).[1]   That such clerics were largely non-resident in their cathedrals or jurisdictions does not affect the argument, certainly not so far as concerns the deans and archdeacons whose *personal* attendance was required by the " praemunientes " clause of the episcopal summonses to parliament ; and the cathedral prebendaries, upon whose services the king had first call, undoubtedly for the most part kept in touch with their chapters, occasionally as a matter of duty as well as of interest, and certainly some of them acted as their parliamentary proctors.[2] Absenteeism from prebendal stall or ecclesiastical office among the king's clerks was perhaps one factor present in the mind of the author of the *Modus* when he proposed the exclusion from the lower clergy in parliament of the deans, archdeacons, and the proctors of cathedral chapters. The main abuse to which he objected was most probably, however, that the existing system under the " praemunientes " clause resulted in too many king's clerks being present among the lower clerical *gradus* in parliament. The author of the *Modus* was evidently confident that he knew which of their two capacities, as civil servants or as ecclesiastical dignitaries or officials, was the more likely to affect the parliamentary conduct (and perhaps especially the attitude to clerical taxation in aid of the Crown) of such of the king's clerks as were deans, archdeacons, and cathedral canons.

If, as I suggest, the author of the *Modus* objected to the way in which the king's clerks were enabled by their ecclesiastical preferments to intrude upon the representation of the clerical estate in parliament, his feelings must have been further exacerbated by the fact that some of the bishops and most of the parliamentary abbots often failed to attend parliament[3] and then very frequently appointed king's clerks as their proctors. In parliaments that were ill-attended by prelates and lower clergy alike— and there were many such in the early fourteenth century—the

[1] *Report on the Dignity of a Peer*, iii. 309.   [2] Edwards, op. cit. p. 92.
[3] J. S. Roskell. " The Problem of the Attendance of the Lords in Medieval Parliaments ", II 162-5.

king's clerks must together have sometimes been predominant in the sessions of their order.

The problem posed by the dual capacity of the king's clerks with respect to parliament cannot, of course, be regarded as new in 1321 or thereabouts. If we look at the lists of the " clerici de consilio " individually summoned to parliament under Edward I after 1295, we find a number of such clerks actually designated in their writs as dean or archdeacon, and these would therefore attend as " clerici de consilio " and also, by virtue of the " prae-munientes " clause, as ecclesiastical dignitaries. To the Lent parliament of 1300, for example, were personally summoned as king's clerks the deans of Lichfield and Wells and the archdeacons of Chester, Richmond, and the East Riding of York.[1] Perhaps we need to expand the tag " Quod omnes tangit, ab omnibus approbetur ", and make it read, " What touches all should be approved by all, including many of the king's clerks ".

In his paper on the *Modus*, Professor Galbraith considered the question of the possible identity of the author of the tract, and came to the conclusion that the author was " a working official, preferably a Chancery official ".[2] Going one stage further, he found himself " left to infer that the author is in all probability the clerk of the parliament magnifying his office as bureaucrats are wont to do ". Then, going one stage further still, he named " a man who fills the bill " : William Airmyn, " custos rotulo-rum " from 1316 to 1324 and probably clerk of the parliaments. We have already met with William Airmyn as canon of York, London, Lincoln, Lichfield, Hereford, and Salisbury, and as archdeacon of the East Riding of York ; and we found him to be one of a formidable group of king's clerks, in number nearly a score strong, who, as deans and archdeacons, would cease to be personally summoned to parliament under the " praemunientes " clause and who, as members of cathedral chapters, would cease to be represented by proctors or to act as cathedral proctors them-selves, if the recommendation of article II of the *Modus* were

[1] *Dignity of a Peer*, op. cit. iii. 115.
[2] Galbraith, op. cit. p. 89. Miss Clarke and Professor Morris, to judge from their conjectures, would probably not have disagreed with Professor Galbraith's conclusion.

followed, with its restriction of the lower clergy in parliament to the proctors for archdeaconries. It was one of the objects of the *Modus*, we may believe, to prevent or at least check the adulteration of the lower clerical *gradus* in parliament by ecclesiastical dignitaries whose chief concern as king's clerks was to serve the king. If so, for William Airmyn, or any other Chancery clerk, to have written the *Modus* would have been a " traison des clercs ", indeed. And unless we can credit the Chancery clerks with a large-minded capacity for devising self-denying ordinances, we may not only rule out William Airmyn as a possible author of the *Modus* but even deny to the Chancery a right to be considered as the milieu from which the *Modus* emanated.

Whoever the author of the *Modus* was, he knew enough about how parliament worked and what it did, to propose important changes in its structure, procedure, and functions. But a knowledge (such as is demonstrated in the *Modus*) of the writs of summons or of the writs *de expensis*, or even of the clerical work of parliament, was surely not confined to Chancery clerks. The Chancery clerks were to have, of course, their place and functions in the parliament of the *Modus*, along with the chancellor. But the increase (in the *Modus*) in the number of clerks of parliament, which Professor Galbraith regarded as the natural act of a bureaucrat " magnifying his office ", was simply a consequence of the tract's separation of the " pares parliamenti " into five *gradus*, to each of which a separate clerk just had to be assigned if ever it was to be allowed to function independently. Besides, the *Modus* (article XIV) does not expressly state from which branch of the civil service the expanded corps of parliamentary clerks with special functions was to be drawn, a point worth noticing, because not only were the chancellor's clerks to be in attendance, but also the clerks of the chief justice and the clerks of the treasurer and other officials of the Exchequer. Moreover, even if the two principal clerkships of parliament were to be monopolized by the Chancery —and it is not so stated in the *Modus*—it was to be by one or two justices that their enrolments were, if at all, to be scrutinized and corrected. Regarding the fees of parliamentary clerks, it is provided by the *Modus* (article XVI) that only those not already in receipt of royal fees or wages are to be paid two shillings a day, and only half this amount if they be " ad mensam regis ". Parliamentary clerkship was perhaps designed by the author of the *Modus* as a career open to talents and not confined to Chancery clerks alone. However this may be, there seems no doubt that such financial regulations of the *Modus* as touch the clerks of parliament are restrictive in tone. And this fact is confirmed by article XXV with its requirement that the clerks are not to deny (" non negabunt ") transcripts of process and must charge no more than a penny for ten lines (and not even that from a needy suitor). Even the width of their vellums is prescribed as 10 inches, although here the *Modus* may only be stating the current width of the rolls in Edward II's reign.

There seems, in fact, to be precious little magnification in the *Modus* of the parliamentary rôle of the Chancery. The chancellor is inevitably referred to on a number of occasions along with other officials. But nothing exceptional is said of him, save that when he finds a plea difficult it is to go for settlement to the special committee of twenty-five, chosen by the earl steward, the earl constable, and the earl marshal. This is practically the solution propounded at greater length in the Lancastrian tract about the duties of the steward of England, by which this proposal of the *Modus* may well have been inspired.[1] And the general tone of *that* tract anent the chancellor's part in hard and ambiguous legal causes is not likely to have recommended itself to any Chancery clerk, let alone the chancellor. Moreover, while the chancellor is noticed in the *Modus* in these ways, the Chancery itself is never mentioned at all. Nor is there any special mention of the Chancery clerks as such. These are perhaps omissions of some relevance, if we are considering the possibility of a Chancery provenance for the *Modus*. One way for a Chancery author to magnify his office would surely have been to appropriate at least the principal clerkships of parliament to the Chancery at a time when (in the reigns of Edward II and Edward III) the single clerk of the parliament was still (as Professor Galbraith admits) " not necessarily a Chancery clerk ". Another way would have been to anticipate the historically impending transference to Chancery

[1] L. W. Vernon Harcourt, *His Grace the Steward and Trial of Peers* (1907), p. 165.

of the custody of the parliament rolls. The *Modus*, however, actually lays down, in article XV, that the two master-copies of the principal rolls of the parliament are to be surrendered (before the departure of parliament) into the keeping of the treasurer and kept in the Treasury.

Especially in view of this last fact, the *Modus*, at the time of its production, is likely to have had a stronger interest for the Exchequer than for the Chancery. With this possibility in mind, it is worth noting the important emphasis (in article II) on the summoning of prelates, secular and religious, on the basis of tenure by barony, and more especially the recommendation (in article III) that the summonses of barons be normally restricted to those with lands equal to the (supposititious) feudal content and monetary value of an earldom or barony. With its reference to the twenty knights' fees of an earl and the $13\frac{1}{3}$ fees of a baron, this article obviously recalls the arrangements of Magna Carta (as modified in the *Confirmatio* of 1297) for the payment of reliefs on succession to the baronies of earls and barons and to individual knights' fees not held by barony.[1] The suggestion in article III of the *Modus* that lay magnates be summoned after this fashion, perhaps betrays, or was designed to appeal to, the "Pipe-roll mind". In 1321, moreover, the Exchequer was doubtless being made very well aware (if ever it needed to be reminded) of the knight's fee as the basic unit of the feudal structure: on 14 January 1321 letters close had ordered the sheriffs to proclaim that all tenants-in-chief by knight service should deliver into the Exchequer (before the quindene of Michaelmas) information about all their demesne and subinfeudated fees.[2] Elsewhere in the *Modus* its author is preoccupied with the financial incidentals of parliamentary meetings, the fees of the clerks of the parliaments and the expense-allowances of the commons apart: article IX provides a detailed set of proposals for the imposition of formidable fines for non-attendance of £100 or 100 marks depending on the status of the defaulting individuals or communities. (For this purpose the duplicate sealed warrants of the elected proctors and lay representatives

[1] Clarke, op. cit. p. 197.

[2] F. Palgrave, *Parliamentary Writs*, i. 537, no. 10.

were, of course, essential as a check on attendance.) And then there are some occasional enumerations of the higher-grade members of the Exchequer staff present in parliament *ex officio*, a feature conspicuously lacking in the case of the Chancery staff, whose head alone is specifically referred to in the *Modus*. For instance, in article VIII it was laid down that on the second day of the parliament the treasurer, chamberlains,[1] and barons of the Exchequer are to be in attendance, and in article XIV the seats for all these officers " at the king's left foot " are noticed.

One further point in favour of an Exchequer as against a Chancery background for the *Modus* is that the exclusion from parliament of those clerical representatives who were king's clerks first and only secondarily local ecclesiastical dignitaries, would not have affected the Exchequer as it would have done the Chancery. Certainly, the staff of the Exchequer was by no means so exclusively clerical as was the Chancery. The proportion of lay to clerical barons of the Exchequer, for example, over the whole reign of Edward II was twelve to eleven, and in 1321 itself it was four to three in favour of the lay element.[2] Moreover, of the seven barons of the Exchequer in 1321 only one, Robert Wodehouse, was a pluralist holder of cathedral prebends ; and, of the rest of the more dignified members of the Exchequer staff who were king's clerks, only the chancellor of the Exchequer (Hervey Staunton) and one of the two chamberlains (Master James de Ispania) held any cathedral stall. Not one of the king's clerks employed in the Exchequer in 1321 held a cathedral deanery or an archdeaconry, the holders of which offices were excluded by the *Modus* from attendance in parliament in their proper ecclesiastical capacity.

[1] Some doubt has been expressed whether the word " chamberlains " in this context ought not to be read in the singular, and be taken to refer to Hugh Despenser the younger, who was king's chamberlain from 1318 until his death (save during his short exile in 1321), and not to the chamberlains of the Exchequer. But the best texts of the *Modus* certainly give the word in the plural (Clarke, op. cit. p. 204), and the interposition of the word *camerarii* between references to the treasurer and the barons of the Exchequer confirms, in fact, the interpretation I have accepted (cf. Vernon Harcourt, op. cit. p. 164, where, in the tract on the Stewardship of England, the Exchequer officials are given as the treasurer, barons and chamberlains). [2] Tout, *Chapters*, ii. 193n.

So far as the problem of the authorship of the *Modus* is concerned, I should hesitate to do more than suggest that the tract was written by someone who possessed an expert knowledge of parliament, was aware of the ecclesiastical practices of the northern province of York, knew enough of the alliance in 1321 of the earls of Lancaster and Hereford and of their recent aims and activities to be able to appeal to their sympathy and interest, and desired to reform the scheme of clerical representation in parliament in order to resurrect (and in some ways transform) the general parliament of estates of 1295. That the *Modus* here and there draws special attention to the Exchequer and its officials, and especially to the head of that office as the proper custodian of parliamentary records, might be taken to suggest that the author was someone bent on attracting the interest of this still most important office of State and appealing to its departmental *amour propre*.

Certainly, the reform of clerical representation envisaged in the *Modus* is not likely to have excited the disapproval of Walter Stapeldon, bishop of Exeter, treasurer of the Exchequer from 18 February 1320 to 25 August 1321, when he was exonerated (it was said) at his own request. Stapeldon had not achieved the episcopate by way of a career in the royal administration. His background, rather, was an academic one : he had once been a professor of canon law in the University of Oxford and already (in 1314) had founded Stapeldon Hall (now Exeter College) for poor scholars going up to Oxford from his diocese. One of the Lords Ordainer appointed in 1310, he was politically a moderate man, and in the summer of 1321 (when still treasurer of the Exchequer) he was one of the bishops who vainly tried to mediate between Edward II and the earls of Lancaster and Hereford.[1] After the royalist triumph at Boroughbridge, he was once more appointed treasurer on 9 May 1322 and so was enabled to continue, down to 1325, the important work of reform at the Exchequer which he had already begun in his first spell of office. His own forthright attitude to the great current problem of ecclesiastical representation in parliament had been one largely dictated by his

[1] *Dictionary of National Biography*, xviii. 979-80.

principles or prejudices as a diocesan bishop. In 1315, according to his own episcopal register, he alone of all the bishops refused to act upon either the " praemunientes " clause of the episcopal writs of summons or the provincial mandate of *venire faciatis* : on that occasion he probably led the resistance of the clergy to the breach of their liberty implied in the form of summons and regarding their right to make grants only in their own convocations, an attitude which then probably cost him his place in the royal council.[1] Careful though he was of ecclesiastical privilege, Stapeldon nonetheless regarded parliament as of supreme importance. When, in December 1321, the award of exile against the Despensers was declared erroneous and revoked in a meeting of convocation which he himself did not attend, and his personal consent to the repeal was demanded by the king, Stapeldon took his stand on the need to seek proper parliamentary authority : his answer was that only in parliament should its acts be abrogated.[2] As Miss Clarke put it, " Stapeldon, like the northern clergy at Sherburn, insisted on the exclusive competence of Parliament, at least for the matters under consideration ". The reform of ecclesiastical representation in parliament suggested by the *Modus*, in order to make parliament the real representative organ of the commonalty of the realm lay and clerical alike, may very well have been intended to appeal to such a mind as Stapeldon's, and perhaps came from someone, directly or indirectly, in contact with him.

As there is so much in the *Modus* suggesting some connection between its author and the Exchequer, the question arises whether he may not have been even a member of its staff, and not that most important one of the Chancery masters, William Airmyn, who was Professor Galbraith's candidate for the honour. In view of the startlingly magnified place given to the chamberlains of the Exchequer among those members of the king's council whose *ex officio* attendance in parliament was required in the *Modus* (article VIII, " De Modo Parliamenti ", and article XIV, " De Locis et Sessionibus in Parliamento "), it may be of some interest, when considering the possible identity of the author of

---

[1] Clarke, op. cit. pp. 134-6.   [2] Ibid. pp. 169-70.

the treatise, to inquire who were the two chamberlains of the Exchequer in 1321. One of the chamberlains was Master James de Ispania, canon of St. Paul's, who for a short time in 1322 was receiver of the King's Chamber : hardly the sort of man to whom the treatise could be attributed. The other chamberlain was Master William Maldon. And if we were to entertain the idea of an Exchequer provenance for the *Modus*, it would be unwise to assert that Maldon was an impossible choice as its author. Formerly a public notary, he had been a chamberlain of the Exchequer since September 1315. He had certainly some proper experience of parliament : he had been one of the two receivers of petitions of Gascony, Wales, Ireland, and Scotland in the Lincoln parliament of January 1316,[1] when he must have been made well aware of the adverse effects of the delayed arrival of some of the magnates and the failure of several others to appear at all,[2] a by no means abnormal situation, but one which the *Modus* proposed to discourage by the levy of formidable amercements (article IX " De inchoatione parliamenti "). More recently (since August 1320), as chamberlain of the Exchequer, Maldon had been directly associated with Stapeldon in a great overhaul of Exchequer and Treasury and other records.[3] If we were to go so far as to postulate William Maldon as the author of the *Modus*, his close involvement in the re-arrangement of Treasury records, a process which lasted from August 1320 until about January 1322,[4] would well consort with the concern of the author of the *Modus* that the Treasury should be *the* repository for the rolls of parliaments (article XV, " De principalibus clericis parliamenti ") and with that author's knowledge of the rolls themselves (article XXV, " De transcriptis recordorum et processuum in parliamento ").

There remains the possible requirement of a North Country connection, conceivably a connection with Yorkshire (or even the city of York), to be fulfilled by any author of the *Modus*, because

---

[1] *Rotuli Parliamentorum*, i. 350.   [2] Roskell, op. cit. pp. 163-4.
[3] Tout, *The Place of Edward II in English History* (2nd edn.), p. 170.
[4] *Essays in Medieval History presented to T. F. Tout* (ed. A. G. Little and F. M. Powicke), V. H. Galbraith, " The Tower as an Exchequer Record Office in the Reign of Edward II ", pp. 231 ff.

of his occasional Lancastrian bias, his evident knowledge of the Lancastrian treatise on the office of Steward of England (perhaps produced shortly before the *Modus* in 1321, when Lancaster was negotiating for support from the magnates and clergy of the northern shires in his pseudo-parliaments at Pontefract and Sherburn-in-Elmet), his awareness of the practice of proctorial representation in the northern convocation by archdeaconries and his adaptation of it to his scheme for the proctorial representation of the lower clergy in the parliament of the *Modus*, and also because of his particular reference in the *Modus* (noted by Morris) to the mayor and citizens of York among the civic recipients of writs of summons, the only other city specifically named being London (article VI, " De civibus "). There is no reason why its author's special interest in York and in the representational usages of the northern convocation (which met there, of course) should necessarily drive us to seek his identity in someone personally connected with the northern metropolis. If the *Modus* was written about 1321, its author may be looked for in someone connected with York merely officially, especially if he knew much about the parliaments of Edward II (which he evidently did). Between 1314 and 1320 parliament had sat at York on no fewer than four occasions, and was to do so twice again in 1322. But not only had York been recently the scene of parliaments. From September 1319 to February 1320 the Exchequer itself had operated from York, and it was to migrate there again in April 1322, because of the Scottish war. And on both occasions of the removal of the rolls, writs, and treasure of the Exchequer from Westminster to York, William Maldon, as one of the two chamberlains, was senior officer in charge of the large convoy of carts employed in the flitting.[1] It is a fair assumption that in each case he worked in York throughout the stay of the Exchequer.

[1] *Essays in Medieval History presented to T. F. Tout* (ed. A. G. Little and F. M. Powicke), D. M. Broome, " Exchequer Migrations to York in the Thirteenth and Fourteenth Centuries ", pp. 291 ff., for the migration of April 1322. For that of 1319 see Exchequer, L.T.R. Memoranda Roll 12 Edward II, P.R.O., E 368/89, mem. 159d (*brevia irretornabilia*, Trinity term) and Exchequer K.R. Memoranda Roll 12 Edward II, P.R.O., E. 159/92 (*irretornabilia*, Trinity term), mem. 5d.

All this suggestion that the *Modus* may be attributed to William Maldon, a chamberlain of the Exchequer when the tract was very possibly composed, rests on the slender foundation of its magnification of his office, if magnification it was. It is to be doubted whether any attribution of authorship could rest upon anything more solid than mere conjecture or hypothesis quite unsusceptible to proof. The authorship of the *Modus* is almost bound to remain an open question. It is in any case perhaps the least important of the problems posed by the *Modus*.

A far more crucial one of those problems is, as I have suggested, that which is posed in the clause " De clero " (article II) concerning the reform of clerical representation in parliament. What the *Modus* says about the place in parliament of the elected representatives of the lay communities of shire, city, and borough, was, as the later history of parliament has shown, full of great prospective significance. Within less than a generation of the probable date of composition of the *Modus* the representatives of the clerical communities of diocese and cathedral-chapter had seceded for all practical purposes from parliament proper. And it is more than doubtful whether any change in the unit of proctorial representation (as suggested in the *Modus*) would have retarded or reversed this development. When the *Modus* was produced, clerical representation in parliament was already foundering in the shallows of clerical privilege : summoned at the king's request, the convocations were to be the assemblies in which the separatist instincts of the clerical order soon found satisfaction. The author of the *Modus*, in proposing a reform of clerical representation designed to give a greater interest to the lower clergy in the working of parliament, was perhaps swimming against the tide. But the reform proposed in the *Modus* relating to this subject has at least some significance : it helps to illumin-ate that slow change of opinion which conditioned the grafting onto the older curialist tradition of parliament, of the newer principle of the constant representation there, by processes of election, of local communities. The most important single item in the doctrine of the *Modus* is the novel construction its author placed on the word " community ". His proposed reform of clerical representation was entirely of a piece with his general theory : the "communitas parliamenti" ought to be the sum of the local communities, clerical as well as lay, ecclesiastical as well as secular, all of whose representatives should be chosen by local election.

THE MEDIEVAL SPEAKERS FOR THE COMMONS IN PARLIAMENT [1]

THE late thirteenth-century parliament was an union of estates in which the elected representatives of shires and other corporate bodies, knights, citizens and burgesses, and the lower clergy, frequently had a due but inferior place and function. Parliament was still fundamentally a special session of the king's court. However dissimilar from and superior to other royal courts it became, a court parliament fundamentally remained and the continued hierarchical ordering of medieval English political society predetermined that its judgements should continue to be the work of its non-representative, aristocratic elements whose judicial function is emphasised by their description as peers. By the end of Edward II's reign, despite the contemporary feudal reaction, the elected representatives of secular communities had come to be considered an essential element in parliament's constitution and already the eventual bicameral nature of parliament was being adumbrated in their practice of meeting outside the great council of magnates. There, apart, they were already coming to regard themselves as entrusted with the task of formulating petitions and at the end of the fourteenth century this, coupled with the exercise of their right to grant or withhold taxation, was more clearly their main function. The Commons had already their place, then, in the constitutional scheme of parliamentary monarchy. Historically, however, it was a subordinate place and even the Commons' realization of their common political identity, for socially they were still heterogeneously composed, was perhaps thrust upon them, partly by the contrast of their own position as representatives with the lords who represented only themselves, and partly by the king's need to deal with them, especially in matters financial, as one group and not several. The clear emergence of the Commons' speaker in 1376, seemingly the Commons' own contribution to their rather rudimentary organisation, was a sign of their realization of the tactical value of unity between knights, citizens and burgesses, although his election down to Tudor times from among the knights of the shire does show, as do other phenomena, the continued political pre-eminence of this *gradus* in the lower house.

We may no longer agree with Stubbs' idea that in the fourteenth century the Commons had sufficiently transformed their position in parliament to have

[1] This paper was read at a meeting of the medieval section of the Anglo-American Conference of Historians at the Institute on 8 July 1949. I have added references and footnotes and here and there developed my themes.

achieved in a lasting form the political and constitutional initiative there, but the reaction against this view has been too severe in its attribution to the Commons of ineffectiveness and even, at times, of a certain myopia in their dealings with the king and Lords. This has been alleged to be an unfortunate result of short parliaments, of a Commons' personnel inevitably subject to variation, and of the general political immaturity of the rising middle class, a combination of these factors resulting in the Commons in parliament being exploited to the profit of the king or, if he is unpopular and aristocratic sentiment in powerful quarters is hostile to him, to the advantage of this baronial opposition. An investigation of the careers of the speakers, of the circumstances in which the speaker is elected (in so far as they can be ascertained), and of his privileges of speech secured by the official acceptance of his 'protestations' should throw light on this political problem and on others of more constitutional importance.

Examining the origin of the Commons' speaker we need not look too remotely. We need not consider the case of Sir Henry de Keighley[1] who in 1301 acted for the community of the realm in parliament as a whole, and not alone for the Commons. When next, so far as we know, parliament resorts to a 'procurator' or 'prolocutor universitatis' it is to provide for 'a corporate act of feudal defiance, transmuted into the will of the commonalty', the renunciation of homage to Edward II through the mouth of Sir William Trussell.[2] He, too, speaks not for the Commons alone, but for the commonalty of the realm. The Commons were only slowly at this time learning, under direct suggestion, to deliberate as estates apart and, even more slowly, to realize their identity of interest as representatives of communities in contrast with those who represented themselves and enjoyed as peers of parliament judicial functions which they, the Commons, did not share.[3] When, in the parliament of April 1343, for the first recorded time the Commons speak in the presence of the king and Lords through the mouth of a named person, they use the services of this same Sir William Trussell, but he is not one of themselves.[4] Thereafter until 1377

---

[1] Madox, *Exchequer*, ii. 108; Palgrave, *Parliamentary Writs*, i. 104, cited *ante*, ix. 7.

[2] M. V. Clarke, 'Committees of Estates and the Deposition of Edward II,' *Historical Essays in honour of James Tait*, ed. J. G. Edwards, V. H. Galbraith and E. F. Jacob, pp. 42–3.

[3] H. G. Richardson and G. O. Sayles, 'The Parliaments of Edward III (cont.),' *ante*, ix. 1–15.

[4] *Rotuli Parliamentorum*, ii. 136*b*. In July 1340 Trussell had been one of those sent by Edward III from Bruges to declare to parliament the facts of the military situation across the Channel. On 30 April 1343 it was Sir Bartholomew de Burwash who, as better qualified than the chancellor, expanded the latter's declaration of the causes of summons with special reference to the truce recently concluded with the French king in Brittany, but it may well have been Trussell who, as an expert in diplomatic affairs (*D.N.B.*, lvii. 270), was on this occasion entrusted with the job of enlightening the Commons in detail and apart. Certainly, on the following day, he did no more than report their assent to the continuance of the truce. On the day after this announcement, the knights of the shire, and others of the Commons came before parliament to report their advice on the problem of keeping the law 'en son droit cours, en manere q'ele soit owele as Poures et as Riches.' There was no mention of Trussell.

there is no mention on the rolls of the parliaments of any other individual speaking for the Commons in parliament. Nor need we be surprised at this silence. When the Commons communicated with the king or Lords in the course of a session they would normally seem to have done so through a small deputation composed of round about a dozen and appointed *ad hoc*.[1] This is of the sort and size the duke of Lancaster obviously anticipated when, on 9 May 1376, Sir Peter de la Mare insisted on *all* the Commons being admitted into the parliament chamber;[2] it seems not unlikely that the speaker would be one of this small deputation, that it might even nominate him itself, in any case that he would probably be chosen for that single occasion only—'a la journe'. But it is quite probable that even as late as 1376 the Commons were content to communicate with the king through an intermediary who was not one of themselves. Walsingham tells us that in the Good Parliament for a time this service was performed by Sir Richard Stury, one of the knights of the chamber, who acted as go-between,—*referendarius*[3] Walsingham calls him—between Edward III and the Commons. He carried the king's wishes to the knights and theirs to the king until, slandering the doings of the knights by saying that they meant to depose the king like his father before him, he was banished from

---

[1] In the parliament of March 1340 twelve knights of the shire 'queux les Communes voleint eslire' (actually thirteen are named), to whom six citizens and burgesses were added, sat daily with nine prelates and lords, supported by the treasurer and four justices, hearing and trying petitions, some of which were made into statutes (*Rot. Parl.*, ii. 113*a*). Little more than a year later the king conceded that the commissioners ordered to make inquiry into the conduct of royal ministers should be examined in his presence 'devant les Grantz et certeynes persones des Communes' (*ibid.*, 131*a*). In 1348 a very select committee of prelates, lords and justices, to the number of six, were asked for by the Commons to expedite unanswered common petitions preferred in this and the previous parliament, in the presence of four or six of the Commons elected by themselves (*ibid.*, 201*a*). In 1352 Chief Justice Shareshull declared the causes of summons and then told the Commons to elect twenty-four or thirty from amongst themselves; these were to have speech with some of the lords in the Painted Chamber on the following day and then join their fellows in the chapter-house of the abbey and inform them of what had transpired (*ibid.*, 237*b*). The request to the lords in 1373 for the appointment of a committee to assist them in their discussions was made by a deputation of 'ascons des Communes' who made their approaches 'en noun de touz' (*ibid.*, 316*b*). On 9 May 1376, when De la Mare protested against the exclusion of many of his fellows from the parliament chamber, the duke of Lancaster observed, reports the Anonimalle Chronicle, 'Sire Peirs, ceo ne serroit meistre de tauntz de comunes entrer pur doner respouns, mes dusz ou tresz purrount soeffirè a une foitz, come ad este use avaunt ces hures.' (*Anon. Chron.*, p. 84). In 1378 the Lords protested against the Commons' demand for a committee of lords to deliberate with them in their house of assembly, saying that the custom was 'qe les Seigneurs elisoient de eux mesmes un certaine petite nombre de vi ou x, et les Communes une autre tielle petite nombre de eux mesmes, et yceux Srs et Cões issint esluz deussent entre-comuner en aisee manere, sanz murmur, crye, et noise.' The Commons agreed and certain lords and Commons were chosen 'en petite et resonable nombre, par manere come ent ad este usez d'ancienetee.' (*Rot. Parl.*, iii. 36*b*).

[2] *Anonimalle Chronicle 1333–81*, ed. V. H. Galbraith, p. 83.

[3] A word later used as an alternative to describe the *prelocutor* of the lower house of Convocation, who first appeared, although not then *sub eo nomine*, in 1399. (I. J. Churchill, *Canterbury Administration*, i. 378.)

court.[1] In 1376, the evidence seems to suggest, the Commons were for the first time using the expedient of a speaker who, as one of themselves privy to their counsels, *continued* to speak before the king and Lords *for the duration* of the parliament. After this time communication between the Commons and the Lords, or with the king for that matter, need not of course be restricted to action through the speaker or even through one of their own number: early in 1382 Walsingham[2] tells us that when William Ufford, earl of Suffolk, collapsed and died on his way up the stairs to the chamber where the Lords were in session he had just been chosen by the knights of the shire 'ad pronunciandum ex parte illorum negotia reipublice' and the Commons are known to have had an elected speaker of their own number in this parliament. And there are, of course, other and much later instances of such practices in the medieval period.

An air of improvisation hangs about the initial activities of De la Mare as continuing speaker in 1376, if we may trust the account of the *Anonimalle Chronicle*, but that he was fairly early in the session intended by the Commons to be their continuing speaker is reasonably clear. It was not De la Mare who, on 30 April, invited speeches from the knights in the chapter-house at the outset of this second day of the session although, after five or six of his fellows had already spoken from the lectern, he did then rehearse the points they had made and added his own counsel. No question of choosing a speaker to bear the 'onus verbi'[3] *need* of course arise until the Commons were prepared to go before the king and the Lords of the council of parliament (and this they were not ready to do for yet another nine days), if the Commons were not in the habit of electing a continuing speaker to act for the whole of the parliamentary session. On Friday, 9 May, when the Commons for the first time since the opening of parliament appeared again before the Lords, the duke of Lancaster, presiding over the Lords as the king's lieutenant, asked the assembled Commons, 'Quel de vous avera la parlaunce et pronunciacion?' De la Mare replied to the effect that 'par commune assent il averoit les paroles a la iourne.' On the Monday following, 12 May, perhaps labouring under the misapprehension that De la Mare had acted three days before for that occasion only, Lancaster again demanded of the Commons once more assembled in the parliament chamber, 'Qi parlera?' De la Mare's answer to the duke's probably innocent and customary query was a testy reference to his appointment, by common assent, on the previous Friday

---

[1] *Chronicon Angliae* (Rolls Series), ed. E. M. Thompson, p. 87; Walsingham is better informed of the doings of the Good Parliament than some have been prepared to allow. His mistaken description of the Commons meeting 'in capitulo Sancti Pauli,' which has sometimes been held against him, is an obvious slip on his, or a copyist's, part: his informant, Sir Thomas de la Hoo, knight of the shire for Bedfordshire, who dreamed in the chapter-house of seven lost gold florins, in his perplexity as to their origin and significance, made his enquiries in the choir of the *monks* (not canons), Walsingham tells us (*ibid.* 70).

[2] *Chronicon Anglie*, p. 333.   [3] *Ibid.*, p. 73.

to have 'la parlaunce a cest foiz (this time of parliament?).' This was perhaps an
enlargement on what had been explicit in the exchanges between John of Gaunt
and De la Mare on the former occasion but it was, I think, certainly implicit in
the request made on that day to De la Mare, by common assent of the Commons,
to assume 'la charge pur eux d'avoir la sovereinte de pronuncier lour voluntes
en le graunt parlement avaunt les seignours.' [1]

The Commons, and presumably most keenly among them their speaker,
were determined that their impeachment of the king's unworthy ministers
should take the form of a maintenance of their accusations in common, in order
to eschew at all costs what Latimer evidently desired, namely, the appearance of
these accusations proceeding from an 'especiale persone' who might subsequently be regarded as a false accuser open to the penalties of the statute
of 38 Edw. III. Had it not been that the Commons insisted on giving their
charges the appearance of proceeding from common clamour, one might have
been tempted to see in their choice of a speaker a paradoxical desire to give their
criminal accusations just that appearance of individual plaint which, short of
presentment by a jury, the common law demanded. But from the first De la
Mare insisted that 'ceo qe une de nous dist touz diount et assentount,'[2] and he
meticulously made protestation of his right to be corrected by his fellows:
'fesaunt toutz vois protestacione devaunt toutz qe yssy sount, qe si ieo rien
mesdy [missay] en ascune poynte qe ieo me sumet al coreccion et amendement de
mes compaignouns.' This was the later formally allowed protestation of the
formally admitted speaker, in all substance (it was here, of course, no more than
a claim unenrolled by the clerk of the parliament and, so far as the Anonimalle
Chronicle discloses the facts, passed without comment). Once the protestation
became an act which required royal concurrence it presupposed a privilege
granted to the speaker rather than to those for whom he spoke, and I shall have
more to say later about it in this connection, but in the first place, as a claim
which apparently met with no response either by way of objection or acceptance,
it seems to have been an expression of something that was almost implicit in the
charge De la Mare undertook at the Commons' request, namely, a reciprocal
safeguard for himself and for the Commons too: it allowed the speaker's utter-
ances, if uncorrected, to pass for what had been assented to by his fellows and,
at the same time, it did not allow any divergence on his part from what it had
been agreed he should say, to go unchallenged by the Commons. Both Commons
and speaker are thus theoretically protected by his protestation from the consequences of any personal indiscretion or under- or over-statement on his part. In
the circumstances in which it was uttered, on 12 May 1376, this protestation
was highly necessary; it immediately preceded the first attack in the parliament

---

[1] *Anonimalle Chronicle*, pp. 83, 85.
[2] *Ibid.*, p. 83.

chamber on Latimer and Lyons. De la Mare's protestation makes it quite clear that the very real dangers of their impeachment had been fully realised.

Sir Peter de la Mare, perhaps more clearly than any of his successors in the medieval speakership, educated as well as represented the opinion of the Commons (les [maters] enfourmant pluis avaunt q'ils mesmes [les Communes] ne savoient).[1] The continuing speaker clearly began his institutional career as a stimulating leader of debate and political opposition. In the course of the fifteenth century his appointment was of increasing procedural importance not only because private petitioners of all classes were more and more anxious to gain the backing of the Commons for their bills and, at times, might address their requests expressly to the speaker and the knights of the shire and Commons,[2] but also because later in the century there was evident need to safeguard the smooth passage of common petitions of official origin requiring the Commons' assent. In 1376, however, the speaker had some distance to go before his Tudor functions as a chairman controlling the expedition of bills in the lower house presumed a procedural neutrality which allowed him no more than a casting vote.[3]

In the course of the six years following the assembly of the Good Parliament parliament met seven times and in all but one of these parliaments (April 1379) we know the name of the Commons' speaker, from the parliament roll itself. The rolls of the two parliaments of 1382, if the Commons elected a speaker, do not disclose his name. Sir James Pickering functioned as speaker a second time in February 1383 just as before him De la Mare and Sir John Gildesburgh, he in successive parliaments, had already twice acted in this capacity. And then eleven parliaments went their way with the rolls vouching no reference to the speaker's name or activities. In January 1394 Sir John Bussy acted as speaker and again in both parliaments summoned to meet in 1397. Thenceforward the name of the speaker is known for every valid parliament. The discouraging omission of the speaker's identity in the parliament rolls for a period of ten years in the middle period of Richard II's reign may, I think, be explained away as a lapse, if lapse is the right word, on the part of the clerk of the parliament responsible for the engrossing of the rolls. It would be unlikely that the Commons on their own initiative, or for lack of it, should suspend in 1383 a practice they are known to have already and recently employed eight times, but

---

[1] *Anonimalle Chronicle*, p. 82; cf. A. F. Pollard, 'The Authorship and Value of the *Anonimalle Chronicle*,' *Eng. Hist. Rev.*, liii (1938), 600, *et seq.*

[2] A. R. Myers, 'Parliamentary Petitions in the Fifteenth Century,' *Eng. Hist. Rev.*, lii (1937) 401–4; *Rot. Parl.*, iv. 499a; A. R. Myers, 'Some Observations on the procedure of the Commons in dealing with bills in the Lancastrian period,' *University of Toronto Law Journal*, vol. iii, no. 1, 65; S. B Chrimes, *English Constitutional Ideas in the Fifteenth Century*, p. 174.

[3] 'The Order and Usage howe to keepe a Parliament, collected by John Vowell alias Hooker (1571), Brit. Mus., Harleian MS. 1178. fo. 22.

fortunately we need not rely on speculation. The rolls of the parliaments of April 1384 and 1395 are like others in not disclosing the speaker's identity but the former[1] does note that when parliament, at its outset, was adjourned for five days the Commons were ordered to occupy themselves profitably in the meantime by treating 'de la persone qi auroit les paroles en cest Parlement pur la Commune' to the end that 'pur l'election de tielle persone le Parlement my fuist tariez come ad este devant ore'; the 1395 roll notes that after making the 'pronunciatio' the chancellor ordered the knights, citizens and burgesses, to assemble in either the chapter house or frater of the abbey of Westminster on the following day and elect him who should speak for them.[2] When the Commons are thus officially instructed to elect him we can be sure that as part of the mechanism of parliament the speaker has arrived and come to stay: the royal command to elect and the royal ratification of the Commons' choice once made, converts his function into an office. We must soon face the possibility of more sinister results.

In the parliament of April 1384, when for the first time the Commons were told to elect a speaker the chancellor also warned parliament to expedite the king's charge and not create diversions. It was an old complaint of governments that parliaments were only too ready to proceed to discuss grievances and suits requiring remedy to the neglect of the king's business; sundry devices had in the past been adopted to preclude failure to adhere to the proper order of parliamentary action, and to secure respect for that 'regimen parliamenti' which Richard II in 1387 drew from his judges at Nottingham belonged to him as part of his prerogative. The usefulness of the continuing speaker among the Commons as a controller of discussion there, and not simply as one who transmitted its outcome, may well have already been realised and appreciated, and it is possible that, even early in the history of his office the speaker, became less of the leader De la Mare had been and more of a manager of the conduct of business in the lower house, although the distinction is a fine one; we must, however, be careful to bear in mind, that there is more evidence for the view that in parliament the speaker acted as the Commons' agent, than for the opinion that in their own assembly he managed them and their proceedings in either the king's interest or the lords'.

It would be as well to face at this juncture one important problem. How far was the speaker imposed on the Commons from above? In 1571 even, according to John Vowell's 'Order and Usage howe to keepe a Parliament', service could be paid to the requirement in the election of the speaker 'that the King ought not to make any choise or cause anie choise to be made of any knight, cittizens, burgesses . . . [or] speaker of the common house . . .; but they must be elected and chosen by the laws, orders, and customs of the realm, as they were wont and ought to be', but the next clause is significant: 'and the kinges good

---

[1] *Rot. Parl.*, iii. 166a.   [2] *Ibid.*, 329a.

advise yet not to be contemned'.[1] Was the Commons' election of their speaker in pre-Tudor times usually or even ever concocted; was it a 'put-up' job, a mere formality? Pollard seems to have thought it was.[2] Noticing the circumstances of De la Mare's election in 1376 he acknowledged that here was no 'concealed nomination' by the Crown but was of the opinion that afterwards this became 'the almost invariable method of determining the speaker's election', and in 1397, he thought, the speaker 'became—and remains—a government nominee elected by the Commons'.

It must be admitted that it is impossible to solve this problem conclusively for no generalisation will cover the whole of the period. In the last quarter of a century before the advent of the Tudors there is incontrovertible evidence that the speaker is frankly paid by the king for his services as such, although not uniformly as seems to have been the case in the next century:[3] following the Coventry parliament of 1459 Sir Thomas Tresham secured an annuity of £40;[4] the speaker of Edward IV's first parliament, Sir James Strangeways, had to wait until the next was in session before he procured his reward but it was the substantial sum of 125 marks when it came;[5] in 1478 William Alyngton got £300.[6] These facts, though suggestive, prove nothing about the circumstances of election. It is true that when in 1489 Sir Thomas FitzWilliam, recorder of London, had been elected to sit for the city in Henry VII's third parliament, he was immediately considered for the speakership.[7] The speaker had been invariably a knight of the shire, unless a break with tradition had already been made in 1485,[8] and so, sometime in the six weeks ensuing before parliament met, FitzWilliam was returned for Lincolnshire.

Can this state of affairs in which the Commons' election is a pure formality, their choice being dictated to them, be projected backwards in time? The formal evidence of the parliament rolls is against it but then this is no cause for wonder; reading between their lines, however, we do discover some evidence which may help to vindicate the Commons' continued independence in this important issue. There are a few instances of the speaker being changed in the course of a parliament. In 1399 John Doreward replaced Sir John Cheyne on the day after his election[9] and there is little doubt that the latter's supersession, ostensibly because of infirmity and an inaudible voice, was dictated by outside pressure and due to the fact that he was unacceptable to archbishop Arundel as 'infestus ecclesie'.[10]

---

[1] B.M. Harleian MS. 1178, op. cit., fo. 23ᵛ.   [2] Eng. Hist. Rev., liii (1938), 600, 602.
[3] B.M., Harleian MS. 1178, op. cit., fo. 22ᵛ.   [4] Cal. Pat. Rolls 1452–61, p. 577.
[5] J. C. Wedgwood, History of Parliament, Biographies 1439–1509, p. 820.
[6] Ibid., p. 9.   [7] Ibid., p. 337.
[8] H. G. Richardson, 'The Commons and Medieval Politics,' Trans. Royal Hist. Soc., 4th Ser., xxviii. 38, n. 2.   [9] Rot. Parl., iii. 424b.
[10] Johannis de Trokelowe et H. de Blaneforde Chronica et Annales (Rolls Series), ed. H. T. Riley, pp. 290, 301.

But whereas the reign of the first Lancastrian began with an official rejection of the chosen speaker, the reign of Henry V began with the rejection of their speaker by the Commons themselves because, at the king's behest, he had exceeded his powers as their agent.[1] William Stourton may well have been, as was formally alleged, physically as well as in other ways from the Commons' point of view infirm, but this incident clearly shows how much of a reality, at this point, was the right of the Commons to elect their speaker and how much of a reality was even their right to elect a fresh speaker after the royal acceptance of their first choice; and how free, without any doubt, was their *second* choice in 1413 is clear from the fact that they elected the man (John Doreward, the same who was their second choice in 1399) who had led their opposition to unauthorised acts on the part of Stourton which had been prompted by the king. Sir John Tyrell's replacement in 1437 may perhaps be more safely attributed to illness (the reason formally noted in the parliament roll), for he died before the year was up. So did Stourton in 1413 but Tyrell was superseded when the session had, as it turned out, only a week to run.[2] The replacement of Thomas Thorpe in 1454[3] had a distinctly political flavour; he had fallen foul of the duke of York and the duke would have none of him. It is true, of course, that the speaker's usual, initial request to be exonerated from the office was a pure formality—only once, in 1449, was the 'excusation' of a speaker-elect allowed.[4]

Next to nothing is known of the procedure adopted by the Commons in electing their speaker. We may not lay much store by Walsingham's statement when discussing the election of Sir Thomas Hungerford in the Bad Parliament of 1377;[5] he described him as chosen by the shire knights alone *and* as 'electus . . . a majori parte ad pronunciandum verba communia.' Nearly half a century later, in 1420, however, we know from the domestic report of the parliamentary burgesses of Bishop's Lynn that the speaker's election might still be so real as to be contested when more than one nomination was made, and that a count might be taken, at any rate if the contest were close, to decide between the claims of the nominees.[6] It would be dangerous to infer, of course, from the

---

[1] *Rot. Parl.*, iv. 4*a*, 4*b*, 5*a*.   [2] *Ibid.*, iv. 502*a*.   [3] *Ibid.*, v. 240*a*.
[4] *Ibid.*, 171*b*.   [5] *Chronicon Angliae*, p. 112.
[6] Cited by M. McKisack, *The Parliamentary Representation of the English Boroughs during the Middle Ages*, p. 142, from the archives of the Corporation of King's Lynn, Gildhall Roll, 8–9 Henry V: 'Et [Thomas Brygge] dicit quod Rogerus Hunte et Ricardus Russell nominati fuerunt ibidem prolocutores, tamen dicit quod, examinacionibus inde factis, Rogerus prevaluit, et habuit plures voces iiij^{or} &c et optinuit officium prolocutoris parliamenti.' As Miss McKisack suggests, it is much more likely that the unsuccessful nominee was John Russell, knight of the shore for Herefordshire in this parliament, who had previously sat in the parliaments of April 1414, 1417, and 1419, and was to be speaker in 1423 and 1432 (but not 1450, as Miss McKisack says), and not the only Richard Russell sitting in 1420 who was returned for the small borough of Dunwich and for the first time at that. To push back this application of the majority principle to the speaker's election (nine years before its observance was required by statute in the conduct of the shire elections to parliament) to the time of the emergence of the office itself perhaps requires too uncritical a faith in Walsingham's veracity, but

fact that the clerk of the parliament took care to note that Tyrell's election in 1427 had been reported[1] as made 'unanimiter' that a contested election was normal, but it may well have been frequent. Nomination as a preliminary to election may have afforded the king or council an opportunity for disclosing their desires, but there is nothing in this mere supposition to suggest an infringement of the Commons' freedom of action. Moreover, had the Commons' choice been dictated to them, it would be difficult to account for their frequent delay in presenting their speaker beyond the time allowed by the chancellor when he ordered them to proceed with the election. Before the end of Henry IV's reign the Commons were told to elect and present their speaker on the second day of the session and, judging from the chronology of the rolls, they invariably conformed to this requirement at this time; but from 1413 down to 1427, although this customary injunction was continued, they almost consistently failed to obey it, normally presenting on the third day, but occasionally taking longer, even though at times the chancellor's command specified the *hour* at which they were to elect and the *hour* at which they were to present.[2] In 1426 they apparently

his statement, in view of the paucity of the evidence on this point, is certainly worth consideration. So perhaps, too, is even his note that the speaker in 1377 was chosen by the shire-knights only. It is very interesting in this connection to recall King James I of Scotland's intention in 1428, just four years after his return from his long exile in England, to apply English methods of parliamentary representation and perhaps procedure to Scottish parliaments. Two or more 'commissaris' from each shire were to be elected in the head court of the bailiwick, and were to be returned 'with ful ande playne power of al the laif (laity) of the sherrefdome,' in order to absolve the small barons and free tenants from their feudal liability to attendance at parliaments and general councils. These commissaries were presumably to be the counterpart and assume the rôle of the English knights of the shire. Once returned they were to chose, it was ordained, 'a wise and ane expert man callit the common spekar of the parliament quhilk sal propone all and sundry nedes and causes pertening to *the commonis* (the italics are mine) in the parliament or generall consal.' (*The Acts of the Parliament of Scotland* (1814), ii. 15, § 2.) We are reminded by Rait that this use of the word 'commons' is, as late as this time, unparallelled in the records of the Scottish parliament and that when it next recurs in the acts of 1585 and 1587—these acts established the parliamentary representation of shires—it was again associated with the barons and freeholders and not with the representatives of the royal burghs as well, for the latter constituted a clearly differentiated third estate. But was James's idea that the speaker elected by the shire-commissioners should speak for the Commons of parliament in the extended, comprehensive English sense of this term? If this were so and James were consciously imitating English methods of procedure, as he was, seemingly, English methods of representation, might we not be led tentatively to wonder (*a*) whether the election of the speaker for the English Commons was not left, even at this late date, with the knights of the shire, and (*b*) how much more likely was such a practice at the end of Edward III's reign? So far as Scotland was concerned suffice it to say that the ordinance did not apparently take effect, the Scottish parliament retaining its system of clearly defined estates, clerical, feudal, and burghal (R. S. Rait, *The Parliaments of Scotland*, pp. 195, 518–20). My thanks are due to Mr. E. W-M. Balfour-Melville for directing my attention to this Scottish ordinance of 1428.   [1] *Rot. Parl.*, iv. 317*a*.

[2] In 1413 the chancellor ordered the Commons to meet at 'sept del clokke a matyn' on the second day of parliament to elect their speaker and to present him an hour later; Stourton was presented on the fourth day of parliament (*ibid.*, iv. 3*b*, 4*a*). In 1437 the chancellor on the opening day told the Commons to assemble on the morrow and elect their speaker before the eighth hour, when they were to present him; they presented Tyrell not on the day or at the time appointed, but on the day after, that is, the third day of the session (*ibid.*, iv. 495*b*, 496*a*).

took ten days to come to a decision.[1] It is true, of course, that in 1427[2] they began a practice, only spasmodically reported in the rolls, of announcing to the Lords the person of their choice but requesting the Lord's mediation to secure a respite before they made formal presentation, and in 1484[3] they declared to the Lords that they had made an election on the second day but did not then name their choice and presented him on the fourth day. Moreover, it must be pointed out that, in 1485, when we have the domestic report[4] of the Colchester burgesses to rely on for the circumstances of the speaker's election, although in accordance with the king's pleasure he was not presented until the third day, he had been elected between 9 and 10 o'clock on the second, and it must be admitted that in the case of FitzWilliam, imposed, as we have seen, as speaker in 1489, the Commons did not present him either until the third day.[5] It may be suggested that the fact that the Commons *seem* earlier in the century to have taken their time in making up their minds should not be interpreted as evidence of free election because towards the end of the century they were taking the same time to present their speaker when, as in FitzWilliam's case, their minds had clearly already been made up for them. This does, I concede, weaken this point in an argument which is stronger on other grounds, but it may well be that here a delay which had in the course of the century hardened into custom had been, originally at any rate and probably for long, of some significance.

That the Commons' speaker was one of their number but virtually imposed upon them is a conclusion which, I think, has arisen from an over-hasty consideration of the fact that they very frequently elected one of the shire-knights who occupied some high administrative office in the civil or preferably household services of the crown, occasionally even sat on the royal council, and was closely connected with the king; or one who, in a period of minority government and conciliar control, was attached to a member or perhaps more than one member of the council, or, in a period of acute strife between factions, to some powerful aristocratic interest outside the council. An analysis of the careers of most of the speakers discloses that they were almost invariably of this calibre. If we were to suppose that a speaker like Sir Thomas Hungerford (speaker in January 1377), John of Gaunt's steward of his estates south of Trent and steward for life of the earl of Salisbury's lands too, could always be relied on to bring pressure of a certain sort to bear on his fellows, we should be unwise to rest content with the assumption that his own opinions were 'fast-dyed' in the colour of his official or aristocratic connections, always provided that these latter

[1] *Ibid.*, iv. 296a.
[2] *Ibid.*, iv. 317a.
[3] *Ibid.*, vi. 238a.
[4] *Red Paper Book of Colchester*, ed. Sir W. Gurney Benham, pp. 60–64 (cited in Wedgwood, *op. cit.*, *Register*, App. xiv. 753).
[5] *Rot. Parl.*, vi. 410a.

did not conflict.[1] Mr. McFarlane has shown us the danger of regarding the members of this professional administrative class, so many of whom and so frequently sat among the parliamentary Commons, as subservient hangers-on whose careers depended on the good lordship of a single great magnate, whose livery and in time of stress whose badge they received, or even on the favour of the king.[2] These men took their fees where they could find them and the only uncomplicated, exclusive loyalty their unquiet minds knew in this period of bastard feudalism and generally unstable government was to their own interests. In any case the Commons would have been hard put to it to find any one of their most influential and experienced members who was not occupied with some office in the household or administrative services of the crown or attached to the service of some great magnate, as administrative agent, feoffee to uses, executor, or counsel, or more probably connected in this and other ways with more than one. Why the Commons exercised their choice in the way they did was probably for the self-same general reasons which actuated the king and magnates when they retained the services of these members of the professional administrative class from which so many of the medieval speakers were drawn: just as the king and magnates required the best counsel available for the regulation of their public and private concerns, so presumably did the Commons want their proceedings conducted with efficiency, especially with regard to the bills they originated or sponsored or merely assented to; and where declaratory emphasis was required when their petitions or conditions were laid before the king and Lords, they required it to be made with a maximum of relevance, cogency and eloquence. Apart from the decade of Henry V's confidently strong rule, the fifteenth century was a period of more or less acute political stress and difficulty, but even when parliament met in times of open dissension and conflict it would seldom be safe to interpret the election as speaker of even an out-and-out partisan, like John Say esquire of the body,[3] in February 1449, or Oldhall, York's chamberlain,[4] in 1450, or Sir Thomas Tresham, controller of the household,[5] in the probably packed session of 1459, as registering more than a certain trend of opinion among the Commons at the beginning of parliament; it need not at all

[1] *John of Gaunt's Register*, vol. i, ed. S. Armitage Smith (Camden Society, 3rd Ser., xx (1911), pp. 114, 153–4, 213; *John of Gaunt's Register 1379–83*, vol. i., ed. E. C. Lodge and R. Somerville (Camden Society, 3rd series, lvi. (1937), 30, 145, 165; vol. ii., lvii. (1937), 407. *Cal. Pat. Rolls 1364–67*, p. 169. Hungerford's connection with the Black Prince, noted by Mr. McFarlane ('Bastard Feudalism', *ante*, xx. 176), seems to have come about *solely* through Sir Bartholomew de Burwash the younger, for whom he acted as lieutenant-steward of the prince's honours of Wallingford and St. Valéry and under-constable of Wallingford's castle in the 'sixties, and with Burwash's death in 1369 this association with the eldest of the King's sons seems to have come to an end. His connection with Lancaster had long been prepared for by the attachment of members of his family to the descendants, in each generation, of the second son of Henry III.

[2] K. B. McFarlane, 'Parliament and "Bastard Feudalism",' *Trans. Royal Hist. Soc.*; 4th Ser. xxvi.; 'Bastard Feudalism,' *ante*, xx. 161 *et seq.*

[3] *Cal. Pat. Rolls 1446–52*, p. 246.   [4] *Ibid.*, p. 231.   [5] *Rot. Parl.*, v. 617a.

imply dictation to the Commons how to elect or an infringement of one of their few liberties.

In determining the Commons' choice the previous parliamentary experience, both as knights of the shire and as speaker, of the talent available must have occasionally counted for much. Out of the 31 speakers of the Lancastrian and Yorkist reigns only 4 had no known previous parliamentary experience[1] and the average number of previous parliaments attended by the speakers was five. The previous parliamentary record of some few of them is very impressive. When Thomas Chaucer, cousin of the Beauforts and chief butler of England, was speaker in 1421 for the fifth time he was sitting for Oxfordshire in his ninth parliament;[2] when Roger Flore of Oakham, steward of the duchy of Lancaster north of Trent since 1416, acted for the fourth time as speaker in 1422 it was on the occasion of his twelfth return for Rutland;[3] when John Russell, from early in Henry IV's reign to nearly the end of Henry V's retained as counsel to the executive of the duchy of Lancaster and Flore's associate as overseer of the will of Edward of Norwich, duke of York, and one of the ducal feoffees, was speaker for the second time in 1432 he was representing Herefordshire for the twelfth time;[4] the parliament of 1433 in which Roger Hunt, a life-long connection of John Lord Tiptoft, a former royal attorney-general, and for the last ten years of his life second baron of the exchequer (1438–48), acted as speaker for the second time, was his eighteenth parliament;[5] Sir John Tyrell, a close connection of the duke of Gloucester, chief steward of the duchy of Lancaster and treasurer of the royal household, when speaker for the third time in 1437 was then up at Westminster for the thirteenth time;[6] William Burley, speaker

[1] Sir Walter Beauchamp (March 1416), William Alyngton (1429), Sir William Oldhall (1450), William Catesby (1484).

[2] M.P. Oxfordshire, 1401, Sept. 1402, 1406, 1407 (speaker), 1410 (speaker), 1411 (speaker), 1413, Nov. 1414 (speaker), May 1421 (speaker), 1422, 1426, 1427, 1429, 1431.

[3] M.P. Rutland, Jan. 1397, 1399, Sept. 1402, Oct. 1404, April and Nov. 1414. March 1416, Oct. 1416 (speaker), 1417 (speaker), 1419 (speaker), 1422 (speaker); P.R.O., Duchy of Lancaster, Accounts Various, D.L. 28/4/9.

[4] M.P. Herefordshire, April 1414, 1417, 1419, 1420, May and Dec. 1421, 1422, 1423 (speaker), 1426, 1429, 1431, 1432 (speaker), 1433; P.R.O., Duchy of Lancaster, Accounts Various, D.L. 28/4/3–11; N. H. Nicolas, *Testamenta Vetusta*, p. 189.

[5] M.P. Huntingdonshire, 1407, 1413, April 1414, 1417, 1419, May 1421, 1422, 1423, 1425, 1426, 1427, 1429, 1431, 1432, 1433 (speaker); Bedfordshire, Nov. 1414, March 1416, 1420 (speaker); *Cal. Pat. Rolls 1405–8*, p. 459; P.R.O., Exchequer K.R., Accounts Various, E. 101/405/22; E. 101/48/4; E. 101/409/2–18; *Cal. Pat. Rolls 1416–22*, p. 412; *ibid. 1436–41*, p. 219; *Cal. Close Rolls 1429–35*, p. 89; *Rot. Parl.*, iv. 267a; *The Register of Archbishop Chichele*, ed. E. F. Jacob, ii. 195.

[6] M.P. Essex, 1411, 1413, March 1416, 1417, 1419, May 1421, 1422, 1425, 1429, 1431 (speaker), 1433, 1437 (speaker); Hertfordshire, 1427 (speaker); *Colchester Oath Book*, ed. Sir W. Gurney Benham, p. 24; *Cal. Pat. Rolls 1416–22*, p. 129; *The Lives of the Berkeleys*, John Smith of Nibley, ii. 40 *et seq.*; *Cal. Pat. Rolls 1422–29*, p. 560; *ibid. 1429–36*, pp. 613–28; *ibid. 1436–41*, pp. 578–94; W. R. Williams, *Duchy of Lancaster Official Lists*, p. 19; P.R.O., Exchequer K.R., Accounts Various, E. 101/408/9–13.

in 1445, was sitting for the fifteenth time;[1] William Tresham, speaker in November 1449 for the fourth time, the then chancellor of the duchy of Lancaster but also to his ultimate undoing connected with the duke of York, was sitting for Northants in his eleventh parliament.[2] These cases of repeated election as speaker, especially in view of the fact that they involve, with the exception of Chaucer, lawyers of long parliamentary experience, incidentally must have done much to establish and define the lines of procedure in the lower house.

Employment in the royal service or aristocratic connections enjoyed by their speakers, the Commons are likely to have found to be to their interest, for, however critical of government finance and whatever other distasteful pressure they ever brought to bear on the executive, their demands would only gain point by being presented through an intermediary acceptable on personal grounds, and this factor's influence on their choice of speaker it is well to take into account; but the nervousness, on occasion, of the speakers, the early speakers in particular, whatever their official complexion, is a clear indication that *they* felt themselves, as speakers, to be anything but government agents. In 1399 John Doreward, a member of the royal council, was anxious to point out[3] that what he said for the Commons should not be taken as proceeding 'de son propre motif ou voluntee singulere', and Sir John Tiptoft, knight of the royal chamber like his father, in 1406 expressly requested resort to his first protestation on no fewer than six occasions.[4] Sir Arnold Savage's second term of office as speaker in January 1404 involved him in such a virulent attack by the Commons[5] on the conduct of the royal household as parliament had not witnessed since Richard II in 1397 had had the initiation of such a proceeding defined as treasonable.[6] Savage, too, was a member of the council[7] and one thing clearly emerges from his second speakership: either membership of the royal council did not preclude its members from giving rein to a critical spirit even in parliament, or the speaker had no choice but to express the complaints or demands of his fellows in the lower house. In 1413 the Commons insisted that their speaker had acted *ultra vires* in having conceded, without their assent, the king's demand to have certain complaints put into writing and Henry V allowed their objection and the speaker's protestation was confirmed.[8] The protestation invariably allowed the speaker to have the words he spoke in parliament amended by his fellows. Hence

---

[1] M.P. Shropshire, 1417, 1419, 1420, May 1421, 1422, 1425, 1427, 1429, 1431, 1432, 1433, 1435, 1437 (speaker), 1439, 1442, 1445 (speaker), Nov. 1449, 1450, 1455.

[2] M.P. Northants, 1423, 1427, 1429, 1432, 1433, 1435, 1439 (speaker), 1442 (speaker), 1447 (speaker), Feb. 1449, Nov. 1449 (speaker); N. H. Nicolas, *Testamenta Vetusta*, p. 23; *Cal. Pat. Rolls 1446–52*, p. 218; *Rot. Parl.*, v. 211–12.

[3] *Rot. Parl.*, iii. 424b.   [4] *Ibid.*, 568b, 569d, 572a, 573b, 574a, 577a, 579b.

[5] *Ibid.*, 523–5.   [6] *Ibid.*, 407b.

[7] *Cal. Pat. Rolls 1401–5*, p. 236; *Cal. Close Rolls 1402–5*, pp. 192, 444; Nicolas, *Procs. and Ordinances of the Privy Council*, i. 222, 238, 244, 246, 295–6; *ibid.*, ii. 83; *Rot. Parl.*, iii. 530a.

[8] *Rot. Parl.*, iv. 4b.

the Commons were here insisting that it allowed *them* to control their speaker's acts in parliament as well as it allowed *him* to safeguard himself against his words being regarded as in any way his own responsibility. They were insisting that he must speak only as they allow him to speak; the protestation embodied *their* right as well as *his* privilege.[1] If the speaker was something of a marionette, most of the evidence goes to show that whatever his personal connections with king or council or individual lords, it was the Commons who pulled the strings which moved him in parliament.

This reciprocal nature of the speaker's protestation has, I think, tended to be overlooked because the protestation has been looked at from a different angle, for it was frequently and significantly accompanied by an apology made beforehand by the speaker for anything he should say in parliament prejudicial or offensive to the king, as in 1378, 1380, 1397, 1398, 1401, 1406 and 1411, and as late as 1449,[2] and sometimes the Lords too were associated with the king in this apology as in 1378, 1380 and 1406.[3] Attention to this recurring clause of the protestation of the early speaker has rightly been drawn on the grounds that it showed that freedom of speech in parliament, as a formal privilege, belonged to him alone of the Commons,[4] and that even he must not transgress the bounds of that 'reverence' which was due from the members of one estate in the realm to those of a higher. Professor Neale's conclusions that the Commons had to

---

[1] The speaker's protestation in the high court of parliament may well be the counterpart of the self-protection that learned counsel was entitled to seek in making an oral pleading on behalf of a client in any court of the king, and counsel for parties to suits before the Lords of parliament could use on occasion a protestation very like that of the speaker. For instance, when in the parliament of 1425 the earl marshal claimed precedence of the earl of Warwick, at one point in the subsequent proceedings Sir Walter Beauchamp (speaker for the Commons in March 1416), counsel for Warwick, requested that he might speak under protestation so that, 'if he saied lesse then he had in commaundement or of his dulle remembrance or foryetfulled lesse (*sic*, foryetfullednesse?) than was profitable to my lordes title or if he of his folie, which God defende, seide more then he had in commaundement,' his principal might be free to make additions or subtractions at his discretion, and that his protestation might be recorded. Similarly Roger Hunt (speaker for the Commons in 1420, 1433), counsel for the earl marshal, later asked to speak under protestation that he might 'resort ayein to reformation of his seid lord Erl Mareshall,' that what he might say should not turn to the displeasure of any of the Lords or of Warwick, and that this protestation might be enacted of record (*Rot. Parl.*, iv. 267*b*, 268*b*). The fact that such protestations were couched in similar form to those of the speaker in no way detracts from the importance and significance of the latter. That the speaker's protestation was no common form merely is clear from the interest which it so clearly attracted on occasion: cf. above and Thomas Chaucer's protestations besides, in 1410 (when the protestation was allowed by the King himself) and in 1411 (when the king was prepared to allow such protestation as had been customary and not otherwise 'qar il ne vorroit aucunement avoir nulle manere de Novellerie en cest Parlement,' whereupon Chaucer requested a postponement to allow his protestation to be put into writing 'plus en especial'). (*Rot. Parl.*, iii. 623*a*, 648*a*).

[2] *Rot. Parl.*, iii. 34*b*, 73*a*, 348*b*, 357*a*, 455*a*, 573*b*, 648*b*; *ibid.*, v. 142*a*.

[3] *Ibid.*, iii. 35*a*, 73*a*, 573*b*.

[4] J. E. Neale, 'The Commons' Privilege of Free Speech in Parliament,' *Tudor Studies presented to A. F. Pollard*, ed. R. W. Seton-Watson, p. 259 *et seq.*

wait until the Tudor period for the concession of a formal privilege of free speech in their own house of assembly cannot be gainsaid. He would accept, I think, the view that these protestations and apologies, coupled with the Commons' concern voiced by their speaker in 1401, 1404, and 1406,[1] that the king should not be moved to animosity against them, or any of their number, by the sinister reports of self-seeking tale-bearers and should pay no attention to any information of their deliberations other than that disclosed by their *accredited* speaker, are evidence that in practice the Commons allowed themselves a considerable latitude of self-expression. The speaker's occasional apology to the Lords as well as to the king does, however, I think, discredit his notion, at any rate so far as the late fourteenth and early fifteenth centuries are concerned, that the Commons in parliament were acting merely as a sort of sounding-board to the Lords, their recognised function as petitioners being exploited in a recrudescence of the old baronial opposition to the Crown.

The speaker's care to disclaim any intention on his part or the Commons' part to give offence to the Lords was no more formal than the apology he made beforehand to the king. To be properly appreciated it should be seen against the background of the political circumstances which prompted the re-affirmation and expansion, in 1378, of the terms of the statute of 1275 touching the crime of 'scandalum magnatum'.[2] In the Good Parliament two peers of parliament (William Lord Latimer, acting chamberlain to the king, and John Lord Neville, then steward of the royal household) had been successfully impeached by the Commons of certain offences which implied grave misgovernance of affairs of state and misconduct about the person of the king. The duke of Lancaster had not then been directly implicated but that his conduct was not above suspicion in these closing stages of the reign of Edward III appears clearly from a significant incident at the beginning of Richard II's first parliament of October 1377. On this occasion, following a request by the Commons for the appointment of a committee of lords to commune with them in their discussions, of which committee Lancaster was one, he protested that the Commons had spoken ill of him and that 'l'en avoit parlez si malveisement de sa persone chose qe droitement serroit entenduz apperte Traison si ce fust voir, qe Dieu defende.' He refused to do anything until these allegations were investigated and, when both Lords and Commons tried to mollify his feelings, went on to say that any 'trovour de tielles paroles par quelles l'en moeveroit legerement debat parentre les Seigneurs du Roialme si fust appert et verroi Traitour' and to demand an ordinance providing for the future punishment of 'tieux parlours et trovours des mensonges.' In 1377 nothing seemingly was done but in the next parliament

---

[1] *Rot. Parl.*, iii. 456a, 523a, 569b.

[2] Statute of Westminster, I (1275), c. 34; stat. 2 Richard II, stat. 1, c. 5; and cf. T. F. T. Plucknett, *Concise History of the Common Law*, pp. 429 *et seq.*

which met at Gloucester a year later the chancellor drew attention to the fact that in different parts of the kingdom there were ill-disposed persons, worthy of the name of 'bacbyters,' who 'moelt communement s'afforcent a dire et controver et conter fauxes, horribles, et perilouses mensonges des Seigneurs et autres, grantz Officers et bones gentz del Roialme, et les font privement notefier et semer entre les Communes et autres et ne les poent ne ne [sic] veullent avouer en appert.' The statute of 1275, whose purpose was to make words which would not otherwise be defamatory actionable if derogatory to the magnates, was confirmed in the Gloucester parliament, but there were some interesting and significant differences between the old and the new statute. The former referred to the danger of discord 'entre le Rey e son pople ou aukuns homes de son reaume'; the latter drew attention to the prospect of debate and discord 'parentre les . . . seigneurs ou parentre les seigneurs et Communes,' and added to the magnates protected by its provisions the chancellor, the treasurer, the clerk of the privy seal, the steward of the household, the justices of both benches, and other great officials of the Crown. In 1388 a second re-enactment of the statute of 1275 allowed the punishment of offenders to lie within the council's jurisdiction.[1] On the close connection between the speaker's occasional apology for what might be said to disturb the Lords and the statute of Scandalum magnatum we have perhaps further light thrown by the pious hope expressed in January 1410 by the king himself when he allowed the speaker's protestation: 'because all the estates of the Parliament were come for the common weal and profit of the King and realm and to make unity and union with one assent and accord, it was certain that the Commons would wish to attempt or speak nothing that would not be honourable, in order to nourish love and concord between all parties'.[2] The occasional oblique reference in the early speakers' protestations to the terms of the statute of Scandalum magnatum clearly shows that the Commons in parliament thought of themselves as liable to be subject to its operation, in other words, that they enjoyed no peculiar privilege of free speech; but the connection between the words of the protestation and the terms of the statute makes the speaker's apologies to the Lords in his protestation anything but an irrelevant inclusion in it.

There are other no less valid reasons, of course, why we should doubt that at this time the Commons were little more than the exponents of the opinions and policies of the upper house of parliament. The frequent inter-commoning between a committee of the Lords and the whole body of the Commons, which has been adduced as evidence of the Commons' subservience was normally secured at the *Commons'* request[3] and, in any case, was an innovation which the

---

[1] *Rot. Parl.*, iii. 5*a*, 5*b*, 32*b*; Stat. 12 Richard II, c. 11.   [2] *Ibid.*, iii. 623*a*.

[3] *Ibid.*, ii. 316*b*, 322*a*, 363*b*; *ibid.*, iii. 5*a*, 36*a*, 100*a*, 134*a*, 145*a*, 167*b*, 486*b*, 610*a*; cf. H. L. Gray, *The Influence of the Commons on Early Legislation*, p. 277, n. 173*a*.

Lords were not long in resenting as an impertinence. In 1378 they refused at first to be party to the practice but continued to allow themselves to be subjected to it.[1]

There is no reason, therefore, to believe other than that the speakers, especially in this particular period we are at present concerned with, spoke for the Commons alone in the parliament chamber, and there is every reason to believe that on occasion they were required there to speak, whatever tendentious influence they may have exercised in the debates in the lower house, in terms far from being acceptable to the Lords generally or to those magnates with whom they were connected in particular. In February 1383 the election as speaker of Sir James Pickering with his Lancastrian connection[2] seems not to have affected the Commons' continued preference for the 'way of Flanders' to the 'way of Spain' as a means of attacking France, in the face of contrary opinions among the Lords. There was, indeed, no reason why it should: one of the strongest objections pleaded by the Commons to any alternative to Despenser's crusade was the difficulty of resisting any Scottish incursion if Lancaster or his brothers were out of the country, one which Pickering, as a north-country knight whose main estates were in Westmorland and Cumberland, although he now sat for Yorkshire, was himself likely to have supported and understood.[3] In these years, until, in fact, fear of government resting on the too restricted base of a court party, supporting a king already obsessed with his prerogative, made the greatest of the magnates and the Commons act together in the parliaments of 1386 and 1388, the political temper of the Commons was very much of their own generation. It is the greater tribute to Richard II's powers of perception and political management, even if their exercise only yielded a short-term success, that before the end of his reign his construction of a party among the Lords was matched by his ability to secure a complacent if not subservient Commons.

Early after the 1399 revolution the Commons recovered their place as independent critics. Thomas Chaucer, whose 'novelleries' rallied the all but worn-out Henry IV into angry protest in 1411,[4] may well, in this his third consecutive term as speaker, as before in 1407 and 1410, have been acting in the interests of his cousins the Beauforts and their ally, the prince of Wales, but there seems to be no valid reason for connecting the humiliations of the king at the hands of the shire-knights earlier in the reign, in 1404 and 1406 especially, with any general movement of opposition among the Lords in parliament or with opposition on the part of any particular aristocratic clique. The Lords were, at times, as irritated as the king by the forwardness of the lower house, and not

---

[1] *Rot. Parl.*, iii. 36a; *ibid.*, 100a.
[2] *John of Gaunt's Register 1373–83*, i. 184; Pickering was not, however, so far as is known, a retainer with fee of John of Gaunt.
[3] *Rot. Parl.*, iii. 145b.   [4] *Ibid.*, 648a.

without reason: in the first of the two parliaments of 1404, after drawing attention to the need of repairs in the royal castles and manors, where what should have been the king's profits were granted away, and also to the great cost of the royal household, the Commons requested the king to charge the Lords to give counsel and advice 'sanz dissimulation ou aucune adulation' and, when this was done, themselves requested the Lords to act diligently and loyally 'sanz curtosie faire entre eux en ascune manere', affirming their own intention to do the same.[1] There are no signs of an entente cordiale here and the evidence of Bodley MS. 462 confirms this view of the relations between the two houses in the parliament next but one, the long parliament of 1406.[2]

It would, of course, be fatuous to suggest that it was always thus. As Mr. McFarlane has pointed out,[3] in the constitutional arrangements made at the accession of Henry of Windsor in 1422 the Commons' aspirations of 1406 for the responsibility of ministers to parliament were passed over in silence. Henry V had worked in amicable partnership with his baronage and his Council had been an aristocratic council; on his death the magnates were determined to perpetuate his system. That 'the lower house did not grasp so obvious a moment for asserting its rights' was due, I think, to the fact not that the baronage needed, and was able, to ignore the Commons but that it carried them with it. It may be argued that the Commons in this critical year failed to appreciate the dangers of oligarchical government and the need for a recognition of their own constitutional share in its future control; that, even if they did not realise the risks involved in an aristocratic régime, the political circumstances of the moment would make their criticism seem unpatriotic; and that, moreover, their not being asked to make any grant of direct taxation weakened their power of effective criticism; but the evidence seems to suggest that the Commons were quite prepared to fall into line behind the Lords and were genuinely more appreciative of their policy than blind to its defects. We need not necessarily think of the Commons as only effective when they were in opposition. Even so, the opportunity of 1422 was an opportunity lost.

The initiative held by the Commons in the first half of Henry IV's reign was lost in 1422 for more than two centuries. For the rest of the fifteenth century it is difficult not to recognise their general subordination to the government of the day and their more than occasional subservience to particular aristocratic, or even royalist, interests and parties. But this may be only on the face of things. As the fifteenth century progressed the rolls of the parliaments became less communicative of the domestic proceedings of the Commons than they had been for the last three decades of the fourteenth century and the first decade of the

---

[1] *Rot. Parl.*, iii. 524*a*.
[2] *The St. Albans Chronicle 1406–1420* (from Bodley MS. 462), ed. V. H. Galbraith, pp. 2–3.
[3] K. B. McFarlane, 'England: The Lancastrian Kings,' *Camb. Med. History*, viii. 388–90.

fifteenth. The decline or rather suspension of the writing of full-scale, comprehensive chronicles of the type which the scriptorium of St. Albans was still able to produce in Henry V's reign means, too, that there is little that can be used to eke out the official records of parliamentary proceedings. Nevertheless, there are signs from time to time that the Commons could still take, when they felt so moved, a strong and critical line which put them sometimes at variance with the Lords, sometimes into disfavour with the administration. In 1425, for example, over the conditions attaching to the Commons' grant of tunnage and poundage there was 'moche altercacyon bytwyne the lordys and the comyns'.[1] In the sessions of 1439–40 there were difficulties between the Commons and the government over its mercantile policies especially with regard to the 'hosting' of alien merchants; the Commons won the day in spite of an adjournment to Reading and in the face of strong resistance from the court.[2] Again in the parliament whose three sessions (the first two at Westminster, the third at Leicester) lasted, with roughly a month's break after the first and second, from 6 November 1449 to 5/8 June 1450 there was a repetition of this antipathy. The Commons not only contrived the impeachment of the king's chief minister, the duke of Suffolk; when the king demanded a subsidy for the defence of Normandy, they withstood, so says Dr. Thomas Gascoigne, 'plures minas et a rege et a suis juvenibus consiliariis,' refused to be intimidated by the rumoured prospect of parliament's indefinite continuance with all its attendant expense, and in the end voted a graduated income-tax instead of the normal subsidy, and that only in return for an act of resumption. Moreover, probably as a result of their objections to the cession of Maine and Anjou or maybe to the conduct of the war, the Commons had drawn from the king (and perhaps the Lords) the demand, 'quod communitas Anglie non intromitteret se de factis regis et dominorum.'[3]

The speaker for the Commons in this unusually drawn-out parliament of 1449–50 had been William Tresham, apprentice-at-law. It was the duke of York who stood to gain most by the disgrace and elimination of Suffolk and by the collapse of his shaken policy towards France, and there are clear indications of a connection between York and Tresham: Tresham had for over a year been one of the ducal feoffees, and his life was to end in tragedy on 23 September 1450 as a direct result of his Yorkist attachment. He had, however, risen as a careerist lawyer in the service of the Crown to the chancellorship of the duchy of Lancaster during the years when Suffolk had been 'priviest of the King's counsel' and had enjoyed an important place on the duchy council, and he had already been three times speaker in the course of this short period (in 1439, 1442, and 1447). It

[1] Gregory's Chronicle, cited in W. Stubbs, Constitutional History of England, iii. § 331 n.
[2] Cambridge Medieval History., op. cit., viii. 401.
[3] Thomas Gascoigne, Loci e Libro Veritatum, ed. J. E. Thorold Rogers, pp. 189–90.

will not do to write him off as a Yorkist partisan any more than as a devotee of
Suffolk's; his allegiances must have been in a state of flux in this time of national
calamity and threatening strife. And it would be an over-simplification, too, of
the Commons' attitudes at the beginning of and throughout this parliament of
1449–50 to describe the lower house as pro-Yorkist in its political sympathy.
We know that there were Yorkist elements in its composition[1] and their influence can be discerned in the Commons' first choice as speaker of Sir John
Popham who had long, probably all his life, been connected with the house of
York. But Popham saw fit to seek and find exoneration from the office; and that
Tresham, the Commons' second choice, was not unacceptable to the government
of the day is clear from his retention, however inadvisable, in the chancellorship
of the duchy of Lancaster, although there was ample time in which to bring about
his dismissal between the dissolution of parliament, early in June, and his murder
nearly four months later.[2] It would be going beyond the evidence to suggest
that as speaker he engineered the downfall of Suffolk; the part he played in that
manœuvre, as in others, of the Commons in this parliament was doubtless a part
they assigned him to play, and *their* temper was one informed by a deep sense of
national frustration and discomfiture rather than, at this point, by a belief in the
saving graces of the exiled York.

In attempting to assess the political as distinct from the constitutional importance of the Commons in the later Middle Ages, particularly with regard to
the political relations between the Lords and the lower house, with due respect
to Mr. Richardson,[3] it seems to me that we cannot always take the long view.
And this is peculiarly the case with the Commons' speaker. Because at the end
of the medieval period there are signs that his election had degenerated into a
mere formality, we must not assume that this had always been the case; what
evidence the rolls of the parliaments and other sources supply, suggests that it
was not so. Some attempts at aristocratic and royal manipulation at the circum-
ference, in the elections of the knights of the shire and increasingly in those of
the parliamentary burgesses, there may always have been in greater or lesser
degree, but we must not assume that at the centre, in the election of their speaker,
the Commons were not normally left with freedom to act in accordance with
their own devices and desires. At times in this matter they may have been subjected to influence, and at times this may have been difficult to distinguish from
pressure, but that before the advent of the Tudors they were ever customarily
subjected to interference in, and to a clear infringement of, their liberty of

---

[1] Wedgwood, *op. cit., Register*, pp. 133–144.
[2] Wedgwood (*op. cit., Biographies*, p. 872) is in error in stating that Tresham was supplanted by
John Say in July 1450. Say assumed office as from 22 September, the day before Tresham's death.
(P.R.O. Duchy of Lancaster, Accounts Various, D.L. 28/5/7.)
[3] H. G. Richardson, 'The Commons and Medieval Politics,' *op. cit.*

election is pure conjecture. In any case, whatever undiscovered evolutions resulted in his election there is little justification for believing that the speaker, whatever his personal inclinations may have been, was able to speak other than as the Commons allowed him. He was the delegate, not the representative, of the elective elements in parliament who by the end of the Middle Ages had come to be regarded as embodying the will of the commonalty of the realm. It was a full consciousness of the medieval traditions of his office which in 1523 prompted Sir Thomas More to act in a way which, according to his son-in-law Roper, drew from Wolsey the complaint, 'Would to God you had been at Rome, Master More, when I made you Speaker'.[1]

---

[1] *The Life of Sir Thomas More, by William Roper*, ed. E. V. Hitchcock (1935), p. 19.

THE PARLIAMENTARY REPRESENTATION OF LINCOLNSHIRE DURING THE REIGNS OF RICHARD II, HENRY IV AND HENRY V

The period from the accession of Richard II in 1377 to the death of Henry V in 1422 was, for the most part, a time of great social and political unrest, which touched at some point every level of English society. Recovery from the Black Death of a generation earlier had been slow, partly because of recurrences of the pestilence. In 1381 there was the short but very severe and disturbing outbreak of the Peasants' Revolt. Lollardy, encouraged by schism in the Papacy, was a cause of real and constant anxiety to English churchmen; and covetous eyes were being cast at ecclesiastical property by men who found the doctrinal aspects of Lollardy quite unattractive. For much the greater part of the period there was enmity towards France. It was financially difficult to maintain a state of open belligerence, and, moreover, there was confusion over diplomatic purpose and military strategy. Richard II long favoured and eventually achieved an accommodation with the French. On this account, but also for other reasons, there were serious quarrels between the king and some of the most powerful of the nobility. At times, these resulted in savage proscriptions of political opponents (of which parliament was the scene), first by one party and then by the other, until, in 1399, disastrously embroiled in "the first attempt of an English king to rule as an autocrat *on principle*" (V. H. Galbraith), Richard II was deposed. His fall was brought about by an overwhelming rebellion led by his cousin, Henry of Bolingbroke (the son and heir of John of Gaunt), who replaced him on the throne. This revolution of 1399 was a shock to the monarchy, and Henry IV's reign was also an unquiet time, socially, politically, and even constitutionally. Parliament provided something of an outlet for dissatisfaction, discontent and dispute; but there was open rebellion in England, and also in Wales, and when revolts had been suppressed, there was tension and disaffection, even in the Lancastrian royal family. Early in his reign Henry V experienced a recurrence of insurrection and treachery. Following his father in 1413, he proved to be very efficient as a ruler at home and also as a soldier in France, where he soon renewed the conflict of the previous century and won considerable success. In this policy of aggression overseas he carried the nobility and the country generally with him; but Henry V died with his triumph in France patently incomplete. Without his masterful personality to guide it, his ambitious foreign policy eventually foundered: and, in the aftermath at home, what with the country's "want of governance and unwillingness to be governed" (to use Mr. Colvin's phrase), so did his dynasty. This, rudely painted in primary colours, is the backcloth of our stage.

Knights of the shire and burgesses had together been coming up to parliaments, at first spasmodically and then with a greater regularity, since 1265. By 1377 the appearance of these elected representatives of local communities, two knights from each of thirty-seven counties in England and two burgesses from each of nearly a hundred towns, had been entirely habitual for about half a century. What little we know of how knights of the shire were then elected is derived from very fragmentary evidence. The fourteenth century produced no statute relating to the manner of holding elections. Some light is thrown on their conduct in the fifteenth century when disputes occasionally followed contested elections and complaint was made to higher authority in some detail, and when remedial statutes laid down rules for the future. With regard to the later mediaeval period as a whole, an evaluation of the main forces influencing the election of knights of the shire to this parliament and to that requires some degree of reliance upon evidence that is even generally inferential, for instance, upon what is known about the careers and the social and family relationships of individual knights of the shire. One must be prepared to rate highly the personal and fortuitous elements in any single electoral situation; but there are likely to have been certain impersonal factors in operation, registering some impact on electoral proceedings. It is sometimes difficult, however, to measure that impact.

Looking at a list of the knights of the shire elected for Lincolnshire to the forty-four parliaments which met in the forty-five years between the accession of Richard II (1377) and the death of Henry V (1422), or rather to the thirty-nine for which the returns for this county are known,[1] one is immediately struck by the considerable number of local men and families represented in it: thirty-two knights of the shire elected, twenty-eight families involved. The average individual attendance of the Lincolnshire knights in this period was at between two and three parliaments[2]; but as many as nine of them (as the returns stand) sat for the county only once. Clearly, whether it was honour or burden to be chosen, election to parliament went the rounds of the Lincolnshire gentry at this time. Even so, there were notables with some influence on the life of the shire who never represented it in parliament at all. More than half of those who in this period acted as sheriffs, even part of whose official business it was to hold the shire elections, were never themselves elected; and yet many of the knights of the shire (roughly half) did act as sheriffs. If parliamentary service had been grudgingly undertaken, fewer of the sheriffs of the time, it may be imagined, would have eluded that duty. Competition was probably an important ingredient of the electoral process.

Lincolnshire was so big in area, and its gentry of substance so numerous, that dominance on the part of any family or even of any family-group was

[1] The electoral returns for Lincolnshire to the parliaments of 1410, 1415, October 1416, 1417 and 1419 have not survived.
[2] See Appendix. Nine knights of the shire sat only once; seven, twice; eight, three times; five, four times; two, five times; and one (Sir John Bussy), ten times.

rather improbable. Inevitably, some of the families to which the knights of the shire of this period belonged were related by ties of kinship or marriage: Tilneys with Rochfords and Skipwiths, Skipwiths with Hawleys, Hawleys with Copuldykes, Suthills with Pouchers. Through the Constables of Flamborough, the families of Copuldyke, Cumberworth, and Hilton were linked up. None of these connections had a compelling influence on elections. There is a surprising absence of even family tradition in parliamentary service. Of the twenty-eight families to which the known knights of the shire between 1377 and 1422 belonged, only four had supplied knights to earlier parliaments (the families of Rochford, Boys, Tothby, and Copuldyke[3]); members in the direct line of barely one out of every four of these twenty-eight families sat for the county in parliament at any later time, and even then it was often only after a long interval. No Dimmock of Scrivelsby, for instance, is known to have been returned after Sir John Dimmock (the first of the hereditary King's Champions of this name) was knight of the shire in Richard II's first parliament until the reign of Edward VI. We know of no Armyn sitting in the two centuries between 1385 and 1589. Certainly, this period under review produced no local parliamentary dynasty comparable with, say, the Stanleys and Haryngtons of Lancashire or the Vernons of Derbyshire. Within the period 1377–1422, there were only four knights whose fathers had had parliamentary experience: the father of the Sir John de Tothby who sat in the first two parliaments after the Peasants' Revolt had been elected thirty years before; Sir William Bussy had been returned for the last time less than four years before his son, Sir John, was first chosen in 1383; the father of Sir Thomas Hawley of Utterby and Girsby, who was elected in 1399 and again to the Coventry parliament of 1404, had sat in three of Edward III's later parliaments; Robert de Cumberworth was knight of the shire in 1393 and 1395, his son Thomas three times under Henry V and twice under Henry VI (between 1414 and 1437). Sir Robert and Sir Godfrey Hilton who sat for Lincolnshire just once each under Henry V (in 1416 and 1421 respectively)—the former of whom was more at home in the East Riding of Yorkshire, the latter an immigrant into Lincolnshire society as husband of the Luttrell heiress to Irnham until (as a result of a second marriage) he later came to prefer Hampshire—were the only brothers elected for Lincolnshire in this period. In only one case did the parliamentary experience of any Lincolnshire family involved in representing the county in the course of this half-century run into three consecutive generations: the son and grandson of Richard Welby, knight of the shire in the last parliament of Henry V's reign, sat for Lincolnshire in 1450 and 1472 respectively.

This is not, of course, to suggest that previous experience of parliamentary service on the part of individuals was held of no account in the Lincolnshire

[3] Sir Saier de Rochford, M.P. 1343; Sir John de Boys, M.P. 1355; Sir William de Tothby, M.P. 1351; Roger de Copuldyke, M.P. 1316.

elections of the late fourteenth and early fifteenth centuries. In only five instances between 1377 and 1422 (so far as we know) were both knights of the shire serving for the first time, and three of these five cases happened right at the beginning of this period (in 1380, 1381, and 1383), the other two thirty years later (in 1411 and 1416). The Lincolnshire electors, it may be implied, were disinclined to choose for the shire two novices, men without previous acquaintance with parliament. Statistically considered, individual re-elections seem to have been not infrequent—nineteen occasions in the elections to the thirty-nine parliaments of the period under review to which the returns are known—but half of these instances are accounted for by the recurrent re-elections of Sir John Bussy in the 1390s. His case apart, re-election was relatively unusual: and only once in the reigns of Richard II, Henry IV and Henry V did it happen that both the knights of the shire elected to one parliament were re-elected to the next. After sitting in the Cambridge parliament of 1388, Sir John Bussy and Sir Philip de Tilney were chosen to go to Westminster in January 1390.

The question of age as a qualification for parliamentary service is another general circumstance worth bearing in mind. The dates of birth of the knights of the shire of this period are only very exceptionally known, but the dates of death of all but a few can be ascertained. Such calculations suggest that middle age was more highly regarded as a qualification than youth. Half (sixteen) of the Lincolnshire knights died within fifteen years of their *first* election to parliament, and most of these (twelve) within five years of their last return. When, as happened more frequently under Henry V, a young man was elected, it was almost invariably along with someone much older.

For the greater part of this period under review, there were no statutes in being to limit the choice of knights of the shire by defining qualifications for election. The election of lawyers practising in the royal courts had been prohibited by enactment in 1372, and, at the same time, so had the election of any sheriff during his tenure of office. The former restriction on the return of men of law was limited in scope, and obviously it left plenty of room in parliament for up-country lawyers; but although a few of the Lincolnshire knights of the shire were descendants of lawyers of considerable repute, two of them being actually sons of royal judges, I have not been able safely to identify as professional lawyers themselves any at all from among the Lincolnshire parliamentary knights of this period.[4] The requirement about the

---

[4] Sir John de Tothby, M.P. in 1381 and May 1382, was grandson of Gilbert de Tothby, a royal serjeant-at-law from 1315 until his death in 1330, who acted as a justice of assize after Edward III's accession (R. C. Dudding, *History of Alford with Rigsby and Ailby*, p. 54 ff.).

Sir Richard Hansard was M.P. in January 1404, 1413, November 1414, May 1421 and 1423. His maternal grandfather was Chief Justice Gascoigne (*The Genealogist*, IV, 112–3).

John de Meres, M.P. in 1407, was grandson of Roger de Meres, who had been made king's serjeant-at-law in 1366–7, promoted Justice of the Common Bench in 1371 (Foss, *Judges of England*, iii, 463–5; Harleian Society, *Lincolnshire Pedigrees*, ii, 663), and who,

sheriffs gradually gained firm local support throughout the country, and certainly in this period under consideration Lincolnshire returned no acting sheriff of its own nor one from any other county.

A sense of the integrity of the county and also a feeling of respect for good family and establishment in landed possession in the county were generally uppermost, we may safely imagine, among the factors influencing the parliamentary elections in Lincolnshire to take the course they did. Certainly, the elections in this period reflect a ready acceptance of the idea that those who represented Lincolnshire should be Lincolnshire men or, if not (as very occasionally), then men who at any rate held lands and at least sometimes resided in the county. The principle of the statute of 1413, requiring actual residence in a county on the part of electors and elected alike when the writs of summons were issued, had long and constantly been observed in Lincolnshire so far as the knights-elect are concerned, and the county's sense of its "worship," a feeling for its own identity and responsibility as a community, had been exemplified without stint in the character of the men it returned to parliament long before 1445, when parliament recognized the need of a statute requiring county representatives to be "notable knights of the same counties for which they shall be chosen, or otherwise notable esquires, gentlemen born, of the same counties as shall be able to be knights, and no man to be such knight which standeth in the degree of a yeoman or under." Most of the Lincolnshire knights of the shire between 1377 and 1422 were proper, belted knights at the time of their first election, and others assumed the rank and dignity of knight bachelor before their parliamentary careers, such as they were, came to an end. (The proportion of knights by rank to esquires was three to one.) All of the knights of the shire were possessed of landed estate within the long boundary of the county, and a majority was resident in Lincolnshire and nowhere else, in spite of the fact that a fair number of them (certainly no less than one out of three) held lands outside the county, almost entirely,

---

by 1369, had also been a member of John of Gaunt's council (*John of Gaunt's Register*, ed. S. Armitage-Smith, ii, 356) and by 1372 the Duke's steward at Boston (*ibid.*, i, 67).

John Skipwith, M.P. in 1406, 1407 and April 1414, was the second son of Sir William Skipwith, who was appointed Justice of the Common Bench in 1359, held the office of Chief Baron of the Exchequer from 1362 until 1365 (when deprived), was made Chief Justice of the King's Bench in Ireland in 1370, and in 1376 was reappointed Secondary Justice of the Common Bench, from which he retired in 1388 (Foss, *op. cit.*, IV, 88–94; W. O. Massingberd, *History of the Parish of Ormsby-cum-Ketsby*, p. 67; *Lincolnshire Pedigrees, op. cit.*, iii, 895).

William Tirwhit, M.P. in March 1416, 1423 and 1426, was the son and heir of Robert Tirwhit, Justice of the King's Bench from 1409 until his death in 1428 (Foss, *op. cit.*, IV, 369; *Lincolnshire Pedigrees, op. cit.*, iii, 1018).

it may be said, in neighbouring shires.[5] Those whose outside interests prevailed over their Lincolnshire concerns were very exceptional. No more than five of the thirty-two shire-knights of this period were ever sheriffs outside Lincolnshire,[6] and rarer still were those ever elected to parliament for another county.[7] In its parliamentary representation at this time, Lincolnshire kept itself to itself, a statement which would not be true of some other counties.

Within the larger unit of the county of Lincolnshire, there then were, as there still are, regions enjoying a distinct and self-conscious identity of their own: the parts of Lindsey, of Kesteven, and of Holland. Three regions: two knights of the shire. Where, regionally, lay the most important influence on elections? Any conclusions are bound to be touched with ambiguity; but this is, nonetheless, a fair question to put. Commissions of the peace, commissions of array, commisssions to assess and collect taxes, and often commissions of sewers (that is, land-drains), were severally issued for each of the three regions, and appointments to serve on these commissions contained few coincidences of personnel. Administrative convenience had perpetuated divisions that were more basic, geographically and historically. Within the community of the county were the communities of its three regions, sometimes described as such, for example, in petitions to the king, in presenting which, although aware of their separate identity, these communities sometimes combined.[8] Now and

[5] Sir John Bozoun, occasionally M.P. between 1383 and 1386, had lands in Nottinghamshire; Walter Tailboys, M.P. 1383–8, in N. Riding, Yorkshire, and Northumberland; Sir John Bussy, M.P. 1383–98, in Nottinghamshire, Rutland and W. Riding, Yorkshire; Sir Gerard de Suthill, M.P. 1391–1402, in Nottinghamshire, and W. Riding, Yorkshire; Sir John de. Copuldyke, M.P. 1397–1406, in Norfolk and Suffolk; Sir Richard Hansard, M.P. 1404–1423, in E. Riding, Yorkshire; John Poucher, M.P. 1411, in Wiltshire; Sir Thomas Cumberworth, M.P. 1414–37, in E. Riding, Yorkshire; Sir Robert Hilton, M.P. 1416, in E. Riding, Yorkshire; William Tirwhit, M.P. 1416–26, in Essex, Northamptonshire and E. Riding, Yorkshire; Sir Robert Hagbech, M.P. in 1420, in Huntingdonshire, Cambridgeshire, Norfolk and Suffolk; Sir Godfrey Hilton, M.P. in 1421, in Nottinghamshire and Yorkshire.

[6] Sir John Bozoun was sheriff of Nottinghamshire and Derbyshire in 1381–2; Sir Philip de Tilney, of Cambridgeshire and Huntingdonshire in 1383–4; Sir Robert Hilton, of Yorkshire in 1417–8, 1423–4, 1427–8; William Tirwhit, of Yorkshire in 1435–6; Sir Robert Hagbech, of Cambridgeshire and Huntingdonshire in 1413–4 (P.R.O., Lists and Indexes, no. IX, List of Sheriffs, passim).

[7] Sir John Bussy was elected to the parliament of 1391 for Rutland as well as for Lincolnshire (but his writ de expensis was addressed to the sheriff of Lincolnshire, not Rutland); Sir John de Rochford, M.P. for Lincolnshire in 1390, 1394, 1397 and 1399, was elected for Cambridgeshire to the Gloucester parliament of 1407, which proved to be his last, for he died in 1410; Sir Robert Hilton of Swine (near Hull), M.P. for Lincolnshire in 1416, was returned for Yorkshire in 1419, 1425, 1426 and 1427.

[8] In 1330 a petition to the King and Council was presented by the men of Kesteven and Holland, complaining that, although the prior of Sempringham had been appointed by the King to collect tolls from horses and carts carrying merchandise through the hamlet of St. Saviour's at Bridgend for the upkeep of the crossings, the prior had made no provision, with the result that the bridges had become so dilapidated that passage had to be by boat; and requesting that auditors should be appointed to examine his account of receipts (Rot. Parl., ii, 32). Another petition, attributed to Edward III's reign, but not to be precisely dated, was put forward by the commune of Kesteven, Lindsey, and the citizens of Lincoln, about the destruction of fresh-water mills which, if the sails of the wind-mills were unable to turn, resulted in a want of bread in these parts (ibid., 403). In 1334, les gentz de la communalte de Kesteven acted alone in petitioning King and Council to authorize the removal of impediments to the free flow of the Witham and the Brant (ibid., 77).

then, however, one region was not above exploiting its distinctiveness at another's expense.[9] These divisions, and the differences and disputes which they bred, were of real significance, if only spasmodically manifested. In this context, allusion may also be made to the competition between Lincoln and Boston in the middle decades of the fourteenth century for possession of the status of a staple port,[10] and there are other intimations of inter-regional tension and local self-consciousness.

An examination of the results of the parliamentary elections in Lincolnshire between 1377 and 1422 reveals the interesting fact that on no more than six occasions were both of the knights of the shire from the same region of Lincolnshire.[11] On all but two of these occasions they were Lindsey men who were

[9] In March 1371, parliament granted to Edward III the sum of £50,000 to be raised by a levy of 22s. 3d. on each parish, it being understood that there were some 40,000 parishes in England. It did not take very long for it to dawn on the government—this at least is to to its credit—that the number of parishes had been optimistically exaggerated and that there were actually fewer than 9,000: and so a "shadow" parliament was specially convened to Winchester in June following to put things right. This the Winchester meeting did, by raising the charge per parish to 116s., and then departed. Difficulties in Lincolnshire seem to have been greater than at Winchester, so much so that in August royal letters close (*CCR*, 1369–74, 248–9) went to the Lincolnshire commissioners for the tax, ordering them to make a move, in haste and on pain of forfeiture. These last words were unusual and harsh, but justifiable: for the writ expressly alludes to the complaint of the men of Lindsey that, though the parishes of Holland were richer than their own (and those of Kesteven as well), the men of Holland refused to assist them, because, even if in the past they had been taxed with the men of Kesteven, they had never been taxed with the men of Lindsey. Now the intention of the grant had been that, in every county, the richer parishes should help the poorer, without consideration being given to county administrative divisions, such as hundreds or wapentakes, and so on. This intention was being contravened in Lincolnshire, the royal writ insisted, and the levy delayed as a result; and the collectors and overseers of the tax were ordered to ensure that the equitable design of the grant was observed. So doubtless it was, but the collectors later on thought that they were entitled to special expenses in putting an end to disagreements between the different parts of the county (if a petition, no more precisely dated than belonging to Edward III's reign, is to be attributed to the time of this upset, as I think it may) (*Rot. Parl.*, ii, 403).

Over a quite different issue, the making of criminal presentments, there was constant trouble (*altercations et debates*) between the men of Holland and Kesteven because of the uncertain whereabouts of the boundary between them in the marshlands of the Welland and the Witham, where the marks had been covered by silt and the debris of fresh-water floods. Moved by whom we know not, the Commons, in the parliament at Northampton in 1380, petitioned for a Chancery commission to renew the boundaries and to sign and mark them by pales, fosses and crosses of stone, by which men might the better tell them for what they were. Probably because of the strife of the Peasants' Revolt of the following year, nothing was done; and it was not until this petition, reproduced *verbatim*, had been submitted in the parliament of January 1390 that a commission was set up and, superintended by the sheriff (a Holland man himself), a perambulation of the bounds was held, following which the ancient metes were re-set by twelve jurors from Holland and a like number from Kesteven (*Rot. Parl.*, iii, 95, 272).

[10] P. Thompson, *The History and Antiquities of Boston and the . . . Hundred of Skirbeck*, Boston, 1856, p. 55; *Rot. Parl.*, ii, 332.

[11] From Kesteven, in 1378, Sir John Auncell (J.P. in Kesteven) and Sir William Bussy of Hougham were elected together; from Holland, in October 1382, Sir Robert de Leake of Sibsey and William Spayne of Boston (both J.P.s in Holland); from Lindsey, in 1402, Sir Henry de Retford of Castlethorpe and Sir Gerard de Suthill of Redbourne (both J.P.s in Lindsey); from Lindsey, in October 1404, Sir Henry de Retford and Sir Thomas Hawley of Utterby and Girsby (both J.P.s in Lindsey); from Lindsey, in April 1414, John Skipwith of Ormsby and Sir Thomas Cumberworth of Somerby (J.P. in Lindsey); from Lindsey, in March 1416, Sir Robert Hilton of Swine (who held the manor of Fulston and lands in Aylesby) and William Tirwhit of Kettleby and Buslingthorpe.

so returned together. The monopoly of one seat for ten years (1388–98) by Sir John Bussy of Hougham in Kesteven gave an over-all preponderance to this region under Richard II, but otherwise there was then a rough equality between the different parts. The tale is quite different after the revolution of 1399. Thereafter the balance is tilted markedly towards Lindsey, especially at the expense of Kesteven. Not once between 1399 and 1415 was a Kesteven man elected, unless it was to the single parliament in these years (that of 1410) for which the returns have been lost. In fact, to put the picture into sharper focus, we may say that from even 1388 to 1415, for more than a quarter of a century, that is, the only Kesteven man elected was Bussy. His many returns in the first half of our period result in something of a distortion. In so far as the parliamentary representation of the shire provides a valid index of any regional superiority in local politics, Lindsey was the most important region, and then came Holland. Of the thirty-two knights elected in the period regarded as a whole, fifteen were Lindsey men, eleven were from Holland, and six from Kesteven.[12] The holding of the shire elections at Lincoln may have had some effect on all this. Very likely it had; but if we remember that time and again under Richard II it was possible for two or even three elections to go by without a Lindsey man appearing in one sequence or a Holland man in another,[13] we can only regard the influence of regional feeling on any single election as a very marginal factor. On elections as they came and went there are likely to have been more potent influences directly at work.

The administration of Lincolnshire, so far as the interests of the Crown were concerned, was as in most other English counties. The local, county concerns of the central government—the holding of the judicial assizes apart—were taken care of by local men authorized by royal commission to occupy the established offices of sheriff, escheator, and justice of the peace, or to act as collectors of various royal dues, commissioners of sewers, members of committees of enquiry into abuses both public and private, and as members of other *ad hoc* tribunals of different kinds. The offices of sheriff and escheator normal changed hands once a year, but other appointments varied, most royal commissions on which local men served being, however, of limited scope and uncertain duration. A man of good local standing who belonged to a landed family with an assured place in the society of the county sooner or later was almost bound to get a royal command to do public services of one kind or another. Being chosen to perform such "chores" attested rather than created, although it might increase, his local prestige and influence. Like serving as a knight of the shire, these duties were part of the *cursus honorum* of the country gentleman.

---

[12] There are 31 instances of a man from Lindsey having been elected, 24 from Holland, 22 from Kesteven (Bussy's elections numbering ten).

[13] No man of Holland was elected to the parliaments of February and October 1383 and April 1384; no man of Lindsey to the parliaments of September 1388 and 1390 (January and November).

Appointment by the Crown as a justice of the peace came at some time the way of all but a very few of the Lincolnshire knights of the shire under Richard II, Henry IV, and Henry V. Possession of the commission of the peace was, however, by no means a condition or even qualification for election to parliament. In Richard II's reign, in fact, there were almost as many knights of the shire who were not J.P.s at the time of their election as were; and in each of five out of the thirteen parliaments which sat in the 1380s it so happened that neither of the two shire-knights was then on the commission of the peace in any part of Lincolnshire.[14] Such a situation only occurred once under the first two Lancastrian kings.[15] One would hesitate to suggest that the royal administration under Henry IV and Henry V, in choosing as local justices men who, as knights of the shire, evidently enjoyed some measure of local approval, was in closer sympathy than before with the needs of the county, as those needs were locally felt. (A much more subtle method of appraisal than that would be required.) But even if this were so, and a man became a sheriff, or escheator, or J.P., or took part in more casual enterprises operating by royal authority and also happened to be elected as knight of the shire, we should have to be careful not to conclude that the two sorts of recognition, the royal and the local, were necessarily connected in any politically significant way. We must guard against blandly identifying a local royal official or commissioner, or even a local retainer of the king, taking special fees as such and perhaps with interest at Court, as a royal nominee if and when he was elected to parliament, and against seeing in his election the result of some direct act of royal dictation, intervention, or interference. Rigging of elections is likely sometimes to have taken place,—at his deposition Richard II was charged with packing his last parliament, and rebels against Henry IV complained of the need for free elections—but the rigging is likely to have been in the main locally contrived by local men for their own benefit. This is not to say that it could not be managed now and then to subserve the royal along with other important interests. Whatever the particular influences working to bring about their election to parliament for the county, royal officials and retainers undoubtedly were returned from time to time as knights of the shire in the period under review. In Richard II's reign, however, these

[14] When elected to the parliament of January 1380 neither Sir William Bussy nor John de Boys was a J.P., although both had formerly held the commission of the peace, the former in Kesteven, the latter in Lindsey. Sir John de Tothby and Sir Robert de Leake were not J.P.s when returned in 1381. Leake became one in Holland a year later; but Tothby was again not a J.P. when re-elected to the parliament of May 1382, nor was his fellow-knight, Sir William Armyn. The latter was still not a J.P. when returned in 1385 along with Sir Philip de Tilney. The latter had not yet become a J.P. when elected to the Merciless Parliament of 1388; nor was his colleague on this occasion, Walter Tailboys, a J.P.
[15] Neither of the two knights of the shire in March 1416 was then a J.P. in Lincolnshire. The senior knight, Sir Robert Hilton, was a J.P. in the East Riding of Yorkshire and in the liberty of Beverley, but was never appointed to the commission in Lincolnshire. His fellow-knight, William Tirwhit, became a J.P. for Lindsey only in 1432.

occasions were few, and, in such instances as there were, the effect of an additional personal connection generally needs to be taken into the reckoning.[16]

Now and then there is evidence to suggest a close relationship between a particular knight of the shire and some member of the parliamentary peerage resident or controlling property in the county. Sir John Auncell of Poynton, elected four times running, first to Edward III's last parliament early in 1377, in October later in the same year to Richard II's first parliament, to the Gloucester parliament of 1378, and then again to Westminster in 1379, from October 1377 until his death in the autumn of 1380 the Exchequer lessee of the royal castle and manor of Somerton and a moiety of Carlton-le-Moorland at 50 marks a year (perhaps the greatest single one of the leases of royal property in Lincolnshire at this time), was a servant of Archbishop Neville of York and a justice of the peace in the archiepiscopal franchises of Beverley and Ripon as well as in Kesteven.[17] Sir John de Tothby, shire-knight in 1381 and re-elected in 1382, was the archbishop's tenant (by knight service) at Tothby and in his manors of Lissington and Rigsby.[18] Sir Walter Tailboys of Kyme, shire-knight in 1383, 1386, and in the Merciless Parliament of 1388, who was related through his mother with the Umfravilles, was to be one of

[16] William Spayne of Boston, knight of the shire at Northampton in November 1380 and in the Westminster parliament of October 1382, at these times was collector of customs and subsidies in the parts of Holland. A wool merchant himself, he had been a royal wool-factor in 1347, a purveyor of victuals for Calais in 1356 and of fish for the royal household in 1360 (CFR, 1347–56, 9; ibid., 1356–68, 4–5; CPR 1358–61, 451). He was a collector of the 1377 poll-tax in Boston (CFR, 1369–77, 389), was sheriff of Lincolnshire in 1378–9, and was again holding this office at the time of his death in the spring of 1385 (ibid., 1377–83, 113; ibid., 1383–91, 76, 93). He was deputy to the Chief Butler of England at Boston by 4 November 1382 (CPR, 1381–5, 180). Spayne's closest connections, however, were with the Duke of Lancaster.

Sir John de Moulton, M.P. in 1373, 1383 (October) and 1384 (April), was a former retainer and eventually an executor of Humphrey de Bohun, Earl of Hereford, Essex and Northampton (ob. 16 January 1373). In December 1373 he was retained by Edward III with an annuity of 100 marks, first payable at the Exchequer but in April 1375 made chargeable on the royal revenues from Lincolnshire and in January 1378 confirmed as such by Richard II (CPR, 1370–4, 375; ibid., 1374–7, 92; ibid., 1377–81, 111). It was almost certainly this Sir John de Moulton who was made Mayor of Bordeaux by Edward III on 9 April 1375 and apparently held office there until superseded on 18 April 1382 (T. Carte, Catalogue des Rolles Gascons, François et Normands, i, 162), and who by October 1384 had become lieutenant of the Marshal of England, which he still was in November 1385 (CCR, 1381–5, 431; ibid., 1385–9, 31; CPR, 1381–5, 509). He died in May 1388 and was buried in Lincoln Cathedral (A. Gibbons, Early Lincoln Wills, 62).

Sir John Bussy, M.P. in 1383 and in each of Richard II's last nine parliaments (September 1388–January 1398), sheriff of Lincolnshire in 1383–4, 1385–6 and 1390–1, was retained by Richard II as a "King's knight" on 4 December 1391 and granted an annuity of 40 marks. By 1397 he was a member of the royal Council. He had been a member of John of Gaunt's retinue, however, from about 1382, and in 1394 he became Chief Steward of the Duchy of Lancaster north of Trent. He also had his connections with the De la Poles and the Beaumont family (see my biography of Bussy in Lincolnshire Architectural and Archaeological Society, Reports and Papers, Vol. 7, part 1, pp. 27–45).

[17] Regarding Auncell's interest in Somerton, see CFR, 1377–83, 16, 221, 235; CPR, 1377–81, 61, 377, 564. For his connection with Archbishop Neville of York, see CPR, 1374–7, 224, 227, 240, 314; ibid., 1377–81, 47, 90–1, 97.

[18] R. C. Dudding, op. cit., p. 59; Feudal Aids, iii, 238.

the overseers of the will of Robert Lord Willoughby of Eresby in 1396.[19] Three years later, Sir Gerald de Suthill of Redbourne, shire-knight in 1391 and 1402, was to act in a similar capacity on behalf of Philip Lord Darcy, and Sir Henry de Retford, shire-knight in 1401, 1402, and at Coventry in 1404, was his fellow-overseer of Lord Darcy's testament.[20]

The nobleman who, directly or indirectly, could exert the greatest amount of pressure on the Lincolnshire elections in the last quarter of the fourteenth century would seem to have been John of Gaunt, Duke of Lancaster, eldest surviving son of Edward III and premier peer of England, the possessor of the great appanage of the Duchy of Lancaster, and, as such, the dispenser of an enormous patronage in offices and fees: a born schemer if an uneasy one, imaginative, thrustful, and eventually circumspect in his public policies. Although Lincolnshire saw little of his person, the ducal influence was ever present. He held, among other things, the considerable rights and lands there that had once belonged to the Lacies. By his first marriage, with Blanche of Lancaster, he had come into their title of Earl of Lincoln. He had many rent-paying tenants in the county, and also men holding their lands of him by the tenure in chivalry, which meant enjoyment of the wardship and disposal in marriage of a tenant if he succeeded when still under age. Bolingbroke Castle had been the birthplace of his son and heir, the later Henry IV. Even his mistress, Katherine Swynford, whom he eventually made his third Duchess, was a Lincolnshire lady, if only by adoption. Three out of the Duke's last five most important estate-managers (the chief stewards) north of Trent, and this during the greater part of the twenty years before his death in 1399, were Lincolnshire men.[21] It would be a matter for astonishment if Lancaster's officials or mere retainers were not to be found among the Lincolnshire knights of the shire in the later years of the fourteenth century, when the Duke's interest in politics was constantly of the keenest.

Either advantage was not always pressed or the electoral suffrages of the gentry were not always automatically commandeered, but in the first half of the reign of Richard II oftener than not a ducal official or retainer was not elected to parliament. The exceptions were Sir Ralph de Rochford, a member of the Lancastrian military retinue, who was elected in 1379[22]; William Spayne of Boston, a wool-exporter in a big way of business and, between 1367 and 1375 and again from 1377 until his death in 1385, a collector of royal customs

---

[19] Tailboys was a great-nephew of Gilbert de Umfraville, third Earl of Angus (*CFR*, *1430–7*, 328; *CCR*, *1392–6*, 102; Harleian Society, *Lincolnshire Pedigrees*, iii, 945). A. Gibbons, *op. cit.*, 91. Lord Willoughby was regularly summoned to parliament from 1376 until his death in August 1396.

[20] A. Gibbons, *op. cit.*, 98. Lord Darcy was summoned to all Richard II's parliaments, and died on 24 April 1399.

[21] Sir William Hawley of Utterby, from 1 November 1379 probably to 1386 (he was certainly in office in July 1383); Sir Philip Tilney, in office from 20 April 1389 to mid-1394; Sir John Bussy from mid-1394 until early in 1398 (R. Somerville, *History of the Duchy of Lancaster*, i, 367).

[22] *John of Gaunt's Register*, *op. cit.*, i, 32.

and subsidies in the port of Boston, who was the Duke's feodary (or warden of fees and franchises) in Lincolnshire and Nottinghamshire at the time of his election as knight of the shire to the Northampton parliament of 1380 and to the second of the two Westminster parliaments of 1382, and who, on the latter occasion (at least), was also acting as purveyor of supplies of stockfish at Boston for the ducal household[23]; Sir John Bussy, one of the Duke's knights bachelor, who was elected in 1383[24]; and Sir Philip de Tilney of Tydd who was elected in 1385 and to the Merciless Parliament of 1388, when the Duke himself was in Spain.

In the second half of Richard II's reign it was a rather different story. To the Cambridge parliament of September 1388 Bussy and Tilney went up together, and also to the next parliament which met at Westminster in January 1390, Tilney by this time having been recently appointed as the Duke's steward of his estates north of Trent and as an *ex officio* member of his council.[25] This proved to be Tilney's last election, although parliament was to meet again

---

[23] For Spayne's activities in the export-trade in wool, see *CFR, 1347–56*, 9; *ibid., 1369–77*, 235; *ibid., 1377–83*, 41, 59; *CPR, 1350–54*, 144; *CCR, 1349–54*, 7, 344, 458, 571; *ibid., 1377–81*, 30. For his connection with John of Gaunt see *John of Gaunt's Register, 1372–76*, ed. S. Armitage Smith, i, 56, 65; ii, 27, 188; *John of Gaunt's Register, 1379–83*, ed. F. C. Lodge and R. Somerville, i, 25; ii, 58–9, 216, 256; R. Somerville, *op. cit.*, i, 128n, 376. William Spayne of Boston was feodary of the Lancastrian estates in Nottinghamshire by 3 December 1371, and by 5 February 1372 in Lincolnshire as well. He occupied both offices concurrently until June 1384. His office of feodary or steward of fees in Lincolnshire was renewed by indenture on 7 April 1383, during the Duke's pleasure; the lordship of Bolingbroke and the Fens were excluded from his commission, but he was to be surveyor of all bailiffs elsewhere in the county. See note 16 above.
[24] *John of Gaunt's Register*, ed. S. Armitage Smith, i, 9.
[25] Tilney was appointed Chief Steward in the northern parts of the Duchy of Lancaster on 20 April 1389 and held office until his death shortly before 18 July 1394, when his will was proved (R. Somerville, *op. cit.*, i, 125n, 367; A. Gibbons, *op. cit.*, 83). He had been made deputy to the King's Chief Butler at Boston by November 1378 (*CPR, 1377–81*, 282), following his brother Frederick, merchant of Boston, who had also been collector of customs and subsidies at Boston in 1351–4, 1363–5, 1372 and 1377. Sir Philip retained the deputy-butlership until November 1382. He was heriff of Cambridgeshire and Huntingdonshire in 1383–4 and of Lincolnshire in 1386–7 (*CFR, 1383–91*, 7, 151). On 11 March 1390 he was made a J.P. in the Lancastrian liberties in Yorkshire, three days after being appointed a commissioner of oyer and terminer, following a complaint by the Duke of Lancaster of long continued infringements of his franchisal rights in the castle and bailey of Lincoln by the civic authorities (*CPR, 1388–92*, 140, 220, 270), and on 11 May following he was again made a special commissioner at Lincoln, regarding an alleged persistent invasion of the dean and chapter's rights of jurisdiction over the cathedral close, again by the mayor and bailiffs of the city (*ibid.*, 271). He served on a considerable number of royal commissions, for example, on those of array and of sewers. Early in 1386 he was made an executor of Richard de Ravenser, an important Chancery clerk who had been keeper of the hanaper of the Chancery from 1357 to 1379, treasurer to Queen Philippa from 1362 to 1367, and archdeacon of Lincoln from 1368 (*CCR, 1389–92*, 148; A. Gibbons, *op. cit.*, 68); and in July 1391 Sir Robert Swillington, chamberlain to John of Gaunt in 1376–7, also made Tilney an executor of his will (A. Gibbons, *op. cit.*, 77; R. Somerville, *op. cit.*, i, 364). In 1387, 1388 and 1389, Tilney was Alderman of the Gild of Corpus Christi in Boston, of which his brother, his brother's wife, and his own wife and children were members (P. Thompson, *op. cit.*, 117; *CPR, 1388–92*, 9). He was also one of those tenants of Richard II's Queen, Anne of Bohemia, who were licensed on 23 September 1392 to establish the Gild of St. Mary and a gild-chantry in Boston parish church (*CPR, 1388–92*, 192, 195). It was in the churchyard at Boston that Tilney elected to be buried, according to the terms of his will, which, drawn on 4 April 1394, was proved by the Bishop of Lincoln on 18 July following (A. Gibbons, *op. cit.*, 83).

four times before he died in 1394; but Bussy of Hougham quite monopolized one of the county seats until his execution at Bristol in July 1399, shortly before Richard II's deposition. Although, in 1391, Bussy became a *royal* retainer for life with a substantial fee of 40 marks a year charged on the king's revenues in Lincolnshire, and eventually was an intimate member of the royal council and, perhaps one may say, permanent Speaker in parliament, he remained so influential a member of the Lancastrian entourage as to be promoted to follow Tilney as chief steward in the northern parts of the Duchy, an office which he continued to hold until the end of his parliamentary career, although not to the end of his life.[26] Bussy was no ordinary man. Long-standing retainer of John of Gaunt and now a retainer of Richard II too, he was a great power in Lincolnshire, and in the country at large he was a figure of some political stature: a symbol of that alliance between the still young, increasingly ambitious and autocratic king and the eldest of his royal uncles, upon the continuation of which in the 1390s to a large extent depended the internal peace of the kingdom.

It is worth noting that none of the four men who were Bussy's later fellow knights of the shire in Richard II's reign—John de Rochford (in November 1390, 1394, September 1397), Gerard de Suthill (in 1391), Robert de Cumberworth (in 1393, 1395), Sir John de Copuldyke (in January 1397)—was a retainer of the king, but that certainly one and almost certainly another two were members of the Lancastrian affinity. Evidence of this is the alacrity with which, in one way and another, Henry of Bolingbroke, Lancaster's heir, recognized their existence, or perhaps we should say their support, after his return from banishment to claim the inheritance of which Richard II had dispossessed him on Lancaster's death early in 1399, and when he had made himself king. Rochford, Suthill, and Copuldyke all sat (by special summons) in great councils assembled by Henry IV in the early years of his reign, as well as in one or another of his earliest parliaments.[27] Sir John de Rochford, a kinsman of Sir Philip Tilney (we may note), went as shire-knight to Henry IV's first parliament in 1399 and was there and then re-appointed steward of the Duchy of Lancaster honour of Bolingbroke, continuing to hold this post until May 1407. He had already been John of Gaunt's steward in the manor of Ingoldmells in 1395–6. His brother, Ralph, had long been a member of Henry IV's personal company, even in the days of his expeditions to Prussia and Lithuania and the Holy Land in the early 1390s, and was now one of the

---

[26] Bussy had been replaced in the chief stewardship by the spring of 1398.
[27] *Proceedings and Ordinances of the Privy Council*, ed. N. H. Nicolas, i, 158, 160.

select group of the knights of the King's Chamber.[28] Gerard de Suthill of Redbourne, who was to be for a second time knight of the shire in Henry IV's third parliament in 1402, was knighted by Henry in the Tower on the eve of his coronation.[29] Sir John de Copuldyke of Harrington (near Spilsby), who was to be elected to the Westminster parliaments of 1401, 1404 and 1406, was Henry's first appointee to the shrievalty of Lincolnshire on 22 August 1399, that is, over a month before Richard II's deposition had even been accomplished.[30]

After 1399, when Henry IV possessed the Duchy of Lancaster as his own private inheritance and kept its administration separate from that of the Crown-lands, no proper duchy official of importance was elected for Lincolnshire to any of the parliaments of Henry IV and Henry V for which the returns have survived. But a majority of the knights of the shire for Lincolnshire under Henry IV were certainly retainers of his, and, whatever its dimensions and by whatever methods its influence was brought to bear, the duchy interest in the county is likely to have helped promote their election. The man who accompanied Sir John de Copuldyke to Westminster in 1401 and Sir Gerard de Suthill in 1402, and who went to the Coventry parliament of 1404 along with Sir Thomas Hawley of Utterby and Girsby (now himself retained as a king's

---

[28] R. Somerville, *op. cit.*, i, 575; *Lincolnshire Notes and Queries*, VII, 173. Regarding Sir Ralph de Rochford, see *Expeditions to Prussia and the Holy Land made by Henry, Earl of Derby, 1390–1 and 1392–3*, ed. L. Toulmin-Smith (pp. 51, 123, 131, 133, 138, 265) and Exchequer, Q.R., Accounts Various, Wardrobe, P.R.O., E.101/404/21. Sir John was sheriff of Lincolnshire in 1391–2, 1400–1 and 1409–10; Sir Ralph, in 1404–5 and 1407–8. Sir John served on many casual royal commissions, and under Henry IV was made a J.P. in Kesteven as well as Holland. On 18 February 1400 he was given for life the office of steward of all the Lincolnshire estates of the late Thomas Holland, Earl of Kent, Richard II's nephew, who had recently been executed for treason by the men of Cirencester (*CPR, 1399–1401*, 201). On 17 August 1401, Bishop Fordham of Ely made him (for life) constable of the castle of Wisbech and steward of his hallmoots and leets there and in certain episcopal lordships in Norfolk, appointments which were confirmed under the Great Seal (*ibid.*, 534). John Rochford was Alderman of the Corpus Christi Gild of Boston in 1381–6, 1391–4, 1397–9 and 1409. A collector of historical notes to the last, he died on 13 December 1410 (*Dictionary of National Biography*, XVII, 74).

[29] C. L. Kingsford, *Chronicles of London*, p. 48. While M.P. in 1402, Suthill was made sheriff of Lincolnshire (on 29 November). Between February 1385 and February 1386 only was he a J.P. in the East Riding of Yorkshire, but he was on the commission of the peace in Lindsey from February 1392 to November 1399 and from May 1401 until his death on 1 August 1410. He served on many occasional commissions.

[30] Sir John de Copuldyke had already been sheriff of Lincolnshire in 1393–4 and M.P. in January 1397. He became a J.P. in Holland in May 1401 and served until his death in 1408, in the meantime campaigning with Henry IV as a "King's knight" in the war in Wales against Owen Glendower (*CPR, 1401–5*, 307) and acting as escheator in Lincolnshire in 1406–7. He was a feoffee of William Lord Willoughby of Eresby in certain estates in Northants, Cambs. and Suffolk (*CCR, 1409–13*, 17, 20). He joined the Corpus Christi Gild of Boston between 1405 and his death (P. Thompson, *op. cit.*, 118). For Sir John's will, see A. Gibbons, *op. cit.*, 114. Dated Palm Sunday 1408, it was proved at Sleaford on 3 May following.

knight with a fee of £40 a year)[31] was Sir Henry de Retford of Castlethorpe and Carleton Paynell.   A member of the army which John of Gaunt had taken to Spain in 1386 as well as (since November 1393) a retainer of Richard II, Retford had found no difficulty in changing sides in 1399 and not over much trouble in getting his existing royal annuity confirmed by the new king.[32]   On the second of these three occasions of parliamentary service (in 1402) Retford was Speaker for the Lower House.   He had served in Henry IV's campaign in Scotland and, more recently, had been active in the royal expeditions against the great rising in Wales under Owen Glendower.   He was again to be in the field with Henry IV in 1405 when a royal army went north into Yorkshire to suppress the rebellion that was led by Archbishop Scrope of York and the young Earl Marshal (Thomas Mowbray), being then, in fact, one of the tribunal—a sort of court-martial—which pronounced sentence of execution against them.   Of the remaining five men who sat in parliament for Lincolnshire in Henry IV's reign, none received special fees as a royal retainer; but Sir Richard Hansard of South Kelsey, who went up to Westminster in

[31] Sir Thomas Hawley had already been M.P. for Lincolnshire in Henry IV's first parliament of 1399   His father, Sir William, when already a firm retainer of John of Gaunt, had been appointed on 1 November 1379 as chief steward of the Duchy of Lancaster north of Trent (excluding Lancashire) and, although superseded before he died at Bayonne in Aquitaine in 1387, was still in office in July 1383 (R. Somerville, *op. cit.*, i, 367; *John of Gaunt's Register, 1379–83, op. cit.*, i, 9, 14; ii, 331).   Sir Thomas was as a member of Henry IV's expedition to Scotland in the summer of 1400, and on 8 May 1401, by way of recompense and as a "King's knight," was granted for life an annuity of £40, charged on the royal Exchequer (*CPR, 1399–1401*, 486).   Immediately afterwards, he was made a J.P. in Lindsey and served until July 1408, except when he was sheriff of Lincolnshire (November 1405–6).   He continued to be a royal retainer in the next reign (*ibid., 1413–6*, 225) and joined Henry V's first expedition to Normandy in 1415, fighting in the Agincourt campaign with a retinue of two men-at-arms and six archers.   Pledges for repayment of his wages, including a sword decorated with ostrich feathers (valued at £22) which had been Henry V's when he was Prince of Wales, were not redeemed in favour of Hawley's executors until 1430–1 (N. H. Nicolas, *The Battle of Agincourt*, 380; App., 17).   Sir Thomas had died between 29 June 1419 (the date of his will, for which see *The Register of Archbishop Chichele*, ed. E. F. Jacob, ii, 191–5) and 20 May 1420 (when probate was allowed at Lambeth in the Prerogative Court of Canterbury in the Archbishop's presence).   It is worth noting that Sir Thomas and his fellow-M.P. in 1404, Sir Henry de Retford, had been associated in 1387 as executors to Sir Thomas's father, Sir William Hawley (Lincolnshire County Record Office, MS. Register of Bishop Buckingham of Lincoln, fol. 341ᵛ).

[32] Having served on Richard II's expedition to Scotland in 1385 with a retinue of one man-at-arms and two archers (*English Historical Review*, LXXIII, N. B. Lewis, "The Last Medieval Summons of the English Feudal Levy, 13 June 1385," 19), Retford had taken out "letters of general attorney" on 12 April 1386 as being about to accompany John of Gaunt's expedition to Spain.   He certainly went, for he was at Bayonne in Gascony in June 1387 (see the last reference in the previous note).   He was sheriff of Lincolnshire for only four weeks in November–December 1389 and again (for the usual year of office) from October 1392 to November 1393, immediately after which Richard II retained him for life at 40 marks a year.   Between September 1394 and April 1395 he was with Richard II's army in Ireland, and in April 1397 went on a royal embassy to Paris, Avignon and Rome, the unrealized aim of which was to end the papal schism.   In the following year, November 1397–8, he was again sheriff.   His royal annuity was renewed for life on 25 February 1401, after service in Scotland in the previous year.   He was once more sheriff of Lincolnshire in 1406–7.   He died shortly before June 1409.   (For references and further details of Retford's career, see my biography in *Lincolnshire Architectural and Archaeological Society, Reports and Papers*, Vol. 7, part 2).

January 1404, was a Duchy of Lancaster tenant.[33]   John Skipwith of Ormsby, who sat in successive parliaments in 1406 and 1407, in the interval between which he became controller of customs and subsidies at Boston, was uncle to William Lord Willoughby of Eresby, and his son married Lord Willoughby's daughter.[34] Evidently, this family connection was a close one. Lord Willoughby had supported Henry of Bolingbroke in the rebellion which brought him to the throne and was a member of the royal council. Sir Thomas de Willoughby, this Lord Willoughby's brother, who in 1411 was elected to the first parliament to meet after the peer's death, had been until recently one of two partners sharing the right to farm the petty customs at King's Lynn since the beginning of the reign.[35] Hansard, Skipwith and Willoughby were all again returned to parliament in the reign of Henry V.

Whatever influence on elections the Bishop of Lincoln was able to exert in these years is likely to have assisted those who stood well with the king.

[33] *Feudal Aids*, iii, 269. Sir Richard Hansard was also M.P. for Lincolnshire in the parliaments of 1413, November 1414, May 1421 and 1423. He was a J.P. in Lindsey from 1406 to 1423 and from 1424 to 1432, royal escheator in Lincolnshire in 1415–6, and sheriff in 1419–20. In September 1407 he had acted with Suthill as arbiter between the priory of Newstead-on-Ancolm and its tenants in the manor of Cadney Howsham. In October 1411 at Wrawby he had supported Justice Tirwhit at a "love-day" between him and William Lord Roos. According to a petition presented in the next parliament (November 1411), Tirwhit admitted to bringing a threateningly large retinue and force to the meeting, asked the King's pardon and offered to apologize to his opponent. He also undertook to take Sir Richard Hansard and a few other friends to make a special apology to Lord Roos at Belvoir Castle for their part in the affair (*Rot. Parl.*, iii, 649–51). In November 1414 Hansard had farmed (for £8 a year, payable in the Exchequer) the estates of the alien priory of Winhale, a cell (in his own parish of South Kelsey) of the Norman abbey of Séez, the lease being renewed for 24 years in 1423 (*CFR, 1413–22*, 81; *ibid.*, *1422–30*, 65). He served on a number of local royal commissions, for example, of array, of sewers, and for raising Crown loans. He died in 1428.

[34] John Skipwith, second son of William Skipwith, a justice of the Common Bench, became the controller of customs and subsidies at Boston on 1 March 1407, was confirmed in office at Gloucester on 3 November following but superseded a few weeks later (on 17 December following) (*CPR, 1405–8*, 297, 373, 382). His sister Alice married Robert, fourth Baron Willoughby, and was mother of William, the fifth Baron. The latter's daughter married John Skipworth's son Thomas (W. O. Massingberd, *History of the Parish of Ormsby-cum-Ketsby*, 67, 81; *Harleian Society, Lincolnshire Pedigrees*, iii, 895). John Skipwith's wife was Alice, daughter of Sir Frederick Tilney of Boston, and he had close relations with the Tilney family. He was also apparently on good terms with his sister Margaret and her husband, Sir Henry Vavasour of Hazlewood (Yorks.) and Cockerington (Lincs.): in 1414 Sir Henry left him a black horse, and in 1415 his sister bequeathed him all her nets for catching fish and foxes (Surtees Society, *Testamenta Eboracensia*, i, 363). In 1397 Skipwith had been seriously at odds with John Lord Welles (*CCR, 1396–99*, 130). He also had a dispute, in 1414, with Sir Thomas Hawley over the will of Thomas Mussenden esquire, of which Skipwith was an executor (*ibid.*, *1413–9*, 188–9; N. H. Nicolas, *Testamenta Vetusta*, 162), in spite of the fact that one of his sons, Patrick Skipwith, had married one of Hawley's daughters, and that Hawley had been one of his feoffees (J. O. Massingberd, *op. cit.*, 74–5). John Skipwith was sheriff of Lincolnshire in 1394–5 and a J.P. in Lindsey from May 1404 to February 1407, and he served on a number of other, more casual royal commissions in the county. He was M.P. in 1406, 1407 (at Gloucester) and in 1414 (at Leicester). He died on 15 July 1415 and was buried at Covenham (J. O. Massingberd, *loc. cit.*).

[35] Sir Thomas de Willoughby of Boston, M.P. for Lincolnshire in 1411 and 1414 (November), was the third son of Robert Lord Willoughby of Eresby who died in 1396. After being divorced in 1381 from Katherine, daughter of Sir Thomas Friskney (A. Gibbons, *op. cit.*, 91), he married Elizabeth, a daughter of his step-mother Elizabeth (herself the daughter of William Lord Latimer) by her first husband, John Lord Neville of Raby (*The Complete Peerage*, ed. H. A. Doubleday and Lord Howard de Walden, vii, 474–9;

Bishop Buckingham, in origin a professional civil servant, who came to the see in 1363, had been politically of little account long before his resignation in 1397. But his successor, Henry Beaufort, who was bishop until 1404, was Henry IV's half-brother, and young Beaufort's successor, Philip Repingdon, was Henry IV's confessor and close friend. No particular member of the episcopal household or retinue during this period, however, has it been found possible to identify among the parliamentary representatives of Lincolnshire.

The reign of Henry V (1413–22) saw the resumption of the war against France with a greater measure of studied concentration of purpose and of urgent activity than had characterized even its successful episodes in the previous century. The war entailed long periods of absence on campaign on the part of the king and of many of the more energetic members of the nobility and of the gentry of the country as a whole. What effect this had on the parliamentary representation of Lincolnshire between 1415 and 1419, we cannot say, because the accidental gaps in the electoral returns to the parliaments of these years are unfortunately especially wide for this county. (For only one of the five parliaments which met in these years have they survived, that of March 1416). But the continued absence of the type of royal retainer which had so prominently figured in the county representation in the first half of Henry IV's reign, is worth noting among the knights of the shire whose names happen to have come down to us. Although more young men than had generally been the case served in those parliaments of Henry V's reign for which we have returns for Lincolnshire, only one of them is known to have joined Henry V's first expedition to France in 1415 when he took Harfleur and humiliated the French army at Agincourt:[36] William Tirwhit of Kettleby

---

[36] Sir Thomas Hawley (M.P. in 1399 and 1404) and Sir Thomas de Willoughby (M.P. in 1411 and 1414) were members of the royal retinue for Henry V's first French expedition, but neither was a young man.

Papal Letters, V, 129; *CPR, 1452–61*, 396; A. Gibbons, *op. cit.*, 90–1). Thomas may well have been "the lorde Willuby brother" who was knighted by Henry IV on 12 October 1399, the eve of his coronation (C. L. Kingsford, *Chronicles of London*, 48). Certainly he had been knighted by 17 December 1399, when he and John Toup were given the right to farm the petty customs at Lynn for five years (as from Michaelmas 1399) for an annual sum of £114 payable in the Exchequer, a grant which was extended on 28 October 1404 for six years (as from Easter 1404) (*CFR, 1399–1405*, 32, 281). His fellow-farmer at Lynn was in the custody of the sheriffs of London in March 1405 when, as a royal debtor, he was ordered to be transferred to the Fleet prison (*CCR, 1402–5*, 448). Sir Thomas himself was twice pardoned outlawry, once in January 1404 for debt to a London mercer, again in November 1414 for a debt to a London draper (*CPR, 1401–5*, 339; *ibid., 1413–6*, 215). He had been sheriff of Lincolnshire in 1403–4, his brother, William Lord Willoughby, being one of his sureties (*CFR, 1399–1405*, 231), and he was a J.P. in Holland from May 1406 to February 1407 and from February 1412 until his death in 1417. He was also made a commissioner for sewers between Boston and Wainfleet and in Lindsey in November 1410, and in Holland in February 1412. On 5 July 1415 he took out royal "letters of protection" as being about to accompany Henry V, as a member of his retinue, on his first expedition to France. In 1404 and 1416 he was Alderman or Warden of the Gild of St. George in Boston (*CPR, 1401–5*, 388; *ibid., 1416–22*, 62), and he held the same office in the Gild of Corpus Christi there in 1406 and 1407 (P. Thompson, *op. cit.*, 118). (For a brief abstract of his will, dated 20 August 1417, see A. Gibbons, *op. cit.*, 145.)

(near Brigg) and Buslingthorpe (near Market Rasen); and Tirwhit's retinue comprised no more than three unmounted archers.[37]   This was the period in which the Hiltons of Swine (in Holderness) got elected, Sir Robert[38] to the parliament of March 1416, Sir Godfrey[39] to that of May 1421, the former seemingly making do with election in Lincolnshire and perhaps exploiting

[37] William Tirwhit, son of Robert Tirwhit, Justice of the King's Bench, was M.P. for Lincolnshire in 1416, 1423 and 1426.   As an esquire, he served in Henry V's retinue on the French expedition of 1415 (N. H. Nicolas, *The Battle of Agincourt*, 385), and in 1420–1, by which time he had been knighted, he was made captain of Montjoie, St. Germain-en-Laye, and Poissy (T. Carte, *op. cit.*, i, 353).   He probably did not campaign abroad after Henry V's death in 1422, certainly not continuously, but it was not until 1428 that he began to be appointed to local royal commissions.   He was a J.P. in Lindsey from July 1432 until his death in 1450–1, in the meantime acting as sheriff of Yorkshire in 1435–6. Sir William's mother was Alice, daughter of Roger Kelke of Kelke (Yorks.) and Barnetby (near Brigg, Lincs.), and his wife was Constance, daughter of Sir Anselin St. Quinton of Brandsburton (near Beverley, Yorks.).   His Yorkshire ties were probably strong: he founded a chantry at Beverley Minster.   He also built a chantry-chapel at Higham (in Waltham-stow, Essex) and a hospital of two chaplains and seven poor bedesmen at Glanford-Brigg (in Wrawby, Lincs.) (*CPR, 1441–6*, 41).   His main estates were in Lincolnshire: the manors' of Buslingthorpe, Kettleby Thorpe, Firsby, Nettleton, Bigby and Wrawby, and lands in Stallingborough, Scawby, Ingham, Fillingham and Elsham (*Feudal Aids*, iii, *passim*).

[38] Sir Robert Hilton, M.P. for Lincolnshire in 1416 and for Yorkshire in 1419, 1425, 1426 and 1427, was sheriff of Lincolnshire in 1414–5 and of Yorkshire in 1417–8, 1423–4 and 1427–8.   He held lands in Lincolnshire at Fulstow (near Lough) and Aylesby (near Grimsby), but usually he lived at Swine in Holderness (*Feudal Aids*, iii, 261, 354, 362). As a "King's esquire," he was granted for life by Henry IV on 7 November 1399 a retaining fee of £32 a year, chargeable on the wool-customs of Hull (*CPR, 1399–1401*, 63).   This royal annuity was confirmed in June, 1413 and February, 1423 (*ibid., 1413–16*, 43; *ibid., 1422–9*, 55).   In the meantime, Hilton served on many local royal commissions, mainly in the East Riding of Yorkshire, being a J.P. there and in the liberty of St. John of Beverley from 1401 until 1424, in the West Riding also in 1414–5, and in Yorkshire as a whole in 1419.   He was never a J.P. in Lincolnshire.   He died sometime between 7 December 1429, when he made his will, and 22 December 1431, when it was proved at York.   He left no male issue, two daughters being his coheirs.   His wife Joan, daughter of Sir Robert and sister of Sir Marmaduke Constable of Flamborough, died a widow in 1432 (Surtees Society, *Testamenta Eboracensia*, ii, 16, 23).

[39] Sir Godfrey Hilton, M.P. for Lincolnshire in May 1421, by his marriage with Hawise, daughter of Sir Andrew Luttrell, sister and heir of Sir Godfrey Luttrell of Irnham, and widow of Sir Thomas de Beelsby (who died in 1415), came into lands in Lincolnshire (at Irnham, Horsington, and Stickford), Yorkshire (at Hooton Pagnell) and Nottinghamshire (at West Bridgford and Holme Pierpoint) (A. C. Sinclair, *A History of Beelsby*, p. 26; *Feudal Aids*, iii, 341; *CFR, 1413–22*, 277, 425; *CCR, 1422–9*, 8).   Hawise died on 24 March 1422. Sometime between 1426 and 1436, Sir Godfrey married Eleanor, daughter of John Lord Welles and widow of Hugh, son of Thomas de Poynings, Lord St. John, of Basing (Hants.), as a result of which marriage he lived at Chawton (Hants.) as well as at Irnham (*The Complete Peerage*, ed. G. H. White, XI, 330).   Besides Chawton, he held, in right of his wife, the manors of Shirborne St. John and Abbotston and the advowson of Selbourne Priory (Hants.) and the manors of Barnham, Bridham and Middleton (Sussex) (*CCR, 1454–61*, 374–5).   He continued to hold (by the courtesy) his first wife's lands in Lincolnshire and Yorkshire until his death in 1459 (*CFR, 1452–61*, 248), and he also held land in his own family's Yorkshire estates at Swine and Winestead (in Holderness) after his brother Sir Robert's death (*CPR, 1429–36*, 275).   Sir Godfrey seems to have made something of a military career under Henry V and Henry VI, royal letters of protection or of general attorney being issued to him, as being about to proceed to France, in 1418, 1421, 1423, 1424, 1433 and 1434 (T. Carte, *op. cit.*, ii, 235, 242, 249, 256, 279, 282).   In May 1425 when the muster of his retinue (among others) was ordered to be held at Dover and Calais, it numbered no fewer than 40 men-at-arms and 120 archers (*CPR, 1422–9*, 299, 302). It may well have been military preoccupations which largely prevented his appointment to any royal commissions at all until 1442 when he first became a J.P. in Hampshire, an office which he retained until his death in 1459.   In 1446 he also became a J.P. in Kesteven, where he continued to serve until November 1458 (*CPR, passim*).

his very recent status as sheriff. (Sir Robert had been sheriff of Lincolnshire from 10 November 1414 to 1 December 1415.) He was not even a justice of the peace in Lincolnshire, nor in 1421 was his brother, Sir Godfrey. Most of the other knights of the shire of Henry V's reign were J.P.s, but they do not seem to be a very interesting lot.[40] Generally, they appear to have been content with the "small change" of squirearchal experience. Sir Thomas Cumberworth of Somerby, knight of the shire in the Leicester parliament of 1414 and the Westminster parliaments of 1420 and December 1421 and (later on) of 1425 and 1437, is an exception. He was soon (in December 1422) to be required by Henry VI's Council to take charge of Charles, Duke of Orleans, the most important of the royal prisoners of war taken at Agincourt, which he did from May 1423, and, after Orleans (in December 1429), of John, Duke of Bourbon, who died in his custody in January 1434.[41] Sir Godfrey Hilton of Irnham is another exception.

[40] For John Bell, M.P. in 1413, see pages 72-3 and note 44; for Sir Richard Hansard, M.P. in 1413, 1414 (November), and 1421 (May), note 33; for John Skipwith, M.P. in 1414 (April), note 34; for Sir Thomas Cumberworth, M.P. in 1414 (April), 1420 and 1421 (December), note 41; for Sir Thomas de Willoughby, M.P. in 1414 (November), note 35.
Sir Robert Hagbech, M.P. in 1420, held the manor of Hagbech Hall in Whaplode and lands in Holbeach (Lincs.), Washingley (Hunts.), Litlington (Cambs.), and also in Norfolk and Suffolk (*Feudal Aids*, ii, 476; vi, 408; *CCR, 1409-13*, 14; *CFR, 1437-45*, 302). He was a J.P. in Holland from June 1410 to February 1412 and from November 1413 to July 1424, in the meantime acting as sheriff of Cambridgeshire and Huntingdonshire in 1413-4. He was sometimes a royal commissioner for sewers, arrays and Crown loans, mainly in Holland (*CPR, passim*). In June 1406 he had been embroiled with Sir John Littlebury, William Lord Roos and William Lord Willoughby standing surety in Chancery for his good behaviour (*CCR, 1405-9*, 134). A retainer of the Duke of Clarence, Sir John Colville, in 1420 made him one of his feoffees in lands in the Isle of Ely and Norfolk (*ibid., 1419-22*, 107).
Richard Welby, of Moulton, M.P. in 1421 (December), was the son of Roger Welby, who was sheriff of Lincolnshire in 1396-7 and died in 1410, and brother of Adelard Welby, B.C.L. (A. Gibbons, *op. cit.*, 144). Frequently a commissioner for sewers in Holland from 1411, and sometimes also in Kesteven, he only became a J.P. (in Holland) in February 1422, but he remained a J.P. until March 1444. In 1412 he was a member of the Gild of Holy Trinity in Boston (*CPR, 1408-13*, 362). He was sworn to keep the peace along with many other Lincolnshire notables in 1434. He died in 1455. His son (Richard) and grandson (another Richard) were M.P.s for Lincolnshire, respectively, in 1450 and 1472.
[41] N. H. Nicolas, *Proceedings and Ordinances of the Privy Council*, iii, 10, 79, 134; iv, 44, 51, 201; *Rot. Parl.*, IV, 339, 438; *CPR, 1429-36*, 461. Sir Thomas Cumberworth, M.P. for Lincolnshire in 1414 (April), 1420, 1421 (December), 1425 and 1437, was the son and heir of Sir Robert de Cumberworth, M.P. in 1393 and 1395. Sir Thomas was a J.P. in Lindsey from January 1414 to February 1416 and from February 1419 to his death in 1451, in the meantime being sheriff of Lincolnshire in 1415-6 and 1430-1. He served on many royal commissions in Lincolnshire, especially commissions of array and for raising Crown loans. It was during his second shrievalty that, in January 1431, a settlement was made in a dispute (over tenements in Theddlethorpe and elsewhere in Lincolnshire) between Walter Tailboys senior and Sir John Keighley, Keighley being supported by Humphrey, Duke of Gloucester. Cumberworth had clearly been Tailboys' friend in this business (*CCR, 1422-9*, 329; *ibid., 1429-35*, 110, 114-5). Later in the same year (in March) he backed up Hamond Sutton, a merchant-stapler of Lincoln, when Sutton had to undertake to appear in Chancery to answer certain demands of his fellow-staplers at Calais (*ibid.*, 112). Cumberworth made his will on 15 February 1451 and died shortly afterwards, being buried at Somerby where he had established a chantry. He made (among others) small bequests to Cardinal Kemp, Lord Cromwell and members of his own family and household. The will contained the unusual provision that "my body ly still, my mowth opyn unhild [uncovered] XXIV owrys, and after laid on bere withowtyn anythyng y opon to covert bot a shert and a blak cloth with a white crosse of cloth of gold, bot I wyl my kyste [chest, coffin] be made and stande by, and at my bereall giff it to hym that fillis my grave"(A. Gibbons, *op. cit.*, 174).

The later parliaments of Henry V sometimes did little more than pass time, and perhaps this generated an apathy which had its effect on the quality of the men elected, in Lincolnshire as well as elsewhere. With the king, and also most of the great men who counted, out of reach, it may have seemed to many that, for the time being, there was likely to be little of interest in parliamentary service, and those knights and esquires whose names were something to conjure with in politics either actually were, or seem to have been, "otherwise engaged" when parliaments met in the last few years before Henry V's death, except when in the parliament of May–June 1421 the king himself was at home in England and present—the only one of the last five parliaments of his reign which he attended. This was when young Sir Godfrey Hilton was returned for Lincolnshire. His homage for his wife's lands at Irnham and elsewhere was taken while he was up at Westminster. Four years later (in 1425) he was to go to France to join the Duke of Bedford, the Regent, with a very large retinue of forty men-at-arms and one hundred and twenty archers. His main future interests were no more to be in Lincolnshire than his origins had been.[42]

Of the knights of the shire of this period of the early fifteenth century, the least socially estimable in the eyes of his contemporaries may well have been the man who was elected (along with Sir Richard Hansard) to Henry V's first parliament, held at Westminster in May 1413: John Bell, merchant of Boston, who, so far as is known, sat only this once. As long ago as 1383 he had been appointed the king's receiver-general for the estates of the earldom of Richmond in Lincolnshire.[43] From 1390 until 1420, apart from a few months in 1401 and between February 1410 and April 1413, Bell was a collector, in the port of Boston and in the customs-area between Wisbech and Grimsby, of either tunnage and poundage or the customs and subsidies on exported wool, other staple commodities, and cloth, and the petty customs; for the greater part of these thirty years he was collector of *all* these various royal imposts levied on merchandise passing into or out of that port and its district.[44] In the first year or so of Henry IV he had been the king's alnager, that is, official inspector and measurer of cloth manufactured for the market and collector of the fees for this service, in the parts of Holland.[45] Two years passed, and in November

[42] See above, note 39.

[43] *CFR, 1383–91*, 5, 22.

[44] John Bell was one of the two collectors of the petty customs, the wool customs, and the subsidy on cloth at Boston from May 1390 to February 1397, from August 1401 to May 1403, from December 1404 to October 1405, from February 1407 to February 1410, and from April 1413 to October 1420; and he was one of the two collectors of tunnage and poundage between June 1390 and March 1401, between March 1403 and February 1410, and between April 1413 and October 1420 (*CFR, passim*). His occupation of these two offices of revenue-collection coincided between June 1390 and February 1397, March and May 1403, December 1404 and October 1405, February 1407 and February 1410, and between April 1413 and October 1420.

[45] *CFR, 1399–1405*, 38, 89 (Bell held the office of alnager from 17 October 1399 to 30 November 1400).

1402 he became deputy at Boston to the Chief Butler of England, whose job it was to control the royal rights of prisage of wines in the ports and to buy for the royal household.[46]   Two years later still, and in 1404–5 Bell was the king's escheator in the county as a whole.[47]   On and off, during the last twenty years of his life, he was a justice of the peace in Holland.[48]   He obviously had a head for business and, as doubtless he profited others, so clearly he profited himself.   He lived in Boston and became Alderman of the Corpus Christi Gild, holding this socially attractive position for three years together, from 1395 to 1398.[49]   As far as is known, he held no land outside the town in his own clear right; but as early as in 1392 he had had the wherewithal to lease for ten years from the trustees of Richard II's Queen (Anne of Bohemia) the manor of Wykes in Donington (between Boston and Spalding), a parcel of the Lincolnshire lands of the honour of Richmond (of which Boston itself was a member, and of which he himself may still have been receiver-general), at the seemingly very high rent of £100 a year.[50]   Following this, soon after Henry IV's accession (in November 1399), he had acquired the wardship of a third of the manors of Skirbeck and Beausolace and, later again (in June 1408), the wardship of lands in Algerkirk and Fossdyke, all of which were also tenancies of the Richmond fee.[51]   Apparently, he did not succumb to the urge to rusticate, which so many successful merchants of this time found impossible to resist.   He had thriven in Boston and in Boston he continued to live and do business, clearly as one of its wealthiest merchants and men of affairs.   His career has much in common with that of William Spayne, knight of the shire in 1380 and 1382, who was also a Boston merchant.[52]

This was a period in which the barriers between gentility, on the one hand, and professional and business life, on the other, seldom if ever intact, were being more commonly breached.   The son of one of the tycoons of the York-shire wool-trade operating from Hull had become Earl of Suffolk in 1385.

[46] CPR, 1401–5, 169. No note of any other appointment as deputy-butler at Boston appears in the Patent Rolls before 5 December 1411, when William Somercotes was appointed.

[47] Bell was appointed escheator on 10 November 1404 and acted for a year, as was usual (CFR, 1399–1405, 272).

[48] He was a J.P. for Holland, May 1398–May 1406, February 1407–June 1410, February 1411–January 1418, October 1418–July 1420 (CPR, passim).

[49] P. Thompson, op. cit., 117; CPR, 1396–9, 342. By 1392 Bell was also a member of the Gild of St. Mary of Boston (ibid., 1391–6, 192), and in 1396 he was one of a number of Boston people licensed by the Crown to found yet another fraternity in Boston parish church (ibid., 1396–99, 19–20).

[50] CPR, 1396–9, 319.

[51] CFR, 1399–1405, 15; ibid., 1405–13, 32; CPR, 1405–8, 443. Bell served on a large number of local royal commissions of different sorts, commissions of sewers, commissions of arrays, commissions for raising royal loans (in August 1404 he and three other Boston merchants received security, on the customs due from their own wool-exports, for a loan of £100 to the Prince of Wales for the Welsh war), and commissions interfering with trade and shipping at Boston in the interest of the Crown (CPR, passim). He was a feoffee-to-uses of (among others) Sir Thomas de Willoughby (note 35), Sir Ralph de Rochford (note 28) and Sir Thomas Dimmock (Lincs. Notes and Queries, VIII, 209; CCR, 1413–9, 86; CPR, 1413–6, 327).

[52] See pages 63–4 and note 23.

It was nothing exceptional for merchants to invest in land, whether by purchase or by lease, and for their sons to move up in the social scale and become gentry; but it is something worth comment when, within the passage of a generation, two Boston merchants, continuing in trade, whatever else they did as well, could represent in parliament, however casually, their shire. Before very many years had passed after Bell's election in 1413 such a phenomenon was to recur. In his twenties and thirties, Hamond Sutton, the great wool-stapler of Lincoln, many times represented his city in parliament. In his forties, by which time he had put on social weight but had remained a merchant still, on three occasions (in 1431, 1435 and 1439) he represented his county, which he had already administered as sheriff in 1428-9.[53] Many of the lawyers and country-gentlemen of the time were becoming ready to sit in parliament for some borough, if they could not get in for their county. To this development members of the merchant class were making little or no demur, even if it meant their own exclusion, so that for a merchant still in business to sit in parliament for a county is something to marvel at. It says a great deal for the integration of middle class society in later mediaeval Lincolnshire, rural and urban, that the contemporary trend in parliamentary representation, which was to go far in the fifteenth century towards converting the House of Commons into an assembly of country gentlemen at the expense of the bourgeoisie of the towns,[54] was occasionally reversed in that county. This is not to say that the Lincolnshire parliamentary boroughs of this time which we have been considering were not themselves susceptible to those nation-wide tendencies in borough representation to which I have just alluded. Robert Walsh, one of the city of Lincoln's representatives in most of the parliaments of the last years of Henry V and the first few years of his successor, was a gentleman and probably also a lawyer, although resident in the city, and Richard Duffield of Barton-on-Humber, who almost completely monopolized one of the Grimsby seats between 1420 and 1435, was a lawyer holding the office of clerk of the peace in the parts of Lindsey from before his parliamentary experience had begun until after it had ended.[55]

Nothing has been said directly, until just now, about the parliamentary representation of the boroughs of Lincolnshire. In the period particularly dealt with in this paper (1377 to 1422) the only Lincolnshire towns electing to parliament were Lincoln and Grimsby. Stamford had not sent burgesses to parliament since the reigns of Edward I and Edward II, and it only resumed its representation, because it was a town favourably affected towards the Yorkists, in the reign of Edward IV. Grantham, and for the same reason, only then first began to be represented in parliament. Boston had sent up men to two parliaments in the middle years of the fourteenth century, but

[53] J. S. Roskell, *The Commons in the Parliament of 1422*, p. 224.
[54] *Ibid.*, Chapter VII.
[55] *Ibid.*, p. 233, p. 174.

then it waited two centuries before beginning to be regularly represented under Mary Tudor.[56]   So was completed the tale of Lincolnshire parliamentary boroughs as they have existed down to very modern times.

The all but total exclusion of Boston from parliamentary representation in the mediaeval period is rather striking.   Its port was next in the kingdom after London in the fourteenth and fifteenth centuries as a place for shipment of wool for the Calais market.   It was also very prominent among those east coast ports in which the merchants of the Hanseatic League concentrated the bulk of their large import trade in Baltic produce and their large export trade in English cloth.[57]   Boston's failure to be a regular mediaeval parliamentary borough is not so remarkable as at first sight might appear, at least not in its domestic consequences.   The richness of the social life of this busy place in the later mediaeval period, and especially in the fourteenth century, is nowhere better attested than in the proliferation of its religious gilds.[58] Not the least important feature of the activity of these fellowships was the prominent place allowed in it to the gentry of the neighbourhood, probably even many of whom had houses in the town.   Most of those knights of the shire for Lincolnshire who came from the parts of Holland were members of one or more of these Boston clubs[59]; a number of them occupied the chief

[56] Stamford is known to have returned parliamentary burgesses in 1295, 1298, 1302, 1305, 1306 and 1322, after which there is wide gap until 1467.   Grantham's first known parliamentary burgesses were elected in 1467 also.   Boston elected representatives in 1352 and 1353, but afterwards none until 1553.   One early return from Louth is recorded in 1306, but even then the name of the single burgess elected was cancelled in the writ *de expensis*.   (See *The Official Return of Members of Parliament*, under these dates.)

[57] In 1353 a staple had been fixed at Lincoln, for which Boston was merely the out-port, and then, in 1369, Boston was itself made a staple-town.   The "communities" of the counties of Lincoln, Nottingham, Leicester and Derby petitioned in the parliament of 1376 that the staple be put back to Lincoln, stating that it had been removed to Boston "par brocage et pur singuler profit . . . a grant damage des ditz Comuns."   The King, in refusing the request, said that the bill had not been avowed in parliament and that, in any case, the staple was well established at Boston for the ease of the people and the profit of the realm. In 1381 Boston was one with Newcastle upon Tyne, Hull and Yarmouth, in being chosen as a coast-town from which passports could be obtained (P. Thompson, *op. cit.*, 55; *Rot. Parl.*, ii, 332).

[58] Gilds were established in Boston with the following dedications: St. Botolph, Corpus Christi, St. Mary, SS. Peter and Paul, St. George, Holy Trinity, St. Katherine, SS. Simon and Jude, "Postill" (The Apostles), Holyrood, Fellowship of Heaven, and Seven Martyrs.

[59] Sir Ralph de Rochford, M.P. 1379, had been one of ten appointed to assist the Alderman of the Corpus Christi Gild of Boston in 1350 (P. Thompson, *op. cit.*, 117); William Spayne, M.P. in 1380 and 1382, was 'a member of the Corpus Christi Gild by 1349 and its Alderman in 1376 and 1377 (*ibid.*, 116; *CPR, 1348–50*, 364); Sir John de Copuldyke of Harrington, M.P. in 1397, 1401, 1404 and 1406, was admitted to the Corpus Christi Gild between 1405 and 1411 (P. Thompson, *op. cit.*, 118); John de Meres of Kirton-in-Holland, M.P. in 1407, was himself a founder-member of the Trinity Gild at Spalding, but members of his family had joined the Corpus Christi Gild at Boston; Sir Thomas de Willoughby, M.P. in 1411 and 1414, was Alderman of the Corpus Christi Gild in 1406 and 1407 (P. Thompson, 118) and also of the Gild of St. George in 1404 and 1416 (*CPR,1401–5*, 388; *ibid.,1416–22*, 62); John Bell, M.P. in 1413, was a member of the Gild of St. Mary in 1392, a founder-member of the Gild of SS. Peter and Paul in 1396, and Alderman of the Corpus Christi Gild in 1395, 1396, 1397 and 1398 (P. Thompson, 117; *CPR, 1391–6*, 192; *ibid., 1396–9*, 19, 342); Richard Welby of Moulton, M.P. in 1421, had been a party in 1412 to a grant of property in Boston to the Holy Trinity Gild (*CPR, 1408–13*, 362).

office of a gild, the Aldermanship; and occasionally it even happened that they were knights of the shire when actually filling that office. Sir Philip de Tilney of Tydd was Alderman of the Corpus Christi Gild when knight of the shire in the two parliaments of 1388.[60] So sometimes was Sir John de Rochford when knight of the shire in the 1390s.[61] Thus Boston was doubtless occasionally represented in parliament, if only indirectly and informally.

Here in Holland at least we find the old distinctions between "country" and "town," between "landlordism" and "trade," no longer possessing much social relevance in the late fourteenth century. The erosion of these distinctions in parliamentary representation on a nation-wide scale is, in the present state of our knowledge, one of the most important aspects of the development of English political society in the fifteenth century. How far the Lincolnshire towns offered intimations of it in the history of their own late fourteenth and fifteenth century parliamentary representation, is a problem to which the local historian has already made some contribution[62]; but there is still plenty of freedom of movement, for those with the enterprise to use it, in this particular field of local parliamentary history.

[60] See note 25.
[61] See note 28.
[62] J. W. F. Hill, *Medieval Lincoln*, 279–80.

APPENDIX

LIST OF KNIGHTS OF THE SHIRE FOR LINCOLNSHIRE, 1377–1421[63]

Date of Meeting of Parliament	Place of Meeting	Names of Knights of the Shire
13 October 1377	Westminster	Sir John Dymmok, Sir John Auncell
20 October 1378	Gloucester	Sir William Bussy, Sir John Auncell
24 April 1379	Westminster	Sir Ralph de Rochford, Sir John Auncell
16 January 1380	,,	Sir William Bussy, John de Boys
5 November 1380	Northampton	William Spaigne
3 November 1381	Westminster	Sir John de Tothby, Sir Robert de Leake
7 May 1382	,,	Sir John de Tothby, Sir William Armyn
6 October 1382	,,	Sir Robert de Leake, William Spaigne
23 February 1383	,,	Sir John Bozoun, Walter Tailboys
26 October 1383	,,	Sir John de Moulton, Sir John Bussy
29 April 1384	Salisbury	Sir John de Moulton, Sir John Bozoun
12 November 1384	Westminster	Sir John Bozoun, Sir Robert de Leake
20 October 1385	,,	Sir Philip de Tilney, Sir William Armyn
1 October 1386	,,	Sir Walter Tailboys, Sir John Bozoun
3 February 1388	,,	Sir Philip de Tilney, Sir Walter Tailboys
9 September 1388	Cambridge	Sir John Bussy, Sir Philip de Tilney
17 January 1390	Westminster	Sir John Bussy, Sir Philip de Tilney
12 November 1390	,,	Sir John Bussy, John de Rochford
3 November 1391	,,	Sir John Bussy, Gerard de Suthill
20 January 1393	Winchester	Sir John Bussy, Robert de Cumberworth
27 January 1394	Westminster	Sir John Bussy, John de Rochford
27 January 1395	,,	Sir John Bussy, Robert de Cumberworth
22 January 1397	,,	Sir John Bussy, Sir John de Copyldyke
17 September 1397	,,	
27 January 1398	Shrewsbury (by adjournment)	} Sir John Bussy, John de Rochford
6 October 1399	Westminster	Sir Thomas Hawley, Sir John de Rochford
20 January 1401	,,	Sir Henry de Retford, Sir John de Copuldyke
30 September 1402	,,	Sir Henry de Retford, Sir Gerard de Suthill
14 January 1404	,,	Sir John de Copuldyke, Sir Richard Hansard
6 October 1404	Coventry	Sir Henry de Retford, Sir Thomas Hawley
1 March 1406	Westminster	Sir John de Copuldyke, John Skipwith
20 October 1407	Gloucester	John Skipwith, John de Meres
27 January 1410	Westminster	Not known
3 November 1411	,,	Sir Thomas de Willoughby, John Poucher
14 May 1413	,,	Sir Richard Hansard, John Bell
30 April 1414	Leicester	John Skipwith, Thomas Cumberworth
19 November 1414	Westminster	Sir Thomas de Willoughby, Sir Richard Hansard
4 November 1415	,,	Not known
16 March 1416	,,	Sir Robert Hilton, William Tirwhit
19 October 1416	,,	Not known
16 November 1417	,,	Not known
16 October 1419	,,	Not known
2 December 1420	,,	Sir Thomas Cumberworth, Sir Robert Hagbech
2 May 1421	,,	Sir Richard Hansard, Sir Godfrey Hilton
1 December 1421	,,	Sir Thomas Cumberworth, Richard Welby

The following abbreviations have been used in the footnotes:

CCR = Calendar of Close Rolls.   P.R.O.   = Public Record Office.
CFR = Calendar of Fine Rolls.   Rot. Parl. = Rotuli Parliamentorum.
CPR = Calendar of Patent Rolls.

The article printed above was read as a paper at the Annual General Meeting of the Lincolnshire Record Society held at Lincoln in 1957.

[63] Abstracted from The Official Return of Members of Parliament, Part I, Parliaments of England, 1213–1702, pp. 197–300.

THE SOCIAL COMPOSITION OF THE COMMONS IN A FIFTEENTH-CENTURY PARLIAMENT

IN an address given at the eighth Congrès Internationale des Sciences Histor-iques held at Zurich in 1938, Sir Maurice Powicke emphasized the need to study the history of the medieval English parliament in its relation to the nature of English society; and, in view of the fact that historians were being driven to consider the environment of parliament, he suggested that 'the value of subse-quent work on parliament lies, not in explanation, but in description'.[2] In the light of these remarks some of the results of a systematic analysis of the member-ship of the Common House of a single, late medieval parliament, looked at from the point of view of its social composition, may not be without some interest: a single Lancastrian parliament, the first parliament of the reign of Henry VI, which met at Westminster on 9 November 1422 and sat until 18 December. There is no particular reason to believe that the knights of the shire and citizens and burgesses who represented their several communities in this parliament of 1422 were not typical of any nearly contemporary parliament; it is, fortunately, a parliament for which all the names of the elected representa-tives are known from the returns to the writs of summons, save those of the burgesses of Dunwich[3]; moreover, it was the scene of activities which were of considerable immediate, and consequential, importance.

The political circumstances in which the parliament met are fairly well known and require no more than a brief notice. On 31 August 1422 Henry V had died prematurely at Bois de Vincennes near Paris. Two and a half years before, in the treaty of Troyes, the success of English arms and diplomacy had secured recognition of the legality of the English conquests in France north of the Loire and the reversion of the Crown of the Valois. Difficulties there had been in the Anglo-Burgundian alliance, and here and elsewhere difficulties were to increase. Especially important among them were the financial and military

---

[1] This paper was read at a meeting of the medieval section of the Anglo-French Conference of His-torians held in All Souls College, Oxford, in September 1949. I have added some references and here and there developed my themes.

[2] *Études présentées à la Commission Internationale pour l'Histoire des Assemblées d'États, L'Organi-sation corporative du Moyen Age à la fin de l'Ancien Régime*, iii. 134–5.

[3] *Return of the Name of Every Member of the Lower House, 1213–1874*, H.C. (1878), LXII. i. 302–4.

strain on England, likely to accrue from the need to complete the French conquest by reducing dauphinist France, and the prospect of a long minority in both realms: a long minority, because Henry V left to succeed him an infant whom he had never seen; in both realms, because less then two months after Henry V's demise Charles VI of France died also, and, in accordance with the treaty of Troyes of 1420, Henry of Windsor succeeded him as his heir. The greatest difficulty the English government had to face, especially where England was concerned, was an insuperable one: the absence of a monarch capable of exercising his authority at a time when kings ruled as well as reigned. But so far as England went, the council had already arrogated to itself the functions of executive power: the desire of Humphrey, duke of Gloucester, Henry V's younger surviving brother and at the late king's death his lieutenant in England, for an unqualified regency in England as distinct from a limited protectorship was foredoomed to disappointment, although not without protest from him.

By this time parliament had been a distinct political and constitutional phenomenon for over a century and a half and was by now something more than a realization of the medieval doctrine of consent; it had become a factor in government likely to stay in English constitutional life. It was the highest court of the realm and yet had features of which no inferior court could boast, for it had also become a representative assembly. It was a court but a unique court, different and distinct from other courts, because—so common lawyers were thinking at the end of the fifteenth century—it represented all men, and, therefore, to it and to its acts every man was a party.[1]

The parliament of conjoined estates in the form conceived by Edward I scarcely outlived the reign of his son. For soon after the deposition of Edward II the proctors of the inferior clergy virtually seceded from the parliamentary assembly, preferring to meet the financial demands of the Crown in their provincial convocations. By the beginning of Edward III's reign, however, the elected representatives of the secular communities of shire and borough had come to be considered an essential element in parliament's constitution. The contrast between them and those summoned by individual writs, the king's preference for dealing with them, especially in matters financial, as one group and not several groups, and the defection of the proctors of the lesser clergy, predetermined that the knights and burgesses should early realize a common political, and eventually constitutional, identity.[2] The increasingly closer association with the Commons of the business of presenting petitions of general import confirmed this tendency to consolidation: by 1363 they had already been allowed the services of a 'commun clerc' (alias 'sub-clericus parliamenti'). Edward III did occasionally resort to the device of separate negotiation with

[1] S. B. Chrimes, *English Constitutional Ideas in the Fifteenth Century*, pp. 78–9.
[2] H. G. Richardson and G. O. Sayles, 'The Parliaments of Edward III (cont.)', *ante*, ix. 1–15.

assemblies of merchants, but only for a time. By the end of the fourteenth century what came to be theoretically recognized in the fifteenth century was already implicit in the structure of parliament: parliament had come to be composed of but three estates of the realm, the lords spiritual, the lords temporal, and the elected commons. The latter represented communities of different social importance and historical traditions, shires and boroughs; they represented, in fact although not formally, different sectional interests in the nation, but, conscious of the need of corporate solidarity, they realized in parliament quite clearly their political identity as one estate of the realm. And yet the consciousness of the old *gradus* of knights of the shire, citizens and burgesses, inescapably persisted among the Commons themselves, even in that very institution which most clearly demonstrated (from 1376 onwards) the corporateness of the medieval Commons, their common speaker.[1] He, until Tudor times, was invariably a knight of the shire.[2] The Commons were one estate in parliament, but in the first half of the fifteenth century private petitioners seeking the Commons' backing for their bills saw fit from time to time to address them to the knights of the shire alone.[3] And as late as 1475 Justice Littleton could illustrate the binding nature of a majority decision in terms which might be taken to suggest that the legislative capacity of the Commons was still the monopoly of the knights.[4] Among the still formally differentiated *gradus* of the Commons the shire-knights were a still superior *gradus*.

The Lancastrian government through the medium of parliamentary statutes had mainly confined its interest in parliamentary elections to the problems of electoral discipline. But in 1445 it was laid down by statute that knights of the shire should be notable knights or else such notable esquires or gentlemen of birth as could support the estate of knighthood and not men of the degree of yeomen or below; and it was found necessary at the same time to reiterate the terms of a statute of 1413 which demanded that the parliamentary burgesses should be resident in the boroughs for which they were elected.[5] It was obviously still felt that the knights of the shire and the parliamentary burgesses should in their personal quality reflect the different status of the communities

---

[1] See my article on 'The Medieval Speakers for the Commons in Parliament', *ante*, I V 31–52.

[2] It is just possible that a break with tradition was made in 1485, but see H. G. Richardson, 'The Commons and Medieval Politics', *Trans. Roy. Hist. Soc.*, 4th Ser., xxviii. 38, n. 2. It is neatly significant of the changes which had come over the character of borough representation during the fifteenth century that the first parliamentary burgess definitely known to have been elected as speaker (in 1533) was a member of a long chivalrous family and was himself knighted by Henry VIII at his presentation for the office: Sir Humphrey Wingfield, burgess for Great Yarmouth.

[3] A. R. Myers 'Parliamentary Petitions in the Fifteenth Century', *Eng. Hist. Rev.*, lii. (1937), 401–4; *idem*, 'Some Observations on the Procedure of the Commons in dealing with Bills in the Lancastrian Period', *University of Toronto Law Journal*, iii, no. 1, 65.

[4] S. B. Chrimes, *op. cit.* (Appendix of Extracts from Year Book Cases), 373.

[5] *Statutes of the Realm*, 23 Hen. VI, c. 14; *Rot. Parl.*, v. 115–16.

they represented, but the need for statutory measures to enforce such requirements shows   that in practice forces were at work which were tending towards a
closer cohesiveness of the different social elements composing the Lower House
of parliament. It will be my aim in analysing the personnel of the Commons in
1422 to show how far and in what ways by that date the recognized unity of the
Commons as a *political* estate in parliament conformed to the way in which they
were socially composed.

The general validity of the findings of an enquiry largely restricted to a single
parliament will, I think, be the more readily accepted if a very brief consideration is given to the problem of the continuity of service in the Commons. At
this time, a period of short but fairly frequent sessions, the normal 'carry-over'
from parliament to parliament was only about a fifth, and of those members of
the Lower House re-elected to successive parliaments the greater proportion
came not from the shires but from the boroughs. Repeated election rather than
re-election is, however, a safer guide to parliamentary experience in the case of
both knights of the shire and burgesses. The average number of parliaments
attended in the course of their careers by the shire-knights of 1422 was six,
and less than one out of ten sat on this one occasion only. Some few knights
had almost uninterrupted parliamentary careers extending over a quarter of a
century; and more of them sat quite continuously but for shorter periods.
Repeated election among the parliamentary burgesses was roughly of the same
order, for they were anything but 'men of business reluctantly diverted from
their private affairs for occasional public service' as Pollard thought they were.
At least two out of every three of the Commons in 1422 had previously sat in
parliament; out of the seventy-four knights of the shire only nineteen at most
were newcomers.[1]

Of the 188 known burgesses elected to Henry VI's first parliament most
were resident in the boroughs returning them. If we exclude the Dorset, Wiltshire, and Cornish boroughs, only one out of ten burgesses was in the strictest
sense a non-resident; and even if we include the returns for the twenty-four
parliamentary boroughs of these heavily represented counties we may still say
that over threequarters of the 1422 burgesses were resident in the boroughs
for which they were elected. There are few signs at this moment of a tendency
to that wholesale 'invasion' of the parliamentary boroughs by outsiders which
later fifteenth-century and Tudor conditions were to accelerate, or of the practice of 'carpet-bagging'. As many as twenty-six of the 188 burgesses of 1422
on other occasions were returned for other boroughs, but of these only five
ever sat for boroughs outside their own counties. Most of the parliamentary

---

[1] The number of newcomers would almost certainly be reduced if the returns to the parliaments of
1410, 1411, April 1414, 1415, March 1416 and October 1416 were not so incomplete. For the last
of these parliaments (October 1416) only the Dunwich burgesses are known of all the Commons.

burgesses of 1422 were resident in-burgesses of the boroughs they represented and many of them were members of the class which supplied the administrative elements in the boroughs themselves: in this connexion it is interesting to note that the then mayors of Wareham, Hull and Winchelsea represented their boroughs in 1422,[1] and six more burgesses had been mayors in the previous administrative year.[2] Again, to Westminster in November 1422 there came as parliamentary burgess one of the then bailiffs of Dartmouth, Colchester, Ipswich, Great Yarmouth, Huntingdon, Shrewsbury and Scarborough.[3]

The trading and mercantile interests were fairly well represented among the burgess members of the Lower House by some forty *identifiable* merchants at least, all resident in the boroughs returning them. The all-important export trade in wool was represented by six of the most influential members of the Calais staple, Of these was one of the two aldermen members for London, Thomas Fauconer. already three times master of the Mercers' Company; he was keenly interested in the Flanders wool trade and had long-established connexions with the big

---

[1] Respectively, Walter Reson, M.P. for Wareham in March 1416, 1420, May 1421, 1423, 1425, 1427, 1431, 1432, and for Melcombe in 1419, who was also collector of customs in the port area of Melcombe in 1422 (after first being controller of customs) and deputy to the chief butler of England there and at Weymouth (J. Hutchins, *History and Antiquities of Dorset*, i. 82; *Cal. Pat. Rolls, 1413–6*, p. 333; *ibid., 1416–22*, pp. 12, 175, 392; *ibid., 1422–9*, pp. 65, 177; *Cal. Fine Rolls, 1413–22*, pp. 203, 291–2, 294; *ibid., 1422–30*, pp. 20, 24–5, 108, 152, 196); John Fitlyng, M.P. for Hull in 1406, 1407, 1411, 1413, 1419, May 1421, 1422, 1423, 1425, 1427, and 1431 (Exchequer, L.T.R. Memoranda Roll, 1 Hen. VI, P.R.O., E 368/195); and John Tamworth, M.P. for Winchelsea in 1419, 1422, 1427, and for Hastings in 1435 and 1445, who was also in 1422 collector of customs and overseer of the tronage at Chichester and on 28 January 1423 was made deputy-butler at Winchelsea (*Cal. Fine Rolls, 1413–22*, pp. 381, 383; *ibid., 1422–30*, pp. 20, 53, 108; *Cal. Pat. Rolls, 1422–9*, p. 8; for his mayoralty see *Sussex Arch. Collections*, viii. 234).

[2] John Cook, of Exeter, M.P. for Exeter in 1422 (R. and S. Izacke, *Remarkable Antiquities of the City of Exeter* [1724], p. 73); Ralph Hunt, of Bath, M.P. for Bath in 1417, 1422, 1423, 1426 (Parl. returns, P.R.O., C. 219/12/6); John Mascall, of Southampton, M.P. there in December 1421, 1422 (J. S. Davies, *History of Southampton*, p. 173); John Shell or Shelley, of Rye, M.P. for Rye in 1410, 1417, 1420, December 1421, 1422, and for Sandwich in 1426, 1429, 1435; Richard Russell, of York, M.P. for York in 1422, 1425, *York Memoranda Book* (Surtees Soc., CXXV), ii. 103; and Thomas Poge, of Nottingham, M.P. there in 1420, December 1421, 1422, 1423, 1427 (Stevenson, *Records of Nottingham*, ii. 428).

[3] Thomas Ayssheldon (Dartmouth), M.P. for Dartmouth in 1420, 1422, 1429, 1433, 1437 (Hist. MSS. Comm., *Fifth Report*, p. 602 *b*); John Sumpter (Colchester), M.P. for Colchester in March 1416, 1419, 1422, 1423, 1427 (W. Gurney Benham, *Colchester Oath Book*, p. 102); Thomas Astylle (Ipswich), M.P. for Ipswich in 1422 (Nicholas Bacon, *Annals of Ipswich*, ed. W. H. Richardson, p. 92); John Colles (Huntingdon), M.P. for Huntingdon in May 1421, 1422, 1423, 1425 (*Cal. Close Rolls, 1422–9*, 73); Hugh Rasyn (Scarborough), M.P. in 1422 and perhaps sometime 'magister scolarum grammaticalium', *Testamenta Eboracensia* (Surtees Soc., XXX), ii. 209; as bailiff he accounted in the exchequer for the farms and issues of the borough on 24 November 1422 (Exchequer, L.T.R., Mem. Roll, 1 Hen. VI, P.R.O., E 368/195); John Perle (Shrewsbury), M.P. for Shrewsbury in 1406, 1422, 1423 (*Trans. Shropshire Arch. and Nat. Hist. Soc.*, iii. 243); Robert Elys (Great Yarmouth), M.P. for Great Yarmouth in November 1414, 1420, May 1421, 1422 (F. Blomefield, *Topographical History of Norfolk*, xi. 324).

Italian exporting firms as well.[1] The other five Calais staplers[2] were returned
from Hull, York, Lincoln, and Nottingham, towns in the basins of the Trent,
Humber and Ouse, whose main lines of communication with the continent lay
through the ports of Hull and Boston, and whose main sources of supply were
the Yorkshire and Lincolnshire wolds and the moorland sheep-runs of the
Pennines. And there were a few more whose interests and activities in this line
of business are less easy to discern. Other branches of import and export trade
were represented too, along with the distributive trades in the hands of internal
middlemen. And some of those whose careers suggest the increasingly English
participation in foreign trade represented also the interests of native ship-owners.
Both the London aldermen returned to parliament exported and imported in
their own vessels[3]; so did John Bourton, the great Bristol merchant, who retained his share in his town's interest in the importation of Gascon wines even
when later he began to dabble in the Icelandic trade.[4] Among those who had
profited by the opportunity which the resumption of the French wars had
afforded for taking up government contracts was one of the barons of the Cinque
Ports, John Tamworth, the same who was mayor of Winchelsea; earlier in this
very year, 1422, he had been engaged in freighting across the Channel both
reinforcements and livestock for the support of Henry V's armies in France.[5]
Tamworth was at this time one of the two collectors of customs and subsidies in
the customs area which had its centre in the port of Chichester.[6] He was only
one of several of the 1422 parliamentary burgesses occupied in this sphere of
administrative activity under the authority of the Crown; men in close touch
with most branches of commercial operation on the one hand, and, as accounting

---

[1] A. B. Beaven, *Aldermen of London*, ii. 2. *Cal. Close Rolls, 1399–1402*, p. 149; *ibid., 1405–9*, p. 478;
ibid., 1413–19, p. 36; *Cal. Pat. Rolls, 1401–5*, p. 214; *ibid., 1413–16*, p. 277. Fauconer was M.P. for
London in 1411, March 1416, December 1421, 1422, 1423.

[2] William Bowes, M.P. for York in March 1416, May 1421, 1422, 1426, 1431 (*Cal. Pat. Rolls,
1405–8*, pp. 321, 414); Richard Russell of York, for whom see above, p. 156, n. 2 (*ibid.*, pp. 321, 414;
ibid., 1422–9, p. 349; *Rot. Parl.*, iv. 474 *b*; *Test. Ebor., op. cit.*, ii. 52 where, in his will of 1 December
1435, he bequeathed £20 and £10 to be divided, respectively, 'inter yconomos de Yorkes Walde de qui-
bus emi lanam' and among those of Lindsey in Lincs.); Hamond Sutton, M.P. for Lincoln in March
1416, 1420, May 1421, 1422, 1423, 1425, 1426, knight of the shire for Lincs. in 1431, 1435, 1439
(*Deputy Keeper's Reports* [*D.K.R.*], xlviii. 293, 357; *Rot. Parl.*, iv. 474 *b*, 484 *b*; N. H. Nicolas,
Proceedings and Ordinances of the Privy Council, v. 278; *Cal. Pat. Rolls, 1446–52*, p. 53); Robert Holme
of Hull, M.P. for Hull in December 1421, 1422, 1423, 1427, 1431, 1435 (*Cal. Pat. Rolls, 1422–9*,
p. 385; *Cal. Close Rolls, 1429–35*, p. 112); Thomas Poge, for whom see above, p. 156, n. 2 (*Cal.
Pat. Rolls, 1422–9*, p. 348).

[3] Thomas Fauconer (e.g. Rymer, *Foedera*, viii. 727); John Michell, M.P. for London in 1411,
1420, 1422, 1426, 1427, 1435 (he had a ship at Newcastle-on-Tyne in November 1415, *Cal. Close
Rolls, 1413–19*, p. 236).

[4] *Cal. Pat. Rolls, 1416–22*, p. 180; *D.K.R.*, xlviii. 361, 365; *Rot. Parl.*, v. 38a.

[5] *Cal. Pat. Rolls, 1413–16*, p. 421; Exchequer, Issue Roll, Easter 10 Hen. V., P.R.O., E 403/655,
mems. 3, 8, 18; Exchequer, Receipt Roll, Michs. I. Hen. VI, P.R.O., E 403/703, mems. 6, 7.

[6] See above, p. 156, n. 1.

officials, with the Exchequer on the other. The port officials of one sort or another returned in 1422, drawn with only two exceptions from the ports of the south and south-west coastal areas, numbered no fewer than thirteen. John Exton, elected at Chichester, for instance, was Tamworth's fellow customer there and shared with him also the office of controller of tronage and pesage of wool and other staple commodities in the same port. Among the port officials were four or five deputies of the chief butler of England, whose primary concern was the surveillance in the ports of the royal rights of prisage on imported wines.[1]

[1] For John Exton, see *Cal. Fine Rolls, 1413–22*, pp. 381, 383; *ibid., 1422–30*, pp. 19, 25, 53. The other customs officials were Walter Reson, M.P. for Wareham, for whom see above, p. 156, n. 1 ; John Hawley (M.P. for Dartmouth in 1410, 1411, 1413, November 1414, May 1421, 1422, 1423, 1425, 1427, 1429, 1431, 1432), collector of customs from April 1413 to May 1417 and from November 1421 to May 1425 at Dartmouth and Exeter (*Cal. Fine Rolls, 1413–22*, pp. 4, 14, 70, 72, 113, 129, 381, 383; *ibid., 1422–30*, pp. 2, 3, 25, 53–4, 60), and deputy-butler at Dartmouth by patent of 10 December 1422 (*Cal. Pat. Rolls, 1422–9*, p. 8); John Gonne (M.P. for Bridgwater in 1422 and 1437), a collector of customs and joint-controller of the tronage and weighing of staple commodities at Bridgwater from 12 July 1421 until February 1423 (*Cal. Fine Rolls, 1413–22*, pp. 380, 381, 383; *Cal. Pat. Rolls, 1416–22*, p. 378); William Balsham (M.P. for Melcombe in 1422, 1429, 1432, 1435, 1437, 1442, and for Lyme in 1431), from March 1410 until his death in 1444, except from 23 January to 8 December 1412, controller of customs at Melcombe, and from October 1415 and April 1421, respectively, until February 1423, controller of customs at Exeter and Dartmouth in S. Devon and at Bridgwater in N. Somerset (*Cal. Pat. Rolls, 1408–13*, pp. 156, 243, 361, 458; *ibid., 1413–16*, p. 333; *ibid., 1416–22*, pp. 337, 398; *ibid., 1422–9*, p. 50; *ibid., 1429–36*, pp. 298, 323; *ibid., 1436–41*, p. 476); Robert Treage (M.P. for Bodmin in 1413, 1420; for Helston in March 1416, 1419; for Liskeard in 1417; for Lostwithiel in May 1421, 1422; for Truro in December 1421, 1425), from July 1414 to November 1423 collector of customs in and between Plymouth and Fowey, and in February 1426 appointed havener in Cornwall and at Plymouth (*Cal. Fine Rolls, 1413–22*, pp. 69, 71, 204–5; *ibid., 1422–30*, p. 125); John Cory (M.P. for Launceston in 1410, Nov. 1414, 1417, May 1421, 1422, 1423), from 26 April 1419 to 4 November 1423 controller of customs in and between Plymouth and Fowey, and appointed collector of customs in the same area on 4 November 1423, and reappointed on 22 July 1425 (*Cal. Pat. Rolls, 1416–22*, pp. 215, 392; *ibid., 1422–9*, p. 50; *Cal. Fine Rolls, 1422–30*, pp. 53, 55, 61, 89, 90, 94, 108); John But (M.P. for Barnstaple in 1402; for Bodmin in 1413, November 1414; for Liskeard in 1417; for Truro in 1422, 1425), in November 1402 appointed deputy-butler at Tawmouth, was by patent of 24 May 1413 made deputy-butler there and also at Barnstaple, Plymouth, Fowey, Falmouth, Penzance, and in all other Cornish ports, and in November 1418 was still holding the office at Tawmouth and Barnstaple (*Cal. Pat. Rolls, 1401–5*, p. 169; *ibid., 1413–16*, 10; *ibid., 1416–22*, p. 175); John Cook, 'draper' (M.P. for Exeter in 1422), on 26 November 1422, in the middle of the 1422 parliament, was appointed mayor of the Exeter staple and acted until 14 November 1423 (Patent Roll, Supplementary, P.R.O., C 67/25); Robert Vessy, 'chapman' of Exeter, *alias* citizen and fishmonger of London (M.P. for Exeter in March 1416, 1422), ended a year of office as constable of the Exeter staple while sitting in the 1422 parliament, having been during the same year, 1421–2, senior bailiff of the city, and in November 1423 was to begin a long appointment as collector of customs and tunnage and poundage at Exeter and Dartmouth (Patent Roll, Supplementary, *loc. cit., Cal. Fine Rolls, 1422–30*, pp. 53–4, 60, 90–1, 95, 108, 152, 196–8, 200); John Fruysthorp (M.P. for Old Sarum in December 1421, 1422), on 4 November 1422 was appointed troner of wools, etc., at Southampton (*Cal. Pat. Rolls, 1422–9*, p. 6); Robert Whelpington (M.P. for Newcastle-on-Tyne in 1413, November 1414, 1422, 1423), had been appointed on 10 November 1418 controller of customs and subsidies at Newcastle (*Cal. Pat. Rolls, 1416–22*, p. 174); Thomas Urswick (M.P. for Lancashire in May 1421, 1422), receiver of the duchy of Lancaster estates in the county palatine, was on 10 December 1422 appointed deputy-butler at Liverpool, and in May 1429 the commission was extended to include Lancaster and all other Lancashire ports (*Cal. Pat. Rolls, 1422–9*, pp. 8, 537).

Such local positions of royal appointment men of burgess status were best fitted to fill by training and circumstance. But instances are not lacking where they are found to be pushing themselves up into positions of royal appointment of greater local influence and social prestige. John Hawley of Dartmouth, for example, besides his office as customer of Dartmouth and Exeter, had in 1422 for nineteen years been occupying the position of feodar and escheator for the duchy of Cornwall property in Devon and Cornwall, and he was one of the justices of the peace for Cornwall.[1] Such men as Hawley were on the fringe of the armigerous class. And many of the parliamentary burgesses of 1422 were of the same middle stratum of society as included the squirearchy proper, and were closely linked with the lesser land-owning class, if but seldom by birth at any rate by ties of interest and business connexion; and some of them had even acquaintance in aristocratic circles.

Quite clearly the old distinctions between 'town' and 'country', between 'landlordism' and 'trade' were breaking down in parliamentary representation as they had been doing in other directions for long enough. It is well, however, to bear some important facts in mind. It is true that merchants, especially the leaders of the commerce of the capital, were less than ever averse to investing the profits of trade in landed estate and that some of them were coming to regard themselves and to be accounted as 'gentlemen'. The burgess element proper in the nation was not, however, enlarging its outlook and aspirations in the sphere of parliamentary representation. Nine of the parliamentary burgesses of 1422 at some time or another also sat as knights of the shire.[2] But only one of them was a merchant, the sometime mayor of the Calais staple, Hamond Sutton of Lincoln, who later represented his shire in three parliaments in the 1430's. The others were lawyers and/or country gentlemen. The approximation in this period of the type of man returned from the boroughs to the type of man returned from the shires was due mainly to the fact that the country gentry and the professional élite of the shires were slowly but surely realizing that the sole approach to the privilege of a return to parliament did not lie through election in a county court. The movement was one of the land-owning and retainer and

[1] *Cal. Pat. Rolls, 1401–5*, p. 213; *ibid., 1413–16*, p. 256; *ibid., 1422–9*, p. 285; *ibid., 1436–41*, p. 56.

[2] Nicholas Assheton (M.P. for Liskeard in May 1421; for Helston in 1422, 1423, 1425, 1427, 1435; for Launceston in 1431, 1432; for Cornwall in 1437, 1439), for whom see below, p. 165. John Hody (M.P. for Shaftesbury in December 1421, 1422, 1423, 1425, 1427; for Dorset in 1431; for Somerset in 1433, 1435, 1437), for whom see below, p. 165; Robert Darcy (M.P. for Newcastle-on-Tyne in 1402; for Essex in March 1416, 1419, May 1421, 1423, 1425, 1426, 1432, 1439, 1445; for Maldon in 1422), for whom see below, p 162; John Langley (M.P. for Chippenham, Wilts, in 1422; for Glos. in 1429, 1432, 1435, 1437, 1442); Robert Whitgreve (M.P. for Stafford in 1411, March 1416, and in all 14 parliaments between 1420 and 1437, and in 1442; for Staffs. in 1445, November 1449), for whom see below, p. 162; John Harpour (M.P. for Stafford in 1419, 1420, May 1421, 1422, 1423, 1425, 1427, 1429; for Staffs. in 1431); John Mynors (M.P. for Newcastle-under-Lyme in 1419, 1422; for Staffs. in 1420, 1431, 1437); John Seymour (M.P. for Ludgershall in 1422; for Wilts. in 1435, 1439, 1445); Hamond Sutton, for whom see p. 157, n. 2. The first six of these nine were lawyers.

professional classes down into borough representation, rather than one of the mercantile class up into a social position from which its members would be able to seek election to parliament for the counties. In some senses the merchant class in the fifteenth century was achieving greater social recognition, and was being encouraged to lose what sense of social inferiority still lingeringly attached itself to merchantry, but it was virtually beginning to renounce its political place in parliament. This was not so in the case of the big centres of commercial activity like London, Bristol, Norwich, York, and Hull, but it was so in very many of the smaller boroughs, especially those far distant from Westminster. Of the twelve parliamentary burgesses returned from Cornwall in 1422, for instance, only one, so far as is known, was a merchant.[1]

Considering some of the parliaments of Edward IV's reign in her book on *The Parliamentary Representation of the English Boroughs during the Middle Ages*, Miss McKisack was of the opinion that, as a result of a 'great influx of the country gentry', 'at least one half of the borough representatives were not true burgesses', and she claimed that in consequence there had been something of a 'revolution' in the composition of the Lower House of parliament.[2] In a house which always included 74 knights of the shire who were almost invariably all gentlemen-born,[3] this 'fifty-fifty' division of the parliamentary burgesses into 'gentry' and 'proper burgesses' tilted over the social balance among the Commons in favour of the gentry. The wholesale Tudor creations of parliamentary boroughs, very largely the answer to demands from magnates desirous of extending their control of parliamentary patronage, of course did nothing to stem this continuing revolution in the composition of the Commons—it did in fact promote it. Professor Neale has shown us[4] that by the end of the sixteenth century the statutorily-qualified resident burgesses elected to parliament tended to be no more than a quarter of those returned by the parliamentary boroughs. As a result 'instead of one gentleman to four townsmen [which would have been

---

[1] Robert Trenerth (M.P. for Liskeard in December 1421; for Truro in 1422) a Cornishman with interests in the tin trade who married the widow of a pewterer of London, where he was a member of the Mercers' Company (*Cal. Close Rolls, 1405–9*, p. 275; *Cal. Pat. Rolls, 1429–36*, p. 170; R. R. Sharpe, *Letter Books of the City of London*, Book I, p. 140; *Feudal Aids*, i. 223).

[2] *Op. cit.*, pp. 109, 113.

[3] Thomas Frowyk, esquire (M.P. for Middlesex in 1419, 1422, 1427, 1432, 1435), was elder brother to Henry Frowyk, who represented London in the 1422 and other parliaments, but, though the mercer came of a family influential for its goldsmith members in Edward I's reign, they were of the third generation of the family since its rustication at South Mimms, near Barnet. (*London and Middlesex Arch. Soc. Trans.*, iv. 260; F.C. Cass, *History of South Mimms*, pp. 68 *et seq.*) The only 1422 knight of the shire who, to my knowledge, began his career as a merchant was John Greville esquire of Chipping Campden and Sezincote, who was knight of the shire for Glos. in April 1414, 1419, May 1421, 1422, 1423, 1425, and 1427. In 1395, certainly, Greville was still a Cotswold wool-merchant like his father, William, whose brass at Campden describes him as *quondam civis Londonie et flos mercatorum lanarum tocius Anglie*. (*Cal. Pat. Rolls, 1391–6*, p. 627).

[4] J. E. Neale, *The Elizabethan House of Commons*, p. 147.

the ratio if the statutes relating to the residential qualification of parliamentary burgesses had been observed] Elizabeth's later parliaments contained four gentlemen to every townsman'. In the Yorkist parliaments there were roughly two gentlemen to every one townsman[1] whereas by that time (if statutes had been given their full legally-binding force) the townsmen ought to have out-numbered the gentry by three to one. The earlier actual, and still legally re-quired, preponderance of burgesses over gentry had quite clearly ended by the time of Edward IV's death. This 'revolution', and revolution it was (although of course one that was as yet by no means complete), Miss McKisack regarded as the product of the political disturbances of the mid-fifteenth century and as coincidental with the beginnings of civil strife in England; albeit she thought that the substitution of country gentlemen or officials for burgesses proper as the representatives of boroughs in parliament is noticeable as a 'tendency' at least from the beginning of Henry VI's reign. My own feeling is that her more detailed examination of the burgess personnel of the Yorkist parliaments[2] led her to post-date developments that were already well in progress by the time of the accession of Henry of Windsor and to lay too much emphasis on the share of the commotions of the middle years of the century in their generation.

In Henry VI's first parliament the townsmen, in the strict sense of resident burgesses, still outnumbered the gentry among the parliamentary commons by something like five to four. For, as we have seen, in 1422 no more than a quarter of the parliamentary burgesses were non-resident. But we should bear in mind the fact that the remaining three-quarters of the parliamentary burgesses of 1422 were by no means necessarily members of the 'burgess class' proper, that is, men interested in the manufacture or distribution of merchandise of one sort or another. And if we include in our estimate of the gentry who sat for boroughs in 1422 all those who had attained to the rank of esquire, those unconnected with trade who could be described in official documents as 'gentlemen', those who were justices of the peace in their shires, those who were lawyers or acted as administrative agents of estates, and those who from time to time attended *shire* elections to parliament and were among the select number who attested on such occasions the legality of the sheriff's return, we shall be enabled to say that something like half of the parliamentary burgesses might be already, at the beginning of Henry VI's reign, not burgesses in the usually accepted 'class'

[1] This estimate is based on an analysis of the biographies of members of the Commons in the parliaments of 1467–8, 1472–5, and 1478, in J. C. Wedgwood, *History of Parliament, Biographies.*

[2] M. McKisack, *op. cit.,* pp. 106–12. Miss McKisack says (p. 112) that the number of esquires, described as such in the returns of borough elections, increased from one in 1437 to ten in 1459, there being none so described in the returns to the parliaments of Henry VI's reign prior to 1437. This is so, but it is by no means necessarily evidence that men of this status sitting as burgesses were at first absent and then so significantly multiplied; it simply means, I think, that in the second half of Henry VI's reign there was increasingly less reluctance on the part of boroughs to disguise in their returns the fact that they were not electing proper burgesses.

sense of that term, although three out of four were still burgesses in the sense that they lived in the towns returning them. The revolution in the class structure of the Lower House of parliament was clearly already past the stage of being a mere tendency. In the parliament of 1422 the members of the burgess class proper were outnumbered by something like four to three.

Many a town which succumbed in the course of Henry VI's and the Yorkist reigns to the practice of resorting to outsiders was one which, in 1422, was ceasing to look for its representatives in parliament among its merchant and trading elements, but had not yet begun to look for its representatives outside its own limits or its burgess-roll. Cases in point which spring to mind are those of Robert Darcy of Maldon,[1] a lawyer in Crown employment, Robert Whitgreve of Stafford, a lawyer who was one of the tellers of the exchequer,[2] John Warfield of Wallingford, the receiver of the Buckinghamshire family of Stonor,[3] Robert Carlisle junior of Carlisle, a member of Lincoln's Inn,[4] Robert Gilbert of Gloucester, another member of Lincoln's Inn,[5] Richard Duffeld of Grimsby, clerk of the peace for the parts of Lindsey in Lincolnshire,[6] John Forthey of Worcester, clerk of the peace for Worcestershire,[7] William Wood[8] and John Bye,[9]

[1] Robert Darcy (see p. 159, n. 2) was sometime steward of the estates of Henry V's maternal grandmother, Joan Bohun, dowager countess of Hereford (*Cal. Pat. Rolls, 1416–22*, p. 235) and from 10 April 1410 to 23 March 1413 and again from January 1423 to his death on 3 September 1448 (from October 1440 in survivorship with his nephew, Henry Filongley) was clerk of the Court of Common Pleas (*ibid., 1408–13*, p. 219; *ibid., 1422–9*, p. 23; *ibid., 1429–36*, p. 101; *ibid., 1436–41*, p. 471).

[2] Robert Whitgreve (see p. 159, n. 2) was on 18 July 1415 appointed one of the four tellers of the exchequer and his office, continuously held, was confirmed for life by patent of 24 November 1445 (Exchequer, Issue Roll, Michs. 3 Hen. V, P.R.O., E 403/622, mem. 7, etc., *Cal. Pat. Rolls, 1441–6*, pp. 335, 415).

[3] John Warfield, nine times M.P. for Wallingford, 1421–37, was receiver and steward of the Stonor estates between 1415 and 1443 (Royal Hist. Soc.). *Stonor Letters* (Camden Third Series, XXIX), pp. 29, 31, 36, xxii; *ibid.*, (Camden Third Series, XXX), ii. 179–80.

[4] Robert Carlisle junior, six times M.P. for Carlisle 1410–22, J.P. for Cumberland, 1435–71 (except in 1461), was a member of Lincoln's Inn in 1420 (*Admission Book*, p. 1).

[5] Robert Gilbert, eight times M.P. for Gloucester, 1415–32, was for twenty years after 1416 of the quorum of the peace in Glos., and in 1424–5 one of the governors of Lincoln's Inn (*Admission Book*, p. 2; *Black Book*, p. 2); he was escheator for Glos. in 1412–13, 1416–17, 1428–30.

[6] Richard Duffeld, thirteen times M.P. for Grimsby, 1413–49, was clerk of the peace for the parts of Lindsey certainly between August 1420 and November 1444 ('Oxford Studies in Social and Legal History', B. H. Putnam, *Early Treatises on the Practice of Justices of the Peace*, p. 25; P.R.O., E 101, 569/38; *ibid.*, 569/41; E 137, 19/3.)

[7] John Forthey, M.P. for Worcester six times, 1420–31, was appointed clerk of the peace in Worcs. in January 1419 and was still in office at Michs. 1426, being superseded between then and 1439 (Putnam, *op. cit.*, p. 66; Exchequer, K.R. Estreats, P.R.O., E 137, 48/1).

[8] William Wood, six times M.P. for Winchester, 1413–23, and from 1415 to his death in 1431 joint-farmer of the alnage of cloth in Hants, had been recorder of Winchester in 1408 (R. R. Sharpe, *Letter Books of London*, Book I, p. 70).

[9] John Bye, M.P. for Winchester in 1422 only, in 1409 had been, and in 1413 still was, town-clerk of Southampton (A. B. Wallis-Chapman, *The Black Book of Southampton*, i. 109, 115–16, 118, 139),

the ex-recorder and recorder respectively of Winchester, to instance some of the resident burgesses of the legal profession only. From the point of view of a departure from the statutory residential qualification of borough representatives, the change from representation by a lawyer or 'gentleman' resident in the borough to representation by one who was not so resident, was perhaps an important step for the individual borough to take. From the point of view of its contribution to a transformation of the social character of the Commons in parliament its effect was negligible. But even if we examine the problem from the narrower (and perhaps safer) point of view of the fulfilment of the qualification of residence imposed by the statute of 1413, or from the point of view of the effect of the failure to observe it on the general composition of the nominally burgess-element in the Commons, an analysis of the returns to Henry VI's parliaments demonstrates that the real transformation of the character of borough representation had taken place before the middle of the century. The revolution in the character of borough representation was by then already a fact. Already one half of the borough representatives were not true burgesses in the sense of being resident. And this was before the government of Henry VI was submitted to those strains and stresses which brought him ultimately to deposition. The civil wars and commotions of that time do not seem to have been even responsible for a catalytic quickening of the process.

Was there any change, as time moved on, in the character of the non-residential parliamentary burgesses and of those resident parliamentary burgesses who did not belong to the burgess class proper? Something of a change does seem to have taken place. But it was not simply that either neighbouring or resident gentry or resident or local lawyers began to come in for a large share of borough representation (they already enjoyed a considerable share of it) but rather that, by the middle of the fifteenth century, a different sort of gentry was making its way into borough representation in far greater numbers than before: the busy administrators, retainers, and hangers-on of nobles and men of influence, officials and servants of the royal household, and members of the royal civil service, careerists with more clearly marked political affiliations and attachments. Of these types there was no more than a handful among the parliamentary burgesses of 1422; towards the middle of the century they were becoming very numerous. Among these careerists royal officials, men occupied in tending the administrative and legal machinery of the Crown or holding positions of greater or lesser authority in the royal household, some of whom were frequently in attendance on the very person of the sovereign, were especially conspicuous. In fact in 1453 this

but by 1416 he was town-clerk and was later recorder of Winchester, and on 6 November 1422 (3 days before parliament met) he was appointed by Henry IV's widow, Queen Joan, her joint-attorney and receiver in the city and liberty (Hist. MSS. Comm., *6th Report*, pp. 601–2; J. Milner, *History of Winchester*, ii. 306).

Westminster element attained to as high a proportion (17%) of the Lower House as was to be reached by the middle of Elizabeth's reign.[1] It is, of course, important to recognize that this adulteration of the personnel of the Commons by the 'Westminster crowd' was not achieved solely through the exploitation of opportunities that borough representation more easily allowed. Exchequer officials and other civil servants—and they are generally of no very great importance and usually make up only a small group—more often than not did secure election from boroughs. So did those yeomen of the royal chamber and other miscellaneous small fry of the household entourage of the king who were coming to regard seats in the Commons as worth the getting. But when highly-placed household officials like its treasurer or controller, or when knights or esquires of the body royal sat in the Lower House, they were returned almost invariably as knights of the shire. Even the members of the little fragmentary group of ushers of the royal chamber who got themselves elected to parliament were for the most part returned by their county courts. In fact, members of the royal household came generally to form a considerably bigger proportion of the knights of the shire than they did of the parliamentary burgesses.

The return of Sir John Fogge,[2] treasurer of the household and privy councillor, by Canterbury in 1467 was, therefore, something of a remarkable occurrence. But not only because he was an important household official. Here was a *knight* representing a borough, or a city to be exact. The only knights by rank who had previously been elected for a city or borough had been merchant princes of London and even such had been few and far between. Fogge's example was followed by Sir John Scott, privy councillor, in 1472, when he sat for Appleby along with the keeper of the great wardrobe; and another knight then sat for Gatton in Surrey. In the next parliament (1478) Sir John Paston and Sir William Knyvet secured election for Yarmouth and Bletchingley respectively. These were obviously still very exceptional cases, but they illustrate clearly that the breakdown of the earlier distinction in the Commons between the *gradus* of those who represented shires and the *gradus* of those who represented boroughs was far advanced by the end of the medieval period. If we may still describe the Lower House as a '*communitas communitatum*', it must be with some important reservations in mind. Its composition was becoming more homogeneous.

By 1422, as we have seen, this tendency to social uniformity in the Commons in parliament was well marked. But at this stage probably no class contributed to it so much as did the men of law. It is possible to identify as lawyers no fewer than thirty-six of the parliamentary burgesses of Henry VI's first parliament and they were to average, in the course of their careers, an attendance at between six and seven parliaments. They included (apart from those lawyers

---

[1] J. E. Neale, *op. cit.*, p. 302; Wedgwood, *op. cit., Biographies, passim.*
[2] Wedgwood, *op. cit., Biographies*, pp. 339–42.

I have already mentioned as being resident in their boroughs) such men as the clerk of the peace in Surrey,[1] the town-clerk of Southampton,[2] the clerk of the courts of the college of St. George of Windsor whom the borough of Wycombe returned,[3] the abbot of Reading's bailiff in the liberty of the borough of Leominster,[4] John Hody of Shaftesbury, later chief justice of the King's Bench,[5] and Nicholas Assheton, later justice of the Common Bench.[6] The lawyers, sitting in the Commons as parliamentary burgesses or as knights of the shire, some few of them sitting indifferently in either rôle as opportunity and circumstance afforded, quite clearly tended to obliterate the lines of social distinction between the formally differentiated elements of the Lower House, the knights and the burgesses.

Miss Thrupp, in her examination of the criteria of gentle rank in her book, *The Merchant Class of Medieval London*, is of the opinion that 'recognition of the professional man was still, in the fifteenth century, rather grudging'.[7] An analysis of the membership of the later medieval Commons, and especially of the knights of the shire, of whose qualifications gentility was felt to be one of the most important, does not, I believe, support this view—although, I admit, Miss Thrupp had other and quite valid grounds for expressing it. In Henry VI's first parliament the *jurisperiti* were no less than a fifth of the Lower House (incidentally almost double the fraction they might constitute in a later Elizabethan house of commons[8]) and of these the greater *pro rata* proportion was

[1] John Hipperon, M.P. for Guildford in March 1416 and 1422, was clerk of the peace for Surrey by October 1417 and was still in office twenty years later (B. H. Putnam, *op. cit.*, p. 25; Exchequer, Sheriffs' Admin. Accounts, P.R.O., E 101/588, 49).

[2] Thomas Marlborough, ten times M.P. for Southampton, 1395–1426, was town-clerk and one of the three lawyers appointed on 6 November 1422 by Henry IV's widow, Queen Joan, to act as her attorneys in the royal courts and to collect all her revenues. Joan enjoyed the greater part of the fee-farm of Southampton (*The Steward's Book of Southampton*; *The Sign Manuals and Letters Patent of Southampton*, ed. H. W. Gidden, i. 88, 90).

[3] Nicholas Clopton, M.P. for Wycombe in 1422 (A. K. B. Roberts, *St. George's College, Windsor Castle, 1346–1416*, pp. 148, 215).

[4] Richard Wynnesley, M.P. for Leominster in 1422, 1427, 1432, and 1442, was by December 1420 the abbot's bailiff there and as such made the returns to the sheriff of Hereford of the Leominster burgesses elected to all the parliaments between 1420 and 1442, save those of 1426 and 1432 (P.R.O C. 219, bundles 12–15).

[5] See above, (p. 159, n. 2. By 1438 Hody was serjeant-at-law and was made chief justice on 13 April 1440 (*Dict. Nat. Biog., s.n.*)

[6] See above, (p. 159, n. 2). Assheton assumed the coif of a serjeant-at-law in February, 1443, and by Trinity term 1444 was a justice of the Common Bench, an office he held until his death in 1466 (Foss, *Judges of England*, iv. 410).

[7] Sylvia L. Thrupp, *The Merchant Class of Medieval London*, p. 246.

[8] J. E. Neale, *op. cit.*, p. 302. The number of practising lawyers in the parliament of 1584 was 53 out of 460 M.P.'s; my calculation for the parliament of 1422 is 57 out of 262, 37 elected as burgesses, 20 as knights of the shire. Professor Neale, however, is able to say that in 1593 'forty-three per cent. of the members possessed a legal education' (*ibid.*, p. 307). The records of Lincoln's Inn are, unfortunately, the only records of an Inn of Court to have survived from so early a date as 1420, when its Register of Admissions begins.

to be found among the shire-knights; roughly, one out of every four county representatives was a man of law. As a group these lawyer knights of the shire were particularly important because it was from their ranks that those whom it is not going too far to describe as parliamentary figures were drawn, men versed, too, in the expertise of parliamentary procedures.

A few of the most important of these shire-knights learned in the law were in royal employment, members of the lay civil service, in the exchequer, in the administration of the king's private estates of his heritage of Lancaster, and in the administration of the royal household. At the time of their return in 1422 John Wodehouse[1] and John Throckmorton[2] respectively elected for Suffolk and Worcestershire, were the two chamberlains of the Exchequer, that is, in charge, under the treasurer, of the lower exchequer of receipt and issue as distinct from the upper exchequer court of audit and pleas. Wodehouse was also chancellor of the duchy of Lancaster and chancellor of the county palatine. He may well already have become chancellor to Henry V's queen, Catherine of Valois, but this other office of his was by way of being an appendage to his chancellorship of the duchy, a considerable part of Catherine's dowry income being provided from duchy sources. Other ex-officio members of the council of the duchy of Lancaster to be returned in 1422 were its chief steward north of Trent, Roger Flore of Oakham,[3] whom the Commons elected as speaker for

---

[1] John Wodehouse, M.P. for Norfolk in 1410, November 1414, March 1416, 1417, May 1421, and for Suffolk in 1422, was appointed chancellor of the duchy of Lancaster on 4 April 1413, and he held office until June 1424 (W. R. Williams, *Duchy of Lancaster, Official Lists*, p. 2). From 6 July 1415 until his death on 27 January 1431, he was king's chamberlain of the exchequer, his original patent being for life (*Cal. Pat. Rolls, 1413–16*, pp. 52, 57, etc.). Within a few days of this appointment he was made one of the feoffees of those parcels of the duchy which Henry V set aside to fulfil his will, of which Wodehouse was chosen as one of the operative executors (*ibid.*, pp. 356–7, 408; *ibid.*, *1416–22*, p. 172; *Foedera*, ix. 289–93). In 1422 he was steward of the liberty of the abbey of Bury St. Edmund's, to whose abbot in the following year he acted as parliamentary proxy (Exchequer, L.T.R., Mem. Roll, 1 Hen. VI, P.R.O., E 368/195; P.R.O., S.C. 10, no. 2347). The precise date when he became chancellor to Queen Catherine is not known (P.R.O., D.L. 28/5/8) but it was probably very early in Henry VI's reign if not before.

[2] John Throckmorton, M.P. for Worcs. in November 1414, 1420, 1422, 1432, 1433, and 1439, was a tenant and retainer of the Beauchamp earls of Warwick (W. Dugdale, *Warwickshire*, pp. 558–9). From January 1414 to his death on 12 April 1445 he was of the quorum of the peace in Worcestershire. Early in 1419 he began what proved to be a life tenure of the Beauchamp chamberlainship of the exchequer (Exchequer, Issue Roll, Easter 7 Hen. V, P.R.O., E 403, 640, mem. 10; Wedgwood, *Biographies*, 851–2 is here in error). He was to be feoffee, attorney, and later executor to earl Richard. From February 1428 he was under-treasurer of England until his death (Wedgwood, *op. cit.*, p. 851; F. Palgrave, *Ancient Calendars of the Exchequer*, ii. 158; Nicolas, *Proc. and Ord. P.C.*, v. 81).

[3] Roger Flore, twelve times M.P. for Rutland, 1397–1422, and speaker in October 1416, 1417, 1419, and 1422, was appointed chief steward of the duchy of Lancaster north of Trent on 1 December 1416, a position which he held until his death in 1427 together with an *ex officio* membership of the duchy council (Duchy of Lancaster, Accounts Various, P.R.O., D.L. 28, 4, no. 9; W. R. Williams, *op. cit.*, p. 19). He was separately appointed chief steward for Lancs. and Cheshire on 22 February 1417 and was superseded *there* on 9 July 1425 (I owe this information to Mr. R. Somerville).

the fourth time, and John Leventhorpe esquire, knight of the shire for Herts, the receiver-general and attorney-general of the duchy. Leventhorpe is particularly interesting: receiver of Henry IV before he came to the throne, he had automatically graduated in 1399 to the office of receiver-general of the duchy of Lancaster properties descending from John of Gaunt, and had accepted in addition the stewardship of all the duchy estates in the home counties; he proved so indispensable as to be retained in his duchy offices by Henry V at his accession in 1413, the only member of the higher duchy administrative staff to survive the new king's first regnal year; he was unique too, but for a more important reason, namely, in being chosen as an executor by *both* the first two Lancastrian kings. There was no scarcity of employment for men of this type of the professional administrator, if not with the king, then in the fee of one or more of the great magnates as legal counsel, or as feoffee to uses, or as executor, or in some other intimate administrative connexion.[1]

It would perhaps be tedious here to particularize these connexions, attachments, and affiliations, but from the point of view of the social composition of the Commons it is important to recognize that the ties binding most of the shire-knights to many of the more important peers of parliament might not only be of a professional character, but could be and often were ties of family relationship. Lord Berkeley's father-in-law, Sir Humphrey Stafford, himself a not far distant kinsman of the young earl of Stafford, was one of the Dorset knights.[2] The son of one of the Suffolk knights, Sir John Howard, had married the earl marshal's sister.[3] Thomas Chaucer of Ewelme, knight of the shire for Oxfordshire, chief butler of England, a man who had enjoyed some considerable measure of Henry V's confidence and had been five times speaker, was cousin to Bishop Beaufort of Winchester and his brother, the duke of Exeter; Chaucer's daughter was at this time countess of Salisbury, and was to become the first duchess of Suffolk.[4] The young knight just out of his nonage, Sir William Eure[5] of Witton-le-Wear (Durham) and Old Malton (Yorks), knight of the shire for Yorkshire, was son-in-law to one of the foremost of the northern magnates whose political stock had risen as a result of the revolution of 1399, Henry Lord FitzHugh of Ravensworth, the head of a northern baronial family powerful in lands and influence between Swale and Tees; FitzHugh had been chamberlain to Henry V

[1] Duchy of Lancaster, Accounts Various, P.R.O., D.L. 28, 4, 1–11. For his executorship to Henry IV and Henry V, see *Rot. Parl.*, iv. 5; *Foedera*, ix. 289–93; *Register of Henry, Chichele*, ed. E. F. Jacob, (Cant. & York Soc.), ii. 421 *et seq.*

[2] John Smyth of Nibley, *The Lives of the Berkeleys*, ed. J. Maclean, ii. 40–8; *Cal. Close Rolls, 1413–19*, p. 469; *ibid.*, *1419–22*, p. 28.

[3] G. Brennan and E. P. Statham, *The House of Howard*, i. 10 *et seq.*

[4] K. B. McFarlane, 'Henry V, Bishop Beaufort, and the Red Hat, 1417–21', *Eng. Hist. Rev.*, lx. (1945), 327 *et seq.*; *Dict. Nat. Biog.*, *s.n.*

[5] N. H. Nicolas, *The Battle of Agincourt*, p. 32; *Victoria County History of Yorkshire, North Riding*, i. 533.

and then treasurer of England from 1417 to 1421; he was the only one of Henry V's operative executors of baronial rank and he was appointed a member of the new royal council. Ralph, Lord Cromwell, another member of the new council, had his brother-in-law, Sir Richard Stanhope,[1] sitting among the Commons for the sixth time as knight of the shire for Nottinghamshire. Sir William Bonville, knight of the shire for Devon, was the son-in-law of Reginald Lord Grey of Ruthyn.[2] One of the Cambridgeshire knights, Sir Walter de la Pole, was cousin german to the earl of Suffolk.[3] And there are others. It is clear that those of the shire-knights who were without seigneurial attachments, of either interest or kinship, were in the minority, and some of those who had not such demonstrable connexions were related to those who certainly had.

It is not my business here to consider whether or not these personal connexions between the Commons and the Lords in parliament predetermined the political subservience of the former to the latter. Mr. McFarlane[4] has warned us of the dangers of attributing an uncomplicated and exclusive loyalty to those members of the gentry who took fees of retainer from their aristocratic connexions or who served them in some administrative capacity. We must also be aware of the dangers of under-rating the contribution such men must have made by way of counsel to the formulation of the policy, in and out of time of parliament, of the lord by whom they were engaged. These considerations apart, may we not ask ourselves whether these aristocratic attachments on the part of individual shire-knights, and sometimes of burgesses too, did not help to bind together in some sense (as well as divide) the members of the Lower House? As a result of their aristocratic ties, their common membership of aristocratic councils and of committees of feoffees in scattered estates, the mutual acquaintance of individual representatives in the Commons would be artificially but inevitably enlarged. However this may be, we can be sure of one thing: the Common House was filled by men who were by no means complete strangers to one another. And this was doubtless generally the case and always had been so, for men of that landed gentry class which supplied the knights of the shire quite often held estates in several counties. Many of the knights and burgesses of 1422 had sat and stood together in the chapter house of the abbey of Westminster on previous occasions and were to do so again; but this apart, many of them, particularly the shire-knights, were in frequent and close communication both in and between the times of parliamentary session on matters of their lord's concern and their own, and not a few were related by close family alliances of blood.

[1] R. Thoroton, *History of Nottinghamshire*, ed. J. Throsby, iii. 243; *Testamenta Ebor.* (Surtees Soc.), ii. 40.

[2] *Cal. Close Rolls, 1413–19*, p. 199.

[3] H. A. Napier, *Notices of Swyncombe and Ewelme, in Co. Oxford*, p. 291.

[4] K. B. McFarlane, 'Parliament and "Bastard Feudalism"', *Trans. Royal Hist. Soc.*, 4th Ser., xxvi; and his 'Bastard Feudalism', *ante*, xx. 161 *et seq.*

The ties between many of the parliamentary knights and members of the peerage were only the natural outcome of the fact that the landed gentry class was sometimes socially, militarily, and from the point of view of territorial standing, hardly distinguishable from the lower ranks of the titular nobility. It was, of course, members of the group of quasi-baronial proprietors whom from time to time, particularly following the crises of dynastic revolution, the king ennobled by making them the recipients of individual writs of summons to the Upper House of parliament or the beneficiaries of patents of creation. We need only recall at random the Tiptofts, the Hungerfords, the Stourtons, the Wenlocks, the Stanleys, the Staffords of Southwick, and the Bonvilles, who one after another slowly made their way upwards into the titular nobility in the course of the fifteenth century, to realize the absence of any social gulf between the most important of the class which furnished the knights of the shire and the parliamentary aristocracy. Quite a number of the shire-knights of 1422, who did not themselves achieve—although some of them did in their descendants—the distinction of an individual writ of parliamentary summons, could have supported elevation into the ranks of the peerage if only the changes and chances of that world of 'bastard feudalism' had been more favourable to them, for a few of them surpassed and more of them could vie with at any rate the lesser magnates of the Upper House of parliament in the extent and value of their landed estates. The property of Sir John Pelham, in 1422 knight of the shire for Sussex, formerly treasurer of England at the end of Henry IV's reign, had then been worth at least £540 a year (over two-thirds of the *average* baronial income of the time).[1] The manors in Essex and Cambridgeshire alone of Sir John Howard, knight of the shire for Suffolk, yielded about £400 a year, and he held the considerable hereditary estates of his family in East Anglia besides.[2] Landed estate in Oxfordshire, Hampshire, Berkshire, and Somerset, mainly inherited from his great-uncle, Bishop Wykeham of Winchester, brought in similar annual revenues to Sir Thomas Wykeham, shire-knight for Oxfordshire.[3] Besides these men, eleven of the parliamentary knights of 1422 are known to have been possessed of lands worth between £100 and £200 a year, and men like Sir William Palton of Somerset, a first cousin of Lord Botreaux (with his twenty-one manors in the West Country and in Oxfordshire, Warwickshire, and Hampshire), Sir Edmund Hastings of Yorkshire (with his estates in the North and East Ridings, North Durham, and Northumberland),

[1] T. W. Horsfield, *History of Sussex*, i. 315; *Sussex Archaeological Society Trans.*, lxix. 63; *Cal. of Feudal Aids*, vi. 410, 457, 504, 521. The average baronial income taxed to the subsidy of 1436 was £865 including annuities, or £768 without annuities (H. L. Gray 'Incomes from Land in England in 1436', *Eng. Hist. Rev.*, xlix. (1934), 619).

[2] *Cambridge Antiquarian Society Communications*, xv. (Cambs. Subsidy Rolls, 1250–1695), pp. 115, 124; *Feudal Aids*, iii. 581–2, 615, 643; vi. 408, 438–9.

[3] *Dict. Nat. Biog., s.n.*

and his fellow knight of the shire, young Sir William Eure (with his extensive properties in Durham, Yorkshire, and Northumberland, and his coal-mine leases in the South Durham field) must have been worth considerably more. The significance of these income-figures will be the better realized if it is remembered that the total number of English land-owners with annual incomes of over £100 was probably short of two hundred and fifty at this time.[1]

Territorial standing was not the only qualification which the shire-knights of 1422, or of any other parliament, possessed to sit for the communities of the counties from which they came and which they represented in the fullest sense of the word. The class from which they were drawn was the bedrock of medieval English political and local administrative life. In 1422 for something like two centuries it had supplied continuously that element in local government whose employment had become and was to remain so characteristic of the English method, providing, as it did, a balance between the requirements of the central administrative machine and the claims of the locality to sympathetic consideration. The shire-knights and men of their sort knew the needs and were aware of the temper of the communities from which they were returned. Half of the seventy-four knights of the shire of 1422 had previously served in the office of sheriff, and nearly as many, in the office of escheator, some of them in more than one bailiwick. Two out of every three were exercising, at the very time of their return, the justiceship of the peace. Most, if not all, had served on local royal commissions of array, inquest, special oyer and terminer, or other such enterprises of limited scope and duration. To such men a return to parliament was but one stage in the *cursus honorum* of the country gentleman; it was one of the recognitions and privileges rather than one of the penalties of social position.

From what I have said already about the lawyer element among the knights of the shire it will be clear, I think, that the original Plantagenet intention to restrict the class from which the county representatives were to be drawn to those who were *milites gladio cincti* had perforce and, for long, meant very little. It has been shrewdly observed by Sir Maurice Powicke that, in the term 'knight of the shire', the word 'knight' is sometimes not so important as the word 'shire'.[2] It is even doubtful, as Miss K. Wood-Legh has said, whether more than a third of the knights of the shire in the Model Parliament of 1295 had been belted knights.[3] And by 1422 for at least half a century and probably for much longer, the term 'knight of the shire' had been employed as a technical term bearing no necessary relation to, or correspondence with, the rank of those who belonged to the *ordo militaris*. Few of those who served as knights of the

---

[1] H. L. Gray, *op. cit.*, pp. 622, 630.
[2] *Études présentées à la Commission Internationale, op. cit.*, iii. 137.
[3] Miss K. Wood-Legh, 'Sheriffs, Lawyers, and Belted Knights in the Parliaments of Edward III', *Eng. Hist. Rev.*, xlvi. 372–88.

shire in 1422 would have been free from a liability to distraint for knighthood, being qualified by their substance to assume it; but it is interesting to find that as great a fraction as a half of them was, in fact, comprised of knights by rank; many of these, moreover, lived up to their title and followed the profession of arms. Only the co-operation, either direct or indirect, of this class and the class of esquires who, in this period of military service by contract, had attained (for all practical purposes) equality with the knights, had made possible the resumption of the French wars in 1415. Nearly half of the 1422 knights of the shire had been actively involved in the conduct of English military and administrative affairs across the Channel at some time or another in the previous seven years. John Golafre esquire,[1] knight of the shire for Berkshire, had been appointed in the spring of 1418 to the office of receiver-general for Normandy and had held the position until May of the following year. Sir John Bertram, one of the Northumbrian knights, had been made custodian of the castle of Fronsac in the Bordelais in August 1419.[2] In the following year Sir Robert Whitney, shire-knight for Herefordshire, had been appointed captain of the town of Vire in the Côtentin.[3] In May 1421 the lieutenancy of Harfleur had fallen to Henry Mulsho esquire,[4] one of the Northants knights and, two months later, his fellow knight of the shire in 1422, Thomas Chambre esquire, had been appointed captain of the town of Guînes in the march of Picardy.[5] And some of these men were to retain their interest in English affairs in France in the new reign.

It will, I think, have become clear why it happens that occasional contemporary attempts to theorize on the changing structure of fifteenth-century English society suggest a certain intellectual confusion. The classic medieval division of society into *oratores*, *bellatores* and *laboratores*, died hard.[6] In a sermon preached before parliament in 1442[7] the chancellor, Bishop Stafford of Bath and Wells, considering the six steps leading up to the throne of Solomon, with which he compared the realm of England, envisaged six orders of society: the prelacy and the ordinary clergy made up two of these; the *militia*, the estate of chivalry, he left as one order; his *communitas populosa* was comprised of merchants, agriculturists, and artificers. This was basically the old theory and to the Commons among his audience must have seemed to have little relevance to the social facts exemplified in their own composition. Nine years earlier, the same bishop, then as chancellor also, had opened the parliament of 1433[8] with a discourse on

---

[1] *D.K.R.*, xli. 712; *ibid.*, xlii. 320.
[2] *Ibid.*, xliv. 611; Exchequer, Issue Roll, 7 Hen. V.
[3] *D.K.R.*, xlii. 382.
[4] *Ibid.*, pp. 426–7; *ibid.*, xliv. 638.
[5] *Ibid.*, xlii. 371; *ibid.*, xliv. 630, 632.
[6] Cf. S. B. Chrimes, *op. cit.*, pp. 94–6.
[7] *Rot. Parl.*, v. 35; cf. S. L. Thrupp, *op. cit.*, pp. 292–3.
[8] *Rot. Parl.*, iv. 419; cf. S. L. Thrupp, *loc. cit.*, and S. B. Chrimes, *op. cit.*, p. 97, where the sermon is mistakenly attributed to Cardinal Beaufort.

the text '*Suscipiant montes pacem populo, et Colles justitiam*', which text, Stafford claimed, illustrated the '*triplex status regni*'. The mountains of his text comprised, he said, the '*praelati, proceres et magnates*'; the hills, the knights, esquires and merchants; the people, the '*cultores, artifices et vulgares*'. This classification was much nearer the truth of the matter with regard to the composition of the parliamentary Commons. The representatives of shires and boroughs, however wide apart, still were the extremes of political and social influence in their number, and however dissimilar, in social construction and political tradition, were the communities for which they were returned, were becoming as time went on less heterogeneous and more of an amalgam of the middle strata in society, the *mediocres*. By the end of the fifteenth century theory had caught up with the actuality of conditions at its beginning; and the Commons were recognized to be what they had for some time been in fact, a single, the third, estate of the realm in parliament. The 'estate of the Commons', a political concept in its origin, came in the fifteenth century to be a much less inapposite term than formerly, in its implications of an important measure of social unity in the Lower House of parliament.

VII

The Office and Dignity of Protector
of England, with special reference
to its origins [1]

HENRY V died on 31 August 1422 at Bois de Vincennes near Paris, leaving to succeed him as king of England and heir of France Henry of Windsor, a baby of nine months, whom he had never seen. Had he lived less than another two months he would have achieved his ambition and become (by the terms of the treaty of Troyes) king both of England and France, for Charles VI of France died on 21 October. It was Henry V's infant heir who became king of the two realms. A situation of great difficulty was thus created. Constitutionally, it proved of greater complexity in England than in France.

All the post-conquest English kings, except Henry IV, had occasionally gone overseas ; and the provision of a regency in the sense of the appointment of a deputy or (more rarely) deputies for a king incapacitated by absence from England had come, therefore, by long and frequent usage, to raise no difficulties. For such royal absences had normally been of short duration and no serious constitutional strain had ever resulted from them. When Henry V died, however, England was faced for the third time within a century by the problems attendant upon the accession of a king who was incapable of governing his kingdom because still under age. In 1327 Edward III had succeeded to the throne at the age of fourteen years, and in 1377 Richard II at the age of ten. The fact of Edward III's short minority (1327–30) did not irremediably aggravate the effects of Edward II's reign and deposition. But the minority of Richard II (1377–89) had been the cause of acute political and constitutional discomfort. Indeed, it may be said that Richard's deposition in 1399 and the Lancastrian usurpation resulted largely from Richard's minority and his reactions to its consequences for himself and his prerogative. Like Edward III in 1327, Richard II in 1377 had been able, however, to perform from the first some of the formalities of the kingly

[1] I should like to thank Professor E. F. Jacob and Mr. K. B. McFarlane for their criticisms and suggestions when this article was being written.

office—to open parliament in person, for example.   Unlike them, Henry VI at his accession was too young for that, or even to be crowned.   Henry V may have been alive to the potential similarities between the events that followed the death of Edward III in 1377 and the situation which might be produced by his own demise : the conduct of Edward III's two more important surviving sons, John of Gaunt and Thomas of Woodstock, might conceivably be paralleled by that of his own two surviving brothers, John, duke of Bedford and Humphrey, duke of Gloucester, and his legitimated kinsmen, the Beauforts.   However this may be, he was too wary a statesman not to have realized before he died the danger to the Lancastrian dynasty of a long minority.   So far as England was concerned, Henry V tried to safeguard the dynasty by providing in his testament for the royal power to be principally exercised during this minority by his younger brother, Gloucester. France was to be governed by the duke of Burgundy or by Bedford.   The latter arrangement he could provide for without the need of English consent.   The former, so it later became clear, he could not.   This essay is concerned with the immediate constitutional results of Henry V's death, of the appointment by his will of Gloucester to a form of regency in England, and of the ultimate rejection of that act by the magnates of the realm in the first parliament of Henry VI's reign ; with the resulting establishment by parliamentary authority, for the first time in English history, of the office of Protector *eo nomine* ; and, by way of epilogue, with the significance of this first Protectorship in the history of the office and dignity as a whole.

Henry of Monmouth died with comparative suddenness and in France, so England was unprepared for the catastrophe. The news of the king's death on the last day of August 1422 was slow in coming through to England and does not seem to have been generally known here before 10 September.[1]   But this was no great matter.   For comparatively little of constitutional or political moment could be immediately decided in England, simply because some of the leading magnates of the realm were then in France. Of the lay peerage, no more than the three earls of Westmorland, Northumberland, and Devon, and twelve barons had been summoned to attend the parliament of the preceding December, the last of the late reign, under the presidency of Henry V's elder surviving brother, then ' custos Anglie ', John, duke of Bedford. The duke of Exeter, the earls of Warwick and March, Henry, Lord FitzHugh (Henry V's chamberlain), Ralph, Lord Cromwell, and the bishop of London (ex-chancellor of the duchy of Normandy) only came home with the late king's funeral cortège ;   the duke of

---

[1] *Rotuli Parliamentorum* (Record Commission), iv. 194a.

Bedford (whom Humphrey, duke of Gloucester, his younger brother, had succeeded as 'custos' in May 1422 when Bedford rejoined the king)[1] as the regent there naturally stayed on in France. So did the earls of Salisbury and Suffolk. Humphrey, earl of Stafford, who returned to England, and John, earl of Oxford, who did not, were both still in their minority. Not until 5 November was it possible to hold a fairly representative meeting of the great council of prelates and nobles. But what could be done in the interim had been done.

At a meeting of available magnates on 28 September at Windsor where they performed homage and swore fealty, Henry V's chancellor of England, Bishop Langley of Durham, resigned formally into the hands of the infant king the great seal of gold ; and it was there entrusted, again formally by the king, but by the hands of the duke of Gloucester, to the temporary custody of the keeper of the rolls of Chancery, Simon Gaunstede. At this meeting, where the great seal was thus made available for authenticating acts of royal authority, Archbishop Chichele, the bishops of Winchester, Exeter, Lincoln and Worcester, the earl of Ormonde, Lords Talbot, Clinton, and Poynings, and the keeper of the privy seal, are also known to have been present. But there were other magnates there too.[2]

Parliamentary sanction for whatever constitutional form government was to assume under the infant king was evidently then considered necessary. And on Michaelmas day the parliamentary writs of individual summons and the writs authorizing the elections of knights of the shire, citizens, and burgesses, were dated at Windsor.[3] Parliament was to meet on the first possible day after the lapse of the customary minimum period of forty days between summons and assembly, namely, on 9 November. The writs were 'tested' by the king, and not, as had been the case in the late reign at such times as Henry V was absent from the realm, by the 'custos Anglie'. Gloucester himself now received a summons, although neither he nor his elder brother, Bedford, had received one when acting as 'custos'. Gloucester's 'custody' of the realm was clearly considered to have ended with Henry V's demise; with a king present in the realm there could legally be no 'custos' or royal 'locum tenens'. Henry of Windsor was theoretically paramount.

According to the constitutional ideas of the time it seems likely that the legally valid existence of the royal continual council came to an end with the death of the king to whose special service its members were sworn, just as did the commissions held on oath by

---

[1] Gloucester had previously been 'custos Anglie' from December 1418 to February 1420.   [2] *Cal. Close Rolls, 1422–9*, p. 46.
[3] *Reports, touching the Dignity of a Peer of the Realm* (1829), iv. 855–6.

other great officials.[1]   But the summoning of Henry VI's first
parliament was advised by ' the council ' and, dated at Windsor on
29 September, the parliamentary writs of summons were jointly
warranted ' by king and council ' (their issue was actually authorized on the following day ' per dominos et proceres ibidem exis-
tentes ') ; [2] so also were warranted the letters patent renewing the
appointments of the existing treasurer and barons of the Exchequer
(30 September), of the puisne justices of both Benches, the keeper
of the rolls of Chancery, and the keeper of the Great Wardrobe
(1 October), and of the chief justices of the two Benches (6 October).   Certain minor officials' commissions were warranted solely
' by the council ' : that of the king's remembrancer of the Exchequer (30 September), that of the master of the mint in the
Tower and at Calais (1 October), and those of certain Household
purveyors (2 October).   The chief justices of South Wales (7
October), the chamberlains respectively of North and South Wales
(2 October), and the chamberlain of Chester (4 October) were
appointed by advice of the council, and the chancellor, justiciar,
and treasurer of Ireland (4 October), with its assent.[3]   The council
warranted the arrangements required for the Channel crossing and
the reception in England of the funeral cortège of the dead king.[4]
The available lords spiritual and temporal seem to have assumed
that the royal authority had devolved upon them by reason of
Henry V's death and the tender age of his heir.   Being, as one of
their minutes of 1 October alleged,[5] the ' major et sanior pars
omnium dominorum et procerum regni ', it was they who must
act, pending the appointment of a sworn council of the regular
kind, not only as the king's advisers but as virtually constituting
the executive.   After all, this was only in accordance with what
had happened at the very beginning of Richard II's minority, and
in accordance with the doctrine to be explicitly enunciated in 1427
that the lords of the kingdom together might be regarded in such
a circumstance as invested with the royal authority when they met
in a parliament or great council, even if (as was, of course, the case
in 1427) a normal sworn council was in being.   Nevertheless it
may be suggested that this council of magnates and principal
officials, which met in the course of the seven weeks preceding
Henry VI's first parliament, enjoyed only a provisional status in
the sense that it acted as a sort of ' care-taker ' government until
such time as a new sworn council could be properly appointed.
For these lords who had exercised the functions of government
evidently saw fit to seek and secure from the parliament of 1422
its ratification of the most significant of their acts, including the

---

[1] J. F. Baldwin, The King's Council, p. 169.
[2] N. H. Nicolas, Proceedings and Ordinances of the Privy Council (hereinafter cited as
P.P.C.), iii. 3.   [3] Cal. Pat. Rolls, 1422–9, pp. 1–4.   [4] Ibid. pp. 35–6.   [5] P.P.C. iii. 4.

summoning of this parliament itself : ' Fait assavoir, qe conuz la verity cy en Engleterre de la passement le tres noble Roi Henry Quint puis le conqueste . . . et considerez la tendre age de son tres beau fitz et heir nostre tres soverain seigneur q'or est, assemblerent pleuseurs honurables Seigneurs de ceste Roialme, si bien espirituelx come temporelx, pur la iminent necessite de governance de la mesme, si bien pur conservation de la paix et exhibition de Justice, come pur l'exercice des offices au Roi regardantz. Sur qoy diverses Commissions, de lour bone advis, ont issuez desoutz le grande seal du Roi as mentz persones, si bien as Justices, come as Visconts, Eschetours, et autres de ses officers, et auxi ont brieves du Roi par l'advis suisdit issuez a somondre ceste Parlement, a l'entente qe par le commune assemble de toutz estates du Roialme, et lour sages conseilles et discretions, la meillour governance pur la tres excellente Persone et Estat de nostre dit soverain Seigneur, et pur tout le dit Roialme, purroit estre purveu en le dit Parlement, si bien pur la salvation del Roialme, come pur defense de le mesme.'[1]

On 5 November a gathering of certain lords spiritual and temporal took place in the council chamber next the chamber of parliament in the palace at Westminster.[2] This was, of course, two days before the late king's burial and four days before parliament was summoned to meet. Many of the lords had already appeared at Westminster, and so the assembly was somewhat different from the other recent meetings of the magnates, being more fully and representatively attended. For there were present the archbishop of Canterbury, the bishops of Winchester, Durham, Norwich, Exeter, Worcester, Lincoln, and Rochester, the dukes of Gloucester and Exeter, the earl of Warwick, the earl Marshal and the earl of Northumberland, and Lords Ferrers, Talbot, Botreaux, Clinton, Audley, FitzHugh, Poynings, Berkeley, and Cromwell. They were met to consider the terms of the duke of Gloucester's commission to begin, conduct, and end the forthcoming parliament : to supply the place of the king therein. The meeting is especially interesting because in it there came to the surface for the first time (so far as surviving records show) the problem of Gloucester's ambition to be regent or, if this ambition were overborne, of the status he might be allowed in the form of government to be devised for the period of the king's minority. A form of commission had evidently been already drafted and its terms set forth that Gloucester on his royal nephew's behalf was to open, conduct, and dissolve parliament ' de assensu concilii '. This phrase Gloucester interpreted as limiting his power to do these things without conciliar sanction and not, which was just possibly intended, as indicating the circumstances of its authorization.[3] He

---

[1] *Rot. Parl.* iv. 170b.   [2] *P.P.C.* iii. 6–7.
[3] W. Stubbs, *The Constitutional History of England* (Library Edition), iii. § 330, n. 3.

protested that the introduction of this phrase into his commission would be ' in prejudicium status sui ' and that, in any case, no such terms of qualification had been employed in his previous commissions to preside over parliament (as ' custos ') in Henry V's name ; were the phrase to be included, he objected, the lords could keep parliament in being for a year on end if they so wished, ' quod erat contra libertatem suam '. The lords, when asked their opinions, answered that in view of the king's age and for the duke's and their own future security they could not, must not, and would not consent to these or equivalent words being excluded. In the end the duke agreed to their petition and counsel and allowed the letters patent setting forth his commission to be engrossed as they stood. Dated 6 November, Gloucester's commission passed the great seal.[1]

To perform the function of king's commissary in parliament, Gloucester was the obvious choice, being the highest of the blood royal and the premier peer then in England. The hedged-in power to act with the assent of the council was all, however, that the lords would allow him of a distinctive position before parliament met. And Gloucester had to accept the fact of aristocratic solidarity. This had in all probability been largely achieved as a result of Henry Beaufort's sustained opposition to Gloucester, although the bishop, who had much at stake, was not alone prominent among the lords who did not share Gloucester's estimate of his own rights and abilities.[2] The tactical weakness of the position of Gloucester face to face with this immediate problem had been, of course, that over a month before, at the end of September, when a political démarche on his part would have been perhaps less difficult, he had accepted (without any known objection) his obligation to receive and obey a summons to parliament, and simply as duke of Gloucester. It made him no more than one among his peers. For, when on 3 March 1428, seeking from the Lords in the parliament then in session a definition (and presumably an enlargement) of his power and authority as Protector, Gloucester stated that he would absent himself from the parliament chamber until they furnished him with an answer, the Lords were to remind him that he had been summoned to parliament as duke of Gloucester, upon his faith and allegiance, ' as other Lordes be, and non otherwise ' ; and they humbly requested, but in the king's name required, his attendance as being legally obligatory. They also stated that ' in Parlement . . . We knowe no powar nor auctorite that ye have other thenne ye as Duc' of Gloucestre sholde have, [in the event of] the Kyng beyng in Parlement at yeres of mest discretion '.[3] Duke Humphrey's failure at Michaelmas 1422 to challenge his summons to

[1] *Rot. Parl.* iv. 169.
[2] *The Chronicle of John Hardyng*, ed. Henry Ellis (London, 1812), pp. 390–1 ; *Rot. Parl.* iv. 326b.   [3] *Rot. Parl.* iv. 326–7.

parliament simply as duke of Gloucester with its implied denial of any vestigial power and authority that he may well have hoped to salvage from his recent office of ' custos Anglie ', or to claim before parliament met the distinctive position in the government accorded him (as we shall see) in Henry V's will, seriously affected his chances of securing the kind of regency he desired for himself. This being the case, his attitude in the council meeting of 5 November was imprudent. For his expression on that occasion of his fears for his ' status ' and ' libertas ' must have made crystal-clear to the lords there present the bent of his political designs ; his protest against any limitation of his powers as the king's commissary in parliament aroused their seemingly unanimous opposition on this particular point, but a more general antipathy on the part of this important group of magnates may well at this stage have been generated. Moderation on the eve of parliament's assembly would have been Gloucester's better course. Gloucester, however, was not a moderate man ; time-biding subterfuge was a weapon absent from his political armoury. It was accordingly in an atmosphere of disquiet that Henry VI's first parliament met on 9 November, two days after the late king's entombment between the shrine of the Confessor and the chapel of the Virgin in the adjacent abbey church of Westminster. Gloucester's hopes of the regency during his young nephew's minority and in his brother Bedford's absence must, when parliament assembled, have then rested mainly on the possibility of the Lords in parliament as a whole falling in with any wishes that Henry V had expressed on this subject in his written testament or by word of mouth on his death-bed. Henry V had certainly declared his intentions in his will, but what they were *in toto* we cannot be sure, because the testament which he had drawn up on 10 June 1421 at the time of his last departure from England, that testament in which his plans for this country were almost certainly described, has not come down to us.[1] That is why the chronicles of the time are an indispensable even if sometimes an unreliable and incomplete source for Henry's provisions.

It was suggested by Professor Vickers [2] that no serious doubt need be entertained about the details of the political dispositions made by Henry V during his fatal illness at Bois de Vincennes, ' for ', he stated, ' the chronicles are almost unanimous in their assertions '. This is not correct. Leaving on one side for the moment the problem as to whether the chroniclers were right in representing Henry V's political plans to have been formulated and declared merely on his death-bed, we may say at once that the chroniclers are by no means unanimous in their assertions of what transpired at Bois de Vincennes.

[1] See the *Excursus* of this article.
[2] K. H. Vickers, *Humphrey, duke of Gloucester* (London, 1907), p. 103.

This lack of unanimity is not so pronounced a feature of their treatment of Henry V's plans for France and Normandy as it is of their evidence of his intentions regarding England. But what some of them say even about the regency of France is to be taken with a great deal of reserve. It is doubtful whether what did in fact happen there fulfilled so simply, as some of them suggest, Henry V's scheme for France. Eventually the duke of Bedford became responsible for the government of Normandy and the regency of France. This is what all the important extant English chronicles say Henry V had decided before his death.[1] All, that is, except Walsingham : this St. Albans chronicler states that the king had provided for Bedford to be ' custos Ducatus Normannie ', but that the duke of Burgundy, whose alliance and support Henry recognized on his death-bed to be essential to English success across the Channel, should be ' Regens Regis et regni Francie '.[2] The evidence of the French chronicler, Monstrelet, in whose knowledge of Burgundian affairs confidence can be placed, confirms Walsingham's statement, but makes it clear that Burgundy's regency was naturally to be conditional upon his acceptance of it ; if Burgundy were to refuse the offer, Bedford was to undertake the government of France as well as Normandy.[3] This is in fact what came to pass.

[1] T. Livio, *Vita Henrici Quinti regis Angliae*, ed. T. Hearne (Oxford, 1716), p. 95 ; *Vita et Gesta Henrici Quinti*, ed. T. Hearne (Oxford, 1727) [wrongly attributed by Hearne to Thomas Elmham and now known as ' the Pseudo-Elmham '], p. 337 ; *Chronicles of London*, ed. C. L. Kingsford (Oxford, 1905), p. 295 ; Harding, *op. cit.* p. 387.

[2] T. Walsingham, *Historia Anglicana*, ed. T. H. Riley (Rolls Series, 1863–4), ii. 345.

[3] E. de Monstrelet, *Chronique*, ed. L. Douët d'Arcq (Paris, 1857–62), iv. 110. Walsingham's and Monstrelet's evidence is here more precise than that of the other chroniclers, and it seems to conform more closely with the facts of the situation at the moment of Henry V's death. For, then, Charles VI of France, though imbecile and incapable of government, was still alive, and the establishment of a regency of his French ally, the duke of Burgundy, after death should end his own, would perhaps have been a sensible policy for Henry V to suggest. Pending the succession to the French throne of Henry of Windsor (in virtue of his inherited title of heir of France), Henry V, it seems, intended that after his death Bedford should withdraw to Normandy, and ' kepe that contray as wel as the remenant of his conquest on the best wise that God wolde yeve hym grace with the revenuz and profittes therof and do therwith as he wolde do with his oune ', merely of course until Henry of Windsor came of age. This was what William Alnwick, bishop of Norwich and Henry V's erstwhile secretary, and three other lords present at the king's deathbed recollected some four and a half years later (on 25 February 1427) of his intention regarding Bedford's future position in France (*P.P.C.* iii. 248 ; the other three lords to testify were the earl of Stafford and Lords Bourchier and Hungerford). It was clearly Henry V's aim at the last to keep the kingdom of France and his own conquests separate and distinct so long as Charles VI was alive and the succession of Henry of Windsor to the French throne was problematic. Only after the accession of Henry VI as king of France on the death of Charles VI (nearly two months after Henry V's demise) did Bedford's regency of France become a preferable, indeed an inevitable, part of English policy across the Channel. Charles VI's death fundamentally altered the French situation from the English point of view. A Burgundian regency of France for Charles VI was one thing ; for Henry VI, quite another matter.

So much for France. Regarding England, the problem is more complex, and the chroniclers of the time for the most part complicate its elucidation and obscure the issues. For, in purporting to deal with Henry V's arrangements for the government of England after his death, they not only represent them as made when the king was dying, but are far from being unanimous in their descriptions of what then took place. It is not quite proper, however, to speak of the evidence of the chronicles as characterized by 'violent disagreement';[1] because, though the chronicles, English and French together, do not always say the same thing about what occurred at Bois de Vincennes regarding England, their evidence is by no means always contradictory, and, if allowances be made for discrepancies here and there, it is still of great worth. Certainly, the evidence of the English chronicles is very valuable.

On the question of the personal custody of Henry of Windsor all the important extant chronicles, French and English alike, are at one in stating that Thomas Beaufort, duke of Exeter, was willed by Henry V on his death-bed to have an important share in this and the related obligation of the young king's education. The *Vita Henrici Quinti* of Titus Livius of Ferrara, who was writing about fifteen years later, mentions Exeter alone as having been entrusted with the 'mores . . ., custodiam corporis et doctrinam' of the infant prince.[2] But all the other chroniclers associate one or two magnates more with him in this task. Unfortunately, they do not always agree as to who these were. It is, however, most likely that all the magnates named, in one account or another of the chronicles, as personal guardians of Henry of Windsor—the duke of Exeter, Henry Beaufort, bishop of Winchester, Richard Beauchamp, earl of Warwick, and Sir Walter Hungerford, Henry V's steward of Household—were in fact appointed by Henry V, even if they do not appear listed all together in any one single chronicle version of Henry V's settlement.[3]

---

[1] K. B. McFarlane, 'England : The Lancastrian Kings', *Cambridge Medieval History*, viii. 387.

[2] T. Livio, *op. cit.* p. 95.

[3] Along with the duke of Bedford, Henry Beaufort, bishop of Winchester, Exeter's elder brother, had been Henry of Windsor's godfather ' at fontstone ', and one of the London chronicles states that Henry V ' committed the kepinge of Henry his yonge sonne and prynce ' to both the brothers Beaufort (*Chronicles of London, op. cit.* pp. 74, 295). The chronicler, John Hardyng, seems to go too far at one point of his rhyming narrative in describing the bishop as ' hiest gouernor of the kynge [Henry VI] his persone ', for elsewhere he simply makes him coadjutor to his brother, Exeter (Hardyng, *op. cit.* pp. 387, 392). This may well have been what Henry V intended, for the *Gesta Henrici Quinti*, with its full account, also mentions the bishop as being appointed : the two Beauforts were to be ' circa regimen filii mei . . . attendentes ' (*Gesta Henrici Quinti Regis Angliae*, ed. B. Williams [London, 1850 ; English Historical Society], p. 159). To the Beauforts, the *Gesta* is alone among the English chronicles in adding the earl of Warwick (*ibid.*). There seems no reason why we should not accept this piece of evidence and include Warwick among Henry of

Whatever their differences and disagreements, all the chronicles, with the exception of Monstrelet, who quite mistakenly says that Henry V entrusted to Exeter ' le régime du royaume d'Angleterre ' along with the custody of the person of his heir, agree that such of the guardians as they mentioned were charged by Henry V *either* with the custody or education of Henry of Windsor *or* with both. Monstrelet's evidence regarding Exeter can be immediately discounted, because his account contains no allusion to Gloucester's special position, in fact, no reference to Gloucester at all (except for Henry V's warning against future dissensions between him and Burgundy). None of the chroniclers, except Monstrelet, omit in their accounts of what transpired at Bois de Vincennes to refer to the pre-eminent and distinctive position of Gloucester in Henry V's English settlement. But none of them allows him, whatever his special place in the guardianship of Henry of Windsor, any share in the latter's personal custody or education. What, then, was the

Windsor's personal guardians. He was an executor of Henry V's will as were the other guardians, and he may well have been chosen, if only, perhaps, during Henry V's last illness at Bois de Vincennes where he was certainly among the small group of English magnates present when the king made his final death-bed dispositions. Moreover, the notice of his appointment is confirmed by Monstrelet (*loc. cit.*). This French chronicler, however, goes further : he states that the king enjoined Warwick ' que vous demourez tout quoy avecques lui pour le conduire et aprendre selon l'estat qu'il lui appartient, car je ne sçaroie mieulx pourveoir '. But we know that it was Exeter who was specially entrusted with Henry of Windsor's education ; that Warwick, according to Hardyng's Chronicle (*op. cit.* p. 394), acted as the young king's preceptor only after Exeter's death in 1427 ; that there is no reference to Warwick acting as ' magister regis ' until May 1428 ; and that it was a few weeks later still that he was given a formal commission under the great seal to take charge of the boy king's education (*P.P.C.*, *op. cit.* iii. 294, 297 ; *Dictionary of National Biography*, iv. 30 ; Warwick was to retain his care of Henry VI's person up to the time of his appointment as lieutenant of France and Normandy in July 1437). It seems that Monstrelet may here have been in error and deduced Warwick's designation by Henry V as Henry of Windsor's instructor from his later appointment, which was most likely one made *de novo* by the council. There certainly is no confirmation of Monstrelet's further assertion that the three estates of England in 1422 appointed the earl ' au gouvernement de la personne de leur roy '. It is possible, of course, that Henry V appointed Warwick to be a tutor in reserve, to be called upon if Exeter were unable to act or when Exeter died. But even if Monstrelet was quite mistaken about the origins of Warwick's later magisterial position, there is no way round the clear statement of the *Gesta* that he was to be one of Henry of Windsor's guardians or the fact of Monstrelet's reference to him in this connexion (however confused and erroneous in its details). Of all the chronicles, English and French alike, only the *Vita et Gesta Henrici Quinti* (the Pseudo-Elmham) refers to Sir Walter Hungerford, K.G. (who in August 1422 for the last five years had occupied the stewardship of the royal Household and was one of Henry V's executors) as being among those deputed to a special position of trust regarding Henry of Windsor. Hungerford was patron of the unknown author of this Life of Henry V and encouraged him to write it not long before his own death in 1449. According to this account, the king had decided that Exeter and Hungerford were to be ' circa personam filii mei . . . attendentes ' (*Vita et Gesta*, *loc. cit.* ; for Hungerford's patronage of the ' Pseudo-Elmham ', see C. L. Kingsford, *English Historical Literature in the fifteenth century* [Oxford, 1913] pp. 5, 58.) This appointment of Hungerford, though noted in only this one chronicle, is confirmed (see below p. 205) by indisputable record evidence (*P.P.C. op. cit.* iii. 37).

nature of this special place of Gloucester's in Henry VI's guardianship ? This problem is connected with another that has already
been referred to : were Henry V's political dispositions for the
guardianship of Henry VI and the government of England during
his minority simply the hasty, oral declarations of a fevered king
in extremis, which is what all the chroniclers who deal in any detail
with the situation at Bois de Vincennes suggest they were?   These
two problems can best be discussed together.

There is, fortunately, no doubt at all that Henry V intended to
arrange some form of guardianship of his infant heir which would
also make provision for the latter's incapacity to rule his English
inheritance, and that he did so (at least partially and perhaps completely) in a written testament.   Unhappily, as has been suggested,
the chronicle evidence with regard to both these matters is for the
most part not very precise or conclusive.   The testimony of
Monstrelet, as we have seen, is generally unsafe, and regarding
Gloucester's position is useless.   The three extant English
chronicles which refer to Henry V's arrangements for the government of England—the *Vita* of Titus Livius, and the anonymous
Gesta and *Vita et Gesta*—are agreed, however, that Gloucester,
' custos Anglie ' at the time of Henry V's death, was to continue
to be in charge of government in this country.   But the authors
of the *Gesta* [1] and the *Vita et Gesta* [2] are not at all helpful regarding
the nature of Gloucester's proposed authority ; both represent
Henry V at Bois de Vincennes as saying, ' Anglie vero protector
et defensor sit frater meus dux Gloucestrie ' ; which title (with
that of ' principalis consiliarius ' added) was simply what the
parliament of 1422 allowed Gloucester if Bedford were absent.
Nevertheless, they do distinguish Gloucester's position in Henry
V's scheme from the position of those to whom, they say, Henry V
granted the governance of his son : those who were to be ' circa
regimen filii mei . . . attendentes ' (*Gesta*), *alias* ' circa personam
filii mei . . . attendentes ' (*Vita et Gesta*).

The *Gesta* and the *Vita et Gesta*, moreover, very usefully make
it clear that Henry V had drawn up his testament and last will
before leaving England, that there were certain codicils attached
thereto, and that he showed these instruments to the princes and
magnates who were with him in his last hours : ' testamentum
suum, prius in Anglia circumspecte conditum, et alios codicellos sue
voluntatis ultime testativos eis ostendit '.   This was probably the
testament drawn up on 10 June 1421, when Henry V left England
for the last time.   The *Gesta* and the *Vita et Gesta* simply refer to
the testament and codicils in order to state that they contained
certain financial provisions for the payment of the king's debts and

---

[1] *Gesta, op. cit.* p. 159.   [2] *Vita et Gesta, op. cit.* p. 333.

of rewards to his Household servants.[1] There is every reason to believe, however, that one of the codicils contained his arrangements for the government of England during his heir's minority. In a memorandum which Gloucester was to submit to the Lords in the 1422 parliament regarding the title and authority he hoped to gain (I shall refer to the memorandum in greater detail later on), the duke stated that he had been granted ' *tutelam et defensionem principales* of the kyng [Henry VI] ' in a codicil of Henry V's will.[2] This memorandum, citations in Latin apart, was written in English, and these particular Latin words may be presumed to have been ' lifted ' from the codicil of the will, which would almost certainly be written in Latin throughout.   It is very interesting to find some of these very same words of the codicil appearing in the *Vita* of Titus Livius when he describes Henry V's death and draws Henry VI's attention to the claims of Gloucester (Livius's patron) on his gratitude : ' Testamento tamen ante tui [i.e. Henrici sexti] tutelam primasque defensiones et curam Humfredo Gloucestrie duci . . . [Henricus quintus] legavit '.[3]   It is immediately after this statement that Livius refers in his text to the fact that Henry V entrusted to his uncle, Exeter, the ' mores . . . custodiam corporis et doctrinam ' of his heir.   In his reference to Gloucester, Livius was probably working from a copy of the codicil of Henry V's will supplied to him by his patron, and it is possible that in his reference to Exeter's charge he was drawing for his information on the same source, where there may well have been included both some arrangement for the upbringing and education and for the custody of the person of Henry V's heir.   If Exeter's charge formed a part of Henry V's testament and if that testament (as there is good reason to believe) was the one drawn up on 10 June 1421, the arrangement for the education of Henry V's heir, as distinct from the provision for the custody of the heir's person, perhaps assumed that the heir would be of the male sex.   For when that testament was made the heir was as yet unborn.   But by then the queen was some three months pregnant, having (in view of Henry of Windsor's birth on 6 December 1421) presumably conceived within a few weeks of her coronation on 23 February in that year ; and when he drew up the testament Henry V did know that a direct succession was at any rate likely to be assured, and that provision

---

[1] *Gesta, op. cit.* p. 160 ; *Vita et Gesta, loc. cit.* ; Walsingham (*Historia Anglicana, op. cit.* ii. 343) says that Henry V, ' cernens . . . sibi mortem proximam imminere . . . sapienter disposuit, testamentum confecit, et debita sua de suis thesauris et jocalibus superabundantibus solvenda constituit . . . '

[2] For the whole memorandum itself, see S. B. Chrimes's transcript of it in ' The Pretensions of the Duke of Gloucester in 1422 ', *ante*, xlv. 102.   For the difficult problems connected with the testaments of Henry V and the codicil referred to in the memorandum, see the *Excursus*.

[3] T. Livio, *op. cit.* p. 95.

must needs be made for the government of England during a minority in the event of his own early death and for the custody of the child in such a circumstance. That Exeter's charge was referred to in the written testament seems not at all unlikely when it is remembered that Sir Walter Hungerford's charge to attend ' circa corpus Regis nunc [i.e. Henrici sexti] ' was on 18 February 1423 referred to in a council-minute as ' secundum quod testamento Regis defuncti patris sui sibi injunctum fuit '.[1]

It seems reasonably clear that the chroniclers who treat in detail of Henry V's last acts at Bois de Vincennes were informed at any rate of some aspects of what happened there. But their representation of Henry V's political dispositions as merely the verbal commands of a dying king to those who stood by his death-bed, however dramatically satisfying it may be, is by no means the whole truth of the matter. It was not in Henry V's character to be taken by surprise. If, however, the royal will was read out and perhaps amplified or elucidated as the end approached, this would partly account for the manner in which these chroniclers described its political plans as having been orally declared by the king when at the point of death. However this may be, from the evidence of Gloucester's memorandum, Titus Livius's account, and the council-minute referring to Hungerford, it seems fairly certain that, whatever additional or supplementary eleventh-hour arrangements Henry V devised for the custody of his heir, he had already made *some* provision for it and also for the special role that Gloucester was to assume in the government of England during the minority, and that he had done so, before he last left England, in his written will and its codicils.

According to most of the available evidence, the actual custody of Henry of Windsor's person was to rest with a group of magnates amongst whom Gloucester is never included. But, according to the codicil (as cited in Gloucester's memorandum) and Livius's testimony in the *Vita*, to Gloucester had been granted the principal wardship and defence of the infant heir : ' *tutelam et defensionem principales* '. These different pieces of evidence at first sight appear to be contradictory. But they can be reconciled if we assume that in Henry V's mind at the time when he made his will there had been formed an intention to distinguish between the wardship of the inheritance and the custody of the person of the heir. Gloucester was to be in England what Bedford was to be in France. The key to the matter may lie, it is suggested, in the word ' tutela '.

When Gloucester submitted his memorandum to the Lords in the 1422 parliament he referred in that statement to their already

---

[1] *P.P.C. op. cit.* iii. 37 ; the council temporarily exonerated Hungerford to allow him to go overseas.

expressed objection to the word 'tutela' as a term used in Roman law ('a terme of lawe civile'), and to their refusal to allow its use in whatever commission Gloucester was to be granted.[1]   The term itself is worth investigation.   It was by the creation of a 'tutela', which the Institutes of Justinian defined as 'ius ac potestas in capite libero ad tuendum eum qui propter aetatem se defendere nequit, iure civili data ac permissa', that under Roman law the guardianship of a male below the age of puberty was provided for. Even anciently the 'tutela' was normally created in a written testament, and from imperial times its creation in a codicil to a will had been permissible.   In Roman legal usage the administration of the 'tutela' might be vested in a group of persons, but even where this was the case one of them could, and in fact would normally, act in a principal capacity, the others being liable to supervise in a general way or, alternatively, perform special functions.   The actual care of the child need not be undertaken by the 'tutor', but in the managing of his ward's affairs he would be obliged to ensure his maintenance and upbringing out of the heir's estate that was entrusted to his charge.   The Roman 'tutor', in fact, was first and foremost the controller of the property of his ward in the time of the latter's incapacity to administer it himself.[2] This was seemingly what Henry V had intended Gloucester to be. Incidentally his desire to create a 'tutela' explains Henry V's omission of his queen, Catherine of Valois, from the nominated personal custodians of Henry of Windsor, although he appointed her to be one of the overseers of his will : under the Roman law of primitive times she would herself, as a widow, have been subject to a 'tutela' ; certainly there was no place for her, as a woman, in the 'tutela' created by her husband for their son.[3]

Gloucester must have based his claims to the regency of England during Henry VI's minority on the knowledge that what his royal brother had conferred upon him in his will was the principal administration and defence of the inheritance of his heir ; which, if the kingdom could be regarded as the property of the king (and in Henry V's mind it still evidently could be), included the inherited attributes of regality.[4]   In accordance with the classic notions of the 'tutela', Henry V's arrangements for his

[1] S. B. Chrimes, loc. cit.

[2] W. W. Buckland, A Manual of Roman Private Law (Cambridge, 1928), pp. 89–98 ; W. W. Buckland and A. D. McNair, Roman Law and Common Law (Cambridge, 1936), pp. 44–8.

[3] The infant Henry VI seems, in fact, to have regularly resided with his mother until her liaison with Owen Tudor, a member of their joint ménage.

[4] In S. B. Chrimes's English Constitutional Ideas in the Fifteenth Century (Cambridge, 1936), pp. 9–13, there is a discussion of Sir John Fortescue's treatment in his De Natura Legis Naturae of a kingdom conceived of as real property, but real property of a public nature, and of the merits of the Roman law of 'tutela' in connexion with problems of succession to kingdoms.

son's personal custody were a separate and secondary, albeit a related, matter. It is true, of course, that the chronicler Hardyng tells us that Gloucester ' desired to have the kepyng of the kyng ',[1] and in the articles of complaint submitted by Duke Humphrey at Leicester early in 1426 against Bishop Beaufort (then chancellor), he was to describe himself as one ' to whom, off alle persones or that shulde be in the londe, by the wey off nature and birthe yt belongeth to se unto the governaunce off the kynges persone '.[2] But it is important to recognize that in this protest Gloucester made no reference to any right of his to govern the king's person under the terms of Henry V's will ; and it is also important to allow for the fact that Gloucester's protest came some time after Henry V's settlement had been drastically modified by the Lords in the 1422 parliament, when they rejected, as we shall see, Gloucester's Romanist interpretation of the Romanist formulae of Henry V's will.[3]

It is only by assuming that Gloucester already knew of his pre-eminent place in Henry V's plans for this country—and the duke after all was an executor of his will—that we can understand the peculiar reference Gloucester had made to his ' status ' and ' liber-tas ' on 5 November 1422, when his powers as the king's commis-sary in parliament were under discussion by the lords in council. Such a knowledge of his royal brother's intentions may have sus-tained Gloucester in the weeks between the arrival of the news of Henry V's death and the meeting of the first parliament of the new reign ; and his confidence in the value of his political stock, shaken perhaps by the events of the meeting on 5 November, may well have been revived by the reading of the will in its various forms immediately after Henry V's burial two days later. The duke could hardly have been made more sanguine of his prospects, how-ever, by the ' pronunciatio ' or sermon delivered at the ceremonial opening of parliament, which took place on 9 November.[4] It was preached by Archbishop Chichele of Canterbury. This in itself is a sign that the gravity of the occasion was fully recognized.[5]

After the reading of Gloucester's patent of commission as the

---

[1] Hardyng, op. cit. p. 390.   [2] Chronicles of London, op. cit. p. 77.

[3] It is interesting to note a later tradition among common lawyers that Glouces-ter favoured the Civil Law. Polydore Vergil described him as ' skillfull in the lawe which is called civill.' ' Even at this day ', he said, ' the common lawyers, when their pleasure is to find some detestable fault with the civill lawe, which the now they be ignorant of in that more they hate it, bring forth this example of [Gloucester's] severitie ' (Three Books of Polydore Vergil's English History, ed. Sir Henry Ellis [Camden Society, vol. 29], p. 72). I am indebted to Professor Jacob for this reference.

[4] Rot. Parl. iv. 169.

[5] By 1422 it had long been customary for the ' pronunciatio ' or declaration of the causes of summons to a parliament to be made by the chancellor of the day ; but, when parliament met in circumstances of a special political or constitutional nature, the discourse might take the form of a sermon preached by the primate of all England. It

king's lieutenant in parliament, the primate addressed the assembled Lords and Commons, taking his text, *Principes populorum congregati sunt cum Deo,* from a psalm of rejoicing in God as the King of His people.[1]   In his discourse Chichele recommended the new king as the son of his father. God had perfected His creation in six days, and thus perfection was associated with the number *six.* The infant king was the sixth of his name to occupy the English throne. Syllogistically, the perfection of his father's work was to be expected of him.   But the king was now of tender age, and parliament had been summoned to provide for ' la bone governance des tres excellent persone du Roi ', for the maintenance of the peace and the administration of the laws of the land, and for the defence of the realm. The sermon, as reported in the parliament-roll, went on : so that God in His mercy may grant peace and prosperity ' a toutz estates et gents de ceste Roialme ', provision ' pur la governance ' must be made of ' honurables et discretes persones . . . et ceo de chescun estate de ceste Roialme ', men of foresight and God-fearing, imbued with true doctrine, of good conversation and hating avarice. It is quite clear that what had been done in the first parliament of the last minority (October 1377) was being followed as far as possible, and that the roll of that parliament had been carefully scrutinized. Chichele was using very similar words to those which the Commons had used in 1377 in one of their requests.[2] This particular request of 1377 was distinct from another petition [3] of the same time in which they had asked for the appointment of a continual council, and the implication of the rest of this 1377 article (and of the answer it met with) is that the Commons were on that occasion referring simply to the composition of the Household of the new king, which, as a subject of request at all, the Lords of parliament then regarded as ' trop chargeante et dure '. It was not the reconstruction of the royal Household to which Chichele referred in 1422. Nor was it the governance of the king's person in the sense of immediate guardianship, for this was certainly not in question, and parliament was to make no recorded recommendation, or confirmation, of any existing arrangement made for it by Henry V. There can be little doubt that, as the notes on Chichele's sermon in the parliament-roll go on to show, the kind of ' governance ' the archbishop

had been so in the first parliament after Richard II's accession in 1377 when Sudbury had opened parliament, and again at Henry IV's accession in 1399 when Arundel had preached. Except in 1422 the primate never in the fifteenth century officiated in parliament in this way, unless he was also chancellor at the time. Admittedly, when the parliament of 1422 met, there had been as yet no chancellor appointed for the new reign. Even so, the choice of Chichele is significant, for there were others among the prelates who might conceivably have performed this function, either of the ex-chancellors, the bishops of Winchester and Durham, for example.

[1] *Biblia Sacra Vulgata,* Psalmus xlvi. 10.   [2] *Rot. Parl.* iii. 6a.   [3] *Ibid.* 7a.

here had in mind was such as would imply the exercise of the
royal authority ; and his reference to the need for honourable men
' de chescun estate ' suggests the provision of a council representatively constituted on the basis of ' estate '. Some deliberate
attempt, in fact, was to be made to secure in the new council a
balance of ' estates '.

All this, as Chichele is reported to have stated, finding his
analogy in the Old Testament story of the Exodus, was the stuff of
the wise counsel given by Jethro to his kinsman, Moses, ' Duc des
gents de Israel '.[1] Whether Chichele expatiated or not in his discourse upon all aspects of Jethro's advice we are not able to deduce
from the brief notes of the sermon in the parliament-roll. But the
moral of the biblical facts and their appositeness to the present
crisis in English affairs, in any case, would not be lost upon all of
his hearers. Moses had been found by Jethro to be overworked
in fulfilling the obligations of government. And Jethro had told
him that this was no good thing : ' stulto labore consumeris et tu
et populus iste qui tecum est ; ultra vires tuas est negotium, solus
illud non poteris sustinere '. When Jethro had advised the appointment of assistants from among the powerful and worthy,
Moses fell in with the advice given him : ' et electis viris strenuis
de cuncto Israel, constituit eos principes populi '. Gloucester was
Chichele's Moses ; his own was the part of Jethro, priest of
Midian. If he held to the whole of his script Chichele must have
referred to the inferior and subordinate powers of Moses's helpers
in government : ' quidquid autem majus fuerit, referant ad te
[Moysen] et ipsi minora tantummodo judicent '. If he did so, the
archbishop's sermon was a model of the art of the trimmer and of
being all things to all men.[2] But this is all purely conjectural, and
we must beware of the dangers of reconstructing Chichele's sermon
from the short report it gets in the parliament-roll. It remains
very doubtful whether he was disposed to prejudice the issue
before parliament. The emphasis of his discourse seems mainly to
have been on the need for co-operation in government, in the
interests of king and people, on the part of the magnates of the
realm, of whom Gloucester was foremost among those present.
This was as far as Chichele apparently would go. He may have
inferred that government at difficult times like these was best
when shared by a number of suitable persons : the idea that
Fortescue was to have a generation later when he defined his

---

[1] *Exodus*, xviii. 12–27.
[2] Was Chichele inclined to act the trimmer because of suspicions of the ecclesiastical ambitions of his suffragan, Bishop Beaufort of Winchester, whose hostility to
Gloucester's political aims had already been aroused? It is a possibility that must
not be either overstressed or overlooked when taking the political temperature of
this crisis in English affairs.

' regimen politicum ' as ' regimen plurium scientia sive consilio ministratum '.[1] But whether the direction of policy and executive control were to be either monarchical in character, vested, in view of Bedford's absence, in the person of Gloucester, or oligarchical, resting in the hands of the lords of the continual council, was a matter for parliament to decide. It is improbable that scriptural analogies played any further part in the ensuing discussions.

It must have been early in the 1422 session that the Commons in parliament requested [2] to know who should have ' the gouern-ance of this Reme undre our souverain lord [the king] bi his high auctorite '. According to the Lords' answer [3] to Gloucester's request of 3 March 1428 to be furnished with a definition of his authority and power as ' protector and defendour of this Lond ', Duke Humphrey in 1422 had proceeded to make a two-fold claim in parliament to the ' governaunce ' of England : it was his right, ' as wel be the mene of . . . birth as be the laste wylle of the Kyng that was [Henry V] '. The lords spiritual and temporal, prom-inent among them the bishop of Winchester, the duke of Exeter, and the earls of March and Warwick, we are now told, on the earlier occasion had long discussed the claim, in the course of their deliberations searching precedents from past times when kings had been of tender age and consulting learned counsel as to the laws of the land. Finally they had rejected the claim in both its aspects as being not ' grounded in precident, nor in the lawe of the land '. They had politely absolved Gloucester from any wilful intention to contravene or over-reach precedent and law, but had found his claim to have the right of governance by birth incompatible with the law and ' ayenst the rigzt and fredome of thestates of the . . . land ' ; and they had rejected his other claim to have it by Henry V's will, virtually on the same grounds, for ' the Kyng that ded ys, in his lyf ne migzt by his last will nor otherwyse altre, change nor abroge [abrogate] with oute thassent of the thre Estates, nor committe or graunte to any persone, governaunce or rule of this land lenger thanne he lyved '. The 1428 statement then goes on to assert that, in 1422, ' to kepe pees and tranquillite, and to thentente to ese and appese you [Gloucester] hit was avised and appointed by auctorite of the Kyng, assentyng the thre Estatys of this lond ', that in the absence of his brother (Bedford) Gloucester should be ' chief of the Kynges Counsail ', and should have a name different from other councillors, that of Protector and Defender,

---

[1] Sir John Fortescue, *The Governance of England*, ed. Chas. Plummer (Oxford, 1855), p. 112.
[2] S. B. Chrimes, *ante, loc. cit.* ; the request of the Commons, here referred to, does not appear on the parliament-roll, and was perhaps made by word of the speaker's mouth only.
[3] *Rot. Parl.* iv. 326 ; already referred to above, on p. 198.

with such certain powers as parliament had allowed and specified. This settlement was to operate not for the duration of the minority of Henry VI but during the king's pleasure : ' as long as it liked the Kyng '. This statement of 1428 embodied the received interpretation of the lords then sitting in Henry VI's fifth parliament of what had transpired during the first parliament of the reign upwards of five years before. It was a careful statement, obviously drafted with a full consciousness of the importance of the constitutional principles it contained. It is the only evidence upon record that throws light on the circumstances of the achievement of the 1422 settlement.[1] But it is not, of course, the only extant ' record evidence ' of what transpired. For there is also the document, now to be considered in detail, which contains those suggestions and stipulations that were submitted by Gloucester to the Lords in the course of the 1422 discussions : Public Record Office, Parliament and Council (Chancery), 53/12.[2]

On the subject of Gloucester's claim to have the right of governance by birth, this document (we have already referred to it as ' Gloucester's memorandum ') makes it clear that one (seemingly the chief) formal objection of the Lords was based on the precedent of 1377, when Richard II had succeeded to the throne at the age of ten years. Richard's eldest surviving uncle, John of Gaunt, duke of Lancaster, had not been then granted the name or authority of ' governor '—so the Lords in 1422 very properly interpreted the 1377 parliament-roll—and on that occasion, as we know, no regent was appointed (Archbishop Sudbury, in his sermon opening Richard II's first parliament, did in fact refer to Richard himself as given by God to be ' Roy et Gouvernour ').[3] Instead, after the coronation, but before Richard's first parliament met, a great council of prelates and lay magnates nominated twelve councillors who were virtually to act as an interim council of regency : two bishops, two earls, two barons, two bannerets, and four knights bachelor.[4] And then, when parliament did meet some three months later, the Lords, being formally moved to do so by a petition of the Commons, nominated in parliament a salaried council of nine to hold office for one year. In it the different estates were again represented in some sort of proportion : three bishops, two earls, two bannerets, and two knights bachelor.[5] In this council was then vested the exercise of the royal authority.

[1] I am not sure whether the *ex post facto* statement made in the parliament-roll of 1427–8 about the decision taken in 1422 would necessarily make that decision ' of record ' in the technical legal sense. The recording in 1428 of the Lords' refusal in 1422 to admit Henry V's right to nominate a regent during the minority of his heir would, however, I believe, constitute a legally valid precedent.

[2] Printed with introductory notes in S. B. Chrimes, *ante, loc. cit.*

[3] *Rot. Parl.* iii. 3b.   [4] Rymer, *Foedera* (London, 1869), iv. 10.

[5] *Rot. Parl.* iii. 6.

Its composition subsequently underwent changes, but during Richard's earliest years its members were chosen in parliament (here the recent precedent of the ' Good Parliament ' of 1376 was being followed). Of this council Lancaster was not even an ordinary member ; along with his younger brothers (Edmund of Langley and Thomas of Woodstock), as Gloucester's memorandum of 1422 rightly points out, John of Gaunt was merely given power to correct any defaults by way of ' maintenance ' on the part of its members.   The Lords in 1422 might conceivably have harked back to the earlier precedent of Edward III's minority when a standing council of four bishops, four earls, and six barons, headed by the king's cousin, Henry, earl of Lancaster, was appointed to advise the young king in all matters of government.[1]   But the precedent of 1377, so we are told in Gloucester's memorandum, was all that they could find, and they were content with it.   Naturally so, for it was very much to their present purpose : in 1377 it was the Lords who had determined how Richard II's government should be carried on ; the council formed to undertake the work had been chosen by them, and mainly from their own number ; and no special position of pre-eminence had been given to Richard II's nearest kinsman, John of Gaunt.

Clearly by no means despairing or lethargic, anxious to increase rather than to see diminished the power he had recently exercised as ' custos ', insistent that Henry V's testamentary instructions regarding the government of England after his death should be complied with, and dissatisfied with the title of ' Defensor of this Reme and chief counseiller of the kyng ' (which was all apparently at this stage of the debate that the Lords had decided to concede him), Gloucester alluded to the Commons' request to know who should have ' the gouernance of this Reme undre our souverain lord bi his high auctorite ' ; and he submitted that the Lords' allowance of the title of ' Defensor ' left this request in substance as well as technically unsatisfied.   Moreover, the memorandum stated that, although Henry V's codicil had granted Gloucester ' tutelam et defensionem principales of the kyng ', the Lords had raised objection to the word ' tutela ' as a term used in Roman law (' a terme of lawe civile ') : to its employment in any commission to be allowed to Gloucester they ' derst nat agree to for diuers causes '.   Some title, however—the memorandum shows that Gloucester clearly felt—must be found to include the authority implied by the word ' tutela ' or, at any rate, some similar form of authority which would be distinct from and additional to that implied by the word ' defensor ' ; so that the codicil (which the memorandum states that the Lords had accepted) might thus be substantially

[1] Rot. Parl. ii. 52a ; Henry Knighton, Chronicon, ed. J. R. Lumby (Rolls Series, 1889), i. 447, 454.

complied with. The petition of the Commons could only be properly met, Gloucester's memorandum suggested, if he were given the title of 'Governour under the kyng' or another equivalent name. But if the title of 'governour' was not available (because of the absence of support for it in the precedent of 1377), then he was prepared to compromise. More generally well-informed or more thorough in his methods of historical research than his opponents, he expressly based his compromise on the two-hundred year old precedent of 1216, when, at the beginning of the earliest minority after the Conquest (that of Henry III), William Marshal, earl of Pembroke, had been appointed as 'rector regis et regni Anglie'.[1]

At this stage of the 1422 debate when Gloucester's memorandum appeared both sides were seemingly still in a reasonable frame of mind, in spite of Gloucester's unsuccessful bid to act as the king's commissary in parliament on larger terms than the Lords would allow. Dispute there was between him and them, it is true, but no rancorous quarrel between intransigent parties had thus far supervened. For Gloucester's memorandum, at least by inference, represents the Lords as having been quite prepared to accept another title for Gloucester or additions to the title they had already granted him, if more convincing evidence than that of Richard II's time were forthcoming ; or else (and this is perhaps a safer interpretation) the document represents them as being ready to take other adducible evidence at least into consideration : ' and if they coude better recordis haue founde or ellys if my lord [Gloucester] coude any better fynde thei shuld be accepted '. Gloucester, too, was determined to appear accommodating : if the precedent of 1216 were to be accepted he would waive out of modesty one part of William Marshal's title, that of ' rector regis ', ' for that he vil nat desire ne to make his seel of suche auctorite as the seid William Mareschall didde ' ; he was, moreover, so he said, desirous of accepting the other part (that of ' rector regni ') by assent of the council, and he had no objection to the word

---

[1] Perhaps Humphrey's knowledge of the 1216 case was derived from an earlier satisfaction of a personal interest in the history of his predecessors in his own secondary title of earl of Pembroke—he had been created in 1414 earl of Pembroke as well as duke of Gloucester. But that is as may be. Had he known about it and in detail, Gloucester might have done better to turn to the precedent of 1327 than to that of 1216. His ancestor, Henry, earl of Lancaster, had been appointed at the time of Edward III's coronation, by common assent of the magnates, ' capitalis custos et supremus consiliarius regis . . . pro meliori gubernaculo regis et regni ', if these words of the chronicler, Henry Knighton, can be taken as being precisely those of an officially-granted title. We do not know that they can ; but Knighton, a canon of the Augustinian abbey of St. Mary in the Meadows at Leicester, is usually very reliable in matters of detail relating to the earls and dukes of Lancaster who were also, of course, earls of Leicester and the patrons of Knighton's own house (Knighton, *op. cit.* i. 447).

'defensor' being added in order to meet the already expressed 'desir and appointment' of the Lords.[1] All might yet be well : the Lords would perhaps be content with a fresh precedent they had either promised to accept or at least to entertain ; they would perhaps allow a form of authority not dissimilar from that implied by the objectionable word 'tutela', and so the requirement of Henry V's codicil would be substantially satisfied ; the Commons' demand would be answered to all intents and purposes if the title of 'rector regni' were admitted, because it was a name practically synonymous with 'governour' ; and Gloucester's own objection, that the title of 'defensor' was not enough, would be met.

We have, in fact, in Gloucester's memorandum a fair-seeming construction of a still fair-seeming situation. And certainly, at this stage of the discussion, Gloucester would at first sight appear to have been not 'so noyous with to dele', as the chronicler Hardyng [2] would have us believe he was at this critical time. But under the bland terms of his memorandum is concealed what might become the ground of grave misunderstanding and serious disagreement, if not the fact of serious disagreement itself. A perfunctory examination of the document might at first suggest that any dispute there was at this juncture between Gloucester and the Lords was one over forms and words and not their substance. But this was not the case. We receive from his memorandum no indication as to what were those 'diuers causes' moving the Lords to dissent from use of the term 'tutela' in Gloucester's title or commission. Not specified, they were conveniently slid over in the memorandum. But we need not doubt that the Lords' objection to the term was not simply the objection of the legal etymologist. Its potential significance was more their concern than its civilian origin. The Lords may have been made aware that, under Roman law, the 'tutela' was designed to protect the interest of the 'tutor' as well as that of the ward, to protect those who would succeed to his estate if he died while still 'impubes' : 'ubi ius successionis, ibi onus tutelae'. It is true, of course, that in 1422

---

[1] The question as to where Duke Humphrey found his information about William Marshal's appointment raises an interesting problem. Reference to the scriptorium at St. Albans, where he was a friend of Abbot Whethamstead and where in 1423 he became a member of the confraternity, might have produced the title granted to the Marshal in 1216, because Matthew Paris supplies the information in his Greater Chronicle in his notice of the earl's death in 1219. But the allusion in Gloucester's memorandum to the high authority enjoyed by the earl's seal perhaps suggests an awareness that it was as 'rector regis et regni' that William Marshal, along with the papal legate Gualo, sealed the first and second re-issues of the Great Charter in 1216 and 1217 when Henry III had no seal of his own. If this is so, it may indicate that copies of these instruments were still available either in extant chronicles (other than in those at St. Albans where they do not appear) or in royal or other archives, although for legal and general purposes both texts had been superseded by the text of Henry III's third confirmation of the charter of 1225.

[2] Hardyng, op. cit. p. 390.

Bedford was the heir presumptive to the throne, but Gloucester was next after him in the succession, and the Lords may conceivably have felt the force of a criticism of the Roman law of wardship to which Sir John Fortescue was to give expression in his *De Laudibus Legum Anglie* a generation later, when he stigmatized its effect as tending ' quasi agnum committere lupo ad devorandum '. But their main objection to the word ' tutela ' was probably that it implied a right to administer the estate of the ward with a responsibility to account only to him, and not until he reached maturity. In this connexion it is worth recalling Gloucester's intention, as reported to the council in January 1427, to answer for what he had done touching the king's estate to none save Henry VI when he came of age.[1] The Lords in 1422 certainly objected to the authority that the word ' tutela ' implied. And when on 3 March 1428, in order to clarify his doubts about his authority as Protector, the Lords described to Gloucester what they had done in 1422 and their intentions at that time, they made this clear : though to pacify him they had made him chief councillor of the king and devised for him as well a title of official pre-eminence, that title was not ' the name of Tutour [Lieutenant, Governour, nor of Regent], nor no name that shuld emporte auctorite of governaunce of the lond ', but the name of Protector and Defender ' the which emporteth a personell duetee of entendance to the actuell defense of the land, as well against thenemys utward, yf cas required, as ayenst Rebelles inward, yf any were, that God forbede '.[2] In an important session of the council on 28 January 1427, when Bedford had been present, the chancellor (John Kemp, archbishop of York) had already made it clear that the Lords regarded the young king as endowed with his complete royal authority, and that it was only because ' by possibilitee of nature he may not in dede rule ne governe in his oune persone ' that they themselves, whether in parliament, great council, or continual council, had assumed the right to exercise the royal authority, ' as toward that that belongeth unto the pollitique rule and governaille of his lande and to thobservance and keping of his lawes '.[3] If the Lords in 1422 were not prepared to recognize Gloucester's right to a ' tutela ' and make him ' tutour ', they were not likely to appreciate the value of his precedent of 1216 and make him ' rector regni ', a term just as suggestive as the other of a right to control or manipulate the royal prerogative and just as contradictory of their own right as they conceived it.

[1] *P.P.C.* iii. 241–2.
[2] *Rot. Parl.* iv. 326b.   Gloucester seems to have regarded himself as being entitled as Protector to enter and keep any royal castle (cf. the first of the articles of Gloucester's charge against Beaufort, 1426, noticed in Edward Hall, *Chronicle* [1809, London], p. 130).   [3] *P.P.C. op. cit.* iii. 233.

As Mr. Chrimes has pointed out, there is no other evidence than the 'memorandum' supplies that the Commons, to satisfy whose petition Gloucester here pretended was his motive, thought insufficient the title of 'protector and defender of the realm and church in England and principal councillor of the king', which Gloucester was ultimately granted in this parliament : its conferment, in fact, was formally to be made by the advice and assent of the lords spiritual and temporal in parliament 'et auxi de la Commune d'Engleterre assemblez en la mesme'.[1] But whether the Commons were dissatisfied, as Gloucester speciously pretended, or not (and he was not without his friends in the Lower House), the Lords were apparently not over-impressed by his historical subtleties, and his researches proved fruitless. The word 'protector', which was added to his title seemingly after the submission of this memorandum of Gloucester's, conveyed no different kind of authority from that implied by the word 'defender'.[2]

Gloucester's memorandum is interesting enough from the point of view of his (or his literary hacks') historical knowledge or capacity for historical investigation, and for the light it casts on the character and persistence of his political aspirations in 1422. It is even more intriguing, I suggest, for the information it contains about the Lords' reception of the codicil of Henry V's will and its terms, upon which was based (as we know, too, from the Lords' statement in 1428) the main part of Gloucester's claim. The codicil, so the memorandum states, 'was redde declared and assented bi al the lordis', who 'required and preyde' Gloucester to take upon himself the charge it contained, 'behetyng [promising] hym help and assistance'. Ready to fall in with the provisions of the codicil 'as ny as they myght goodly', the Lords 'haue assented for to call my lord [Gloucester] Defensor of this Reme and chief counseiller of the kyng'. This they have done, the memorandum tells us, in spite of the fact that their search for precedents had yielded only that of 1377, which did the opposite of subserving Gloucester's claim by birth. This piece of 'record evidence' of 1422 is, therefore, at first sight transparently at variance with the evidence upon record of 1428 on the subject of the Lords' attitude to Henry V's will at the earlier date. Far from rejecting outright the notion that a reigning king, without the assent of the three estates (presumably expressed in parliament), could nominate a regent to act during his successor's minority—and this was what the Lords in 1428 were to say they had done in 1422—the Lords are clearly represented in this memorandum of Gloucester's as having accepted Henry V's will on this issue and, at first at any rate, as

[1] *Rot. Parl.* iv. 175b.
[2] Apart from the accepted common meaning of the two terms, that this was so regarded at the time is clear from the declaration of the Lords in 1428.

having accepted it completely. It certainly does not represent them as having questioned *on principle* and from the beginning the rightfulness of Henry V's action in leaving the ' regency ' of England to Gloucester by his will alone, and therefore without the concurrence of the estates of the realm. It would appear, unless Gloucester was guilty of fatuous misrepresentation in this statement of his case, that a reconciliation of the two pieces of evidence can only be effected on the basis of some such argument as this : that sometime after this memorandum was drawn up and put forward (its survival among Chancery archives seems to indicate that it was, in fact, submitted to the Lords) the Lords sheered off and altered course about, so that after once accepting the codicil of the will they came to reject it outright as the lawful basis of any part of Gloucester's authority. Precedent was being created in 1422 as well as being cited.[1] Of the discovery of this new constitutional principle that a reigning king could not by his mere authority arrange the form of government to operate during the minority of his successor or, more precisely, nominate a regent,

---

[1] I know of only one case of a royal will embodying dispositions of a political character that was recent in 1422. One of the charges against Richard II at his deposition (*Rot. Parl.* iii. 421a, borne out by the terms of the will itself in J. Nichols, *Royal Wills*, pp. 197–8) represented that in his ' testamentum ' (sealed with the great seal, the privy seal, and his signet), after providing for the discharging of the debts of his Household (to pay these he left £20,000), and the upkeep of lepers and their chaplains at Westminster and Bermondsey (for these he left 5000 or 6000 marks), Richard bequeathed to his successor the rest of his gold on condition that he upheld the acts of his last proper parliament (that of September 1397 and January 1398) and the acts of the parliamentary commission at Coventry on 16 September 1398 and at Westminster on 18 March 1399. If his successor refused this condition, then the dukes of Surrey, Aumale, and Exeter, and the earl of Wiltshire were to have the surplus of Richard's wealth in order to maintain these various parliamentary acts, if need be until death. These acts themselves were on 30 September 1399 represented as erroneous and repugnant to law and reason, and Richard was censured for having so striven to maintain them. This case is not, of course, strictly apposite to the 1422 dilemma. Richard II had tried to influence if not determine the form of the political policy of his successor ; Henry V, to provide for the constitutional form of the government under his successor, a king under age.

In an earlier period when the realm was regarded even more clearly as a feudal inheritance, provision for its government in time of an heir's minority was unquestionably a royal prerogative. In 1253 and in 1272 respectively Henry III and the Lord Edward had each made testamentary provision for the royal government in the event of his dying while a successor was still under age. The former, about to set sail for Gascony, left the custody of his son and heir and other children, *and the custody of the kingdom*, together with all his lands in Wales, Ireland, and Gascony, to his queen, Eleanor, until his heir attained his majority (*Royal Wills, op. cit.* p. 15). The Lord Edward on crusade at Acre treated the governance of the realm after his own and then his father's death as his to dispose of, although Henry III was yet alive when he did so : if after his own death his father should die before his children came of age, *the realm* and all his lands were to remain in the hands of his (Edward's) executors, the archbishop of York, and Roger Mortimer ' ovesk autres prodes homes du reaume, ke il akondrunt si mestier seyt ', until the children came of age (*ibid.* p. 19 ; and cf. Sir F. M. Powicke, *Henry III and the Lord Edward*, ii. 583, 603, 698). As Sir Maurice Powicke says, ' Edward was already king in all but name ' before he left England for the crusade.

nothing appears on the roll of the 1422 parliament : it was not to be made explicit, as we have seen, until early in 1428 when Gloucester refused to attend parliament and the Lords prepared a statement of what had happened in 1422, in order to remind him of his duty.[1]

Gloucester's position in 1422 was, of course, difficult for other reasons than that of his doubtful suitability in the eyes of the Lords for a ' regency ' or that of the absence of recent and accommodating precedents. Despite the slow growth of the doctrine of capacities as applied to the medieval English king and of the theoretical distinction between his office and person,[2] the guardianship of the person of his heir had been dealt with by Henry V as a matter separate from the arrangements he had made for the exercise of the kingly function, and it seems fairly clear that the problem of personal guardianship did not complicate the situation in 1422. There was, however, the difficulty arising out of the fact that the council had come to be a largely aristocratic body and accustomed to perform executive as well as advisory functions, and that the Lords were determined to perpetuate this system of participation and control. There was also the constitutional difficulty arising out of Henry V's settlement of the government during his successor's minority by his will alone, and without the assent of parliament. But there was, too, the added practical difficulty that the person who was by ability and *prior* right of birth best fitted for the chief place in the government of England had been ear-marked for a position which made his continuous presence in England impossible : John, duke of Bedford, regent of France and Normandy. It must have been realized in 1422 that Bedford would want, at some time or another during the minority, and might be required, to return to England ; and it was inconceivable that he, the elder of the king's two uncles and the heir presumptive, should be subjected when he came (even if only for a short time) to some form of superior jurisdiction or authority on the part of his younger brother, Gloucester. Henry V's death-bed dispositions, with their appointment of Bedford to an office outside England, had put him, in fact, into an anomalous position. And that Bedford himself was aware of this is clear from a letter he wrote from Rouen to the civic officials and community of London on 26 October 1422.[3] In this letter he had stated that the ' gouvernaunce ' of England was his as the elder surviving brother of Henry V, and that he had ' chief interesse ' in it after the king ; while requiring the city to do nothing to prejudice his right, he acknow-

[1] See above, pp. 198, 210.
[2] S. B. Chrimes, *Constitutional Ideas*, pp. 34–8.
[3] *Collection Générale des Documents Français qui se trouvent en Angleterre*, ed. Jules Delpit (Paris, 1847), i. 232–3.

ledged that he had no desire to impugn ' the ordonnance or wil '
of Henry V, but did so with a saving for his own right, ' to the
whiche, as we trewe and truste fully that hit was not oure saide
souverain lordes [Henry V's] entente to deroge or doo prejudice '.
And the Lords, too, in making the settlement of 1422, were aware
of the need to consider Bedford's predicament and make some
provision for his superior status within the framework of that
settlement.   In fact it may well have been partially for this reason
that the Lords went back on their acceptance of Henry V's testamentary provisions for the government of the kingdom after his
death.

And to all that related to Bedford, Gloucester was also alive.
So much so, that the whole emphasis of his memorandum was on
the need for his appointment by the Lords on terms which would
materially satisfy Henry V's instructions as set out in his written
will.   In the memorandum Gloucester excluded all *direct* reference
to his claim by birth.   It is, in fact, only from the information of the
Lords' statement of 1428 that we get *explicit* reference to its having
been made.   That he made a claim of this sort we need not doubt,
however, because it is certainly *implicit* in the terms of his memorandum : in the reference to the Lords' researches into the case of John
of Gaunt in 1377, and in the statement that William Marshal, made
' rector regis et regni Anglie ' in 1216, had been ' nat so nygh to
the kyng [Henry III] as my lord [Gloucester] is to our liege lord '.
Gloucester, when drawing up his memorandum was, of course,
aware of the fact that he must take Bedford into consideration :
his own historical researches resulting in the discovery of the
precedent of 1216 were allegedly made so that neither he nor Bedford as well should suffer by reason of any slackness on his,
Gloucester's, part ; his acceptance of any title which he himself
deemed adequate was not to bind Bedford in his absence ; it was
only to expedite the conclusion of parliament and so to pleasure
the Lords that he, in Bedford's absence, was prepared to accept
what he proposed that the Lords should agree to ; and he recognized that, at Bedford's first homecoming to England, what was
now decided in 1422 would have to be reconsidered and perhaps
revised.   Bedford, as a matter of historical fact, was not destined
to see Westminster again until 10 January 1426.   If Gloucester
realized that his brother was likely to be long fettered by his
military and administrative duties in France (as he may well have
done), it was an acute tactical move to represent that any settlement reached during this parliament of 1422 need only be of a
temporary and provisional nature.   Be that as it may, at the end of
his memorandum Gloucester nevertheless made it clear that he
thought that some place of pre-eminence would still have to be
found for him in the government even if, and when, Bedford

returned, in order to fulfil the terms of Henry V's will, and that he envisaged the possibility of a title and authority then being devised to be held both by him and Bedford : ' and thenne bothe his brothir and he for to stonde at large if them like or for to accepte the seid thing forthe upon hem and take . . . [com?] mission to them bothe in suche form as thay both will be avised '.   Gloucester was clearly pinning his hopes to Henry V's will.

Gloucester's attempt in this memorandum of his to jockey or cajole the Lords into a position which, after reflexion, they were no longer prepared to accept was doomed to frustration.   Cunningly devised though the memorandum had been, its conception had seemingly been ill-advised.   It certainly did not produce the result that Gloucester hoped for : the Lords ultimately decided on the twenty-seventh day of the parliamentary session (5 December) that Bedford, when in England, should be ' Regni Anglie et Ecclesie Anglicane Protector et Defensor ac Consiliarius Principalis domini Regis ', and that during Bedford's absence from the realm Gloucester should occupy that same and no higher position.   The appointment was not made for the duration of the king's minority, but was to last expressly during his pleasure.[1] This limitation perhaps depended on the current form of the settlement being subject to Bedford's acceptance.   But it meant in effect that the magnates collectively had the power to revoke the Protectorship ; this is implied in the chancellor's statement in council on 28 January 1427 that the right to exercise the royal authority was vested in the Lords in parliament or in great council or, if neither such assembly were in session, in the continual council.[2]   The act of appointment proceeded from the royal authority, but was made ' de assensu et avisamento Dominorum tàm Spiritualium quam Temporalium in presenti Parliamento existentium, necnon de assensu Communitatis Regni Anglie existentis in eodem '.   Letters patent, exemplifying the commission and dated on 5 December 1422, were engrossed and passed the great seal, being warranted by king and council in parliament.   The qualifications of Bedford and Gloucester for the Protectorship were formally specified as ' circumspectio ' and ' industria ', all mention of any right of birth being suppressed ; and there was no reference to Henry V's will in Gloucester's commission.   For God's honour and the profit of king and realm and at the ' requisitio ' of the Lords, Gloucester accepted the commission for himself, protesting that this action did not prejudice his brother's right to assume or decline it.   Here perhaps was Gloucester's ' bolt-hole '.   But considering Bedford's law-abiding nature and his concern for his own rights, it was a narrow one enough and, such as it was, it was stopped by Bed-

[1] *Rot. Parl.* iv. 174-5.   [2] *P.P.C.* iii. 233.

ford's later complete and unconditional acceptance of the settlement. The settlement was a compromise, but only on the face of
things. Gloucester was certainly given titular pre-eminence,
which had not been accorded in any form whatsoever to his grandfather, John of Gaunt, in 1377. But it was a position which fell
short of what Henry V had intended for him and of his own
ambitions. What the Lords in 1422 did was more or less what
their fore-bears had done at Richard II's accession : rejecting a
tutorship and Gloucester's alternative suggestion that he should
be made ' rector regni ', they had provided for the exercise of the
royal authority by themselves.

In the end the Lords had been brought, seemingly, to the view
that in the matter of Bedford's or Gloucester's title it would be
better if it reflected simply those vaguely-worded primary functions,
undertaken by a king in his coronation oath : the preservation of
peace for the church and for clergy and people. One of the most
important theoretical factors clearly determining the establishment
in 1422 of a protectorship *eo nomine* was that for the first time in
English history the king was so young as to make his coronation
a necessarily long-postponed event. This is made reasonably clear
by the fact that after Henry VI, still in his minority, was crowned
on 5 November 1429, the protectorship came by the Lords' determination to its logical end, the chief councillorship alone remaining
in force. For at his coronation the king, as the 1429 parliament-
roll states, ' Protectionem et Defensionem Regni et Ecclesie . . .
suscepit atque ad eadem . . . protegenda et defendenda . . .
sacramentum prestitit corporalem '.[1] Ten days later Gloucester
laid down his Protectorship in parliament, saving his brother's
liberty to do the same for himself.

The notice of the Lords' decision of 5 December 1422 is followed on the parliament-roll by a grant of certain rights of official
and ecclesiastical patronage to whichever of the two royal dukes
was occupying the office of Protector.[2] He was enabled to nominate royal foresters, parkers, and keepers of warrens in England
and Wales when such offices fell vacant, but the conduct of these
officials once appointed was a matter subject to the jurisdiction of
the whole council and they could be dismissed by it for reasonable
cause ; he might also nominate suitable clerks to vacant parish
churches in the royal patronage that were assessed at values of
between twenty and thirty marks, and to all prebends in royal
chapels but not to the office of dean therein. On such matters the
acting Protector's signet letters were to be sufficient warrants for
the issuing of letters of privy seal to move the great seal. These
rights of patronage reserved to the acting Protector were not

---

[1] *Rot. Parl.* iv. 337a.   [2] *Ibid.* p. 175.

intrinsically related to his office ; they were not, of course, essential to its exercise, but were simply grants by royal favour and in partial consideration of his future labours in office.[1] All other patronage was to be at the disposal of the whole council, except the chancellor's and treasurer's traditional *ex officio* patronage.

On the parliament-roll there next follows a memorandum referring to the subsequent nomination (probably on 9 December 1422) of seventeen 'conseillers assistentz a la governance '.[2] This act, prompted by a request of the Commons, was performed ' by the advice and assent ' of all the lords. The names of the members of the new council were read openly in parliament. That there was no peculiar restrictive significance attached to the word 'assistentz ' is clear from the fact that Gloucester's name headed the list. The only other peer in England of ducal status, the duke of Exeter, as the foremost of the king's personal guardians, was naturally included. Apart from these two, and except for its *ex officio* members, the construction of the council was framed on something like the now time-honoured basis of representation by estates : five prelates (the archbishop of Canterbury and the bishops of London, Winchester, Norwich, and Worcester), five earls (March, Warwick, the Earl Marshal, Northumberland, and Westmorland), and five others of varying status but all knights (the barons FitzHugh and Cromwell, both peers of parliament, and three commoners, Sir Walter Hungerford, Sir John Tiptoft, and Sir Walter Beauchamp). These collectively submitted the conditions on which they took office in a paper schedule of five articles written in English.[3] This schedule, after the Lords had approved its contents, was carried down to the Commons for their

---

[1] In 1424 it was to be decided that the acting Protector should receive 8000 marks a year as salary for attending the Council, the next highest fee being £200. When Bedford came to England in 1426, however, Gloucester was allowed 3000 marks as chief councillor next to his brother. After the abolition of the protectorship in 1429 he was granted 2000 marks as chief councillor and twice that amount as ' custos ' when the king was absent from the kingdom. These sums were raised to 5000 and 6000 marks respectively in 1431 (Baldwin, *op. cit.* pp. 174–6).

[2] *Rot. Parl.* iv. 175b. The letters patent appointing Bedford to be Protector when he was in England, and Gloucester when he was not, were dated 5 December 1422. They were warranted by king and council in parliament. But the roll of the 1422 parliament tells us that the choice of the other councillors ' assistentz a la governance ' *followed* these appointments ; and for the purposes of the payment of its members the royal council was later not considered to have been re-constituted, ' auctoritate parliamenti ', until 9 December 1422 (*P.P.C.* iii. 157, 203 ; the date, ' ix° die Novembris ', at p. 155, J. H. Ramsay decided in his *Lancaster and York*, i. 326, n. 4, must have been ' a clerical error '). The council in parliament may, therefore, be said to have been sufficiently constituted when the lords spiritual and temporal were duly assembled. Where were the magnates of the realm, convened to parliament by the king's summons, there was (or might be considered to be) his council in parliament. The ' official ' nucleus of the new council had, of course, already been supplied on 16 November by the appointment of a chancellor, treasurer, and keeper of the privy seal. (*Rot. Parl.* iv. 171–2.)   [3] *Rot. Parl.* iv. 176a.

perusal by a delegation from the Upper House.   The Lords would
have their views ('lour entent').

The Commons scrutinized the whole schedule apparently with
care and suggested an amendment to the first article which the
Lords later accepted.   This article stipulated that the choice of
justices of the peace, sheriffs, escheators, and sea-port and other
officials should lie with the council, except those appointments left
with the acting Protector and those customs appointments already
resigned by Henry V to Bishop Beaufort as part of the security
which the latter had demanded for the repayment of his loans to
the Crown.   The Commons now pointed out that a proviso of
non-prejudice should be inserted on behalf of those who had the
authority (either by inheritance or by grant for life) to appoint to
certain of these offices as of right.   The other articles of the
schedule were not changed.   One of them reserved to the council
the control of the exercise of the feudal rights of the Crown, the
bestowal of wardships and marriages and other 'casueltees', 'and
that indifferently atte the derrest with oute favour or eny maner
parcialtee or fraude'.   Another provided for the custody of the
royal treasury and the keeping of secrecy about its contents.
Another was an administrative device : the clerk of the council
was to be required on oath to write day by day the names of all
the lords present at its sessions, 'to see what, howe, and by whom,
eny thyng passeth'.   The remaining one of the five articles was
related to the more important point of procedure within the council
itself and deserves special consideration.

In Richard II's first parliament the Commons had asked that
the continual council should be enlarged by eight persons 'de
diverses estatz et degrees' and that important business should not
pass without the assent and advice of all, but that for less important
matters the advice and assent of at least four might suffice.[1]   Nine
additional councillors were in fact appointed in 1377, but, as
regards procedure, the Commons' request was answered with a
statement of very limited import : no grant of escheat, wardship,
marriage, or rent, within the Crown's bestowal, was to be made
to any one of the councillors during their year's term of office
except by common assent of all or by a majority vote.   Nothing
was then said of how matters of greater moment were to be decided,
if dissent should arise in the council.   In 1422, the members of
the new council laid it down as a rule that they might proceed to
business if six or four at the least were present, not counting the
ex officio members ; but if 'grete maters' were to be discussed then
the attendance of all or of a majority was necessary.   On the

---

[1] *Rot. Parl.* iii. 6b.   As to what at different times constituted a quorum of the council,
see Baldwin, *op. cit.* pp. 413, 415.

subject of attendance greater elasticity seems now to have been permitted than in 1377.   The appointment of a Protector in 1422 also made a difference : where it had been usual for the council to consult the king, the Protector's advice must be taken.   But as regards procedure, this arrangement was all that was now formally decided upon.

Why there was so little precise definition as to procedure in the stipulations of the councillors-elect in 1422 it is rather difficult to understand, unless there was trouble during the 1422 parliamentary session between Gloucester and the Lords on this topic.   In that case definition would seem to have been an even more urgent necessity, because procedure was a problem hard to distinguish from the subject of the Protector's powers as such and as chief of the council, and also from that of the competence of the council acting without him.   In the memorandum he submitted to the Lords before the settlement of 5 December, Gloucester had set forth some of his views on conciliar competence and the allied subject of conciliar procedure.   He was, of course, then expecting, or hoping for, a greater authority than in fact he was to be allowed, and he expressed himself accordingly.   Firstly, he was prepared to do no 'grete thing', apart from 'certain [unspecified] specialtes', without the advice of the council ; in return, the council was to decide nothing without his advice except matters 'of cours and of commune lawe'.   This he represented as having been already proposed and declared by the Lords.   Secondly, unanimity on the part of the council, he went on to suggest, was not essential : a majority decision was to carry the whole council ; but, if the council were equally divided upon any matter, then that side to which Gloucester adhered was to be accounted the majority (' and that in a metere ther as be like many on both sides the more partie be demed ther as my lord is ').   As regards Gloucester's first point, condescension on his part to take the advice of the council on important issues was converted, as we have seen, by the conditions of the councillors-elect, into condescension on their part to take the Protector's advice on such matters as ' the Kyng hath been accustumed to be conseilled of '.   Regarding his second point, their stipulations ignored it.   Perhaps they felt that time and experience would be on their side.

Time and experience were to illustrate the need for further definition on these as well as other matters.   The council, re-assuming office (with some slight change of membership) in the second parliament of the reign (October 1423-February 1424), was to stipulate *inter alia* that matters affecting the weal of the king and realm and requiring expeditious handling might be decided by as few as six or four councillors, but only if they and also the *ex officio* members (the chancellor, the treasurer, and the keeper of the privy seal) were all of one mind. It also insisted that if there were differences of opinion over any bill preferred in the council, that bill should not pass unless, there and then, there was a majority in favour of it.[1] At Reading, on 24 November 1426, fresh conditions were again drawn up by the council ; and it now decided that never should a majority be comprised of less than four councillors and one official member.[2] Thus far there is no hint, in the council's rules for its own conduct, of that influence on its decisions by its over-mighty members, which Gloucester's memorandum of 1422 suggests he, for one, expected to be able to exert. But in one of these conciliar stipulations of 1426 [3] we gain an inkling of how powerful an influence on his (or Bedford's) part was likely to be brought to bear on conciliar proceedings, especially in event of divided counsels : if there were dispute and the Protector, finding himself among the minority, ' wol sture [stir] that other partie by reson to falle unto hem ', the matter should rest until the following day unless the minority chose to come into line. But then the view of ' the more partie in nombre ' should prevail. Only if there were a tie was the Protector's party to carry the day, which was precisely what Gloucester had suggested in 1422. As the lords of the council were to point out to Bedford in that celebrated meeting of 28 January 1427,[4] when they consciously demonstrated their right to exercise the royal authority by sending for him to attend on them, the execution of that authority rested ' not in oon singuler persone but in alle my said lordes togidres ', saving the authority attached to the office of Protector. Bedford swore on the Gospels—and at this all wept—that he would be governed by the council, ' levyng his oune opinyon but if thei alle thought hit bettre '.[5] Gloucester was visited on the next day by the council at his inn, because there he lay sick. After being reminded of his former attitude of intransigeance, of his statement, ' Lat my brother governe as hym lust whiles he is in this land, for after his going overe into Fraunce I wol governe as me semeth good ', and of his reported intention to answer none save the king, when he came of age, for what he had done touching the king's estate, he protested that he had never intended to govern other than with the council ' as oon of hem and by their advis '.[6]

That the council could thus get its own way and regulate its own procedure and do this when parliament was not in session, and without either reference to it or recourse to its support, argues strongly for the growth of its sense of its own solidarity and its own authority ; in this development its continuous existence with but little change of personnel was an important factor. And, as

[1] *Rot. Parl.* iv. 201b.   [2] *P.P.C.* iii. 150.
[3] *Ibid.* 216–7.   [4] *Ibid.* 238.   [5] *Ibid.* 240.   [6] *Ibid.* 241–2.

a result, its domestic constitutional policies, especially on the subject of the Protector's powers, were remarkably consistent and unwavering. In the years between the parliament of 1422 and the end of the year 1426 it had already been worked out that the council should have control of government when a parliament or great council was not in session, and that its consent was necessary before its chief member could act in even his capacity of Protector in any important issue. And this system worked until the Protectorship came to an end with Henry of Windsor's coronation during the parliament of 1429, and then with certain changes beyond that event.

The settlement of 1422 resulted in the establishment of a Protectorship with safeguards for the ultimate superiority, under the king, of the lords spiritual and temporal whether assembled in parliament, or great council, or the ordinary continual council. It had been achieved after a due consideration of precedents and its essential form, whatever novel features were incorporated into it, owed much to plans of government devised on previous occasions of royal minority, especially to the conciliar arrangement contrived when Richard II became king. The settlement of 1422, with its creation of a limited Protectorship, itself became a precedent ; and the experience gained in achieving the settlement and meeting the inadequacies and the difficulties to which it gave rise was perhaps made use of on those later occasions when the king was himself unable to govern and a Protectorship was again established.

The reign of Henry VI was to see a Protectorship set up on two other occasions : in 1454, when the king became temporarily insane, and again in 1455, when he was once more out of his mind. On the first of these two occasions Richard, duke of York, was chosen by the Lords to take Bedford's and Gloucester's former title and powers by parliamentary authority, and with the same formal limitation that his office was to terminate at the royal pleasure. But there was an interesting, new provision now made necessary. Bedford and Gloucester had been Henry VI's nearest kinsmen and their appointments to act as Protector had tacitly recognized the strength of agnatic ties when the choice of a Protector was under consideration. In 1454 the king's nearest male relative was his son, Edward, prince of Wales. But he was an infant of less than two years, and to have appointed, even formally only, one incapable of government by reason of age to rule on behalf of one incapacitated by imbecility would have been a *reductio ad absurdum* of the Protector's office. Edward's prospective right and title had still, however, to be recognized, and it was provided that when he reached the age of discretion, the office was to devolve upon him if he wished to assume it.[1]   On the second occasion in 1455 the Protector's title, powers, and warrant were as before, but this time it was to be the lords who were to determine in parliament when the royal pleasure should apply the closure. This proviso was in the circumstances a practical safeguard for them, as well as for the king and York himself ; and so was York's undertaking not to proceed in the execution of his office without the approval of a council chosen by the lords, to which was reserved, with an awareness of the statement of 28 January 1427, the ' politique rule and governaunce ' of the land.[2]

No such safeguards seem to have been furnished in 1483 in the next establishment of a Protectorship, when Richard, duke of Gloucester, the only surviving brother of Edward IV, took upon himself the powers of regency on behalf of his twelve year old nephew, Edward V.   The will of Edward IV has not come down to us, but Polydore Vergil says that it committed his sons to Gloucester's ' tuytion ' and that on his death-bed Edward IV appointed his brother as Protector of the realm.[3]   This was the only title by which seemingly Gloucester was later officially described.[4] But it is possible that in the short time between his ' coup ' at the expense of the Woodvilles and his own usurpation of the throne he formally acted as the king's governor, an office which during the late reign and more recently had been filled by the young king's maternal uncle, the earl Rivers.   Certainly Duke Richard's authority with regard to the person of the king was greater than had been Duke Humphrey's in 1422, and this was not because his Protectorship was likely to be brought to an end by an early coronation.   The projected parliamentary sermon of the chancellor, Bishop Russell of Lincoln, which was to have been preached in Edward V's first parliament (which never met, of course) suggests that Edward IV had provided for Richard of Gloucester a kind of authority only a part of which Henry V had desired for *his* younger brother ; it referred to Richard as being not only ' protector of thys Reme ' but also as possessing ' the tutele and ouersyghte of the kynges most roialle persone durynge hys yeres of tendirnesse '. Gloucester was to be the king's ' tutor and protector ' ; he might be expected (so the bishop of Lincoln thought) to acquit himself like Marcus Emilius Lepidus who, when granted by the Roman senate ' the offyce of tutele, defence, and protection ' of the son of Ptolemy, king of Egypt, proceeded to undertake ' thedicacion and conduite of the persone of that yonge prince as in administracion

---

[1] *Rot. Parl.* v. 242–3.   [2] *Ibid.* 286a.

[3] *Three Books of Polydore Vergil's English History*, ed. Sir Henry Ellis (Camden Society, vol. 29), pp. 171, 176.

[4] *Grants, etc., from the Crown during the Reign of Edward V*, ed. J. G. Nichols (Camden Society, vol. 60), pp. 12, 17.

of alle grete thynges concernynge hys Reme '.[1] Designed to include the authority of the tutor, Richard of Gloucester's Protectorship of 1483 became with its ampler powers the nearest precedent in character as well as in time to the office as revived during the next royal minority, that is, on behalf of Edward VI and in favour of his nearest male relative, his mother's brother, Edward Seymour, duke of Somerset.

Whether Henry VIII knew it or not, his settlement of the royal succession and his provisions for a regency during the probable minority of his heir are a miracle of compromise between his own arbitrary will and the experience of the medieval past. Against the contingencies of minority rule he provided, as for the likely hazards of the succession, by act of parliament in 1536.[2]   The form of minority government was thus to be predetermined by statute, but its substance by the king's last will and testament similarly sanctioned beforehand : his heir was to be under the ' governance ' of his natural mother and of such other counsellors and nobles as the king's will should appoint, or, if the queen-mother were dead, then simply of the counsellors and nobles.   Henry VIII clearly admitted the strength and value of the idea that government is best furnished during a minority by a council ; but he took good care to reserve to himself a right to appoint its members.   If his heir were a male, the settlement was to operate until he was eighteen years old ; if a female, until she was sixteen.   To contravene the statute was to commit high treason.   And in his will of 30 December 1546 Henry accordingly entrusted the ' gouverment ' of Prince Edward after his accession to his own executors, who were also to be the ' counsaillours of the Privy Counsail ' of the future king and to have the government of ' all our Realms, Dominions, and Subjectz and of all th'Affairs Publicq and Private ' of the young king or, as it was otherwise expressed in the same instrument, the ' Rule and Charge ' of Edward VI ' in all his Causes and Affaires, and of the hole Realme, doing . . . all thinges as under Him and in his Name ' until his marriage and the end of his eighteenth year.[3]

Henry VIII, therefore, made no provision for the appointment of a Protector or Tutor to be of special pre-eminence in office or dignity.   The authority he granted to his appointees was to be exercised in a co-ordinate manner : they were to act ' with like and equal charge '.   But he left to the executors and councillors he nominated the right to determine, by a majority if need be, the order for their rule and proceeding.   And this they interpreted on 31 January 1547, only three days after Henry VIII's death, as

---

[1] S. B. Chrimes, *Constitutional Ideas*, pp. 177–8.
[2] Statute 28 Henry VIII, c. 7.   [3] Rymer, *Foedera*, xv. 110.

enabling them to appoint the duke of Somerset to the ' furste and chief place amonges us ' and to grant him the title of ' the Protectour of all the realmes and dominions of the Kinges Majestie . . . and . . . the Governour of his moste royal persone '. They had felt it best that one of their number should be ' preferred in name and place before others, to whome as to the state and hedde of the reste ' ambassadors and others might have access, and who would be ' mete and hable to be a special Remembrancer and to kepe a moste certaine accompte of all our procedinges '. But Somerset was required to act always with the advice and assent of his co-executors. On the following day the executors first declared their action to such of the council as were not of their number and then, in Edward VI's presence, to all the lords, who agreed to this modification of the late king's will.[1] On 12 March 1547 a ratification of this act passed the great seal and issued as a letter patent warranted by the king, and Somerset emerged as ' Personae Regiae Gubernator ac Regnorum Dominiorum et Subditorum nostrorum Protector '. On 11 August of the following year his powers as Protector were further defined or, perhaps more strictly, added to, by his creation as ' Locumtenens [Regis] ac Capitaneus Generalis pro Guerris et Bellis ', offices which gave him authority not only to wage war whenever expedient, but also to array subjects, hire mercenaries, exercise martial law, and even to treat with foreign powers.[2] The Protectorship, in its first infancy during the tenure of office by the dukes of Bedford and Gloucester between 1422 and 1429, had clearly put on weight.

When the dignity was once more revived, its holder had in fact destroyed the kingly office and with it the nature of the old constitution itself. The appointment to a Protectorship of the regicidal Cromwell in 1653 doubtless created for the office and dignity he held an association too disreputable ever to permit its later resurrection. In point of fact, Edward VI's was the last royal minority in English history, although not the last to be contemplated as a possible contingency ;[3] but later regencies followed precedents less disturbing to the constitution than those furnished by the historic Protectorships. The office down to the middle of the Tudor period had become progressively more inflated with power with each occasion of its use. With Cromwell it had become completely disassociated from its earliest aim. Until then Protectorships had been established in circumstances of royal incapacity formally to provide for the government of the country until such time as the king could himself more properly assume it ; the Protectorship of Cromwell was theoretically the keystone of an

---

[1] *Acts of the Privy Council of England* (new series), ed. J. R. Dasent, ii (1547–50), pp. 5–7.

[2] Rymer, *Foedera*, xv. 175.   [3] Victoria's was that.

arch of government from which hereditary monarchy had been removed. 'The Lord Protector of the Commonwealth of England, Scotland, and Ireland and the dominions thereto belonging', in whose name writs were to run, was appointed for life.[1] Only in determining that the office should be elective, did the Instrument of Government faintly echo the first creation of the office by authority of parliament in 1422.

Excursus

THE identity of the codicil of Henry V's will that referred to Gloucester's 'regency' is not as easy to establish as at first sight it would seem to be. Shortly before his departure on his earliest French expedition, Henry V drew up his first will at Southampton on 24 July 1415. It was written in Latin and authenticated by the great seal, the privy seal, the signet, and the king's sign manual. It provided *inter alia* for his burial in Westminster abbey, the fulfilment of his father's testament, the payment of his own debts, and the bequest of certain of his own property in cash and moveables (*Foedera* [London, 1704-35], ix. 289-93). Before he left England a second time for France, Henry drew up on 21 July 1417 certain arrangements for the future disposal of those parcels of the duchy of Lancaster already (in 1415) entrusted to a body of feoffees for the fulfilment of his will (with one exception all the executors of the 1415 will were also members of the committee of feoffees). This second will, written in English, took the form of an indenture, to which was affixed the great seal and 'my seel that I use in the governance of myn heritage of Lancastre' (probably the signet of the eagle) ; it was subscribed with the king's sign manual, and the whole document was enclosed under the privy seal (J. Nichols, *Royal Wills*, pp. 236-43). Before he left England for the third and last time, Henry V drew up at Dover on 10 June 1421 yet another will. But this has been lost, and we are ignorant of its contents (*Rot. Parl.* iv. 299b). We may assume, however, that, beginning and ending in Latin, it was written in Latin throughout, as had been the will of 1415 ; we know that it was sealed with the great seal, the privy seal, and the signet. It probably, indeed almost certainly, superseded the 1415 will, and may partly have been drawn up because the royal style of the 1415 will was out-of-date and had, in fact, been so since the conclusion of the treaty of Troyes in 1420 (the 1415 will described Henry V as 'Rex Anglie et Francie', the 1421 will as 'Rex Anglie, Heres et Regens Regni Francie'), and because the king wished to make new and additional stipulations. Perhaps the most compelling reason moving Henry V to make a new will in June 1421 was, however, his knowledge that his queen was then expecting to supply him

---

[1] S. R. Gardiner, *The Constitutional Documents of the Puritan Revolution, 1625-1660* (3rd ed., Oxford, 1906), pp. 405-16.

with a direct heir.   In any case, by 1421, of the original supervisors the duke of Clarence and Robert Hallum, bishop of Salisbury, were dead, and of the original executors, Richard Courtenay, bishop of Norwich, and Sir John Rothenale (see note, pp. 232-3).   No doubt the 1421 will included the still relevant items of the 1415 will, but it must inevitably have embodied new provisions, perhaps, for example, Henry V's known bequests to certain French churches (*Foedera*, x. 346) ;   it certainly established a revised scheme for its execution, with a board of executors double in size what it had been in 1415.   That the will of 1415 was superseded by the 1421 will is suggested, too, by the fact that it was the latter alone, and not the former as well, which Thomas Langley, bishop of Durham, produced on 7 November 1422 (immediately after Henry V's burial) for inspection by the overseer, Archbishop Chichele of Canterbury, and by Bishop Beaufort of Winchester and the dukes of Gloucester and Exeter.   Langley on the same occasion also produced for their inspection a ' codicil ', hastily but laboriously written in English on paper in Henry V's own hand (' thus enterlynet and blotted as hit is '), sealed with the signet of the eagle on 9 June 1421, and included with the testament and will of the following day, 10 June.   Is this the ' codicil ' which was referred to in the memorandum that Gloucester submitted to the Lords of the 1422 parliament, and which gave him that ' tutelam et defensionem principales ' of Henry V's heir which he proceeded unsuccessfully to claim in 1422 ?   It seems unlikely.   The codicil of 9 June 1421 was written in English, and the Latin words cited in Gloucester's memorandum, being a quotation, must clearly have come out of an instrument written in Latin.   Moreover, the codicil of 9 June was addressed primarily to Henry V's feoffees and its terms were most probably confined to supplementing the instructions drawn up for their guidance in 1417.   Fresh instructions to the feoffees were doubtless necessitated in 1421 by the recent death of Henry V's eldest brother, the duke of Clarence ;   because the declaration of 1417, although it provided for the ultimate succession to the duchy enfeoffments of a direct heir of Henry V, in its provisions for the endowment (from the enfeoffments) of only the two youngest brothers, the dukes of Bedford and Gloucester, assumed the likely succession of Clarence to the bulk of the inheritance (Henry V being still unmarried).   It is further possible that the codicil of 9 June 1421 took cognizance of accessions to the inheritance of Lancaster after the recent death of Henry V's grandmother, Joan, the dowager countess of Hereford, whose co-heir the king was (as the heir of his mother, Mary Bohun, Henry IV's first wife).

Two alternative suggestions may be offered.   The first suggestion is that the will of 10 June 1421 itself contained a codicil comprising a statement of, or including an allusion to, Henry V's desires regarding a ' regency ' for England.   For when this will was composed, the queen, having presumably conceived not long after her coronation on 23 February (Henry VI was born on 6 December 1421), was pregnant with a child, whose right to inherit the throne was assured, irrespective of its sex, by the second succession act of 1406.   In the event of Henry V's early death, and of his heir's survival, a long minority was inevitable, and it is most probable that the king provided for a ' regency ' before he last left England and without waiting for the birth of his heir.   The second suggestion is to postulate either a fresh will and codicil altogether or simply a fresh supplementary codicil to the will of 10 June 1421, either of which might have been made in France, subsequent to Henry V's last departure from England and, if this were the case, most probably after Henry of Windsor's birth on 6 December 1421 and possibly when Henry V was on his death-bed.   But this idea of a ' continental will ' or a ' continental codicil ' is quite ruled out by the testimony of all the English chroniclers who deal with the death-bed settlement, except Walsingham.   This St. Albans writer (*Historia Anglicana*, ii. 343) says that Henry V made his will (' testamentum confecit ') when he felt his end drawing near.   But both the *Gesta* (*op. cit.* p. 160) and the *Vita et Gesta* (*op. cit.* p. 333) say that his testament and the codicils of his last will had been carefully drawn up in England, and that it was these which Henry V showed to his lords at Bois de Vincennes (' Testamentum suum prius in Anglia circumspecte conditum et alios codicellos sue voluntatis ultime testativos eis ostendit ').   And the *Vita* of Titus Livius also discloses the fact that the will had been composed before the happenings at Bois de Vincennes : ' testamento tamen *ante* tui tutelam . . . Humfredo Gloucestrie duci . . . legavit ' (*op. cit.* p. 95 ; the italics are mine).   Moreover, when on 29 January 1426 the bishop of Durham was ordered to produce at Leicester, for inspection by the council, ' les Testament et Codicelles conteignantz la darrein volunte ' of Henry V, all he exhibited was the testament of 10 June 1421 and the codicil of the day before (Langley there and then relinquished their custody to the keeper of the privy seal, Master William Alnwick ; the declaration to the Lancastrian feoffees of 1417 Langley retained until he surrendered it to his surviving co-feoffees on 8 November 1435).   I am inclined, therefore, to think that the codicil referred to in Gloucester's memorandum is *either* a Latin codicil included in the Latin will of 10 June 1421 *or* is the Latin will of 10 June 1421 itself, the word codicil being used in Gloucester's memorandum synonymously for ' will '. Of these two last alternatives I prefer the first.   The fact that the bishop of Durham was ordered in January 1426 to produce more than one codicil seems to me to clinch the issue, if the plural form (' codicelles ') may be taken literally.   And taking into account the chronicle evidence, I think that it may.

    Note to the Excursus.   The executors of the will of 24 July 1415 were Henry Beaufort, bishop of Winchester, Thomas Langley, bishop of Durham, Richard Courtenay, bishop of Norwich, Ralph Neville, earl of Westmorland, Thomas Beaufort, earl of Dorset (later duke of Exeter), Henry, Lord FitzHugh, Sir Walter Hungerford, Sir John Rothenale, John Wodehouse, and John Leventhorpe.   Of these, Lord FitzHugh, Sir John Rothenale, and John Wodehouse were charged ' continue intendere executioni hujus nostre voluntatis in loco ad hoc per omnes executores nostros assignando et continue sollicitare donec omnia et singula in hoc testamento nostro contenta compleantur '.   And these three ' working ' executors were to consult with the others over difficulties.   The overseers of the will appointed were Henry V's three brothers (the dukes of Clarence, Bedford, and Gloucester), Archbishop Chichele, and Robert

Hallum, bishop of Salisbury.   In June 1421 Henry V appointed his queen (Catherine of Valois), Bedford, and Chichele as overseers.   As executors he re-appointed those of 1415 who were still available (death had removed the bishop of Norwich and Sir John Rothenale), but more than doubled their original membership by adding the earls of Warwick, Northumberland, and Worcester, Lords Willoughby and Clifford, and Sir Walter Beauchamp, Sir Lewis Robessart, Sir William Porter, Sir Robert Babthorp, and John Wilcotes (Worcester, Clifford, and Wilcotes pre-deceased Henry V).   But then, in 1421, there were appointed to be executors with a controlling authority, the duke of Gloucester (seemingly changing his status as overseer), the duke of Exeter, the bishop of Winchester, and the bishop of Durham in addition to the overseers proper (the last three had been nominated as ordinary executors in 1415). The 'working' executors of the 1421 will were Henry, Lord FitzHugh, Hungerford, Beauchamp, Robessart, Porter, Babthorpe, Wodehouse, and Leventhorpe, of whom only Hungerford, Porter, Babthorpe, and Leventhorpe were still alive in 1432, when they were described as executors and also as 'administratores' in . . . testamento specialiter et nominatim constituti ' (*Rot. Parl.* iv. 172–3, 393.   It was only to the overseer, Archbishop Chichele, and to his own fellow controlling executors, Gloucester, Exeter, and Bishop Beaufort, that the bishop of Durham, after Henry V's burial on 7 November 1422, exhibited the late king's will of 10 June 1421 and the codicil of the previous day (Bedford was in France).   There were three groups involved in the actual administration of the will : the overseers proper, those executors with special powers of control, and the group of 'working' executors. The controlling and the 'working' executors were not, of course, the whole of the executory body.   But what functions the others still surviving in 1422—the earls of Westmorland, Warwick, and Northumberland, and Lord Willoughby—were intended to perform is not clear.   Presumably they shared a general responsibility.   They might be (and were) convened, however, when and as often as the controlling committee of executors, the two dukes and the two bishops, found it expedient to consult them.   (I am indebted for the reference to the overseers of the will of 10 June 1421 in a privy seal warrant [P.R.O., E.404/43] of 18 December 1426 to Mr. McFarlane, whose interest in this problem of the different wills of Henry V has been most helpful).

The above *Excursus* has been, in every important respect, superseded by the article entitled 'The last will and codicils of Henry V', published, in *The English Historical Review*, vol. XCVI (1981), pp. 79-102, by Patrick and Felicity Strong. However, I have retained it, partly because it exhibits certain factual and other details that are still of interest, partly because it affords a contrast between our state of imperfect knowledge of Henry V's testamentary dispositions at the time of its writing and the certainty we now enjoy thanks to Mr. and Mrs. Strong's article.

When my paper was published in 1953, it was true to say that the will which Henry V drew up at Dover on 10 June 1421 was 'lost' and that we were ignorant of its contents. The original document itself is yet to find, but at least we now know its terms; and we also know the terms of the codicils which were added to the will at Bois de Vincennes on 26 August 1422, five days before the king died. For a later fifteenth century copy of the texts of both will and codicils, having been rediscovered in the archives of Eton College by Mr. Strong, the Archivist, has now been published in the above-noted article.

So far as my article proper is concerned, its argument as to the nature of the authority claimed by Duke Humphrey under a codicil of Henry V's will, an argument resting upon the words *tutelam et defensionem principales* contained in the duke's memorandum submitted to the parliament of 1422, remains unimpaired — it is clear that the duke was quoting the exact words of the codicil (codicil [3], E.H.R., vol. XCVI, p.99). It is now clear, however, that my statement (p. 205) that Henry V had made special provision for the duke's role in England during the minority of his heir *before* he last left England (i.e. in the will of 10 June 1421) is erroneous. The codicil in question was one of those which the king added to that will at Bois de Vincennes on 26 August 1421.

PERSPECTIVES IN ENGLISH PARLIAMENTARY HISTORY[1]

THE reaction, mainly exemplified in the work of A. F. Pollard,[2] H. G. Richardson and G. O. Sayles,[3] against William Stubbs's interpretation of the development of the English parliament in the Middle Ages, has in some ways been very salutary. The medieval constitution was a " king-spun " constitution. And it is important to emphasize the authoritarian origin of parliament : to realize that every time the king summoned a general parliament he was exacting a response to his own power of command and seeking his own ends, rather than consciously providing a channel of communication for the nation's will in answer to a demand from below which it would have been imprudent to resist. For, although the representative parliaments of the fourteenth and fifteenth centuries met even frequently, they met intermittently and by no stable rule binding upon the king. It was also necessary to realize that the growing complexity of the royal government and administration demanded a " clearing-house " for difficult questions which parliament could best provide, especially when, with the king and his council at its centre, it was attended by the prelates, lay magnates, and commons ; and that parliament was, in this sense, a necessary complement to the normal administrative machinery. For Mr. Richardson and Dr. Sayles, parliament was " the child of the monarchy and reared by the civil service " as an instrument

[1] A lecture delivered in the Library series of public lectures.
[2] *The Evolution of Parliament* (2nd edn., London, 1926).
[3] H. G. Richardson and G. O. Sayles, " The Early Records of the English Parliaments ", *Bulletin of the Institute of Historical Research* (*B.I.H.R.*), v (1927-8), vi (1928-9) ; " The Parliaments of Edward III," *ibid.* viii (1930-1), ix (1931-2) ; " The King's Ministers in Parliament ", *English Historical Review* (*E.H.R.*), vols. xlvi-vii (1931-2).
H. G. Richardson, " The Origins of Parliament ", *Transactions of the Royal Historical Society* (*T.R.H.S.*), 4th ser., vol. xi (1928) ; " The Commons and Medieval Politics ", *ibid.* 4th ser., vol. xxviii (1946).
G. O. Sayles, *The Medieval Foundations of England* (London, 1948), chap. 27.

of the king's administrative authority.[1]   These critics of Stubbs would seem, however, to have erred in being too eager to define with exactness and precision what, originally, parliament was, especially by insisting that down to Edward III its judicial function was all-important and quite essential, this deduction supplying the chief clue to any proper understanding of its early character.   Despite Professor Plucknett's warning of the danger of making any rigid distinction between early parliaments and great councils,[2] and despite Sir J. Goronwy Edwards's demonstration that the essence of parliament's functions was " not specifically judicial . . . or specifically anything " but rather " consisted in being *unspecific* ",[3] Mr. Richardson and Dr. Sayles have, nonetheless, very recently re-asserted their views.[4]

Mr. Richardson and Dr. Sayles have also consistently " written down " or " disparaged " the rôle of the Commons in medieval parliaments both early and late.   They tell us that in early times the Commons were politically ineffective, this notion being a natural inference from the theory that what then really mattered in parliament was " justice " and not " politics ".   Subsequently, we are told that in later times (when " politics " had become more important than " justice ") the Commons continued to be politically ineffective, this notion being a natural inference from the theory that they had now become subservient to the Lords.   Dr. Sayles has insisted that " the facts point to the subservience rather than the independence of the Commons "[5] ; Mr. Richardson, that " the position occupied by the baronage in parliament . . . largely determined the part played by the Commons ".[6] According to this school of thought, the dominance of the Lords pre-ordained the dependence of the Commons : unless directed

[1] The quotation, from Sayles, *The Medieval Foundations of England*, p. 449, is cited by Edward Miller in *The Origins of Parliament* (Historical Association, Pamphlet, General Series, no. 44), and the words that follow it are his.

[2] T. F. T. Plucknett, " Parliament " in *The English Government at Work, 1327-1337*, vol. 1, ed. J. F. Willard and W. A. Morris (1940).

[3] *Historians and the Medieval English Parliament* (David Murray Foundation Lecture in the University of Glasgow, 1955 ; Glasgow, 1960), pp. 23-24.

[4] " Parliaments and Great Councils in Medieval England ", *The Law Quarterly Review*, vol. lxxvii (1961).

[5] *The Medieval Foundations of England*, p. 464.

[6] *T.R.H.S.*, 4th ser., xxviii. 21.

from above, the Commons were politically of little account. As Mr. Edward Miller has summarized their doctrine, the Commons " long remained in the outer darkness of inessentials ; and even when they emerged into the parliamentary light they were scarcely capable of positive attitudes and soon fell victims to the power of the lords, their masters ".[1] The possibility of the Commons being sometimes " prompted " by the Lords was conceded by Stubbs. But, of course, the views of Mr. Richardson and Dr. Sayles are diametrically opposed to Stubbs's assertion that "under Edward II, Edward III, and Richard II, the third estate claimed and won its place as the foremost of the three ".[2] Stubbs's view, at any rate as expressed in these terms, contains an exaggeration. But must we go to the other extreme of accepting the theory of Mr. Richardson and Dr. Sayles?

Their assertion that the medieval Commons were generally subservient to the Upper House was based upon the frequent connection between individual lords and knights of the shire and also the procedure of joint discussion between the Houses by delegations drawn from each. Mr. McFarlane has objected to the theory that subservience was inevitable because of the existence of personal ties between M.P.s and peers, even though there is evidence of aristocratic influence on shire elections in the fifteenth century.[3] And Sir J. Goronwy Edwards has shown that the procedure of joint discussions by delegations (" inter-communing "), far from assisting the Lords to direct the Commons, is more liable to have had an opposite effect, especially regarding that most important concern of parliaments, the voting of taxes.[4] Political ineffectiveness, indeed, seems to consort ill with the Commons' vital right to withhold assent to taxation (secured well before the end of the fourteenth century), the right to appropriate supplies, and the claim, if only spasmodically made (but when made, not infrequently recognized), to exercise an audit of accounts of expenditure of taxes. Nor does it seem easy to recon-

[1] Miller, op. cit. p. 7.
[2] Stubbs, *The Constitutional History of England* (Library edn., 1880), ii. 332.
[3] K. B. McFarlane, " Parliament and Bastard Feudalism ", *T.R.H.S.*, 4th ser., vol. xxvi (1944).
[4] J. G. Edwards, *The Commons in Medieval English Parliaments* (The Creighton Lecture in History, 1957), pp. 5 ff.

cile political ineffectiveness with the Commons' capacity for init-
iating legislation by common petition.   Mr. Richardson admitted
this capacity in his statement that in the fourteenth century the
Commons' petitions became " the normal basis of legislation ".[1]
He and Dr. Sayles even went so far as to draw attention to the way
in which this development resulted under Edward III in unprecedentedly "repetitive and ill-digested statutes ".[2]   It appears,
however, that they have failed to notice that the royal judges
(provided that their professional ability to produce a tidy draft
was no less than their predecessors') must therefore have been
forced to adhere closely to, and therefore hold in proper respect,
the verbal form of the petitions receiving engrossment at their
hands.   Such a gloss hardly suits Mr. Richardson's suggestion
(on another occasion) that " if the king declared that their [the
Commons'] advice and assent was to be sought in the making of
statutes, we must not read too much into words such as these ".[3]
Is there not some danger that we may read too little or, much more,
nothing at all?   Nor is the theory that the Commons were politically insignificant consistent with what we know of the social
standing and administrative importance of many of the medieval
knights of the shire and not a few of the burgesses, the frequently
long and sometimes intensive parliamentary experience of members,
and the onset of the momentous invasion of borough seats by the
gentry before the middle of the fifteenth century.[4]

How come about these contradictory interpretations of the
rôle of the medieval Commons?   Undoubtedly, one reason is to
be sought in the defects of the evidence relating to the medieval
parliament in general and to the Commons in particular, not least
the sheer paucity of that evidence.   *The Anonimalle Chronicle*
provides a narrative account of some of the Commons' own
sessions in the Good Parliament of 1376[5]; but it is a brief account,
a unique disclosure, and relates to a remarkable session.   That
central source, the *Rotuli Parliamentorum*, records no more of the

---

[1] *T.R.H.S.*, 4th ser., xxviii. 27.   [2] *B.I.H.R.*, ix. 13.
[3] *T.R.H.S.*, 4th ser., xxviii. 32.
[4] J. S. Roskell, *The Commons in the Parliament of 1422* (Manchester, 1953).
[5] *The Anonimalle Chronicle*, ed. V. H. Galbraith (Manchester, 1927), pp. 80-83,
85, 88.

Commons' doings than their formally stated results and does not record how those results were arrived at in the Commons' own house of assembly. Moreover, as Sir J. Goronwy Edwards has stated, the evidence of the parliament-rolls has " a certain quality of fortuitousness ",[1] reducing the value of original finds and making any arguments *ex silentio* very precarious and even dangerous. Even regarding what parliament did as a whole, the rolls provide inadequate information : regarding the internal proceedings of the Commons, virtually nothing at all. What would be needed to appraise the Commons' rôle in " ordinary politics " (to say nothing of " high politics ")—records of their debates, diaries, letters, such as appear in Elizabethan times in all their dazzling irridescence—is absent from what evidence there is of how the medieval parliament worked and of what it did.

Original sources apart, my feeling is that contradictory interpretations and therefore contradictory estimations of the rôle of the medieval Commons have arisen, at least in part, out of an unreal distinction in the treatment of the history of parliament between the medieval and modern periods. Or perhaps I should say, as a result of a misplacing of the frontier between the modern constitution, of which parliament is an indispensable, inevitable and permanent part, and the pre-modern (including medieval) constitution, in which parliament, being dependent directly upon the king's will for its meetings, was an extraordinary and occasional event and not a regular part of the constitution. The eventual achievement of constitutional and political independence by the Lower House has to be examined against the background of parliament's emergence as an essential and regular part of the constitution. If parliament is to control government in a really effective manner, the control applied must be the opposite of intermittent, spasmodic, and uncertain. But especially must this be the case if that control is to be effectively exercised by the elected Commons, for whenever the king dissolved parliament the life of the Lower House was *pro hac vice* extinguished, whereas the House of Lords was, in a sense, only adjourned, albeit indefinitely.[2] However the Commons are elected, however com-

---

[1] *The Commons in Medieval English Parliaments*, p. 4.
[2] Betty Kemp, *King and Commons, 1660-1832* (London, 1957), p. 51.

posed, however privileged, however aggressive, so long as they are dependent upon the king's volition or discretion for their very existence, their control will fall short of reality.[1] The basic pre-condition of control of government by the Commons is that parliament should meet regularly. Not until the end of the seventeenth century was this requirement conclusively admitted.

A limitation of the royal prerogative of summons had soon been recognized as a practical necessity by the Long Parliament of Charles I. Or rather this parliament had recognized the need to limit the abuse of that prerogative by omission. And so the Tri-ennial Act of 1641 (signed on the same day as the bill of attainder against Strafford) provided for the meeting of parliament if the king, within three years of dissolving this or any future parlia-ment, failed to summon a new parliament : in this event, if the Lord Chancellor defaulted, the peers were to meet and twelve or more of them might issue the writs ; failing action on the part of the peers, the sheriffs and other returning officers were to hold elections ; failing action on *their* part, the electors were to meet as if the writs had been regularly issued ; and no parliament so unusually convened was to be dissolved without its own consent before fifty days had elapsed from the date appointed for its meeting. This Act of 1641 was repealed in 1664, and, although a new statute re-declared the principle of triennial parliaments, no machinery, alternative to that provided for in 1641, was intro-duced, so that, although Charles II went on to fulfil the intention of the Statute of 1664 in a general sense, he was able to break it in the last years of his reign. So was James II. All that was demanded on this subject in the Declaration of Right was that parliament should meet frequently. And it was left to the Triennial Act of 1694 to provide a solution to the problem of a statutory interval between parliaments which lasted until 1887. In practice, the annual need to pass the Mutiny Act (from 1689) and also to make appropriation of supply ensured that parliament would meet every year. This in itself ended the possibility of long intervals between parliaments.

But if parliament, and especially the Lower House, was to be a vital part of the constitution, this would not only depend upon a

[1] Ibid. p. 16.

limitation of the royal prerogative of summons[1] : it would also depend upon a limitation of the king's right to dissolve parliament at his discretion ; there would need to be a rule controlling the duration of parliaments. Before 1641, the king's right to end a parliament at will, even after only a brief session, had never been effectively disputed,[2] and the Long Parliament's early insistence on a minimum life of fifty days (unless it consented to an earlier dissolution) was conditioned by its memory of the eleven years' tyranny and of Charles I's previous use of his prerogative of dissolution to escape from demands for redress of grievance. After the Restoration, however, and the experience of the Cavalier Parliament, with its sixteen sessions extending over a period of eighteen years, it began to be felt not only that intervals between parliaments should be curtailed, but that the maximum life of parliament should be regulated: " a standing parliament ", resulting from the king's indefinite continuance of parliament, would render the Commons more susceptible to corruption and, therefore, more liable to royal control. The Declaration of Right made no reference to this question of duration of parliaments. The Triennial Act of 1694, however, as well as requiring that not more than three years should elapse between parliaments, also stipulated that no parliament should last longer than three years. The maximum life of parliament was extended to seven years by the Septennial Act of 1716. And this so much longer term soon came to be regarded by the Commons as the principal guarantee of their independence of the king and the House of Lords, with the result that the Act of 1716 was interpreted in the eighteenth cen-

[1] Mr. R. W. K. Hinton, when discussing, in his valuable article " English Constitutional Doctrines from the Fifteenth Century to the Seventeenth " (E.H.R., lxxv. 410-25), the early seventeenth-century problem whether the " good of the commonwealth ", which was the object of legislation, could best be provided by parliament as the highest court of the realm, stressed the effect on this capacity of the king's right to determine when parliament met and how long it sat.

[2] One of the ten questions put to Richard II's judges at Nottingham in 1387 was : " Numquid Rex quandocumque sibi placuerit poterit dissolvere Parliamentum, et suis Dominis et Communibus precipere quod ab inde recedant, An non? " Their answer was in the affirmative and that if anyone proceeded against the king's will " ut in Parliamento ", he stood to be punished as a traitor (Rot. Parl. iii. 233). It would appear that the royal right to dissolve parliament at will had been challenged in the parliament of 1386.

tury as if it prescribed not the maximum but the normal duration of a parliament, a span of life to which every parliament was conventionally entitled.[1]

It is chiefly because of the practical necessity since 1689 for parliament to meet each year and the statutes controlling the use of the royal prerogatives of summons and dissolution that, roughly, the turn of the seventeenth century constitutes the main line of demarcation between modern and earlier parliamentary history. Only then did parliament become a really regular part of the constitution.

Now, there has been no shortage of eloquent advocacy of the theory that parliament, and especially the House of Commons, was set upon a new career in the sixteenth century. For this theory we are mainly indebted to specialists in Tudor history, principally to A. F. Pollard, Sir John Neale, and G. R. Elton ; and it is perhaps not unfair to ask whether these historians may not have been moved unconsciously to exaggerate the significance, for the history of parliament, of the period upon which they chose to concentrate so devotedly. To help substantiate the responsibility of the Tudors for the emergence of parliament in the modern, say, " historic " phase, may they not have run the risk of depreciating the significance of parliament, especially its Lower House, in the medieval, say, " pre-historic " phase? Pollard regarded Henry VIII as having "magnified" parliament,[2] spoke of its being " Henry's extension and not his restraint of parliament that makes his rule unprecedented ",[3] and described the sixteenth century as " the great period of the consolidation of the house of commons ", the time in which it " acquires a weight which makes it the centre of parliamentary gravity ".[4] But parliament's influence upon the course of events was bound to be conditioned and affected by the intermittent character of its meetings. And that the meetings of the Tudor parliament were only occasional, there is no question. They were far less frequent than in pre-Tudor times. Between 1327 and 1485 only forty-two individual years went by in which parliament did not meet. We can count as many such years (43) between 1509 and 1603 ; and of the forty-four years of Elizabeth

[1] Kemp, op, cit. p. 34.
[2] *The Evolution of Parliament*, p. 215.
[3] Ibid. p. 277.
[4] Ibid. p. 160.

I's reign no fewer than twenty-six were quite uninterrupted by any parliamentary session. To apply the test of the medieval suggestion that parliament should meet at least once a year (to do justice to petitioners for grace) would obviously be unrealistic, since this suggestion was only very occasionally made even in the fourteenth century (when the dispensing of " justice " was still a significant function of parliament) and in any case was ineffectual. But if, solely for purposes of comparison between pre-Tudor and Tudor times, we apply the criterion of frequency thought proper or adequate in the seventeenth century, we find (a) that between 1327 and 1485 only twice did three years and more elapse without parliament meeting, and that these two occasions fell very late in that period (namely, in 1456-9 and 1478-83), and (b) that in the Tudor period, during which thirty-three parliaments met, such an interval occurred no fewer than ten times, half of these under Elizabeth I. Meeting at well-spaced intervals, Elizabeth's parliaments in fact were few. As her Lord Keeper explained as late as 1593, " Her maiestie hath euermore been most loth to call for the assemblie of her people in parlement, and hath done the same but rarely ".[1] And clearly some of her subjects must have readily sympathized : as Sir Thomas Smith had put it in 1560, " What can a commonwealth desire more than peace, liberty, quietness, little taking of base money, few parliaments. . .?"[2]

But, of course, we must ask whether, if Tudor parliaments were fewer than those of the medieval period, this was compensated by a tendency for parliament to run to a plurality of sessions and/or to enjoy a longer life. In the medieval period, down to the end of Henry V's reign in 1422, a single session had sufficed for all save nine parliaments (1328-9, 1332-3, 1371, 1381-2, 1388, 1397-8, 1406, 1410, and 1416), of which only one (1406) ran to three sessions. But under Henry VI and the Yorkists two out of every three parliaments had two or more sessions (four in 1445-6, seven in 1472-5), whereas under Tudor rule barely half sat for more than a single session. (The eight sessions of the Reformation Parliament of 1529-36, the four sessions of the parliament of

[1] J. E. Neale, " The Lord Keeper's Speech to the Parliament of 1592-3 ", E.H.R., xxxi (1916), 130.

[2] J Strype, The Life of Sir Thomas Smith (Oxford, 1820), p. 192.

1547-52, and the three sessions of the parliament of 1572-83, were quite exceptional.) Turning to the question of mere duration, we find that a parliament under Edward III lasted on average for three weeks, during the following half-century for twice as long, and under Henry VI for more than twice as long again : and this average duration of about three months under Henry VI is characteristic of the sixteenth century (provided we exclude the quite unusually long Reformation Parliament with its eight sessions totalling the equivalent of ten months). Less frequent and fewer in number though they were, Tudor parliaments did not as a general rule last longer, in terms of time spent in actual session, than Henry VI's and other later medieval parliaments.

But it is on more immediate grounds than these that we should perhaps be wary of accepting Pollard's estimate of the significance of the Tudor period in the history of parliament, especially of the Lower House, and particularly his emphasis on the partnership between king and Commons as a great landmark. Dr. Elton subscribes to Pollard's view that parliament entered upon its proper career in the sixteenth century.[1] He, however, is evidently uneasy about this ascription of novelty to the community of interests between king and parliament, even especially when he is concerned with the effect on the Commons of their share in promoting the ecclesiastical changes made by the Reformation Parliament. Speaking of Henry VIII and Cromwell's employment of parliament and statute to make their revolution legally enforceable, he suggests that we waste no time " in admiring their penetration in choosing parliament as a partner, because in fact they never had any choice ".[2] And that the implicit meaning of these words is that the medieval development of parliament holds at least some importance for Dr. Elton is brought out in a subsequent remark of his : " the polity which Cromwell wanted rested not on the supremacy of the king, but on the supremacy of king in parliament. Of course this was not totally new ; all medieval development stood behind this flowering of parliamentary monarchy."[3] At the same time Dr. Elton holds by Pollard's main thesis that parliament underwent a species of conversion in

[1] G. R. Elton, *England under the Tudors* (London, 1955 [reprinted 1959]), p. 14.   [2] Ibid. p. 167.   [3] Ibid. p. 168.

the sixteenth century. But if, as Dr. Elton says, the principal achievement of Henry VIII's reign, the supremacy of the king in parliament, was " *not totally* new " [my italics[1]] this is hardly to say that, although the achievement might owe something to the medieval parliament, this something amounted to very much. In fact, Dr. Elton expresses himself more succinctly, if not very much more helpfully : " building upon the medieval foundations but erecting *something quite new* on them [my italics again], the Tudors and their ministers produced the composite sovereign body of the king in parliament."[2] It all depends on how important to a structure you regard its foundations. Personally, I would prefer (even if I trusted the metaphor) not to discriminate too positively between these parts of the edifice. We may, however, quote against Dr. Elton the judgement of Pollard that the effect of the Act of Proclamations of 1539 was to free the supreme head of the church from subjection to parliamentary conditions in the exercise of his supremacy.[3] And also (although with greater conviction) we may quote against Pollard, Dr. Elton's estimate of the effect of the Commons' participation in the ecclesiastical work of the Reformation Parliament : from 1529 " the Commons ", says Dr. Elton, " experienced a few short and rather spurious years of primacy, at first (1529-31) because they were the natural mouthpiece of anti-clericalism, but then simply because Cromwell sat there. . . . In 1539 when he sat in the Lords, all the important bills were introduced there first."[4] Nonetheless, in general Dr. Elton holds by Pollard's main thesis that it was in the sixteenth century that parliament entered upon its proper career. So, in his great trilogy, does Sir John Neale.[5]

What is basically important to Sir John Neale is (1) to dis-

[1] G. R. Elton, *England under the Tudors* (London, 1955 [reprinted 1959]), p. 168.   [2] Ibid. p. 14.
[3] *The Evolution of Parliament*, p. 268. Dr. Elton's objection to this view of the Act seems to depend upon his deduction that, because the Act was seldom used for the purpose mentioned, it was not intended to be so used (" Henry VIII's Act of Proclamations ", *E.H.R.*, lxxv (1960), 213, n. 2).
[4] Op. cit., pp. 174-5.
[5] J. E. Neale, *The Elizabethan House of Commons* (London, 1949) ; *Elizabeth I and her Parliaments, 1559-1581* (London, 1953) ; *Elizabeth I and her Parliaments, 1584-1601* (London, 1957).

pose of the legend of Tudor despotism, (2) " to banish the old illusion that early Stuart parliaments had few roots in the sixteenth century ",[1] and (3) to establish that by the end of that century " parliament had become a political force with which the Crown and government had to reckon ", this being " a change . . . brought about by developments in the power, position and prestige of the House of Commons ".[2] But Sir John Neale's more particular task is to elucidate these problems by discovering the " vital significance ", for the growth of parliament, of the reign of Elizabeth I.[3] Well aware of the fewness of her parliaments and the brevity of their sessions—only ten parliaments, comprising thirteen sessions averaging less than ten weeks each in duration, and with an average gap of over three years between each session[4] —he makes it abundantly clear that the age was still one of personal monarchy and rightly insists that parliament was not an ordinary but an extraordinary part of the constitution, and that it was none of its business to exercise supervision over the government of the country. But he achieves the first of his basic aims. And if we treat as Elizabethan anticipations of early Stuart conditions the conversion of patronage into " a political weapon ",[5] " the growing disputatiousness of the Commons "[6] who were learning " the ineradicable lesson of defying their Sovereign "[7] (partly through the medium of " the concerted preparation behind many of the agitations "),[8] and the desire of the " opposition " members to initiate bills and to frame the agenda of parliament,[9] we may concede that Sir John Neale achieves even the second of his basic aims. But what of the third of his basic aims?

At least some historians would take the view that not later than the end of the fourteenth century parliament " had become a force with which the Crown and government had to reckon ", and that this was so from then on. (Not that to say the whole of this is necessarily to say very much.) We may therefore concentrate

---

[1] *Elizabeth I and her Parliaments, 1559-1581*, p. 11.   [2] Ibid. p. 16.
[3] *The Elizabethan House of Commons*, p. 12.
[4] Ibid. p. 381.   [5] Ibid. p. 241.   [6] Ibid. p. 382.
[7] *Elizabeth I and her Parliaments, 1559-1581*, p. 421.
[8] Ibid.   [9] Ibid. p. 28.

rather on the statement that whatever " change " took place had been " brought about by developments in the power, position and prestige of the House of Commons ". Sir John Neale has himself summarized developments in the position of the Commons between Henry VIII's accession and Elizabeth I's : " the House of Commons had acquired the right—not the exclusive right—to control the attendance of its Members ; it had created for itself the right to enforce its privilege of freedom from arrest ; it had invented a power to imprison offenders against its privileges and its dignity ; it had converted an uncertain prescriptive enjoyment of free speech into a formal privilege possessing revolutionary possibilities ; it had even established precedents for punishing licentious speech by Members, thus covertly encroaching on the jurisdiction of the Crown, though on each occasion it took care to recognize that discipline in such matters belonged to the Sovereign. In brief, it had arrogated to itself the functions of a court ".[1] This is a fair statement. But it cannot be over-emphasized that its validity depends upon the qualifications and reservations, the language of scholarly caution, with which the writer has wisely tempered his assertions. Moreover, it is of first-rate importance to recognize a distinction between privileges which affected the power of the Lower House over its own members and towards the public, and those which affected its power to control or influence the government.

Of all these privileges mentioned by Sir John Neale the most important was the privilege of free speech. That, following Sir Thomas More's claim for freedom of speech in 1523, Henry VIII " had allowed opposition in parliament " (Elton[2]), is a statement which would have been more meaningful and conclusive had there not existed a " natural community of interests between him and his parliaments " (Elton[3]), and had the Commons done more than "exploit More's conception of the privilege as licence to oppose any bill or motion " (Neale[4]). The Commons' right to speak and vote against government measures, won by the time of Elizabeth I's accession, was something negative. What Elizabeth's

[1] *Elizabeth I and her Parliaments, 1559-1581*, p. 19.
[2] *England under the Tudors*, p. 171.   [3] Ibid.
[4] *Elizabeth I and her Parliaments, 1584-1601*, p. 435.

reign produced, says Sir John Neale, was an opposition which " wanted to initiate : to introduce bills and motions of their own, to frame the agenda of parliament ",[1] and needed freedom of speech in order to do so. But when we are considering the *power* of the Commons in that period, surely what we must ask is, first, whether the privilege upon which that desire depended for its realization was actually enjoyed, and, second, whether that desire itself was fulfilled.

What chiefly upset the relations between Elizabeth and her Commons in the first half of her reign was the question of the royal succession and, more especially, religious and ecclesiastical issues. And " the conflicts and divergences " between them were such that " there was not a session free from collision of some sort ".[2] But there is no doubt that the Commons' enlarged claim to freedom of speech was contested. What is more, it was generally contested by the queen with success. Elizabeth, as Dr. Elton says, " put precisely those things out of bounds which the opposition wished to discuss ",[3] and the defence of freedom of speech itself in 1576 by Peter Wentworth only resulted in his imprisonment in the Tower (where he remained until, after a month, the queen remitted her displeasure). Admittedly, it was the Lower House itself which, startled by Wentworth's excessive use of what it was his aim to defend, appointed a committee of all the privy councillors who were M.P.s to decide his punishment.[4] But it can be of small comfort to the protagonists of the view that the Commons were developing political muscle at this time that, in this particular instance, the Commons were exercising their right of committal only to the detriment of their claim to freedom of speech. Wentworth's propensity to bold utterance again resulted in his committal in 1587. Then, at the outset of the parliament of 1593, Elizabeth defined liberty of speech in terms which went far to repudiate the Commons' claim. The Lord Keeper, having on the queen's behalf told the Speaker to suppress " any bill that passeth the Reach of a subiectes brayne to mencion", explained that what she would allow was "liberall but not licentious speech,

---

[1] *Elizabeth I and her Parliaments, 1559-1581*, p. 28.   [2] Ibid. p. 420.
[3] *England under the Tudors*, pp. 268-9.
[4] Neale, *Elizabeth I and her Parliaments, 1559-1581*, pp. 318-29.

libertie therefore but with dew limitacion ". " The uerye trew libertie of the house ", went on the Lord Keeper, " was to say yea or no to Bills ": a member might briefly explain his reasons, but his freedom did not extend " to speak there of All causes . . . and to frame a forme of Relligion or a state of gouernment as to their idle braynes shall seem meetest ": no ruler " fitt for his state " would tolerate " such absurdities ". Already, the Lord Keeper had made it clear that membership of the House would not protect from punishment any M.P. who overstepped the bounds of "loyaltie and good discretion ": he ended his advice by saying that the queen hoped that " no man here longeth so much for his ruyne " or " to make such a perill to his own saffetye " as to offend, especially now that she had made the Commons "partakers of her entent and meaninge ".[1] Wentworth's third imprisonment, along with the imprisonment or sequestering of six other members,[2] for trespassing beyond the limits of discretion later in the same session, suitably enforced the queen's warnings. What Wentworth's imprisonments for audacious speaking surely indicate is that the right he claimed was largely illusory in practice. Evidently, such treatment did not succeed in gagging Wentworth, but the example made of him and others can only have had its effect on some less foolhardy than they. Although parliament, by Sir John Neale's showing, was less tractable than used to be thought and " there was not a session free from collision of some sort ", that the queen was able to control her Commons and curb their fantasies is surely a tribute less to the growing power of the Lower House than to the continuing power of the sovereign. In controlling her Commons Elizabeth sacrificed little if anything, certainly nothing vital, of her prerogative. Restiveness in opposition is not power, although it may lead to a claim to it. A claim to power, important though it is, is not the same as power acquired and put to effective use. Bickering, wrangling, petulance and

[1] Neale, *E.H.R.*, xxxi (1916), 136-7. This version of the speech is far superior to that of D'Ewes's *Journals* which included the following words: "Priviledge of Speech is granted, but you must know what privilege you have, not to speak every one what he listeth, or what cometh in his brain to utter that ; but your priviledge is I or No." Another version has " your priuiledge is for such speech as shall be used with Iudgement and sobrietye " (ibid. p. 128).

[2] Neale, *Elizabeth I and her Parliaments, 1584-1601*, p. 278.

resentment are nothing of themselves. What counts is not the passion with which men create or enter into opposition, but that this opposition, whether passionate or not, should be successful in attaining its ends. Elizabeth's policy towards parliament was co-operation—and through members of her Privy Council in the Lower House she was in a fair way to obtain it—but, if she failed to obtain it, then mastery. In Sir John Neale's considered judgement, " from the constitutional point of view, the most important theme in our story is the relationship of the Puritan Movement to parliamentary development ".[1] We may use his own words as comment : that by 1601, " there was no longer a Puritan organization in the background, and the fanatical mentality of bygone assemblies was in disrepute ".[2] So much for the threat to personal monarchy and the preparation of the constitutional revolution of Stuart times.[3]

Elizabeth I's last parliament of 1601 witnessed no shortage of free speech, or of indignation, in the debates over royal monopolies. Indeed, there was a considerable amount of virulent abuse. But under the early Stuarts what the Commons conceived as their right to free speech was many times so honoured in the breach as to leave it at best precarious : illusory in practice. For those who spoke indiscretely or intemperately were liable to be punished in some way. We may recall the imprisonment of Sir Thomas Wentworth and three other members after the Addled Parliament of 1614, when five more were forbidden to leave London and another four were dismissed from the commission of the peace. During the next parliament, in November 1621, occurred the arrest of Sandys along with Selden, James I himself explaining his reasons : " we think ourself very free and able to punish any man's misdemeanours in parliament, as well during their sitting as after ; which we mean not to spare hereafter, upon any occasion of any man's insolent behaviour there that shall be ministered unto us."[4] And this was no idle threat : the Commons'

---

[1] *Elizabeth I and her Parliaments, 1584-1601*, p. 436.
[2] Ibid. p. 437.
[3] Ibid. p. 435.
[4] *Select Statutes and other Constitutional Documents illustrative of the reigns of Elizabeth and James I*, ed. G. W. Prothero (Oxford, 1894), p. 310.

protestation of 18 December, which included an assertion of their right to liberty of speech in discussing all questions of public concern, the king ripped out of their Journal with his own hands and, having dissolved parliament, imprisoned Sir Edward Coke and four other M.P.s (including Selden) and sent another four to act unwillingly as royal commissioners in Ireland. Charles I's second parliament (1626) witnessed the committal to the Tower of Eliot and Digges for alleged insolence of speech, and, following Charles's next parliament (1628-9), Eliot again and this time no fewer than eight other M.P.s were fined and sent to prison by the King's Bench, Eliot dying there in 1632, Valentine remaining in confinement until the Short Parliament of 1640. Their conduct stigmatized by the king himself as " disobedient and seditious ",[1] these M.P.s had been afforded no protection by privilege or right. Moreover, it was not until 1667 that these judgements were reversed as illegal and " against the freedom and privilege of Parliament ".[2] Meanwhile, several M.P.s had again been imprisoned after the Short Parliament. The famous attempted arrest of the Five Members for high treason in January 1642 was an infringement more dramatic, of course, but mainly because of Charles's personal intervention, his visit to the Lower House with an armed escort, and the escape of his intended victims with the connivance of the House. Not until the Bill of Rights was any constitutional safeguard found for freedom of speech, protection being then supplied by the reservation to parliament of all cases involving the privilege. Such privileges and rights as freedom from arrest at private suit, the right of the House to expel a member (exemplified in 1581 and 1585), the determination of contested elections and decisions upon the legality of returns (1604), are important evidence of the growing corporateness of the Commons, but, relative to the power of control of royal government by parliament, they are unsubstantial. Freedom of speech in the Commons, however, was a *sine qua non* of effective participation. Neither Tudor nor early Stuart parliaments enjoyed it without question and in comfort.

No one is likely to forget Professor Wallace Notestein's im-

[1] T. P. Taswell-Langmead, *English Constitutional History* (10th edn. by T. F. T. Plucknett), p. 422.   [2] Ibid. p. 424 n.

portant contribution in the Raleigh Lecture of 1924, entitled "The Winning of the Initiative by the House of Commons ".[1] What he most memorably demonstrated, in underlining the growing contentiousness of the Commons under James I, was how much of this was due, negatively, to the king's failure (until 1614[2]) to influence elections with a view to enlisting a majority of supporters among the Commons, to the inadequacy in both number and competence of the Privy Councillors in the House, and to the king's inability to keep the Lords firmly on his side ; positively, to the growth of " an entirely new Committee system " (especially the growth of the Committee of the Whole House), by which the Speaker's power was restricted and the power of the opposition leadership given greater scope. But, as in the struggle for freedom of speech, so in these new developments, what was being fashioned was the wherewithal to secure power, not power itself. The new institutions, or rather practices, were means to an end. Control ultimately depended on such, but by their invention and use control itself was not established.

One of the obvious ways of testing the control exercised by parliament over the royal government and administration is to enquire (a) whether parliament could properly require the sovereign to appoint important officials and councillors acceptable to it, (b) whether, once so appointed, these were effectively made answerable to parliament, and, (c) by what procedure parliament could, if gravely dissatisfied with any aspect of their public conduct, bring them to book.[3] During the medieval period, only in a

[1] *Proceedings of the British Academy*, vol. xi. This lecture was separately published by the Oxford University Press in 1924 and reprinted photographically in 1949.

[2] I regard Professor Notestein's opinion about royal interference in the 1614 elections as confirmed by the evidence contained in Chap. iii of Mr. T. L. Moir's book, *The Addled Parliament of 1614* (Oxford, 1958). That there was " no great conspiracy to pack the lower House " (ibid. p. 163) is not necessarily at variance either with Mr. Moir's evidence in Chap. iii or the implication of his statement that " the resentment of the gentry at ' interference ' in local elections found tumultuous expression during the session " (ibid. p. 54).

[3] Cf. Charles I's definition of the rôle of the House of Commons : " an excellent Conserver of Liberty, but never intended for any share in Government, or the chusing of them that should govern " (his answer to the Nineteen Propositions composed by Sir John Colepeper, Chancellor of the Exchequer, and Viscount Falkland, Secretary of State, 21 June 1642, [John Rushworth], *Historical Collections*

royal minority or when the affairs of the realm were so out of joint as to need drastic reforms requiring the appointment of officials and councillors whom parliament could trust, was the exclusive right of the Crown to appoint its own ministers at all disputed. This exclusive right to appoint was generally not disputed under either Tudors or Stuarts. But in the fourteenth and early fifteenth centuries there had been at least some occasions when parliament had felt moved to interfere. Moreover, on some of these and at other times the Commons had used the process of impeachment at the bar of the Upper House to secure the punishment of officials and others for crimes and misdemeanours offensive to the Crown and detrimental to the public weal. In the Good Parliament of 1376 the King's Chamberlain and the Steward of the Household (both of them peers), in 1386 the earl of Suffolk, the ex-Chancellor, in 1388 the royal judges, and in 1397 Archbishop Arundel, were all brought to trial in this way, in each case, save the last, in despite of the king and against his will. After Richard II's reign the procedure of impeachment was only once again used in the medieval period, namely, in 1450, when the duke of Suffolk was subjected to it. Thereafter it fell into abeyance until revived by the Commons in 1621. When seeking punishment for political offenders, the Tudors had in fact preferred to use Star Chamber or, if and when they used parliament, to initiate state trials by bills of attainder introduced in the Upper House. Whether or not the Tudor Commons were unequal to the strain of making impeachments, they did not in fact do so. It was, therefore, a medieval instrument which was revived in 1621 against the Lord Chancellor (Bacon) and was used again in 1624 against the Lord Treasurer (Cranfield), each of whom was condemned for bribery. Between then and 1688 there were about forty cases of impeachment. The Commons would have used it against Buckingham in 1626, had not Charles forestalled them by dissolving parliament. Early in the Long Parliament they put it to unprecedentedly extensive use against Strafford, Laud, Finch (the Lord Keeper), Windebank (Secretary of State), thirteen of the

(London, 1721), iv. 731). For a discussion of the general constitutional significance of Charles's statement, see C. C. Weston, " The Theory of Mixed Monarchy Under Charles I and After ", *E.H.R.*, lxxv. 429.

bishops, and six judges. And so on and so forth. To the last quarter of the seventeenth century, in the trial of Danby in 1679, belongs, however, the formulation of two very important problems in the history of the procedure, important for what their settlement would imply, namely, that impeachment, whatever it had been originally, was not now at the suit of the Crown. The two problems were : (a) was a royal pardon pleadable to an impeachment by the Commons that was depending? and (b) did impeachment abate if parliament were prorogued or dissolved? The first question, important because a royal pardon could be used to screen ministers of the Crown from parliamentary justice and so render entirely nugatory their pretended responsibility, was answered to the detriment of the prerogative in the Act of Settlement of 1701. The second was to be answered in the same spirit, but not until 1791 (during the impeachment of Warren Hastings), the reason for the long postponement of a settlement of this crucial issue of principle being that the procedure itself had become anachronistic and moribund " as the criminal law gradually embraced a wider variety of financial misdeeds, and as the growth of ministerial responsibility provided a sufficient sanction against ministers whose political conduct gave offence ".[1]

Earlier in this paper, I have referred to the importance, for parliamentary legislation by statute, of petitions promoted by the Commons. It was in the fourteenth century that these became " the normal basis of legislation " of this kind, provided they were agreed by the Lords and assented to by the king. Even though from the middle of the fifteenth century onwards parliamentary law-making became increasingly officially-inspired, the Lower House inevitably remained the source of origin of much of the legislation issued with parliamentary authority. Legislation by petition from below was, however, subject to a royal power to make amendments which seem not to have required " reference-back ", and in any case depended absolutely upon the royal assent. The sovereign's right to veto bills was unquestioned in both theory and practice, a vital and cherished part of the prerogative. In theory it still survives. But for how long did it survive in practice? When did the Crown effectively cease to

[1] Taswell-Langmead, op. cit. pp. 590-601.

dispute what both Lords and Commons willed to have law? In the medieval period, the veto was freely used. Under Elizabeth I it could still be extensively used, at least on occasion.[1] It is true that its use became infrequent under the Stuarts, but this was because they preferred to use their dispensing power, Charles II and James II a suspending power as well. And the revival of the royal veto under William III can best be understood in the light of the recent declaration, in the Bill of Rights, that these special powers of dispensing and suspending were illegal except when used with parliamentary consent, which was virtually to vitiate their prerogatival character. William III's revival of the veto was a cause of disappointment, and it was short-lived.[2] Only once, in 1708, did Anne refuse her assent to a bill (the Scottish Militia Bill), since when that faintly derisive formula, *Le Roi s'advisera*, has never been used. As Miss Betty Kemp has said, " As far as legislation went, parliament seemed to have vindicated its supremacy and, in this sphere, not only to have deprived the King of independent power but also to have deprived him, in practice, of his position of equality with the other two parts of parliament ".[3] In future, the Crown, if opposed to a parliamentary bill, would need to defeat it in its earlier stages by political contrivance.

The question of parliamentary control of government sooner or later imposes an enquiry into taxation, to secure parliamentary sanction for which was the main single object of the summoning of most parliaments before this was made regular at the end of the seventeenth century. Upon direct taxation, subsidies levied throughout the land generally on men's lands or goods, and also upon the regular continuation of indirect taxation, the customs and subsidies on imports and exports, depended the royal administration, especially during an emergency or in the conduct of a foreign policy resulting in military enterprise abroad and entailing heavy expenditure. The acid test of the power of parliament lies in its control of these revenues.

[1] Cf. the message from the queen delivered by the Speaker to the Commons on 27 February 1593 : " it is in my power to assent or dissent to anything done in Parliament . . ." (Prothero, op. cit. p. 125).
[2] Kemp, op. cit. pp. 26-27.   [3] Ibid. p. 27.

Recognition of the need for the consent of parliament to both direct and indirect taxation had been secured in the medieval period. And that this consent was then a reality was, so far as direct taxation is concerned, sometimes convincingly demonstrated by a refusal by parliament to meet the demands of the Crown and, so far as indirect taxation is concerned, by changes in the rates of the customs, by variations in the period for which these grants were made available, and even, although only very occasionally, by dramatic token suspensions of the customs for brief intervals of time.[1] Let me hasten to add that under Edward III the consent of the Commons had become equally essential with that of the Lords, and that in 1407 it was established that the Lords should merely assent to what had been granted independently by the Commons who were, moreover, literally to be left with the last word, since the final declaration of a grant was then reserved for their Speaker[2]: by 1455 the Lords' power of amendment extended in practice only to a reduction of the amount of a grant, not to its enhancement.[3] In view of the assertions of historians of parliament in the Tudor period that the power of the Commons was perceptibly growing in that period, it is necessary to point out that even the long-established and elementary right of the Commons to initiate all money bills was jeopardized so late in Elizabeth I's reign as 1593. When, on this occasion, the Lower House had offered two subsidies, and the government had succeeded in getting the Upper House to make a bigger grant, the Lords demanded a conference with the Commons where Burghley stated that they insisted on *three* subsidies. Sir Francis Bacon objected that this amendment, as it stood, was a breach of the Commons' privilege. But apparently all that he could do to protect this privilege was to suggest that the Commons should themselves offer the three subsidies the Lords had already proposed : and it was this grant which finally passed.[4] " In this

[1] Such suspensions occurred in 1381 and 1385 (*Rot. Parl.* iii. 104b, 204b).

[2] *Rot. Parl.* iii. 611. Reference was expressly made to this precedent in the dispute over the subsidy in 1593 (Sir Simonds D'Ewes, *Journals of all the Parliaments during the Reign of Queen Elizabeth* [London, 1682], p. 485b).

[3] S. B. Chrimes, *English Constitutional Ideas in the Fifteenth Century* (Cambridge, 1936), p. 361.

[4] Neale, *Elizabeth I and her Parliaments, 1584-1601*, pp. 300-10.

serious clash between the houses—the first in the century—the Commons ", says Dr. Elton, " had successfully protected their right to initiate all money bills."[1] So, in a sense, they had. But we can hardly fail to observe that the price of protection eventually paid by the Commons was their acquiescence in the outcome of the original offence. It was not until 1678 that the Commons *finally* made good their claim that money bills must originate in their House. But they were then able to add to this the stipulation that, although the Lords might still reject their money bills, they could not amend them, not even by reduction.

The power of parliament and especially of the Commons has always depended in the last resort upon control of taxation. This control was subject to a contraction throughout the Tudor period, partly because parliament was ready to allow all of the Tudor monarchs at the beginning of each of their reigns and for life the customs-dues and tonnage and poundage, which together formed a very substantial and certainly highly necessary part of the regular revenues of the Crown. The fact that these grants were " in the bag " from the beginning of a reign meant that the bargaining power of the Commons was reduced *pro tanto*. For grants for the life of the king there were, it is true, medieval precedents (in 1398,[2] 1415, 1453, 1465, and 1484) : each one of the successors of Edward III, save Henry IV, had enjoyed such a vote. The grant made to Edward IV lasted eighteen years. The other pre-Tudor grants, however, had been in the event short-lived, so that all of them together accounted for no more than about a third of the period involved. Moreover, of all the medieval kings who received this mark of parliamentary approbation, only Richard III did so in his first parliament, that is, as though it were a matter of course. Then, however, the grant of the customs and tonnage and poundage did become just that : from this time forward they were never withheld until, in Charles I's first parliament, the Commons refused to grant the subsidies for more than a year. Charles, insisting that they should be voted him for life as before, was therefore only claiming what each of his last seven predeces-

[1] Elton, *England under the Tudors*, p. 462.

[2] Richard II's grant extended only to the wool-subsidy, tonnage and poundage not being included. Later grants for life covered all of these subsidies.

sors had been allowed. Evidently the Lords felt much as the king did; at least they rejected the limitation. Perhaps Charles had a right to *expect* a grant for life. But no more. And there is no doubt that the Commons, following medieval precedents, had every right not to make such a grant, unless their right of consent was to be set aside as unreal or negligible. We may admire the stubbornness of the Lower House over this issue, but we shall avoid any risk of exaggerating their power to enforce their right if we remember that Charles collected the taxes in question without any parliamentary authority, continuing to levy them even after 1629, when he actually renounced all right of his own conceiving. So long as the king was fully entitled to dissolve parliament at his pleasure and was able to use this prerogative to choke opposition when it became intolerable, it was next to impossible for the Commons to secure the abolition of levies collected by mere royal authority, especially if, as for example in the case of impositions under James I and ship-money under Charles I, there was current at the time some genuine doubt as to their illegality. The Commons' power was still permissive : in the last resort it depended, as their existence did, upon the king's will. It could be argued, of course, that Charles's wilful exaction of levies legally requiring the Commons' consent without that consent helped to produce the explosion which brought his system crashing to the ground and eventually cost him his head. But had the years made him wiser, more appreciative of the need for accommodation and compromise, and careful to avoid the appearance of duplicity, he might still have escaped the graver consequences of his financial, as well as other, policies.

The Tudor period witnessed a contraction in parliamentary control of taxation, not only because tonnage and poundage, etc., were granted for a reign once and for all at its outset, but also because the Tudors sometimes resorted to very profitable extra-parliamentary forms of financial levy, such as benevolences and forced loans (which parliament now and then abjectly sanctioned in retrospect, treating them as taxes or, in the case of loans, cancelling the king's indebtedness).[1] But not only for this reason.

[1] In 1495 parliament sanctioned the benevolence of 1491, and in 1529 and 1544 it released the king from any obligation to repay forced loans.

To be effective, parliamentary control of taxation must needs contain more than recognition of the elementary principle of simple consent. If parliament was really to control taxation, it was necessary that it should be able to make its grants conditional upon their appropriation to specific purposes, and to ensure that these appropriations were adhered to, either by the appointment of special treasurers supervising the receipt and expenditure of grants or simply by audit of accounts. Medieval parliamentary grants, from 1340[1] onwards, were with a fair constancy tied to expenditure in certain directions, mainly to finance war or measures for defence. The appointment of special treasurers or receivers in charge of tax-funds and the use of audit (or view) of accounts were also resorted to at the Commons' demand.[2] It is true that both these last devices were always precarious, were employed only spasmodically (and even then by royal condescension), and that after Henry IV's reign the first was hardly ever used and the second not at all (so far as the records show). But, under Yorkists and Tudors alike, *all* of these devices were in abeyance. In fact, appropriation to specific objects was not to be resurrected until 1624,[3] was then not again re-introduced until

[1] See G. L. Harriss, " The Commons' Petitions of 1340 ", *E.H.R.*, lxxviii (1963), 628, 642-3, 645-6.

[2] Special treasurers of moneys voted for the wars were in office in 1377-9, 1382, 1385-7, 1390-1, 1404-6, and 1450. Audits of their accounts were allowed to the Commons in 1378, 1379, 1404, and 1406.

[3] It was not as if the need for a clause of appropriation in the subsidy bill had never, in the meantime, entered the heads of M.P.s. At the beginning of the parliament of 1593 the Lord Keeper gave out that the principal reason of its meeting was " preparation of aid . . . against the mighty and great forces of the King of Spain, bent and intended against this Realm ", and the Commons' Committee for the aid soon advised a grant of two subsidies. According to D'Ewes's *Journal*, Nathaniel Bacon, himself one of the Committee, supplemented its report with a statement that some of the members had proposed that " the present necessity of the Causes moving them to offer the said double Subsidy " should be " set down and inserted in the Bill ". And the *Journal* then goes on to relate that Serjeant Harris desired " in the subsidies to have it set down, that those Subsidies be to maintain a War impulsive and defensive against the Spaniard ". The main point of this intervention (as the next speaker, Sir Walter Raleigh, made clear) was to ensure that a state of open war with Spain should be declared. Nonetheless, the wish that the grant should be specifically appropriated to such a war was itself so strongly felt as to result in a demand that this condition should be " inserted into the preamble of the said Bill " (op. cit. pp. 477-8). The burden of the long

1665, and was only made invariable after the Revolution of 1688. And audit, although revived in 1624 and 1641, was only indisputably re-established in 1667.

Now, what I have been trying to do is to demonstrate that if we seek for " a great divide " in the history of parliament and especially of its eventually dominant House, we can best find it in the seventeenth century, in the late seventeenth century, or about the turn of the seventeenth century. And the so many convergent indications of a fundamental change in the position of the Commons appearing in the late seventeenth century may perhaps drive us to ask ourselves whether the Tudor period can have been so really important for the history of the development of the Lower House as is sometimes made out. And if we decide that that degree of importance is hard to substantiate, then perhaps we should ask, too, whether the medieval Commons can have been so immature and ineffective as is also sometimes made out, not least by those who exaggerate the importance of their Tudor successors. Now it would appear that the real break in the history of the Commons comes not with the Tudor period, even though it was then that the Reformation enlarged the scope of the intervention of parliament in public affairs, and that religious and ecclesiastical questions produced quite unprecedented states of emotional tension, especially among the Commons. Nor does this break come with the abolition by the Commons of

and eloquent preamble to the subsidy bill was, admittedly, the need to furnish the defence of the realm. But, although it was made evident that the King of Spain was the enemy meant, the object of the expenditure of the grant was given no greater particularity than " for our Defence " (*Statutes of the Realm*, vol. iv, part 2, p. 867). Specific appropriation had obviously been evaded in the drafting.

The appropriation of 1624 was of quite a different order : it was " for the defence of this your Realme of England, the securing of your Kingdom of Ireland, the assistance of your neighbours the States of the United Provinces and other your Majesties friends and allies, and for the setting forth of your Royall Navie ". Seven sworn treasurers were appointed, their expenditure to be controlled by warrant of the members of the Council of War. The treasurers were to account to the House of Commons which was empowered to commit offenders to the Tower, and these were to remain as close prisoners until delivered by the order of the House. The offences of peers were to be brought to the notice of the Lords who were to have similar powers of committal (*Statutes of the Realm*, vol. iv, part 2, pp. 1247, 1261-2).

both the Monarchy and the House of Lords in 1649, because at that point the old constitution was merely suspended for a time. It comes, rather, with the end of the power of the Crown to govern effectively without parliament. And as soon as parliament has made itself indispensable and even inevitable (but when the peers have established their freedom to disobey the royal summons to attend) we can say that parliament has moved into a significantly new phase of its history. The constitution of the *ancien régime* is now really at an end : not moribund, but defunct. What the Tudor Commons had been creating by organizing their own self-discipline, for example, controlling their own attendance, sending to prison offenders against their privileges, keeping their own *Journal*, and so emphasizing their corporateness, was not power, much less authority, but merely potentiality. Or rather what they had done was to add by these developments to an already existing potentiality, the potentiality furnished by the medieval Commons, at the same time allowing that medieval potentiality to be diminished or to lose some of its value by disuse, it being left to the seventeenth-century Commons not only to exploit and fulfil that Tudor potentiality, but also to re-discover and salvage what had been lost of the medieval potentiality, and to do the first of these things all the more effectively by doing the second as well. The seventeenth-century lawyers, searching for precedents in the parliamentary records of the fourteenth and fifteenth centuries appropriate and apposite to their own situation, mistakes of interpretation though they committed from time to time, suffered from no delusions as to the importance and relevance of the work of their medieval forebears. What, in my opinion, actuated them was a consciousness of continuing or recurrent constitutional and political realities or situations. The basic English constitutional and political problem of what we call later medieval and early modern times was how to control a monarchy which, though at no time despotic, was never less than a monarchy. The Tudors, in taking into partnership the community of which parliament was the microcosm, were using the familiar Plantagenet expedient: participation in government at the sovereign's command. But if we regard parliament, as certainly some medieval Englishmen were capable of doing, as a means of limiting monarchical authority[1]—the expression of a *dominium politicum et regale*—the Tudor period was generally one in which the traditions of the medieval Commons were not, so far as the Commons' relations with the royal government are concerned, substantially extended ; and if in some respects they were expanded, we should recognize that in others they underwent a contraction. It was only in the seventeenth century when the state of the monarchy prompted and the national situation permitted it, that such of those medieval traditions as had been in abeyance and yet were valuable, experienced a real and now revolutionary re-quickening.

[1] Hinton, op. cit. pp. 410-17.

INDEX TO VOLUME I

[Contractions: archbp. for archbishop; bp. for bishop; kg. for king; qn. for queen; † for died]

Abbotston (Hants.) V 70
Abingdon, abbot of II 167
Agincourt, battle of II 181; V 67, 69, 71
Airmyn, Richard III 425; William III 425-7, 429, 432-3, 438
Aiscough, William, bp. of Salisbury II 189
Alexander III, kg. of Scotland II 160
Algerkirk (Lincs.) V 73
Alnwick, William bp. of Norwich VII 200, 222, 232
Alyngton, William IV 43; William his grandson II 38
Anglo-Burgundian alliance VI 152
Anjou IV 50
Anne, qn. of Richard II; V 73; VIII 468; her tenants V 64
Anonimalle Chronicle II 201; IV 33-5; VIII 451
Appleby (Westm.) VI 164
Appleby, Robert de III 426
Archdeaconries III 429-30
Arches, court of III 426
Armagh, province of III 429
Armyn, family V 55; Sir William V 61, 77
Arras, congress of II 187
Arundel, John, bp. of Chichester II 204; Thomas, archbp. of Canterbury II 176-7, 179; IV 38; VII 207; VIII 466
Assheton, Nicholas VI 159, 165
Astylle, Thomas VI 156
Audley, Hugh de, earl of Gloucester (†1347) II 166
Aumâle, Edward, duke of (†1415) VII 217; and see under York.
Aumeney, Simon de, abbot of Malmesbury II 202
Auncell, Sir John V 59, 62, 77
Avignon V 67
Aylesby (Lincs.) V 59, 70
Ayscough, William, bp. of Salisbury II 203
Ayssheldon, Thomas VI 156

Babthorp, Sir Robert VII 233
Bacon, Sir Francis VIII 466, 469; Nathaniel VIII 472
Baldock, Robert III 426, 429
Balliol, Edward II 165
Balsham, William VI 158
Bangor, see II 178, 183-4, 190; bps. of II 163, 190, 195
Bardelby, Robert III 425, 427-8
Bardney, abbot of II 190
Bardolf, Thomas, lord (†1408) II 180
Barnetby (Lincs.) V 70
Barnham (Sussex) V 70
Barnstable (Devon) VI 158
Barton-on-Humber (Lincs.) V 74
Bastard feudalism IV 42
Bath (Somerset) VI 156
Bath and Wells, see of II 183, 190; bps. of II 159, 181
Battle, abbot of II 182, 190-1
Bayonne (France) V 67
Beauchamp, earls of Warwick: Guy (†1315) II 162-3; Richard (†1439) II 179, 183-4, IV 45, VI 166, VII 194, 197, 201, 210, 222, 233; Thomas (†1401) II 160, 170, 176; earl of Worcester, Richard (†1422) VII 233; Beauchamp of Powick, John, lord (†1475) II 190, 204; Beauchamp (of Somerset), John de (†1336) II 173; Sir Walter IV 43, 45; VII 222, 233; William, lord St. Amand (†1457) II 190
Beaufort, family IV 48; VII 194; Edmund, duke of Somerset (†1455) II 190, 192-3; Henry, bp. of Winchester II 180-1, 184-6; V 69; VI 167; VII 195, 197-8, 201, 207, 209, 215, 222-3, 231-3; John, earl of Somerset (†1410) II 176, 180; Thomas, earl of Dorset later duke of Exeter (†1426) II 180, 184-5; VI 167; VII 194, 197, 201-2,

1

8

Vickers, K.H. VII 199
Victoria, queen VII 229
Villiers, George, duke of Buckingham (†1628) VIII 466
Vire (France) VI 171
Vowell (*alias* Hooker), John IV 37

Wainfleet (Lincs.) V 69
Wake, Thomas, lord (†1349) II 168
Wakering, John, bp. of Norwich II 182; VII 197
Waldby, Robert, archbp. of York II 177
Wales, marches of III 412; north, chamberlain of VII 196; south, chief justice and chamberlain of VII 196; Edward, Prince of (†1376) IV 42; Edward of Lancaster, Prince of (†1471) II 189, 191, 195; VII 226-7
Wallingford VI 162; castle and honour IV 42
Walsh, Robert V 74
Walsingham, Thomas, chronicler IV 33-4, 39; VII 200, 232
Waltham, abbots of II 161, 167, 179, 182
Waltham, Roger III 427
Wareham (Dorset) VI 156, 158
Warenne, John de, earl of Surrey (†1347) II 161, 173, 202
Warfield, John VI 162
Washingley (Hunts.) V 71
Welbeck, abbot of II 165
Welby, Adelard V 71; Richard V 55, 71, 75 77; Roger V 71
Welland, river V 59
Welles, John, lord (†1421) II 171; V 68, 70; Lionel (†1461) II 190; Richard de, lord Willoughby (†1470) II 191
Wells, cathedral chapter III 427; dean II 173; archdeaconry III 429
Welsh bps. II 174
Wenlock, family VI 169
Wentworth, Peter VIII 461-2
Wentworth, Thomas, earl of Strafford (†1641) VIII 453, 463, 466
Westminster, palace Painted Chamber IV 33
Westminster, abbey II 176; church VII 199; Confessor's shrine II 176-7; VII 199; chapter house IV 33, 37; refectory IV 37; abbots of II 167-8, 175, 177, 179-80, 184-5, 188-9; lepers VII 217
West Bridgford (Notts.) V 70
Westmorland IV 48
Weymouth (Dorset) VI 156
Whaplode (Lincs.) V 71

Whelpington, Robert VI 158
Whethamstead, John, abbot of St. Albans VII 214
Whitgreve, Robert VI 159, 162
Whitney, Sir Robert VI 171
Wilcotes, John VII 233
William III; VIII 468
Willoughby, lords: Robert (†1396) V 63, 68; William (†1409) II 180, V 66, 68-9, 71; Robert (†1452) VII 233; and see under Welles
Willoughby, Sir Thomas V 68-9, 71, 73, 75, 77
Wiltshire VI 159
Winchcombe, abbot of II 190
Winchelsea (Sussex) VI 156-7
Winchester II 175, 188; V 59; VI 162; city recorders VI 163; see of II 185-6; bp. of II 168; archdeaconry III 421
Windebank, Sir Francis VIII 466
Windsor VII 195; college of St. George VI 165
Winestead (Yorks.) V 70
Wingfield, Sir Humphrey VI 154
Winhale (Lincs.), priory V 68
Wisbech (Lincs.) V 66, 72
Witenagemot I 1
Witham, river V 58-9
Witton-le-Wear (Durham) VI 167
Wodehouse, John VI 166; VII 232-3; Robert de III 425-6, 431, 436
Wolsey, Thomas, Cardinal IV 52
Wood, William VI 162
Wood-Legh, Kathleen VI 170
Woodville, family VII 227; Anthony, earl Rivers (†1483) VII 227; Richard, earl Rivers (†1469) II 190
Worcester VI 162; see of II 182; bps. of II 160-1, 164, 190-1; cathedral chapter III 428; archdeaconry III 421-2
Worcestershire VI 162, 166
Wouldham, Thomas, bp. of Rochester II 174
Wrawby (Lincs.) V 68, 70
Wycombe (Bucks.) VI 165
Wykeham, Sir Thomas VI 169; William of, bp. of Winchester VI 169
Wykes (Lincs.) V 73
Wynnesley, Richard VI 165

Yarmouth (Norfolk) V 75; VI 154, 156, 164
York II 162, 165, 175; III 419, 439; VI 156-7, 160; mayor and citizens III 440;